French Absolutism:
the crucial phase, 1620-1629

French Absolutism:
the crucial phase, 1620-1629

A. D. LUBLINSKAYA

Formerly Professor of Medieval History
Leningrad University

Now Research Fellow, USSR Academy
of Sciences

TRANSLATED BY BRIAN PEARCE

WITH A FOREWORD BY J. H. ELLIOTT

CAMBRIDGE
AT THE UNIVERSITY PRESS
1968

Published by the Syndics of the Cambridge University Press
Bentley House, 200 Euston Road, London, N.W.1
American Branch: 32 East 57th Street, New York, N.Y.10022

Library of Congress Catalogue Card Number: 68-21395
Standard Book Number: 521 07117 8

First published in Russian under the title
Frantsuzsky Absolyutizm v Pervoi Treti XVII veka,
Izdatel'stvo 'Nauka', Moscow–Leningrad, 1965

Printed in Great Britain
at the University Printing House, Cambridge
(Brooke Crutchley, University Printer)

Contents

Foreword

In recent years, historians of Early Modern Europe have been debating (some will consider, *ad nauseam*) the existence, the character, and the extent of a 'general crisis of the seventeenth century'. The debate has engaged historians of many nationalities and persuasions—Marxist, anti-Marxist, neo-Marxist, a-political—but the majority of voices heard in the discussion have been those of historians from the West. The publication in English of Mme Lublinskaya's *French absolutism* is therefore particularly welcome, in that it provides West European readers with the opportunity to become acquainted with the views of a distinguished Soviet historian, whose original researches into the history of seventeenth-century France are here combined with a summary and discussion of the debate over the general European crisis.

In a volume originally intended for a Russian public, it is natural that a considerable amount of space should be devoted to summaries of the views of West European historians and of their contributions to the debate. Although these summaries occupy two entire chapters of Professor Lublinskaya's book, it will be seen that they constitute a good deal more than a mere *réchauffé* of books and articles easily accessible to Western readers. Summary turns out, on examination, to be accompanied by a commentary which is far from anodyne. Professor Lublinskaya is not afraid to take distinguished contributors sternly to task for their failings, and her judgments are frequently supported by comments both shrewd and incisive. But even those historians who consider themselves unjustifiably placed in the dock can hardly fail to be interested, and perhaps even surprised, by the general tenor of the verdict. For this emerges as nothing less than a *critique* of the whole 'general crisis' interpretation of seventeenth-century European history—an interpretation which, in Professor Lublinskaya's words, 'has become a sort of axiom, a point of departure for all discussions, even in those cases where historians are not agreed on a particular interpretation of particular economic and social phenomena or political struggles'.[1]

The great interest of Mme Lublinskaya's conclusion will not be lost on those readers who compare it with Dr Hobsbawm's summary in 1965 of the discussion generated by his original article on 'The crisis of the seventeenth century': 'The fact of the seventeenth-century crisis may be regarded as

[1] P. 80.

vii

established. An explanation of it which would meet with general agreement still remains to be found, and its place in the genesis of modern industrialism also awaits more discussion. I would suggest that it will be found to fit most readily into some elaborated or modified version of the Marxist model of economic development'.[1]

There are models and models; and, in an age addicted to model-making, there is an inherent tendency to give preference to the historical model over the historical fact. It is one of the great merits of Professor Lublinskaya that, while by no means disdaining theory, she remains, as any good historian should remain, deeply impressed by facts. It is as a specialist in the history of seventeenth-century France that she approaches the problem of the 'general crisis', and it is to the detailed exposition of some ten years of French history that the major part of her book is devoted. Since these years, 1620–9, are crucial years in the development of the French monarchy, with the outbreak of the Thirty Years War, the rise to power of Richelieu, and the victory of the Crown over the Huguenots, their study is of outstanding interest in itself, irrespective of any contribution it may make to the understanding of the wider problems of the European economy.

In her four detailed chapters devoted to the France of Louis XIII, Professor Lublinskaya displays a refreshing determination to avoid that 'tendency to anachronism and preconceived opinion' which she detects and castigates in some of her historical colleagues.[2] It will soon be appreciated that this approach yields handsome dividends in the study of a period traditionally dominated, in the eyes of historians, by the towering figure of Cardinal Richelieu. This natural preoccupation with Richelieu has tended to make the early 1620s appear in historical writing as no more than an untidy prelude to his appearance at the centre of the stage, and the later years of the decade as a period in which both policy and events are radically transformed by the genius of a great minister. By means of a meticulous, year-by-year analysis of the national and international situation, Professor Lublinskaya has been able to reveal the powerful element of continuity in Crown policy throughout the decade as a whole, and, in so doing, has given substance and credibility to such figures as La Vieuville, who traditionally flit ghostlike down the corridors of power to disappear into the shadows at the advent of the cardinal.

There is, however, much more here than a rediscovery of forgotten men. Chapter 4 is an important reassessment of the Huguenot question, valuable not only for its analysis of the composition of the Huguenot party, but

[1] *Crisis in Europe*, ed. T. H. Aston (London, 1965), p. 58.
[2] P. 43.

also for its success in setting the problem of the Huguenots within the wider context of the French domestic scene. By unravelling the complexities of the relationship between the Huguenot problem, the opposition of the grandees, and France's precarious international situation, Professor Lublinskaya has made it easier to understand why any French government was bound to give high priority at this juncture to the suppression of the Huguenot 'state within the state'. In this chapter, as in those that follow, the old-fashioned virtues of political and diplomatic narrative, of which Mme Lublinskaya proves to be a stout champion, are amply displayed. But narrative does not dominate to the exclusion of analysis, and politics are not conceived in so narrow a sense as to prevent careful consideration of their relationship to problems of the economy and finance. The author rightly points to the lack of an adequate study of French Crown finances in the age of Richelieu, but her own contribution towards such a study is a valuable one. The role of the financiers was crucial in the life of seventeenth-century France. It was the financiers, grown fat on the profits of war, who became the principal targets of popular hatred in the early days of the Fronde. It was the financiers, comfortably settled in their spacious town houses, who set the style for upper-class urban living in the middle and later years of the century. The nature of their relationship to government is a vital, and often neglected, clue to the effectiveness or ineffectiveness of seventeenth-century states. Chapter 5 of this book provides important evidence about this relationship in the France of Louis XIII.

Professor Lublinskaya's final chapter is devoted to a survey of Richelieu's famous programme for reform, as presented to the Assembly of Notables of 1626. The economic aspects of this programme were admirably examined by Henri Hauser some thirty years ago.[1] But Professor Lublinskaya has been able in this chapter to amplify, and in some cases to correct, Hauser's account, while incidentally providing some new and interesting documentary evidence on the vexed question of the Treaty of Monzón. The most important feature of this chapter, however, is the way in which it allows Richelieu's reform programme to be seen in relation to the formidable political and financial problems of the 1620s, as they have appeared in the earlier chapters of the book. Professor Lublinskaya's treatment of the Assembly of Notables gives a fresh insight into the necessity for financial and economic reform, and makes it possible to gain a clearer idea of the elements of novelty and continuity in the Cardinal's proposals.

In a book that ends with the year 1629, any judgment on Richelieu's stature as a statesman is bound to remain in suspense. In the early years of

[1] *La pensée et l'action économiques du Cardinal de Richelieu* (Paris, 1944).

power it is the problems and the policies which principally impress. One of the most striking features of Richelieu's first years in office is the extent to which both his problems and his policies resemble those to be found on the other side of the Pyrenees, during the opening years of the ministry of his rival, the Count-Duke of Olivares. In the Crown of Aragon the Spanish monarchy has its own version of a 'state within the state' (although at least bereft of religious complications). In the Spain, as in the France, of the early 1620's, the financial position is acute, and an effective foreign policy urgently demands thoroughgoing fiscal and economic reform. Olivares, like Richelieu, is involved in an intricate game of bluff with the great financiers. Like Richelieu, he is besieged by demands for protectionist policies, and, like Richelieu, he gives high priority to the strengthening of the fleet and the launching of overseas trading companies. Like Richelieu, too, he finds his policies thwarted by a combination of apathy and powerful vested interests; and, like the cardinal, he is finally compelled to sacrifice cherished plans for reform in order to meet the appalling financial commitments of war.

Do these similarities between the problems of Richelieu's France and Olivares's Spain suggest, after all, the existence of a 'general crisis' in seventeenth-century Europe? 'Crisis' is a much overworked word these days, and could conveniently be given a rest. But it may well appear to some readers that Professor Lublinskaya, in her anxiety to disprove the notion of a 'crisis of capitalism', has leant over too far in the opposite direction. Readers acquainted with Professor Supple's *Commercial crisis and change in England, 1600–1642*[1] may perhaps feel that she presents an unduly cheerful picture of the English economy in the first half of the seventeenth century. Nor does a study of French mercantilist treatises, however interesting in itself, compensate adequately for the absence of a close investigation of population, agriculture and production, such as has recently been accomplished for Languedoc by Professor Le Roy Ladurie.[2] If Languedoc is in any way representative of France as a whole, then sharp differences seem to have existed between the texture of economic life in a sixteenth century that was conducive to entrepreneurial initiative, and a seventeenth century that favoured the *rentier*.[3]

It seems, indeed, that we are still a long way from being able to pronounce with any degree of confidence on 'the general crisis of the seventeenth

[1] Cambridge, 1959.
[2] *Les paysans de Languedoc* (2 vols, Paris, 1966). It should be pointed out, however, that Professor Ladurie is concerned with agrarian life and has little to say on the question of industrial growth or stagnation.   [3] Ibid. I, 474.

century'. The debate has been useful, in that it has focused attention on certain problems of government, finance, and economic activity, all of which deserved further investigation. It has also served to encourage comparative history, which is capable of adding so much to our understanding of national histories in the Early Modern period. But at the same time it has tended to emphasise how much we still need to know about the development of individual states and societies before 'general' explanations can become anything more than stimulating hypotheses (or, in some instances, positive impediments to intelligent thought). In making her own contribution to the general debate, Professor Lublinskaya has introduced a usefully discordant note from an unexpected quarter. But she has also provided, in her study of the France of Louis XIII, the detailed exposition and analysis which are indispensable if 'general' explanations and comparative history are to be anything more than an amusing *jeu d'esprit*.

J.H.E.

Translator's Note

Writing about the French nobility, Professor Lublinskaya uses the word *znat'* (and sometimes *vel'mozhi*) for those whom contemporaries called *les grands*, and the word *dvoryane* when she refers to the *noblesse d'épée* in general, especially the rank and file of this social group as contrasted with *les grands*. These words have been translated as 'the greater nobles' or 'the higher nobility' and as 'the lesser nobles' or 'the lower nobility', respectively, since to use 'aristocracy' and 'gentry' would imply a distinction between the two strata indicated which did not exist in France as it did in England. Sometimes the name of the higher stratum has been rendered as 'grandees', or 'princes'.

The author's *derzhatel'* and *ispol'schchik* have been put into French, as *tenancier* and *métayer* respectively, since these are the original terms to which the Russian words mentioned correspond in the writings of Russian historians of agrarian relations in France. The *tenancier* was a personally free, but feudally dependent, hereditary possessor of a holding for which a quit-rent was paid to a lord, usually in money. (This quit-rent being called *cens*, the holdings were called *censives*, and the *tenanciers* also known as *censitaires*.) The supreme ownership (*domaine direct*) of land held in this way was retained by the lord, under feudal law—hence the payment of a (fixed) quit-rent— but the peasant was to a large extent free to dispose of the land as he pleased (to sell it, to divide it, to mortgage it, etc.). This form of tenure became established in France in the fifteenth century and lasted until the Revolution. The nearest corresponding term in English land law would be 'copyholder', though copyhold was less firmly guaranteed by the courts than the position of the *tenancier* in France; in some ways, the latter was like an English 'freeholder', but, unlike the freeholder, he was always and necessarily a mere peasant.

The *métayer* held land on a short-term lease which was not subject to feudal law. He had no right to alienate his holding in any way. He leased it, under a written contract, for six to nine years, paying the lord, in kind, a fixed proportion of his crop. He stood in no feudal relationship to the owner of of the land. Marx saw *métayage* as a 'transitional form' between feudal rent and capitalist rent. It developed in France especially from the sixteenth century onward.

When the author writes of 'foreign historians', 'historical writing abroad', and so on, she means, of course, non-Soviet historians and historical writing outside the Soviet Union.

By 'the progressive tasks of absolutism' Professor Lublinskaya means, in accordance with Marxist usage, those changes brought about within the feudal order by the absolute monarchy which centralised the country and in other ways facilitated the growth of capitalism, and in this sense prepared the way for the 'bourgeois revolution'.

Marxists call the stage of capitalist industrial production before the Industrial Revolution the stage of *manufacture* (in contrast to the subsequent stage of machinofacture). Whereas the characteristic enterprise of post-Industrial-Revolution capitalism is the factory, the characteristic of this earlier stage is the *manufactory*, which may be *centralised* (under one roof) or *dispersed* (i.e., the putting-out system in its most advanced form)—consisting in either case of wage-workers who work by hand on the basis of division of labour. A worker who carries out in a manufactory a particular operation which contributes to the production of a commodity is a *detail-worker*. Thus, to quote the classical example, in a needle manufactory the needles passed through the hands of some seventy workers, one of whom drew the wire, another straightened it, a third cut it, a fourth sharpened the ends, and so on. There is a contrast here both with craft production, in which an entire article is made by one worker, and with factory production, in which machinery is used.

My additions to Professor Lublinskaya's notes are given in square brackets. These may add a point of information not available at the time of original publication, or direct the English reader to more accessible sources.

B.P.

Publisher's Note

Professor Lublinskaya has corrected and revised the original Russian text for this translation. She has also abridged the first two chapters, eliminating a number of quotations from works by Western historians which are assumed to be familiar to readers in the English-speaking world.

FRANCE IN 1620

Foreign Enclaves in France		Abbreviations	
O.	Orange	S	Sommières
C.V.	Comtat Venaissin	M	Marsillargues
CH.	Charolais (*to Spain*)	SG	Saint-Gilles
		AM	Aigues-Mortes

▥ Pays d'états

Introduction

The importance of the problems studied in this book is self-evident. The development of capitalism, the changes caused by it in the structure of society, the rise of absolutism, these are the foundations of the entire history of the Western European countries at the beginning of the capitalist era. My choice of this particular period, however, requires some explanation.

In the first third of the seventeenth century all the main distinctive features of each of the countries developing towards the bourgeois form of society became clearly outlined. A new 'hierarchy' of European states, characteristic of the manufactory period of capitalism and of the early bourgeois revolutions, began to take shape.

It was in this period that France assumed its special place in Europe. From being the country of classical feudalism it developed into the country of no less classical absolutism. Just because there was a very close organic connexion between these two stages, it was impossible for France to become the country of classical capitalism. That destiny fell to England. France's lot was a very long-drawn-out preparation for the most radical, and also classical, bourgeois-democratic revolution.

The crucial period during which this particular fate was determined for France, giving her the political hegemony of Europe in the seventeenth century and making her in the eighteenth the centre of the Enlightenment, was the first third of the seventeenth century. Until this period the new and significant beginnings already made in economic life, the social structure, politics and culture, had not yet acquired sufficient stability and firmness. In many countries, early capitalism had proved a fragile and short-lived phenomenon. By the middle of the sixteenth century it had largely faded in Italy, had been broken in Germany and had collapsed in Spain. In France itself the prolonged civil strife of the second half of the sixteenth century had a very harmful effect on the country's capitalist development; the peaceful period of Henry IV's reign was too short, and it was followed by new civil wars. To sum up, in 1610 it was still possible that France might take a road leading to prolonged stagnation and perhaps to decline in capitalist development.

The situation was further complicated by the fact that the strength of the principal political adversary of absolutism at that time, the greater nobles, had not yet been exhausted. Although their ranks had been thinned in the civil wars of the second half of the sixteenth century, they continued to be a group with substantial political weight, and they fought actively for their reactionary programme of decentralisation and maintenance of the old order of things which hindered the development of bourgeois elements. The personality of Louis XIII, incapable of ruling by himself, inspired the grandees with great hopes of subjecting the king to their influence so that he would follow a political course corresponding to their needs. The French princes of the blood, dukes and peers could still hope to gain, at the Court and in the country, positions like those which provided the basis of the power of the feudal grandees of Spain. And this would have been reflected in the entire course of the country's development.

By the end of the first third of the seventeenth century these reactionary pretensions, together with other obstacles, mostly of a political nature, had been overcome. The progressive forces in France—the bourgeoisie and the masses of the people—had played a decisive role in this by supporting the absolute monarchy in its struggle against the grandees and against separatist tendencies. They had proved, even at that time, strong enough to turn the scale in favour of economic and political progress.

These were profound processes, the course and outcome of which were far from fully or always clear to contemporaries. On the contrary, the civil wars and wars against the Huguenots made an impression of something rotten in the state of France and of the instability of the absolute monarchy. Such an impression was all the more convincing in that France's economic position continued to be far from brilliant, and the government's finances were in a lamentable condition. The bourgeoisie was loud in its complaints, and called for a strengthening of protection; the people were starving, and the menace of revolt hung in the air. The government took some measures, but these failed to bring the desired results, for the continually extending Thirty Years War largely paralysed its efforts.

All these political and economic phenomena compel the historian to go outside the usual limits observed in studying the history of a single country (even though taking into account the international setting) and, so to speak, set the country being studied within the system of all-European economics and politics. In the case of the seventeenth century, the historian is very favourably placed, for interesting, broad views are expressed in contemporary historical writing, relating to the complex combination of events in Europe as a whole. The ups and downs of political conflict, involving nearly all countries, the social structure of these countries, and especially the comparatively slow rate of development of capitalism, have in recent years attracted the attention of many historians. In contemporary historiography abroad the theory of 'general crisis' and 'general revolution' in the seventeenth century has become widely accepted.

It is inevitable that the history of France should be given particular attention in the development of these theories, since the general 'state of disorder' appeared in an extremely vivid form in France. On the other hand, one cannot restrict oneself to France alone: a mutual dependence in the development of all the countries of Europe, beginning in the sixteenth century, is a fact beyond dispute or doubt. These are the considerations which have determined the theme and structure of this book, which does not deal only with France, although this country is its centre of attention.

In the first two chapters, on the basis of a critical analysis of the theory of 'general crisis' and 'general revolution' in the seventeenth century, I consider the problem of the peculiarities of the manufactory stage in the development of capitalism as a whole, and the social relations which correspond to this. In the following chapters I endeavour to study the particular situation, between 1610 and the end of the 1620s, of the French economy, in relation to the general economic development of Europe, and of France itself. I review in detail the government's prolonged struggle against the Huguenots, in order to abolish their political autonomy; its relations with the financiers and its financial policy; the plan for economic and financial reforms put forward by Richelieu at the Assembly of Notables in 1626–7; and his activity in the diplomatic sphere. These subjects have been not so much chosen by the author as dictated by the actual course of events in those years.

This work leads on, in respect both of the period covered and of the problems discussed, from my book *France at the beginning of the seventeenth century (1610–1620)* [in Russian] (Leningrad, 1959). The reader will frequently come upon references to the earlier book, as I have endeavoured to avoid repeating much of what has already been examined in detail in another place.

CHAPTER 1

The theory of general economic
crisis in seventeenth-century Europe

FOR a long time the seventeenth century lacked, so far as the whole of Europe and the whole of the century were concerned, a special, resounding epithet to describe it. The title of 'the century of Louis XIV' applied mainly to France in the second half of the century; it was therefore restricted both territorially and chronologically, and did not gain general acceptance. Between its glorious neighbours, 'the century of the Renaissance' and 'the century of the Enlightenment', the seventeenth century seemed somehow not fully defined, lacking in any leading and characteristic feature. It was studied much less than either the sixteenth or the eighteenth.

The situation has markedly altered, however, in the foreign historiography of the last decade. Interest in all aspects of seventeenth-century history has increased, and especially in the economic and social aspects. Many new works of wide scope have appeared, together with new theories which endeavour to systematise the knowledge that has been accumulated, arranging it in some kind of general pattern which will embrace all or most of the countries of Europe, and reveal what it was that determined the common features (or at least the similarity) of the processes taking place in these countries. In these theories, the seventeenth century figures as something special, as a century of very acute contradictions, a century of economic, social and political crisis, of a *crise de conscience*. It has, at last, been given its descriptive epithet, and become the century of 'general crisis' and of 'general revolution', the 'tragic century'.

Many of these conceptions are dubious and even quite unacceptable—in the first place the very idea of 'general crisis' and 'general revolution'—but they are interesting in that they try to penetrate deeply into the essence of events, to track down some sort of fundamental causes of those processes of outstanding importance which were common to all the countries of Europe.

France occupies almost the first place in these theories not only on account of its objectively great role in the history of the entire continent, but also because many phenomena that are nowadays regarded as specific to the 'tragic century' found their most clear-cut expression in France (economic crisis, mercantilism, absolutism, classicism, etc.). Of particular interest in this connexion is the first half of the century, when the contradictions revealed themselves in an especially vivid way, when the time was out of joint and the whole of society in ferment.

The increased interest in the economic history of the seventeenth century is closely linked with the interest that many foreign historians are showing in the important and complicated problems of the origins of capitalism and its development within the womb of feudal society. Very noteworthy in this connexion was not only the appearance, as long ago as 1946, of a book by the British Marxist Maurice Dobb,[1] but also the lively discussion which arose in connexion with this book and which has continued right down to the present time.[2] Soviet historians reacted very quickly to this discussion, in the form of reviews in which they evaluated the ideas of Dobb and the other participants in the discussion and emphasised the methodological interest of the problem being discussed.[3]

The discussion ranged over a wide field of social and economic aspects in the history of Western European countries between the fifteenth and eighteenth centuries, but its most fruitful result was in relation to research on the period which is 'darkest' so far as economic history is concerned, namely, the seventeenth century. Going forward from the sixteenth century, which has been relatively well studied in this respect, historians found themselves in a rather difficult situation, confronted with facts which were not yet adequately explained. In the overall picture they found they were startled by the absence of a forward movement in the first quarter of the seventeenth century, followed by a prolonged stagnation and even decline. This was first and foremost a matter of prices. After the appearance of Hamilton's work on the 'price revolution' of the sixteenth century, a sort of axiom became established among foreign historians, whereby the movement of prices had to be treated as basic in any investigation of economic history.[4] Later on, social conflicts came within historians' field of vision—the numerous peasant and urban revolts of this period. An important part was played in this connexion by B. F. Porshnev's book, *Popular uprisings in France before the Fronde* [in

[1] M. Dobb, *Studies in the development of capitalism* (London, 1946).
[2] *The transition from feudalism to capitalism*, a symposium by P. Sweezy, H. K. Takahashi, M. Dobb, R. Hilton, C. Hill (London, 1954); G. Lefebvre, G. Procacci and A. Soboul, 'Une discussion historique: du féodalisme au capitalisme', *Pensée*, no. 65 (1956); M. Dobb, *The transition from feudalism to capitalism* ('Our History' pamphlet no. 29) (London, 1963).
[3] I. Zvavich, review [in Russian] of Dobb, *Studies in the development of capitalism*, *Voprosy Istorii*, no. 4 (1947); Yu. L. Bessmertny, review [in Russian] of the discussion (see note 2, above), *Voprosy Istorii*, no. 12 (1955).
[4] A very interesting and fundamental criticism of this theory is given in P. Vilar's article, 'Problems of capitalism', *Past and Present*, no. 10 (1956).

Russian], which was published in 1948 and became known abroad after the appearance of a German translation of the whole book,[1] and further after reviews had appeared in the French press, followed by a French translation of the long introduction.[2] Against the background of the seventeenth-century economic depression and class conflict, special significance was accorded to the most important events of the middle years of the century—the English Revolution and the Fronde, the latter described by Porshnev as an unsuccessful bourgeois revolution. A heated discussion arose round these subjects too. In short, seventeenth-century history became one of the most topical of themes. Every fresh piece of work on it, whether in the form of a big book, a basic article or even a short note, contributed to the development of the problem.

One of the earliest and at the same time most many-sided and complete statements of this conception of a general crisis in the development of the Western European countries in the seventeenth century was made by Roland Mousnier, who in 1954 brought out the fourth volume in the Paris series *Histoire générale des civilisations*, under the title: *Les XVIe et XVIIe siècles. Les progrès de la civilisation européenne et le déclin de l'Orient (1492–1715)*.

In the course of eight years this book went through three editions, which testifies to its great success not only among specialists but also with a wide public.[3] It was written in vivid and expressive language, and lavishly illustrated. An extensive section of the book dealt with various aspects of the crisis and how it was overcome. All the progress made in the seventeenth century, its abundant fruits in the field of science and art, giving it the right to be called *le Grand Siècle*, were achieved as a result of the efforts put into the overcoming of the crisis. This, in the author's view, is the historical significance for the world of the Western European crisis of the seventeenth century and its resolution.

Before proceeding to analyse this idea, we must briefly consider Mousnier's views on the history of Western Europe in the previous century. He understands the crisis of the seventeenth century mainly in terms of a comparison with the sixteenth-century boom, which Mousnier, like other foreign historians, calls the economic Renaissance and the capitalist revolution.[4]

It must be mentioned that the entire book, and especially the first half

[1] B. Porschnew, *Die Volksaufstände in Frankreich* (Berlin, 1954).
[2] Review by Jean Bruhat in *Pensée* (nos. 29 and 32, 1950); translation of the preface in *Pensée* (nos. 40 and 41, 1952). In 1963 appeared a French translation of the whole book: B. Porchnev, *Les soulèvements populaires en France de 1623 à 1648* (Paris, 1963) (*École Pratique des Hautes Études, VIe section, Œuvres étrangères*, IV).
[3] A second, revised edition appeared in 1956 (the subsequent references are to this edition), and a third edition, also revised, and enlarged, in 1961.
[4] Mousnier, *Les XVIe et XVIIe siècles*, p. 47.

dealing with Europe, are written more in the form of reflexions on the essential meaning of the processes taking place than of a connected chronological exposition. The author assumes that the reader knows the facts of political history, and he speaks of events only in so far as he is obliged to do this when discussing the economic, social, constitutional and international history of the period. This means that the whole book is rich in constantly moving thought, it enables the author to undertake far-reaching comparisons —in short, it makes the book interesting not only to specialists but also to every type of reader.

Mousnier discusses in fair detail the economic situation in the sixteenth century, describing this primarily in terms of the tempestuous development of commercial capitalism. He deals also with the progress of mining and metallurgy, stressing the appearance in these branches of expensive technical innovations. The development of capitalist relations as a whole, that is, the capitalist exploitation of wage-workers, is given considerably less attention, and agrarian relations are touched on only briefly.

One cannot deny the great part played by merchants' capital in the sixteenth century; everything connected with it leaps to the eye when one first surveys the period. The material contained in the sources—or at least, in those which have been used by historians up to now—also focuses attention on merchants' capital. But in the course of Mousnier's argument a sort of shifting of emphasis occurs, both on the economic and on the historical level. He is inclined to see in the brilliant prosperity of trade, banking and the rest the growth of capitalism in general, and, correspondingly, he sees the decline of trade and the contraction in the scale of credit operations as the decline of capitalism. He expresses this shift of historical emphasis by attributing an all-European, international character to capitalism in the sixteenth century (at least down to 1560) which later on appears to have been lost through the national mercantilist policies of the separate states.

Large-scale trade did indeed link the countries of Europe together economically, and linked them with distant continents, and credit and financial operations ignored state frontiers. The Antwerp stock exchange was established for the merchants of all countries. But let us look more closely at these phenomena. The pages devoted to them are strewn with mentions of the Fuggers, the Welsers, the Hochstätters and so on, to illustrate the bold enterprising spirit of sixteenth-century capitalists, their readiness to undertake risk, and also their close financial and political ties with the absolute monarchies. It is quite natural that Mousnier should see the Fuggers and their like as typical examples of the big capitalists of the sixteenth century. But was their activity really all-European and international? Would it not be truer to

7

say that it was limited to the confines of the Empire of Charles V, and was international only to the extent that (with all possible reservations) that empire can be regarded as international, because it joined together, formally and temporarily, Germany, Spain, the Netherlands and part of Italy? In any case, this activity cannot be called all-European; it hardly affected at all such large and important countries as England and France. Consequently, the extensive scale of the activity of the Fuggers and other German commercial and banking houses was determined entirely by a *political* factor—the large extent of the Empire, of which Charles V made Germany the centre—and not by the characteristics of capitalism itself as such.

The view that capitalist activity on an all-European scale was replaced by nationally confined mercantilism also seems lacking in adequate foundation. Mercantilism, as is well known, was older than 1560 and indeed was developed successfully in England and France before that date. It can be observed, in a special form, in Charles V's Empire too, where for a time the national boundaries of the countries comprising this Empire were obliterated. There it had an especially marked effect on the scale of the financial and commercial activity of the Fuggers and other capitalists. When the Empire of Charles V collapsed, this 'imperial' variant of mercantilism came to an end as well, and distinct Spanish, Dutch, etc., mercantilisms came to the forefront again.

In the first and second editions of his book, Mousnier examines in detail the decline of capitalism which set in in the second half of the sixteenth century. In the third edition, however, he rejects the view that capitalism did decline. Mousnier now considers that, despite the unfavourable political circumstances of this period, economic activity continued to be substantial in all branches of production. Thus, the entire sixteenth century is sharply contrasted, as an epoch of boom, with the seventeenth century as an epoch of crisis.

Mousnier examines the social consequences of the development of capitalism: he defines its mutual relations with the state in the sixteenth century in terms of the giving of credit by bankers to the state, and sees the absolute monarchy as a particular type of capitalist enterprise, operated by financiers.[1]

The structure of sixteenth-century society appears as follows. The capitalist boom and the increase in prices brought the bourgeoisie closer to the *classe des seigneurs* and separated them from the *classes populaires,* and also divided

[1] See on this A. D. Lublinskaya, 'The contemporary bourgeois conception of the absolute monarchy' [in Russian], *Kritika noveishei burzhuaznoi istoriografii. Sbornik statei [A critique of contemporary bourgeois historiography. Symposium]* (Moscow–Leningrad, USSR Academy of Sciences Press, 1961), pp. 374–403 (*Trudy Leningradskogo otdeleniya Instituta istorii, vypusk* 3 [*Transactions of the Leningrad Section of the Institute of History,* III]).

them into various groups. The lords who were impoverished by the rise in prices sold their land to the merchants, who were raised to the nobility and laid the foundations of new noble families. The old nobility, however, did not accept them as equals. Below these ennobled merchants were bourgeois—craft-guild masters, small shopkeepers and craftsmen. At the very bottom of the social ladder were the proletariat—workers in capitalist enterprises, journeymen, craftsmen outside the guilds. Their nominal wages grew very slowly (owing to the resistance of the bourgeoisie, which was supported by the rulers), and their real wages fell. A class struggle began, with strikes and revolts.

In the countryside, farmers of the capitalist type were separated from *tenanciers* (feudal tenants) and *métayers* (share-croppers), whose position grew worse as a result of the increase in prices. Peasant revolts broke out, in which sections of the better-off peasantry often joined, protesting against high prices for imported goods, against the spread of capitalist property and against feudal dues.

A differentiation of classes took place, and a struggle between classes developed which had political and religious consequences.

It is very important to note that in this analysis no place is found for the most important social group (most important not quantitatively but qualitatively)—the merchant entrepreneurs, the section of the big bourgeoisie which did not become ennobled and did not lose its essentially bourgeois character. This is a considerable gap in an analysis of the structure of society in the sixteenth century, a period when the presence or disappearance of a commercial and industrial bourgeoisie played a part of foremost importance, signifying, on the one hand, a movement forward in the direction of bourgeois society and, on the other, decline and stagnation. The destiny of industrial capitalism and the peculiarity of its evolution in the sixteenth century have remained outside the scope of this analysis, which purports to sum up the development of Western European society in the sixteenth century as a whole.

Mousnier begins his analysis of the economic crisis of the seventeenth century with an enumeration of the radical defects inherent in the society of that time, which became more acute as a result of the fall in prices at the beginning of the seventeenth century. He ascribes paramount importance to the disparity between the growth of population and the restricted possibilities of feeding it. Agricultural technique remained at a low level, crop-yields did not improve, famine and disease were endemic, and the redundant part of the population periodically died off. Frequent harvest-failures caused an increase in the price of corn, affecting especially those cereals which the mass of the people consumed. The importation of wheat from Eastern Europe only helped a little, for transport charges were high.

Famines brought economic crisis in their train. They disorganised the life of the countryside, caused the death of wage-workers, the flight of population from the countryside, and the formation of a deprived and miserable proletariat. The high price of foodstuffs compelled nobles and bourgeois to reduce their expenditure, unemployment appeared in the cities, craftsmen sold their products themselves, at a loss, the profits of entrepreneurs declined. The periodical famines intensified the general economic instability and created obstacles to the progress of the economy.

This chronic instability of the economic structure was complicated in the seventeenth century by crises caused by the movement of prices. First the increase in prices slowed down, and then prices began to fall, a process marked by very sharp fluctuations.

The quantity of precious metals imported from America into Europe began to shrink, according to Hamilton's figures, from as early as 1600 onward. The insignificant yearly increase in the supply of precious metals was already inadequate to meet the growing demand for money for commercial transactions. After the 1630s came a sharp reduction in imports of gold and silver, and after the 1650s this almost ceased altogether.

Before 1625–30 prices rose fairly slowly in Europe as a whole, then, after remaining steady for a time, they began a slow decline. After 1650–60 the fall in prices became more rapid, the lowest level being reached in 1660–80. Then they rose a little, until 1700, but in 1700–15 declined somewhat. In England the rapid rise in prices went on until 1640–50.

In a number of countries inflation took place (in the first third of the century, Germany, Spain and some others, and at the end of the century in France), that is, the amount of precious metal in the coinage was reduced.

The consequence was a slowing down of the development of capitalism over a large part of Europe. The insignificant increase in prices reduced the profits of the capitalists.[1] No new enterprises were established, and existing ones were expanded only rarely. The tempo of production declined and the number of unemployed and vagabonds increased.

Furthermore, the seventeenth century was marked by extraordinarily sharp variations in prices, much greater than comparable phenomena in the sixteenth century. These began in the very first years of the seventeenth century (a particularly sharp fall was observed, continuing until 1610–15). The fluctuations bore a partly seasonal and partly cyclical character, with

[1] See the critique by P. Vilar of the thesis about the reduction in profit as a result of the fall in prices (Vilar, loc. cit. p. 21).

cycles of ten to twenty years. Even in England the steady rise in prices was succeeded in 1640–50 by a situation in which sharp fluctuations occurred.

Mousnier considers that it is not possible at present to give a complete explanation of these phenomena, and offers a merely partial one. The causes of these price fluctuations cannot be wars because, given the rudimentary development of exchange in those days, movements of troops and battles could have an effect on prices only in the particular localities where these took place. Unfavourable weather conditions must be taken into account, however, along with the consequences of harvest-failures and the growth of population.

In the seventeenth century the economy of nearly the whole of Europe, with only a few countries excepted, was close to disaster. Too rapid and acute rises in prices, by reducing demand, made trade unprofitable. At the same time, these rises did not last long enough for even the most firmly established entrepreneurs to be able to exploit them to make up for their trading losses by increasing profits and accumulating capital for investment. A fall in prices again set in, and profits vanished. The entrepreneur dismissed workers and withheld payment from creditors. These fluctuations made it impossible to carry out any well-grounded calculations, and discouraged entrepreneurs. Many businesses closed down, while others could not be developed.

Thus, Mousnier concludes, the seventeenth century, lying between two centuries in which price-increases were the characteristic feature, was a period in which economic crisis was uninterrupted, though it varied in intensity.

In analysing this conception one first and foremost feels doubtful about the stress laid on the stagnation of agricultural technique and of demographic movements. These were characteristic of the entire medieval period, along with harvest-failure, famine, epidemics, etc. Mousnier correctly remarks that these defects were inherent in the social structure as such. But then it should be recognised that they were operative in the sixteenth century, too, when there was an undoubted growth of capitalism. It is hard to agree with his view that there was complete stagnation in agriculture, and very low yields. Surely those facts which he has noted in relation to the sixteenth century[1]— the increase in the production of grain for sale, as also of wine, industrial crops, etc.—continued to prevail in the seventeenth? Economic specialisation, including agricultural specialisation, of different regions and countries continued to grow. The migration of countryfolk to the towns increased the number of cash customers for foodstuffs, and the existence of standing armies operated in the same direction. Such phenomena as these—the increase in

---

[1] Mousnier, *Les XVIᵉ et XVIIᵉ siècles*, p. 65.

urban populations and the existence of large armies—would have been altogether impossible if there had been complete stagnation in agriculture and an unchanging volume of agricultural production. In the demographic sphere it is necessary to take into account not only quantitative changes but also qualitative ones.

Of course, famines and epidemics were severe calamities for the population, increasing the death-rate and disrupting normal conditions of life for a certain period of time. But they rarely involved whole countries, affecting, as a rule, only particular regions and not disturbing the forward march of economic development as a whole.

There are no grounds for attributing the high prices for foodstuffs in the seventeenth century only to such causes as harvest-failure or a large influx of precious metals. Such explanations could be relevant to a society with developed capitalist production, in which commodity economy embraced all branches. The nobility and bourgeoisie of the seventeenth century, however, were far from being as dependent on the market for provisions as they were to be later on, even in the eighteenth century. Rent in kind, tithes and payments in kind under *métayage*, played a considerable part in the seventeenth century, making a substantial section of the landowners first and foremost direct consumers of the products of their estates and only in the second place, and to a certain extent, sellers, not buyers, of these products. For this reason the effect of harvest-failures (provided these were not too frequent and did not involve an extensive area) on the productive life of the cities could not be so direct, rapid and prolonged as to disturb it profoundly. Besides which, the urban market and urban production served not only the nobles and bourgeois but the whole urban population, a wide area round about, and, in the seventeenth century, also distant regions and countries. Consequently, the scale of urban production, in which masses of urban craftsmen and workers were occupied, depended to an incomparably greater extent on the general economic situation than on the increase or decrease of demand on the part of the local nobles and bourgeois. These considerations entitle us to see the phenomena mentioned—without denying their importance altogether—as playing a different role in the complex of economic factors in the seventeenth century from that given them in Mousnier's book, and not to regard them as being peculiar to the seventeenth century.

Let us now turn to the analysis of price-movements. This is the process which Mousnier puts in the forefront of his conception.

It is above all necessary to observe that historians have not yet at their disposal a *detailed* picture of price-movements even in the chief countries of seventeenth-century Europe. To judge the impact of this process on the economic life of *particular* countries such information is, however, essential, for in the seventeenth century it was precisely the difference in the rate of development of different countries towards bourgeois society that was increasing. An overall estimate of price-movements for Europe as a whole largely conceals these differences.

Nevertheless, let us take, for lack of anything better, the data which have so far been made available, and let us consider a few periods. It is evidently beyond doubt, so far as at any rate some countries are concerned, that there was a fall in prices at the very beginning of the seventeenth century (that is, in 1600–10 and even in 1610–15). One might draw the conclusion that this period must have seen a very unfavourable economic situation. In fact it was quite the opposite. The low prices did not affect industry adversely. In France, for instance, the first decade of the seventeenth century was a period of boom in manufacture, craft production and agriculture, a period in which the State debt was reduced, the State budget was balanced, and so on. The profits of merchants and manufacturers increased, and they succeeded in becoming considerably richer in these years.

Similar phenomena, though on a lower level, occurred in Spain. Holland was unquestionably prosperous in this period. (England cannot be included in this generalisation, since there prices continued to rise right down to the middle of the seventeenth century.)[1] In short, for the three European countries for which the seventeenth century really was a period of capitalist development (at different rates), that is, for Holland, England and France, the beginning of the century was *not* accompanied by the appearance of conditions unfavourable to this development, despite the reduction in the influx of precious metals and the fall in prices which had already begun.[2]

It must be emphasised that in Spain, Germany and Italy unfavourable conditions for the development of capitalism had taken shape earlier.[3] The stagnation or even the decline of embryonic capitalist relations took place in these countries as early as the sixteenth century, that is, in a period of an acute increase in prices, and was brought about in Germany and Italy by quite different causes. As for Spain, that country's economic development

---

[1] Earl J. Hamilton, 'The History of Prices before 1750', *XIe Congrès International des Sciences Historiques, Rapports*, I (Stockholm, 1960), 152. Some historians consider that not only in England but throughout the northern countries the favourable situation lasted until 1640–50 (see Jeannin's review of Mousnier, *Les XVIe et XVIIe siècles* (3rd edition), *Revue historique*, CCXXX (1963), 180, 181).

[2] It must be mentioned that Mousnier offers only fragmentary and scanty facts of an economic nature for countries other than these. He examines in detail and in all aspects, three countries only: England, Holland and France. A few pages are given to the state structure of Poland and Russia. All the other countries are practically outside his field of view.

[3] Judging by recent research, the economic decline of Italy should not be dated earlier than the middle of the sixteenth century.

was, so far as can be judged, fundamentally undermined precisely by a too tempestuous price-revolution. The other countries of northern, eastern and south-eastern Europe were, even in the seventeenth century, mostly taking only the first steps along the road to the appearance of capitalism or had not yet even started on this road. For this reason their economic life, whether advancing or declining, cannot be estimated in terms of the advance or decline of capitalism.

In the subsequent period, 1615–30, a period of slow increase in prices, one's attention is attracted by the disparity which is beginning to appear between the shrinking influx of precious metals and the rise in prices, which, though slowing down, is still continuing. For this reason the supporters of the theory of a crisis caused by low prices cannot call this period of price-increases an unfavourable one.

In 1630 a sharp fall in the influx of precious metals occurred (it suddenly fell to the level of 1580), but prices in Spain itself remained, on the average, at the previous level, and in other countries fell very slowly. Consequently, the divergence between the two curves (influx of precious metals and move-ment of prices) continued to increase.

After 1650, the influx of gold and silver through Spain almost dried up, and so the relation between this and the movement of prices ceased. Nevertheless, prices still fell slowly.

Further, the years of lowest prices, 1660–80, can hardly be regarded as an unfavourable period for the development of capitalism in England, Holland and France. On the contrary, there can be no doubt that there was economic progress in these years in England and France. It was in the twenty years under Colbert that the development of capitalism in France took a big step forward. The last period of the seventeenth century, 1680–1700, was one which saw a certain rise in prices.

Let us present the picture as a whole, that is, without taking into account short, sharp fluctuations or special deviations in particular countries:

1600–1615	low prices
1615–1630	a slow rise in prices
1630–1650	a slow fall in prices
1650–1660	low prices
1660–1680	very low prices
1680–1700	a slow rise in prices

It is especially important to take into account the fact mentioned above that in 1615–30 the curves showing influx of precious metals and movement of prices did not correspond, and also the cessation of the influx of precious

14

metals from 1650 onward. For this reason one can speak, as regards the century as a whole, except for the years 1600–15, of an *independent* movement of prices, *not* dependent on the influx of gold and silver. This distinguishes the seventeenth century qualitatively from the preceding one. The price-revolution as such ended at the turn from the sixteenth into the seventeenth century.

Mousnier's view that there were *acute* price-fluctuations in the seventeenth century seems, moreover, to be not altogether well-founded. Particular peaks in the curves showing price-movements can occur in very different periods and are due, as a rule, to causes which do not last very long. The cyclical movement of prices in the seventeenth century is marked by rather gentle transitions. As compared with the sixteenth century (with the extremely sharp rise in prices in 1550–60 and again in 1580–90) and with the fall in prices after 1600, the price-curves for the seventeenth century are on the whole more even.

It is also obvious that both the periods of particularly low prices (1600–15 and 1660–80) were at the same time periods of marked boom and growth of capitalism in those countries where one can in general talk of such a pheno-menon in the seventeenth century, namely, England, France and Holland. It is notable that for France, moreover, these were the *only* periods of com-paratively rapid capitalist development in the seventeenth century. These considerations must be given attention when we draw up the balance sheet of the history of France in the seventeenth century.

For this reason the thesis about the slow development of capitalism in a large part of Europe in the seventeenth century begins to look doubtful. If a situation when prices rose very little reduced the profits of the capitalists, why then (if we take France as an example) did these profits rise precisely in the periods when prices were lowest?[1] The largest number of new manu-factories appeared in France precisely in the times of Henry IV and of Colbert, that is, in the low-price periods already mentioned. This means that the view that the tempo of production declined when prices were low is groundless (I will deal with the question of vagabonds and the unemployed later).

Let us now look at the explanations offered by Mousnier. These do not bear on the direction taken by price-movements as a whole, but only on their cyclical fluctuations. It must be admitted that historians as yet have not the information needed to explain completely the complex economic processes of the seventeenth century. But to a certain limited extent this task can be undertaken.

[1] Compare Hamilton's view of the high level of profits not only in the sixteenth century but also throughout the seventeenth (Hamilton, loc. cit. p. 160).

Mousnier does not consider that wars were responsible for price-fluctuations, because in the seventeenth century military operations were localised. This is true, but war must be seen as a whole and not confined to the mere theatre of hostilities. The increase in taxes, the strain on material and human resources, the expanded production of arms and equipment for the armies—these and other phenomena affected the whole country, burdening to a greater or less extent nearly the whole population, and not merely in those particularly unfortunate areas where actual fighting took place. It seems highly probable that temporary fluctuations in prices were to some extent caused precisely by war conditions, though in each separate country this depended every time on specific circumstances.

Mousnier's other ideas about the increase in population and its connexion with price-movements[1] may be well-founded in themselves, but it is hard to apply them to the seventeenth century as a whole as causes of prime importance, and indeed Mousnier himself does not so regard them.

It is more important to analyse Mousnier's conclusion about the catastrophic situation of the European economy in the seventeenth century. True, one must, of course, exclude England and Holland from this conclusion, so that the *only* country, among those already advancing along the road of capitalist development, to which the conclusion applies, is France. In the subsequent chapters I shall examine the conditions for the development of capitalism in France in the first third of the seventeenth century, that is, in a period which I regard as very important for the study of the conditions governing the formation of bourgeois society within the womb of the feudal order. For the moment I note that in all the other countries of Europe, that is, over the greater part of the continent, the seventeenth century either was, or was not, a difficult time for economic development for different reasons in each case, and this was not connected with the development of capitalism in these countries. There are no grounds for extending the thesis about a crisis of capitalism to the whole of seventeenth-century Europe. The general notion of an economic crisis (that is, not necessarily a crisis of capitalist development) is put forward by Mousnier in too sweeping, too summary a form.

It seems to me that one can only formulate a theory about economic development in the seventeenth century if one analyses not just the economic life but the whole complex of social and economic relations and political struggle. For this reason I will first examine the theory of social and political crisis developed in Mousnier's book.

[1] Compare also the critique of the theory of the growth of population as a cause of the movement of prices, in Hamilton, (loc. cit. pp. 157, 158).

As regards Europe as a whole, Mousnier confines himself to a brief remark that in the seventeenth century social antagonisms became more acute, without any change in their essential sixteenth-century character. The importance of particular groups of the bourgeoisie continued to increase, though not so fast as in the previous century. Later, he proceeds to consider the social crisis in separate countries.

In France[1] and other similar countries, he explains, economic instability compelled capitalists to turn to making loans to the state, which was more profitable than industrial and commercial activity. As a consequence, the social importance of the financiers and of financial and judicial officials increased. The sale of offices became widespread almost everywhere, but in France it reached its apogee. Officials possessed their offices as hereditary property, which facilitated the consolidation of a whole 'class'[2] of officials.

At the same time the class of merchant-manufacturers grew in strength. Like the rich craft-guild masters, the merchants controlled large amounts of capital, and founded enterprises for the making of cannon, arms, saltpetre, metal wares, silk fabrics, carpets and clothes. They bought land and acquired State, municipal and ecclesiastical offices for members of their families. In this way they joined in the exercise of governmental authority (*fonctions publiques*) on an equal footing with tax-farmers and officials.

The aim of all these bourgeois was to attain *noblesse*, and they attained it by various paths. But the old nobility despised these pen-pushers and shop-keepers, and all the more because they monopolised expensive offices which had become unattainable for the nobles themselves. And even those offices which were not put up for sale were more and more frequently given by the king to bourgeois—under Henry IV they increasingly filled the king's Council, which formerly had been made up mostly of men from the old nobility. Secretaries of state and ministers were bourgeois who retained, in spite of their titles of marquis, count, and so on, manners and habits alien to the way of life of the old nobility.

Antagonism increased between the lords, who were owners of fiefs, whether they were from the old nobility, officials, merchants or financiers, and the peasants, 'in spite of their community of interests and their tenurial ties'.[3] The lords lived on the peasants' labour, receiving rent and dues from them, in addition to which, part of the state taxes paid by the peasantry found its way to the lords in the form of pensions, salaries and the like. Their income from the land depended, however, to a large extent, on the movement of prices.

[1] I deal with France in more detail than with other countries.
[2] Here and later I retain the terminology used by Mousnier.
[3] Mousnier, *Les XVIe et XVIIe siècles*, p. 154. A community of interest between peasants and landlords is assumed to exist.

In a period of increasing prices, if this resulted from a shortage of food-stuffs, the lords and the larger farmers, who had reserves, were the ones who benefited, being able to sell at high prices. The *métayers* and smallholding peasants suffered; their harvest went in subsistence and seed-corn, and there was nothing left with which to pay taxes and dues.

If the increase in prices was due to other causes, everyone benefited: small peasants, large farmers and lords, especially the latter, for at every renewal of a lease they could increase the rent to be paid, so reducing the farmer's income.

When prices fell, the *métayers* and smallholding peasantry were able to pay their rents and dues in kind with ease (if prices had fallen owing to abundance of produce), but found themselves in difficulties with their money payments, because they were obliged to sell as much as possible immediately after the harvest, which was a bad time, since prices were at their lowest. In such a situation, outgoings for taxes, rent and dues might exceed their total income. Periods like this were also hard for the agricultural workers, and the number of vagabonds grew. Leaseholders likewise suffered, if their leases had been drawn up in a period of high prices.

As a result, concludes Mousnier, inequality and antagonisms between classes grew increasingly. In addition whether prices were rising or falling, taxes, rents and dues frequently exceeded in amount the incomes of the small producers, and then peasant revolts and peasant wars broke out.

Antagonisms also increased in the towns, between the nobles, financiers and officials, on the one hand, and the taxpayers—small craft-guild masters and journeymen—on the other. The official bodies were biased in favour of the oligarchy of big merchant-manufacturers, while they encroached on the interests of craftsmen of all ranks and conditions. The state supported the employers against the workers and journeymen, helping them to escape un-favourable competition, reduce wages and prolong the working day. The angry workers and journeymen formed clandestine unions and struggled against their employers. Their numbers grew and they felt their strength: in 1637 in Paris there were 45,000 workers and apprentices, in Lyons they constituted two-thirds of the population of 100,000. When a flood of poor people and vagabonds poured into the cities, adding their numbers to the unemployed and low-paid workers, urban revolts broke out. Social antagon-isms were fostered by the religious conflicts between Catholics and Huguenots; such clashes easily developed into class struggles if the rich merchant-manufacturers were Huguenots and the workers dependent on them were Catholics.

There is no need here to paraphrase at length Mousnier's description of the economic situation and social crisis in England. He depicts the process of vigorous development of capitalism in seventeenth-century England, with the formation of new classes—industrial bourgeoisie, gentry, workers. There was no economic crisis in England, but the social antagonisms were characteristic of a country where capitalism was developing rapidly. The same applies to Holland as well.

Turning to the political crisis, Mousnier observes everywhere (that is, in England, Holland and France) revolts and civil wars, either open or else maturing in less obvious ways.

In France the war with the Habsburgs gave rise to a constant deficit in the budget. Expenditure increased rapidly. At the same time, possibilities for developing industry were limited, receipts from taxation were inadequate, and every increase in taxes was badly received by the population. The demands of the royal exchequer became causes of revolt, or pretexts for it.

Peasant revolts went on continuously, and in periods when taxes rose substantially there were regular peasant wars, embracing several regions. The town workers rose if bread was dear, unemployment considerable and taxes heavy.

Revolts were especially numerous between 1630 and 1659. They cannot, however, according to Mousnier, be described as a war of the poor against the rich. The rebels attacked only the agents of the exchequer, and the tax-farmers. *Châteaux* and *hôtels* were in danger only in those cases where their owners were upstarts—officials and financiers. The government restored order without difficulty, provided that nobles, officials and bourgeois did not take part. When all classes joined in rebellion, the state found itself in crisis. Mousnier draws the following picture of such a crisis in France of the first half of the seventeenth century.

The revolt of the princes of the blood and the aristocracy against absolutism enlisted the support of the mass of the people, including even the peasantry, he claims. The grandees had extensive *clientèles* in the army and in the provinces, made up of nobles and officials, and these in turn were very influential among the local petty nobility, small bourgeoisie and peasants. All lords wielded enormous influence over their peasants, based on the tenurial ties between the latter and the owners of the land. Hatred on the part of the peasants for their lords arose only when the latter were especially bad. Besides, the nobles and the peasants had common interests which united them against the king and his exchequer. The royal taxes sucked the peasants dry and reduced the incomes of the lords (lower leasehold rents, and in bad years even cessation of payment of rents and dues). The lords often called on their peasants to rise up against tax-collectors, and protected them from oppression by the soldiery during the civil wars. For these reasons the peasants usually followed their lords.

All classes of society readily joined revolts. This was because there were no clear-cut dividing lines between them. Often within a single family some members were military men, that is, noblemen, while others were officials, and yet others were related by marriage to greater merchants or to members of the *parlements*, etc. The close family ties and client-relationships of those days favoured the mutual interweaving of different social groups, from the highest nobility down to the merchants.

The king could not rely even on his officials. The interests of the members of the *parlements* and other high courts were damaged by the various dues demanded from them, which lowered the value and importance of their offices. The increase in direct taxation reduced their income from land, while the increase in indirect taxation hit at their pockets as consumers. They refused to register fiscal edicts even in the very midst of war, and this in some instances paralysed the operations of the government. The Paris *parlement* claimed the right to carry out, along with the grandees, as in 1615 and 1648, the most important political functions, that is, it fought for a monarchy limited by the influence of the aristocracy, while the aim of the royal authority was a monarchy both absolute and founded on the people's acceptance.

In 1648, Mousnier goes on, the *parlement* intended to organise a government, independent of the king, with legislative authority and control over the executive; this meant a first attempt at a separation of powers. The *parlement* pressed for a limited monarchy, and even prepared the way for a republic. Its position was a revolutionary one; it included rejection of a monarchy which united the king with his kingdom and the nation with its sovereign.

This political revolution was, however, fundamentally retrograde. It aimed merely at defence of the present positions of the members of the *parlements* and their allies, who wielded power in the localities in their capacity as possessors of offices and fiefs. It was directed against another revolution which was being carried through by absolutism with the aim of centralisation and, to a certain degree, a general levelling (egalitarianism). Defending provincial and corporate particularism, the *parlements* fought against the strengthening of their rivals, the *intendants* who were appointed by the king and acted in the interests of the king and the public weal, interests which coincided with the general interests of the state.

The *parlements* had one good weapon—protest against taxation. They convinced the French people that they were paying excessively high taxes merely for the sake of the king's glory and the luxury of the court (although at that time the Habsburgs were threatening the very existence of the kingdom, and the wretched court had not even enough money for food). Consequently the people felt respect and affection for the *parlements*, as did the urban bourgeoisie, who were likewise tormented by taxes. As landowners, the members of the *parlements* also enjoyed authority among their own peasants.

The Huguenot party defended their special position, their federalism. The Huguenot lords joined with the grandees and revolted every time that the king particularly needed internal peace because of external war.

Thus, as soon as the grandees gave the signal, says Mousnier, nobles, officials, townspeople, and peasants in the provinces rose in revolt. The nobles called on the population to fight, while the *parlements* forced the storehouses to open where the corn which the *intendants* had collected for the army was stored (for example, in the Dauphiné in 1630), or seized from the royal treasurers the payments which they had withheld, again because of war needs (for example, at Toulouse in 1630). They supported the rebels, and in those cases when revolt was directed only against the king's agents and did not affect their own interests, they refrained from taking the measures they should have taken in order to stop it.

Revolts occurred during the minorities of Louis XIII and Louis XIV, when the princes of the blood put forward their claims to rule, and also in years of harvest-failure, dearth, and war, when, in Mousnier's opinion, national feeling was extinguished; grandees, officials, bourgeoisie, common people, all, so to speak, forgot about the external enemy, and the provinces rose in revolt one after another. More than once the country's fate depended on the outcome of a single battle. If at Lens in 1648 not the French but the Spaniards had won the day, at a time when the Fronde was coming to a head, this would have led to the dismemberment of the state and the shipwreck of French national independence.

To the political crisis in England and Holland, Mousnier devotes only a page and a half. He sees as the cause of the two English revolutions of the seventeenth century the struggle against absolutism on the part of the bourgeoisie and those sections of the gentry which had become capitalistic, fighting for a limited monarchy which would personify their capitalist interests. In Holland, Mousnier mentions the acute conflict between the republican-inclined Dutch bourgeoisie, with their unifying tendency, headed by the Grand Pensionary of Holland (whom they cast for the role of president of a unified republic of the United Provinces), and the Prince of Orange, incarnating the monarchical tendency, based on the nobility of the backward provinces and on all the foes of the capitalist bourgeoisie: the peasants, the workers, the sailors, the army. This struggle divided the country, with varying success for the two sides. The Grand Pensionary got the upper hand in time of peace, the Prince of Orange in time of war. For our purpose here it is sufficient to note that Mousnier treats the English revolutions as bourgeois revolutions[1] and the political conflicts in Holland as antagonisms inherent in a more or less developed bourgeois society. As regards his picture of the social and political crisis in France in the first half of the seventeenth century, however, this calls for detailed analysis.

It is typical that Mousnier does not preface his exposition of the social and political crisis in France with even the briefest of outlines of the development of the French economy in the seventeenth century, whereas for England and Holland he does give some facts of this order. As a result, the picture of social relations and political struggle in France appears to be determined exclusively by the processes common to Europe as a whole, which I have already discussed. The specific reasons for the instability of the economic situation in France, and, consequently, the reasons why part of the French bourgeoisie withdrew from trade and industry, are not mentioned in Mousnier's book.

Not less typical is his tendency, whatever group of the French bourgeoisie he is writing about, whether financiers, officials, or merchant-manufacturers, to show them evolving in one direction only: towards noble rank and *fonctions publiques*. However, taking up the claim of the old nobility of the seventeenth century, Mousnier regards this acquired *noblesse* of theirs as unreal. He continues to treat as bourgeois even secretaries of state and ministers who retained bourgeois habits and manners, although as regards their source of income and place in production and social life they were nobles, and, moreover, not of the first generation.[2] The ennoblement of a *part* of the bourgeoisie (as a result of which two groups, later merged into one, were formed in the French nobility in the seventeenth century—the old hereditary group, landowning and military, and the new group, landowning and official)[3] is interpreted by Mousnier as meaning the absence of any clear-cut dividing lines in the social structure of France. Let us take the example he quotes in this connexion. There could indeed be within a single family (especially from the middle of the seventeenth century to the end of the eighteenth century) both officials and military men, and even in-laws from merchant families, who were themselves not merchants. But this is evidence not of the absence of social frontiers but merely of the consolidation of the noble

---

[1] I shall discuss below other theories which deny the bourgeois character of the English revolution (see chapter 2).

[2] See p. 8, n. 1.

[3] A. D. Lublinskaya, *Frantsiya v nachale XVII veka (1610–1620 gg.)* [*France at the beginning of the seventeenth century, 1610–1620*] (Leningrad, 1959), chapter, 2.

class, in which a fusion was already taking place between two groups, who were abandoning their antagonisms, which had been fairly acute in the second half of the sixteenth century and at the beginning of the seventeenth century.

Mousnier's view on the evolution of the bourgeoisie completely avoids the question of the position occupied by the commercial and industrial bourgeoisie, its social role, its political programme, its attitude to the regulations and taxes existing in the country, its growing opposition to the nobility and the government, and so on. This relegation to the background of the chief force in which the forward march of capitalism was embodied distorts his analysis of the crisis of capitalism, the social structure and the political struggle in France.

It is typical that in dealing with the towns Mousnier mentions first and foremost the growing antagonisms between nobles, financiers and officials, on the one hand, and small masters and journeymen, as taxpayers, on the other. Merchants and manufacturers do not figure in this antagonism, though they should have been included among the taxpayers, especially as the commercial and industrial bourgeoisie expressed their protest against taxation very sharply, since its burden fell directly on them.

Let us turn to the social antagonisms in the countryside. Mousnier looks very briefly at the relations between landowners and peasants on the social plane, and remarks that the source of the landowners' livelihood was the labour (that is, the exploitation) of the peasantry. He explains the nature of these relations, however, without reference to class antagonisms. The decisive factor here too turns out to be the movement of prices and the state of the market resulting from this. One might conclude that the author considers that the fundamental reason why the payments of all kinds they had to make exceeded the income of the small peasantry was merely economic instability, and not increasing exploitation. He associates the increase in the number of vagabonds and beggars only with the fall in prices, and says nothing about the loss of their land by the poorest peasantry.[1] For the sake of brevity it is allowable to lump together all owners of fiefs, disregarding differences in the structure of their estates, in their methods of managing these and exploiting their farmers and peasants. But when class and political struggles are being analysed, such contempt for the differences between the nobility of blood and the new nobility at once warns us of what is to come later. It is impossible not to protest against his allegation that the lords and the peasants had the same interests, even if this is understood to mean joint opposition to the royal exchequer.

[1] Speaking of England, Mousnier mentions the enclosures and the eviction of peasants.

Mousnier devotes a good deal of attention to the peasant and urban revolts of 1630–59, and regards the heavy burden of taxes caused by external war as the main cause. In a general way this view is correct (though it does not take into account the burden of seignorial and capitalist exploitation to which the continually increasing taxes were added), but his analysis of the revolts gives rise to a number of objections.

The fact that risings in town and country were not aimed immediately and directly against *châteaux* and *hôtels*, that is, that the watchword *Paix aux chaumières, guerre aux châteaux!* was not yet clearly voiced, does not justify Mousnier's conclusion that there was no war of the poor against the rich. Analysis of a number of revolts shows that, while beginning as anti-tax outbreaks, they were often transformed into a war of the poor against the rich, and then *hôtels* were attacked; and this not because their owners were 'upstarts' (that is, not real nobles), officials and financiers (it is probable that the rebellious people were blind to this fine distinction) but because officials and financiers were rich men, and in the towns they personified the ruling authority. In the countryside too revolts often developed into attacks on *châteaux*, especially (and this must be emphasised) if these belonged to new nobles, because the latter usually adopted more intensive methods of exploitation, transitional to capitalist methods, on their lands which they had bought from the peasants.

With regard to the participation of other social strata in the revolts, it must be observed that open participation on the side of the rebels was an extremely rare occurrence (I shall discuss revolts by the nobles at a later stage). It would be more correct to call it a certain degree of connivance on the part of the local authorities, which did indeed happen rather frequently, though only, as a rule, in the initial phase of a revolt before it began to affect property, as Mousnier himself admits. He is also right in saying that there were even cases of incitement of the people to revolt by nobles, *parlements* and municipalities. But Mousnier greatly exaggerates the importance of this connivance or incitement both in his evaluation of particular revolts and as a general tendency. In fact, the privileged strata of French society had, each in its own way, definite claims on the government, and counted on being able to satisfy these claims, even if only in part, through pressure on the government. In one way or another they were constantly bringing this pressure to bear; popular revolts in many cases created very favourable opportunities for doing this, which municipalities, *parlements* and nobles were not slow to utilise. This, however, does not justify the statement that they joined in the revolts or that the latter occurred only because of their incitements.

We must particularly consider Mousnier's treatment of the revolts of the higher nobility against absolutism. According to him, the grandees possessed a great influence which penetrated by different channels into the very depths of French society. He considers that because of this the grandees drew into their struggle the mass of the population, right down to the peasantry. This view too is marred by extreme exaggeration. In my study of the civil war of Louis XIII's minority[1] I was able to show precisely the opposite, namely, how very slight the influence of the great nobles was. They did not possess real political slogans that could rally all sections of society. In 1614–20 the grandees found temporary support for their aspirations only in a certain part of the *noblesse d'épée*. During the Fronde the situation was more complicated, but even then the princes of the blood were only able to exploit, not to call forth or direct at their own discretion, an existing social movement, in order to achieve their ends.

Particularly complicated were relations between the *parlements* and the government, and on this point one can largely agree with Mousnier. In my view he defines correctly the reasons for the opposition of the *parlements*, and the general significance of their activity, though one can hardly describe this reactionary activity as a 'revolution'. However, his definitions of the political programmes of the *parlements* and of the absolute monarchy respectively are open to objection.

Mousnier's view that in 1615 the *parlement* fought to establish a monarchy limited by the political power of the higher nobility, and marched together with the grandees, is without foundation. The *parlement* of 1615 is not identical with the *parlement* of 1648. In 1615 the Paris *parlement* had no reason for political opposition to the government, which it supported, nor did it ally with the grandees in order to limit the monarchy. What Mousnier sees as an alliance was in fact a passing tactical manœuvre, undertaken in order to defend a form of ownership of office which was particularly advantageous to the official caste (the *paulette*).[2] The opposition of all the *parlements*, in Paris and the provinces, was formed between the 1620s and 1640s, when the *intendants* were undermining their power and restricting their sphere of activity. They then really did accumulate sufficient reasons to attempt, in 1648, to put their demands into effect. But at the start of the Fronde the

---

[1] Lublinskaya, *Frantsiya v nachale XVII veka*. As regards the social prop of the grandees, namely, the nobility, Pierre Deyon has collected some information about infringement by the government of the tax privileges of the old nobility during the first half of the seventeenth century. These measures were received very badly in view of the general impoverishment of the noble estate, and aroused oppositional moods among them. (P. Deyon, 'A propos des rapports entre la noblesse française et la monarchie absolue pendant la première moitié du XVIIᵉ siècle', *Revue historique*, CCXXXI (1964), 341–56).

[2] Lublinskaya, *Frantsiya v nachale XVII veka*, ch. 4.

essence of the aspirations of the higher officials was not to achieve a separation of powers, or to clear the way for a republic, or even to safeguard their acquired position. The *parlements* wanted to go back to the past, to that age of influence and weight they had enjoyed in the sixteenth century. The events of the Fronde vividly revealed the reactionary nature of their political ideal; and this remained their line ever after, right down to the Revolution itself.

Mousnier depicts absolutism as merely the agent of centralisation, national unity, nationality, the egalitarian principle, as the only consistent defender of general national interests and of the defence of the country against external danger. Not only does this view reflect the theory, long inherent in bourgeois historiography, of the 'above-class' nature of the state, including the absolute monarchy, it also shows an excessive idealisation of the royal power and an oversimplified notion of the tasks confronting this power in the seventeenth century.

Egalitarianism cannot, of course, be proved by a mere calculation of the number of noble, and even ducal, heads cut off by Richelieu, and a comparison of this number with that of peasant and artisan rebels hanged, even though such a comparison is also very instructive. What is more important is that a concrete study of the internal policy of all the rulers of France in that period enables us to appreciate that 'nationality' and 'egalitarianism' were very remote from them.

There can be no doubt about the centralising function of absolutism, which followed the progressive line of development for French state-building to take in that period. But by this activity it was not forwarding the unity and equality of all classes, as Mousnier supposes. It rested on severe exploitation of the mass of the people, and on a scarcely more restrained use of the accumulated wealth of the bourgeoisie, to which at the same time it offered in exchange, however, the many benefits of mercantilism, aid against the workers, and so on, not to mention the fact that centralisation itself was first and foremost of benefit to the bourgeoisie. In relation to both groups of the nobility the policy of absolutism aimed at defending their basic class interests, that is, their property. The absolute monarchy did not meet the openly reactionary demands of the *noblesse d'épée*, and in many cases it directly opposed them—but this is still a long way from 'egalitarianism'.

It is, finally, permissible to ask whether national feeling had really died out in the years of harsh experience of foreign war, when whole provinces rose in revolt owing to the unbearable burden of taxation, thereby hindering the government in its struggle with the external enemy. Could, however, the outcome of a single battle decide the fate of the whole country and lead, in the event of defeat, to the disappearance (*disparition*) of France, as Mousnier suggests?[1] One may think that no viable country has ever disappeared as a result of a single lost battle. It seems likely that so extreme a proposition was put forward in order to underline more sharply still the absence, according to Mousnier, in practically the whole of French society of any 'national feeling'—or let us, rather, call it patriotism.

As regards the first question, only a negative answer can be given to it. The very notion that patriotism could have disappeared from the entire people in a period of heavy calamities is quite unfounded. Did not the French people show a profound and self-sacrificing patriotism in 1636, when, after the capture of Corbie, the road to Paris lay open to the Spaniards? And is it possible to put on the same level the genuine treason of Gaston d'Orléans, Condé, Cinq-Mars, etc., the more or less cautious opposition of the *parlements* and the propertied classes generally, and the revolts of the common people, at last worn out by their privations, whose sweat and blood eventually brought victory in the long and cruel external war? In 1630–59, were military and other burdens distributed in France in accordance with the material capacities of the different classes and estates? Could the people not see that they were being called on to pay more than they possessed, while the rich contributed only a small part of their property? In order to rise up against such an order of things the people needed no agitation by the *parlements*, they could see with their own eyes.

The subsequent sections of Mousnier's book, devoted to the crisis of the first half of the seventeenth century in the realms of art, science, religion and morals, I shall not discuss here.

In summing up the crisis theory as a whole, it must be emphasised that, in the process of analysing Mousnier's argument, the crisis, strictly speaking, has evaporated. What has been made clear is the following: of the three countries studied in the book—England, Holland and France—the first two are exceptions. In the first half of the seventeenth century they experienced not an economic crisis but, on the contrary, an economic boom—an intense development of industrial and commercial capitalism which determined the character of the class struggle, and the revolution in England. As for France (whose history is central to Mousnier's book both as a source of detailed analysis and as a case study of the developments taking place in Europe as a whole), it must be recognised that in this country the 'economic crisis' in the first half of the seventeenth century remains unexamined, since facts are lacking on the development of production, its increase or decline. In other words, the existence of an economic crisis is not established concretely, but

---

[1] Mousnier, *Les XVIe et XVIIe siècles.* p. 166.

inferred from events which are defined as social and political crises. The withdrawal of part of the bourgeoisie from the bourgeois sphere of activity, and their ennoblement, serve as arguments to show that trade and industry declined, popular revolts witness to taxation being too heavy in an epoch of crisis, etc.

Proceeding to the chapter which is devoted to the struggle against the crisis, attention must again be directed towards the material dealing with economic life and absolutism. Mousnier's chief idea is this, that the saviour from all the misfortunes brought by the crisis was the state, or, more precisely, the absolute monarchy. For this reason he begins with absolutism and goes on from that to mercantilism. We too shall proceed in that order, for it is beyond question that one's understanding of economic policy (economic life is examined in this connexion only as the economic policy of the state) must follow closely from one's understanding of the state structure.

Mousnier sees three types of absolutism and three forms of mercantilism corresponding to them—French, Dutch and English. He devotes much attention to the ideology of absolutism and its propaganda, both official and unofficial, ascribing to it very great importance in the overcoming of the political and ideological crises. He draws his general conclusions on the basis of a great deal of comparative material, so that we cannot confine ourselves to France alone in considering it.

Characteristic of the French variant of absolutism (and the Spanish variant had much in common with this) were two systems of government: either a prime minister ruled, under a weak or under-age king (Richelieu, Mazarin, Olivares), or else the king himself was his own prime minister (Louis XIV). In the periods when ministers ruled, a supreme instrument of government was developed, the king's Council. In periods of direct rule by the king all the functions of government were concentrated in his person. Mousnier sees as the reason for this that the king needed to subordinate to himself not only his subjects in general but also, and in particular, his officials, who had become independent through the sale of offices. To achieve this aim the king employed *lettres de cachet* (that is, his personal decisions, despatched to particular individuals or institutions) and made use on an extensive scale of *intendants*, devoted to himself, who in wartime monopolised all power in the provinces. Also at the king's disposal were the army and the political police. The *parlements* lost their capacity to interfere in political life, and even the most important judicial matters were dealt with not by them but by special commissions, the members of which were nominated by the king. A policy like this was, in Mousnier's view, directed towards unity and equality; he calls it revolutionary, preparing the way for the state of modern times.

The same purpose was served by the rise of the bourgeoisie which the kings promoted. During the seventeenth century the kings all recruited their ministers, councillors and *intendants* to a large extent among the official bourgeoisie; by ennobling them they created veritable dynasties of 'bourgeois' ministers, which they counterposed to the dynasties of feudal grandees. The kings formed an official nobility out of their officials, and bound the real nobility (that is, the nobility of blood) to themselves by offering them honours and means of living in the form of military and ecclesiastical offices, pensions, gifts, etc. By this means opposition to absolutism on the part of the grandees and the old nobility was broken down.

'Thus', concludes Mousnier, 'by dividing functions between two classes, but reserving the most important of them to the lesser class, the bourgeoisie, and systematically raising up this class and counterposing it to the other, stronger class, the King brought the class struggle to a point of equilibrium between classes which ensured his personal power and, in the government and the state, unity, order and hierarchy. Also, however, perhaps compelled by war needs and without any intention of changing the social structure of the Kingdom, the King levelled and equalised everyone more and more completely, in service due to the state, total submission and unlimited obedience and, with Louis XIV, the royal power became autocratic and revolutionary.'[1]

I have already examined this point of view in detail, stressing the 'statist' nature of Mousnier's conception and the illegitimacy of identifying the *noblesse de robe* with the bourgeoisie.[2] Here one need only observe that in so far as, in Mousnier's opinion, the kings equalised the position of the old nobility and the official bourgeoisie (and in the given case the latter personifies the bourgeoisie as a whole), the class struggle does not merely reach a state of equilibrium, it vanishes altogether. With the aid of the royal authority and ennoblement, the weaker class is put on an equal footing with the stronger; consequently it no longer needs to fight against its rival, and the latter, having no strength to oppose to the king or to his ministers and other high officials, is obliged to restrict itself to expressing disdain of *un règne de vile bourgeoisie*.

In England, Mousnier tells us, the Stuarts endeavoured through their absolutism both to help the development of the country towards capitalism and to maintain equilibrium between the old nobility, the feudal tenantry and the poor, on the one hand, and the capitalists and the classes dependent

---

[1] Mousnier, *Les XVIᵉ et XVIIᵉ siècles*, p. 236.   [2] See p. 8, n. 1.

on them on the other. The state machine (the king's Council) was developed less than in France, but followed the same line in its evolution. Absolutism was weaker than in France and needed to strengthen its foundations. In their conflicts with Parliament, James I and Charles I resorted to setting up special courts to carry out their intentions. In search of financial resources they sold offices and increased customs duties; Charles I even tried to introduce a direct tax by his own authority alone. But they had no considerable standing army and therefore insufficient power to realise their aims. Never- theless, for a time they managed to concentrate in their hands the principal attributes of absolutism, and through unremitting control over the capitalists and those nobles who carried on commercial agriculture they were able to maintain, for a short period ending in 1640, a state of equilibrium between the old and the new classes of society.[1]

In Holland, says Mousnier, the class struggle made possible the con- centration of power in the hands of the Princes of Orange, and beginning in 1621, war conditions made them *de facto* absolute monarchs. After the end of the war, in 1648, the republican bourgeoisie had their revenge, and the Orange family were deprived of power. However, the bourgeoisie proved weak and incapable of protecting their security and interests; they lost two wars with England and one with France. Caring only about their profits, and being unwilling to pay high taxes for war needs, the Dutch bourgeoisie weakened the army, and thereby aroused the discontent of the masses. Once again basing himself on the latter, William III established his authority in 1672, maintaining it down to the Peace of Nijmwegen, when the scales again tipped in favour of the republican bourgeoisie, who, like the whole country, were hoping for peace and friendly relations with France. Similar situations in which one or the other side was strengthened occurred later on as well.

Mousnier draws the following conclusion from all these facts: 'The United Provinces thus present, from time to time, an example of a régime in which class struggle, external danger and popular pressure cause power to be concentrated in the hands of a war leader who enjoys, owing to his princely birth, a sort of preferential right to this power—an example of a régime, which, without large changes in bourgeois republican institutions, operates as an absolutist régime based on public opinion. It is thus a régime on the borderline between monarchy and dictatorship, and closely resembles the dictatorship of Cromwell, England's Protector after the anarchy of the English Republic. Bourgeois republican régimes, confronted with internal crises and dangers from abroad, have to give place to authoritarian régimes.'[2]

[1] Mousnier, *Les XVIᵉ et XVIIᵉ siècles*, pp. 236–40.
[2] Ibid. p. 242.

I shall not attempt a detailed criticism of this picture of the class struggle in England and Holland. I shall say only this, that however one judges it (and there is much that I cannot accept in Mousnier's view), the main point is that, where England and Holland are concerned, Mousnier mentions the antagonisms between the classes connected with the development of capitalism and the classes opposed to it. These class struggles were indeed the main ones during the seventeenth century in those countries, and determined the course taken by political conflicts there. But in his characterisation of the English and Dutch types of absolutism he leaves unclear very important aspects of this problem. If the Stuarts were protecting the development of capitalism and using their power to this end, why did they need to exercise control over the capitalists, the gentry, and so on, and to establish an equilibrium between the new classes and the old, that is, to protect the interests of the latter? If they protected the old classes from the new, what remains of their help to the development of capitalism? Such questions, and more could be asked, render dubious one of Mousnier's chief propositions, namely, that the absolute rulers directed at their own discretion either a struggle between classes or the realisation of an equilibrium between them.

In his definition of the absolutism of the Princes of Orange, everything comes down to a matter of war or no war. In wartime, absolutism is established, in peacetime it surrenders its position. Owing to their unwillingness to open their purses for the needs of defence, and through their exclusive concern for quick returns, the Dutch bourgeoisie proved incapable of carrying on a war and coping with the internal class struggle. Mousnier's summing-up of them is so categorical that one gets the impression that these are basic features of this bourgeoisie, inherent in this class always and everywhere. But then it remains unexplained why in the sixteenth century the Dutch bourgeoisie nevertheless kept up a hard struggle against Spain and, victorious in this war, established itself in political power. For the entire seventeenth century it is depicted, in the relevant section of Mousnier's book, as a constant and uniform force, only its positions in political struggles and military confrontations being taken into consideration. He does not explain either its situation in circumstances of intense competition from the English (and to some extent the French) bourgeoisie, or its losses during the trade wars of the seventeenth century. For the bourgeois republic of Holland (Mousnier admits that republican institutions remained unaltered) the problem of absolutism has been put in a very oversimplified way, because the retention of political power by a bourgeoisie after the triumph of a bourgeois revolution takes place in a very complex setting, different in many ways from the social and political structure of feudal-absolutist states.

Mousnier begins his study of mercantilism by defining its essential nature.[1] The fundamental purposes of mercantilist policy were to strengthen the state and its economic independence on the international plane. This could be achieved only by concentrating the maximum possible amount of money within the country. However, the stock of gold and silver currency in Europe was very small. It has been calculated that, around 1660, it was equivalent to about fifty milliard French francs of 1928. All the countries of Europe put together possessed in those days a reserve of bullion equal only to the reserve held by the Bank of France at the end of 1929.

This limited supply of monetary resources was the cause of the economic nationalism and the continual war over money between states. Each of them endeavoured to establish a favourable trade balance for itself, so as to attract and retain the maximum possible amount of money. Above all, attention was paid to fostering exports of manufactured goods, because the labour embodied in them exceeded their cost. Colonies were called upon to provide the metropolitan countries with cheap raw material or cheap goods and to buy from them finished goods at high prices.

In Mousnier's view, mercantilism was economic statism, for only the state was in a position to regulate and stimulate economic life in the direction needed. Nor was its aim prosperity as such, or the raising of the standard of living. These were only means to the end, or by-products; the main aim was to strengthen the state. In the first phase of the development of mercantilism (France in the seventeenth century) politics predominated over economics, in the second (Holland in the seventeenth century) economics subordinated politics to itself and the state served the interests of the commercial and industrial bourgeoisie which it had reared. England in 1603–88 displayed an intermediate type of mercantilism.

I have deliberately spent some time setting out Mousnier's theory of mercantilism, because I find expressed here in concentrated form the fundamental features of his whole conception. He formulates very clearly and concisely the principles of mercantilist policy in the very form in which they were conceived and put into practice by the leading European statesmen of the seventeenth century. In other words, his theory merely repeats their theories, it does not delve beneath them, and it gives no estimation of them from the standpoint of an objective study of the process of economic development in the Western European countries. Furthermore, in this form the theory of mercantilism appears only as it was interpreted in state practice, that is, only as state economic policy. Rulers, made directly aware of their dependence on the availability of metal currency, carried out an economic

[1] Mousnier, *Les XVIe et XVIIe siècles*, pp. 242–4.

32

policy calculated to put the necessary resources at their disposal. Their every-day needs impelled them to do this. In their eyes money was the embodi-ment of the nation's wealth, and they obtained it either by way of plundering overseas countries or else by fostering national production, without seeing any particular difference between the two methods. They merely observed the economic situation existing in Europe and in their own countries in particular, and more or less successfully adapted themselves to it in their economic policies. But it would not be correct to identify mercantilism as a whole and in essence merely with state practice in the economic sphere. In the seventeenth century the theory of mercantilism began to be worked out in the sphere of political economy too (and earliest of all in France). Besides the fact that this theory includes the idea of labour as the source of wealth (though labour was understood only as producing money), it is very interest-ing precisely because of those elements in it which did not coincide with state mercantilist policy, and did not coincide with it for the very reason that they were directed to creating more favourable conditions for the development of capitalism as such, and not to partially adapting it to the needs of the state.

Mousnier never raises this question of the nascent contradictions between capitalism and the state. He sees mercantilism as merely a state policy for rescuing the countries of Europe from an economic crisis which had enveloped them.

He sees Dutch mercantilism as the variant most closely approximating to a 'free economy' (*économie libérale*). Having conquered for themselves the position of chief middlemen in world maritime trade, the Dutch were obliged to show a certain tolerance. In their rivalry with England they stood up for the principle of the freedom of the seas (*mare liberum*). But their own trading activity was subjected to regulation by trading companies and super-vised by the state. In a period when there was a shortage of precious metals, freedom for private trade might prove harmful: such a quantity of goods might be thrown on to the markets of Europe and Asia as would exceed the available stock of currency. The consequence would be that prices would fall, entrepreneurs would be ruined, and trade would decline. As a result, in a period of crisis private persons were helpless, while the state was not yet in possession of sufficient means or administrative organs to regulate overseas trade. This role was fulfilled by trading companies, which defined the limits of their activity, possessed monopoly rights in trade with particular countries, and wielded complete political power in the colonies, aided by a standing army and navy. This policy of regulation brought in huge profits. The divi-dends of the East India Company amounted to 25–30 per cent and the value of its shares in 1670 was six times what it had been in 1602. The links between its directors and the state resulted in a sort of merger between the state, the Company and the Bank of Amsterdam. 'Politics and war are instruments of commerce controlled by a capitalist trust.'[1]

The more independent and free organisation of the West India Company made it unstable and brought it to ruin. The chief role in this company was played by its council, and the general meeting of shareholders which examined all matters affecting the company. This company was torn by internal disputes and its policy was inconsistent and feeble.

In the seventeenth century the Dutch conquered the position of middle-men also in the supply of precious metals to Europe. Holland's abundant reserves of capital in the form of metallic currency conferred great political power on this little country.

Mousnier defines English mercantilism as being intermediate between the Dutch and French varieties. The regulation which had begun already under Elizabeth was given a powerful stimulus in the seventeenth century when the English witnessed the rapid recovery of the French economy as a result of encouragement by Henry IV. At the same time the boom in Holland's trade showed freedom of commerce and the role of privileged companies in a favourable light. The development of England's trade demanded govern-mental intervention, but the considerable success already attained by the commercial and industrial bourgeoisie inspired them to oppose regulation and monopoly and strive for free trade, regulated only by general parliamentary legislation.

The early Stuarts did a considerable amount in the field of economic regulation and tried to encourage the development of industry by helping the formation of monopolies, regulating trade and forbidding imports. The revolution, however, established freedom of trade and practically abolished all company privileges. Then, however, the market became oversaturated and it was shown that freedom of trade brought bad results. After the Restoration, Charles II went back to the system of state interference, but on a restricted scale, acting mainly by way of general measures (legislation, customs dues, trade treaties). The monopoly of trade with the colonies was maintained, while the internal economy was allowed to develop freely, with-out control over the quality of goods (which deteriorated) or regulation of prices or wages. The merchant's only incentive was profit.

And so, concludes Mousnier, England owed its prosperity to governmental measures, though the country did not attain Holland's degree of prosperity and the English East India Company was unable to hold its own against its Dutch rival.

[1] Mousnier, *Les XVIe et XVIIe siècles*, p. 245.

French mercantilism, as the most complete and finished form, naturally presents special interest, because the very social and economic structure of France itself demanded intensive intervention by the state. Mousnier devotes much space to analysing it.[1] He considers that both as doctrine and as practice, French mercantilism remained unchanged all through the seventeenth century, and Colbert merely developed it on a grander scale than his predecessors, endeavouring to overcome the severe consequences of the crisis. 'Colbertism' was already inherent in Henry IV (after 1596) and Richelieu (until 1631), as in Louis XIV (after 1661), in their pursuit of mainly political ends: it was impossible to allow gold to leave France, because it might enrich the country's enemies.

In so far as the merchants themselves were not capable of overcoming the difficulties that stood in their way, a complex system of state economic organisation was created, which was to a considerable extent unified under Colbert. So as not to allow any outflow of money abroad, the state created industrial enterprises, being itself often the only purchaser of their products, because the home market was still restricted. The peasants bought so few iron wares, preferring to do their work with wooden implements,[2] that the state took nearly all the iron made in the country for ships, military equipment, building work, and so on. The state organised channels of circulation of money within the country (collection of taxes by the exchequer, payments by the exchequer to contractors and to workers, then again collection of taxes from these people, and so on). The inflow of money from abroad could be increased only by increasing the amount of goods exported. This was why the basis of French mercantilism was industry.

The picture given of the 'manufacturing of manufacturers', even though a familiar one, cannot but support Mousnier's thesis and offer a powerful argument for his statist conception. In the subsequent chapters I shall bring forward material, however, which shows that the absolutist government actually did little on its own initiative and that its chief economic measures were suggested to it (sometimes repeatedly) by the French bourgeoisie, which was far from being voiceless and without initiative, but on the contrary persistently sought for a place in the sun.[3]

At this point something more must be added. The material quoted by Mousnier in the following paragraph, devoted to different types of organisation of industrial production, at once detracts from the statist conclusion which I have just mentioned.

[1] Ibid. pp. 249–56. [2] See on this below, pp. 112, 113.
[3] Jeannin also greatly limits the creative role of the government in the economic field (Jeannin, *Revue historique*, CCXXX, 180, 181).

3-2

Mousnier distinguishes three types of production: in small artisan work-shops, in small enterprises making semi-finished goods (he cites smithies in the Nivernais where they made the separate parts of anchors, which were then put together in a manufactory), and in large enterprises, which he calls factories. He correctly observes that the second type was the most wide-spread (that is, dispersed manufactories linked with centralised ones where the main or final operations were carried out) and the number of workers employed in them both in the towns and also, and especially, in the country, increased steadily. In Picardy, of 25,000 weaving looms 19,000 were in the countryside, and in Amiens alone eight to ten large merchant-manufacturers gave work to 100,000 countryfolk who combined agricultural work with spinning and weaving. At the same time a small number of centralised manu-factories employed plenty of workers; for instance, in a Rouen manufactory where fine linen was made there were already at the opening of the seven-teenth century 5,000–6,000 workers. However, while under Colbert 1,200 pieces of fine cloth were made every year in the big Van Robais manufactory at Abbeville, in Picardy as a whole 100,000 urban and rural workers produced 180,000 pieces of fabric a year.

It is important to emphasise the importance of the decisive quantitative predominance of dispersed manufacture (or, more precisely, of the combina-tion of dispersed with centralised manufacture) when the bulk of the workers were employed in dispersed manufactories. It testifies to the predominance of that type of production which by its very nature is least affected by state intervention and encouragement. In this sphere relations between the mer-chant putters-out and the workers, and also the payment of the latter, are determined spontaneously, depending neither on craft nor on state control. If I can use the expression, in this period it was the sphere of freest enter-prise,[1] something which must be taken into account when defining the overall scope of state encouragement in the field of industry. The govern-ment took no account of the interests of the workers, which it subordinated to the tasks of developing production and cheapening products.

The external trade of France was regulated like that of England and Holland. In the colonies, Richelieu and Colbert tried to establish 'New Frances'. This entire policy in the spheres of industry and trade had great success. French products became famous for their high quality and con-quered the markets of Europe and overseas.

I have said already that Mousnier exaggerates the role of French absolutism

[1] Valuable material on this matter will be found in the substantial and very interesting work by P. Goubert, *Beauvais et le Beauvaisis de 1600 à 1730, Contribution à l'histoire sociale de la France du XVIIe siècle* (Paris, 1960).

in the creation of capitalist industry. There is a similar exaggeration in his estimation of the Dutch and English types of mercantilism.

It is also typical that Mousnier should stress the fatal consequences of freedom of trade, that is, of the absence of state control. In this connexion let us consider the question of companies. In Mousnier's view, these flourished when they were subject to regulations which they themselves imposed, since the Dutch state lacked as yet the means to regulate overseas trade, and in the absence of such regulation they declined. Mousnier explains the need for this regulation by the endeavour to avoid anarchy in the market and in the way prices were formed under conditions of a limited supply of currency.

I consider that the reasons for regulation were different. The Dutch and English trading companies of the sixteenth and seventeenth centuries were, in organisation, successors to the merchant associations of earlier centuries. In both cases, control and regulation within these trading groups aimed to lay down a rate of profit uniform for all, distributed in proportion to the capital invested. This was because at that time free competition between individual units of capital had only recently begun and was developing parallel with the process of accumulation of considerable wealth in the hands of separate persons. The monopoly trade of the companies in distant over-seas markets brought in enormous profits also because it was to some extent based on robbery, either in the 'purchase' of raw material or the 'sale' of European products.

Mousnier says nothing about the decline of the Dutch economy in the second half of the seventeenth century. As he describes it, it remained steadily prosperous, and even successfully competing with the English and French, all through the century; but this was already no longer true by the second half of the seventeenth century.

In subsequent chapters of my book, examining such subjects as the condition of the French economy, the state budget, mercantilism, absolutism, and so on, I shall more than once return to my critique of Mousnier's conception, in so far as this relates to France. But France is not only the cornerstone of the whole theory of the 'general crisis' in the seventeenth century. Detailed analysis of this theory has shown that the author himself excludes England and Holland from the countries in the grip of the crisis. Consequently, France is the only one of the countries of north-western Europe where this alleged crisis is supposed to have shown itself in more or less definite forms. For this reason the answer which the reader will find in the subsequent chapters dealing with France will be at the same time an answer to Mousnier's whole conception.

37

Mousnier's book is noteworthy for the attempt the author makes to view all the historical processes of the seventeenth century from the standpoint of a 'general crisis'. Though the economic aspect receives considerable attention, many other spheres of human activity are also looked at in the book. I now go on to analyse certain writings which are devoted particularly to economic problems. These are all the more interesting because they are the outcome of close research. Furthermore, at the present time foreign historians' attention is chiefly directed to economic subjects of wide scope which are also important for Soviet specialists.

Hobsbawm's long article[1] is mostly concerned with the economic crisis of the seventeenth century. The first part of it appeared early in 1954, when the writer was not yet acquainted with Mousnier's book, which had only recently appeared; in the second part Hobsbawm refers to the book, but it is quite clear that these two researchers formed their ideas independently of each other.

Unlike Mousnier's book, Hobsbawm's article is equipped with an extensive apparatus which enables the reader, on the one hand, to supplement the facts given, and on the other, to judge the reliability and quality of the data used. The first part of the article describes the crisis as such, the second describes how it was overcome.

Hobsbawm's argument is of very great interest. His reading is wide, and based on a large number of valuable sources. His basic thesis is that, starting in the fourteenth and continuing until the seventeenth century, inclusive, the European economy experienced grave difficulties in its development, which were overcome only at the beginning of the eighteenth century. The last phase of this prolonged 'general crisis' occurred in the seventeenth century, especially in the first half; already by the end of the century the crisis was abating, because, in contrast to the situation in previous centuries, in the seventeenth those obstacles which had until then hindered the development of capitalism were at last eliminated. For this reason the crisis of the seventeenth century should not be regarded as being an entirely reactionary phenomenon.

---

[1] E. J. Hobsbawm, 'The general crisis of the European economy in the seventeenth century', *Past and Present*, nos. 5 and 6 (1954). On the significance of this article for discussion of the English Revolution, see L. Munby, 'Some problems of progressive historiography in Britain' [in Russian], *Voprosy Istorii*, no. 5 (1963). Hobsbawm reiterated the main propositions of his article in 1960 (E. J. Hobsbawm, 'Il secolo XVII nello sviluppo del capitalismo', *Studi storici*, Rome, no. 4 (1959–60)). F. Mauro has made some interesting observations in connexion with the problems touched on by Hobsbawm. In his view, if some countries were affected by decline, this took place to the advantage of other areas. Mauro limits the concept of the 'crisis', considering that, at most, one can speak only of stabilisation. He disagrees with Hobsbawm about the retarding effect of the 'feudal framework' (F. Mauro, 'Sur la "crise" du XVIIᵉ siècle', *Annales E.S.C.*, no. 1 (1959)).

Hobsbawm formulates very precisely a division of seventeenth-century Europe into zones which differ in their line of development. In the Mediterranean countries the decline was distinctly marked, and in Germany too (though not yet definitively), as was also the case in Poland, Denmark, the Hanse towns, and to some extent in Austria, in spite of that country's political strength. On the other hand, in Holland, Sweden, Russia and some small countries, such as Switzerland, progress rather than stagnation was observable, and in England an unquestionable advance. France occupied an intermediate position, but in that country, right down to the end of the century, political progress was not reinforced by substantial economic progress. This, in Hobsbawm's view, is the all-European economic balance-sheet of the seventeenth century: it is possible that the gains made by the countries of the Atlantic seaboard did not make up for the losses suffered in the Mediterranean area, Central Europe and around the Baltic. For this reason one may speak generally of the stagnation and even of the decline of Europe's economy in this period.

Hobsbawm regards as evidence of the existence of crisis a number of phenomena among which first place is given to the decline or stagnation of population in nearly all countries apart from Holland, Norway, Sweden, and Switzerland (in England the population ceased to grow after 1630). Only the inhabitants of capital cities and international centres of trade and banking increased in numbers.

As regards industrial production, Hobsbawm notes that only very general data are available. Some countries (Italy, Poland, the greater part of Germany, certain provinces of France) 'were plainly de-industrialised', while in others rapid development took place (Switzerland); in England and Sweden there was undoubtedly a growth of the extractive industries. In addition, a considerable growth was observed, in many parts of Europe, of rural out-work at the expense of urban or local craft industry, and this may have increased the total output. The fall in prices which began in the 1640s[1] can hardly serve as evidence of a decline in production, for it resulted more from a decline in demand than from a reduction in the import of precious metals. However, in the fundamental branch of industry for those times, the textile

---

[1] Hobsbawm considers the price revolution briefly in a special note (*Past and Present*, no. 5, p. 49) and expresses the view that the importance of this factor is usually much exaggerated. Like Mousnier, he corrects the usually accepted view that prices rose right up to 1640, giving figures to show a fall beginning already between 1605 and 1620. The end of the Thirty Years War coincided with an intensification of the crisis, beginning in the 1660s, and reaching its most acute phase (and the lowest point of prices) in the 1660s and the early 1670s. Hobsbawm considers that in general the movement of prices during the seventeenth century tallied with the periods of the crisis.

industry, there occurred, apparently, not only a shift from 'old' to 'new' draperies, but also a decline of total output.

The crisis was more comprehensive in the sphere of trade. What had been the chief trading areas in the Middle Ages—the Mediterranean and the Baltic —experienced a revolution in trade. The Baltic countries began to export, instead of foodstuffs, articles such as timber, metal, and materials for ship-building, and cut down their imports of Western cloth. The figures of the Sound dues show that the high point of Baltic trade was between 1590 and 1620, that there was a falling-off in the 1620s, followed, right down to the 1650s, by a catastrophic decline, and then stability until the 1680s. After 1650 the Mediterranean too was transformed into an area where trade was carried on, for the most part, only in raw materials and local products. On the whole it is probable that in 1620–60 export figures did not rise significantly, and internal trade, except in the case of the maritime states, could hardly make up for the loss in this sphere.

It can therefore be regarded as beyond doubt that European expansion entered a phase of crisis in that period. The Spanish and Portuguese colonial empires shrank and changed their character. It is noteworthy that the Dutch proved unable to maintain the conquests they had made in 1600–40; their empire likewise shrank in the following years.

It is well known that the seventeenth century was an age of social revolts in both Western and Eastern Europe. Some historians have even seen in this fact some sort of general revolutionary crisis which embraces such events as the Fronde, the revolts against Spanish rule in Catalonia, Portugal and Naples, the peasants' war in Switzerland in 1653, the English Revolution, the numerous peasants' revolts in France, the Ukrainian revolution of 1648–54, and even more—the Kurucz movements in Hungary, Stenka Razin's revolt of 1672, the Bohemian peasants' revolt in 1680, the revolts in Ireland in 1641 and 1689, and so on. However, the countries of Europe (apart from Holland and England, with their bourgeois régimes) eventually found a stable state form in absolutism.[1] Hobsbawm considers that even partial acceptance of his argument would mean agreement with his view about the existence of a general crisis in the seventeenth century. At the same time, he immediately makes a substantial reservation to the effect that the countries which underwent bourgeois revolutions (i.e. Holland and England) retained a relative immunity from the crisis. He places the beginning of the crisis approximately in 1620, the peak between 1640 and 1670, with a tendency to improvement appearing in 1680, to be fully realised only from 1720.

[1] Hobsbawm notes that some historians regard the rise of absolutism as a sign of a country's economic weakness, and expresses the view that this problem needs further exploration (*Past and Present*, no. 5, pp. 37–8).

Before going on to the next section of the article, which deals with the causes of the crisis, let us first examine whether Hobsbawm has succeeded, wholly or in part, in showing that there actually *was* a crisis—without going outside the limits of that circle of problems and arguments indicated by the author himself.

Most interesting, for my purpose, is Hobsbawm's main thesis regarding the all-European 'balance' of countries considered in the economic aspect. On one side of the balance he puts, alongside the England which had just experienced the bourgeois revolution, capitalist Holland, and also Sweden, Russia, based on serfdom, and economically insignificant Switzerland. On the other side of the balance he puts the 'de-industrialised' Mediterranean and Central European countries. France figures in neither group, and occupies an intermediate position between them. Thus we see that Hobsbawm essentially has in mind not a crisis of capitalism in one country or another (as Mousnier has), but a crisis of the economy generally, regardless of whether it has assumed a capitalist character or not. Accordingly he puts the question of the overcoming of the crisis differently, because for him the important point is the removal of obstacles to the development of capitalism throughout Europe. In his view, the side of the balance containing the countries which were suffering from crises in the middle of the seventeenth century temporarily outweighed the other, and the all-European balance proved unfavourable for the continent as a whole. One cannot deny that this view, based on recognition of close interconnexions between the development of the separate European countries, has both breadth and originality. It could open up fruitful possibilities for work on the all-European economy of the seventeenth century. It is, therefore, all the more interesting to examine the basis of this view.

The weakest point in Hobsbawm's theory is his analysis of industry; he himself admits the meagreness of the available material. To prove decline he cites only six or seven works dealing with Italy, Burgundy, Languedoc, Strasbourg, Leyden; that is, data in the main of a narrowly local nature. These also provide him with the basis for a statement about the widespread development of rural out-work. However, one thing is clear, namely, that the facts available to him (and the situation is little better today, ten years later) are inadequate for any estimate to be made about rates of development and scope of production in the seventeenth century in Europe as a whole, and in many individual countries. At the same time it is unquestionable that industry in the advanced countries—England, Holland, France, and others— advanced during the century; but this is attributed by Hobsbawm to the overcoming of the crisis.

His view about decline or stagnation in rates of growth of population is also dubious. Opinions on this score are greatly divided, and other views could be brought forward to counter Hobsbawm's. It is probable that on this point too, owing to inadequacy of data, we are not at present in a position to express any definite view.

The question of revolutions and revolts we can leave aside, as the author confines himself to a bald enumeration of them—though this list certainly provokes many objections—and his brief opinion about absolutism.

Only two points remain which are well studied and well elucidated in the article: international trade and colonial expansion. On the first of these the author himself concludes that there was a decline in the Baltic and Levant trades between the 1620s and 1660s. On the second point he records the decline of the Spanish and Portuguese colonial empires, followed in the 1640s–70s by that of the Dutch also.

Let us first look at colonial expansion. The crisis in colonial expansion consisted, in Hobsbawm's view, in the passing of hegemony from Spain and Portugal to Holland (later, I might add, to England). I would comment that this transition signified also a qualitative change in the system: from the predominance of plunder and unequal trade to the establishment of a more or less regular plantation economy and colonisation as such. But this transfer of hegemony cannot by itself serve as an indication or proof of the existence of a crisis of European economy. It reflects something different: the arrival in the arena of colonial expansion, one after the other, of those countries which, by virtue of the level of their capitalist development, were more and more adapted to this expansion, and which in bitter struggle wrested from their predecessors in this field a bigger or smaller share of the booty.

In the last analysis, only one of all Hobsbawm's points remains, in my opinion, namely the undoubted crisis of the Baltic and Levant trades in the 1620s–60s. It is significant that it is this very period in which Hobsbawm considers there was a general crisis.

It seems to me that at the basis of the whole conception of a European crisis there lies, as the only reliable set of facts, the decline of the Baltic and Levant trades.[1]

This raises the question of a different set of causes of the crisis from those discussed in Hobsbawm's article. Should the shrinkage in trade in the Baltic and Mediterranean areas be ascribed to the first all-European war, known as the Thirty Years War, and the other wars which took place in different parts

---

[1] I must observe that Hobsbawm's idea of a 'revolution' in Baltic trade (i.e. trade from the Baltic to the rest of Europe) does not stand up to criticism: grain, and not timber, metals and shipbuilding materials, continued to be the chief merchandise exported.

of Europe between the 1650s and 1670s? This question must arise, and, foreseeing it, Hobsbawm presents his objections. In his view, the war could not be the cause, and merely deepened a crisis which existed already. The war affected only certain parts of Europe, yet there was also crisis where no warlike operations occurred. In addition, the amount of devastation caused by the wars of the seventeenth century has been greatly exaggerated. We now know that even after the unprecedentedly destructive wars of the twentieth century, only twenty to twenty-five years have been needed in order to replace the loss of population, restore capital equipment and attain the previous volume of production. If in the seventeenth century the rate of reconstruction was much slower, it was because wars aggravated the crisis tendencies that existed. Moreover, against the losses caused by war must be set the stimulation war gave to the development of mining and metallurgy, and also the temporary boom in industry in countries not involved in war (for instance, in England in the 1630s). Finally, Hobsbawm asks whether the war itself (he means the Thirty Years War) was not perhaps stimulated by the crisis, and why it went on for so long. However, he considers this a speculative notion and takes it no further.

I have already criticised similar views[1] expressed by Mousnier, and shall return later to considering the question of the influence of war on the state of the economy in the seventeenth century. I think that Hobsbawm's arguments are unconvincing. A certain tendency to anachronism and preconceived opinion is characteristic of them, as of Mousnier's.

After rejecting the war as the cause of the crisis, Hobsbawm proceeds to examine those causes which, in his view, really hindered the development of capitalism. Yes, *of capitalism*, for later Hobsbawm goes on to analyse not the economy of Europe as a whole, whose fundamental features varied, but merely the development of capitalist economy alone. Why was it, he asks, that though capitalism, having appeared at the end of the fifteenth century, developed vigorously in the sixteenth, the industrial revolution had to wait until the eighteenth and nineteenth centuries? What were the obstacles which prevented a more rapid and even growth of capitalism? He considers that these obstacles were (1) the social structure of a feudal (i.e. essentially agrarian) society, (2) difficulties in conquering and mastering overseas and colonial markets, and (3) the narrowness of the home market. If we take into account that the first of these coincides with the third, then we can reduce all these obstacles, briefly, to a single factor—a crisis of effective demand in the home and external markets. Capitalism, in his view, developed slowly and passed through a phase of acute crisis in the seventeenth century because it was not

[1] See p. 16.

43

possible to ensure a growing effective demand, and there was therefore no stimulus to expanding the scale of capitalist production. So as to leave no doubt that he finds the basic cause of the crisis in the sphere of demand, Hobsbawm specifically adds that there were no insuperable obstacles in the sphere of technique to the development of capitalism in the sixteenth and seventeenth centuries. He refers to the work of Nef on the 'first industrial revolution' in England in 1540–1640, and specially stresses the considerable technical progress made in Germany in 1450–1520 (printing, effective fire-arms, watches, development in mining and metallurgy).

Hobsbawm starts from the idea that in order to secure an outlet for the ever-increasing volume of production, a radical break-up of the social struc-ture of feudal society was needed, that is to say, a radical redistribution of labour-power from agriculture to industry, the creation of substantial masses of free wage-workers who would obtain on the market the goods they needed for personal consumption. This process of creating the capitalist home market is called by Hobsbawm, following Marx, the other side of the process of separating the producer from the means of production. He rejects the view that the development of elements of capitalism within the womb of feudal society automatically leads to the creation both of an extensive market and of large numbers of wage-workers. In his opinion this requires the presence of certain conditions, still not quite clear, without which the development of capitalism is held back owing to the general predominance of a feudal structure of society, which limits the potential labour-force and potential demand for the products of the capitalist enterprises. The capitalist or entre-preneurial 'spirit', the striving to obtain maximum profits, is not capable, of course, of carrying through by itself the social or technical revolution needed for the triumph of capitalism. The latter in any case requires the presence of large-scale production of articles in wide demand (such as, for instance, sugar or cotton textiles), and not merely of expensive goods (silk, pepper, etc.) for a narrow circle of well-to-do consumers. The capacity of the market remained restricted, for natural self-sufficient economy was far from being a thing of the past. The growth of production could take place smoothly only within definite limits. When these limits had been attained, the period of crisis began, which was what happened in both the internal and the external markets in the seventeenth century, following the expansion in the fifteenth and sixteenth centuries.[1] This crisis could not be overcome by the 'feudal businessmen', that is, the richest and most powerful merchants, who had adapted themselves to the conditions of feudal society.

As evidence of all this, Hobsbawm quotes the decline of Italy and in

[1] Hobsbawm, *Past and Present*, no. 5, p. 41.

general of the old centres of medieval trade and industry. In his opinion the Italians possessed the largest agglomerations of capital in the sixteenth century, but misinvested it, immobilising it in the construction of buildings, loans to foreign rulers, or the acquisition of immovable property. Hobsbawm shares the standpoint of Fanfani in considering that the diversion of capital from the sphere of production ruined Italian manufacturing industry in its seventeenth-century struggle with Dutch, English and French competitors. However, Italian merchants had already learnt from experience much earlier that the biggest profits were to be obtained by means other than production, and they adapted to the comparatively restricted possibilities that were open to them. If they invested their money in unproductive branches, this was obviously for the simple reason that the 'capitalist sector' offered no scope for a different, capitalistic use of their financial resources. The bulk of Europe's population remained 'economically neutral' in relation to them; they were not consumers of Italian-made commodities. The Italians were so accustomed to making money by providing the feudal world with its trade and finance that it was not easy for them to go over to a different method, especially because the general boom at the end of the sixteenth century, the demand for money on the part of the large absolute monarchies, and the unprecedented luxury of the aristocracies had the effect of postponing the decline of Italian industry and trade until the seventeenth century, when all that remained to the Italians, and that not for long, was their predominance in the sphere of public finance. Hobsbawm sees the cause of this in the fact that the production of luxury articles continued to predominate in Italy. 'But who,' asks Hobsbawm, 'in the great period of luxury buying from 1580 to 1620, would guess that the future of high-quality textiles was limited?'[1]

I have set out in detail Hobsbawm's argument concerning the tempo and the causes of the decline of the Italian economy because I find the line of his thinking on this matter very significant in relation to his general theory. Hobsbawm considers that the prosperity of the Italian textile industry was short-lived because, being aimed at a narrow circle of consumers, mostly abroad, it enjoyed no wide prospects of development and therefore suffered defeat in conflict with foreign competitors.[2] This, for him, was the cause of Italy's decline in the age of the general crisis of the seventeenth century.

In my view, the process of the decline of Italy is depicted by Hobsbawm in an oversimplified way, not because the writer leaves aside many important

[1] Ibid. p. 43.
[2] Hobsbawm considers that at present it is still not possible to regard as proved Cipolla's view that the costs of production of Italian goods were higher than those of goods of the kind and quality produced in other countries.

45

factors for the sake of brevity, but because he gives chief attention to questions of the market. It is impossible to deny the great importance of the market either in general or for the early manufactory stage in particular. But the problem of the decline of the Italian economy cannot be simply reduced to a market crisis. Involved in it as well are such factors as difficulty in obtaining raw material for high-quality textiles, the change in world trade routes, the political division of Italy in the age of growth of large national states, the devastation of the northern part of the country as a result of the wars of the first half of the sixteenth century, and many others. The fate of early Italian (more precisely, Florentine) cloth manufacture was already settled—in the sense that the possibility of substantial expansion was closed to it—in the second half of the fifteenth century, that is, long before the seventeenth-century crisis. It would appear that the contraction in imports of English wool, from which the high-quality Florentine cloth was made, played a quite fatal role in this matter, together with the loss of Eastern markets, Eastern dyestuffs and alum, and so on. But at that time, making up to a large extent for the decline in cloth exports, there was a vigorous development (also in manufactories)[1] of the production of silk fabrics, which all through the sixteenth century and the beginning of the seventeenth encountered no rivals on the European market; only later were they forced into second place by French silks. In addition, French manufacture of high-quality textiles and luxury articles, rising to first place, developed successfully during the seventeenth and eighteenth centuries, steadily expanding the volume of production and conquering the markets of Europe and the world. Just as successfully, it later passed over to the factory stage, without experiencing serious hindrances from the narrowness of the market for its products. It therefore seems to me that it is not a matter of the adaptation of Italian 'feudal businessmen' to supplying goods and money to the upper circles of feudal society, nor of the difficulty of going over to the production of cheap goods for a wide market. It is now becoming more and more obvious how important the cheap textiles were for Italy, and how well they developed in the sixteenth and seventeenth centuries, to serve the internal market. As for the production of luxury articles, the Italian merchant-manufacturers, as Hobsbawm admits, still dominated the European market in the sixteenth century and the first third of the seventeenth, in the very period when a new type of capitalist merchant was emerging. In other words, they were able to adapt themselves to the changed conditions. If they later had to surrender their positions to their

---

[1] It must be especially emphasised that manufacture as the first phase of capitalist production did not disappear from Italy in the sixteenth and seventeenth centuries; it continued right down to the country's economic upswing in the eighteenth century.

French competitors in the luxury-goods industry, this happened not because of any lack of prospects for this branch—for the French luxury-goods industry served the same upper circles of society as the Italian, supplying all countries of Europe and America and bringing in large profits—but for different reasons, rooted in a general economic and political situation which was unfavourable to Italy, making that country incapable of competing on the world market. The manufacture of luxury articles is not in itself inevitably doomed to suffer curtailment in a period of really broad development of capitalism. On the contrary, this branch of industry, though not, of course, the leading one, gets along perfectly well with all the others. Furthermore, the example of France shows especially clearly the importance to it of the external market, since the internal market for luxury articles is inevitably always too narrow. Surely, then, inquiry into the problem of the decline of the Italian economy must follow quite a different course from the one Hobsbawm's idea suggests?

The decline of Italy is seen by Hobsbawm mainly as an example of the inability of 'feudal businessmen' to take the path of developing a capitalist economy on a large scale. His attention is chiefly concentrated, however, on the market crisis confronting West-European products in the markets of Eastern Europe, America and Asia, and in the internal markets of each of the advanced countries of Europe.

Hobsbawm considers that the commercial and industrial expansion of the West-European countries became possible in the fifteenth and sixteenth centuries thanks to substantial importation of foodstuffs from Eastern Europe; these exportable surpluses were made available by the creation of serf agriculture, that is, by strengthening of feudalism, which in its turn had significant consequences. In the first place, it reduced demand on the part of the peasants, or at least compelled them to switch from good-quality Western textiles to cheap locally produced ones. Secondly, the changes in the agrarian system favoured a handful of magnates, while the number of small nobles was reduced, and their prosperity declined (for example, in Poland). Finally, the urban market was adversely affected by the monopolising of export by the landlords. Consequently the expansion of capitalism in the West, stimulating exports of foodstuffs in that direction, led to the strengthening of feudalism in Eastern Europe, and entailed an appreciable decline in demand for West-European manufactured goods, while the markets of the Baltic region were, in the seventeenth century, probably the most important for West-European production. A market crisis was created for the West, and in Eastern Europe intensified exploitation caused the Ukrainian revolution.[1]

---

[1] Hobsbawm has in view the events of 1648–54.

These notions of Hobsbawm's seem to have no foundation. He supports them with references taken principally from Rutkowski's works of the 1920s, which are very much out of date now, and their conclusions doubted. An extensive body of writing has now been devoted to the problem of the 'second enserfment', and it is seen to be much more complicated. In any case it is clear that the intensification of serfdom began a good deal earlier than when exports of landlords' grain[1] had assumed appreciable dimensions. The strengthening of the lords' manorial economy was primarily related to the needs of the internal market, that is, it was first and foremost a result of the internal development of the countries of Eastern Europe. Of course, the peasantry had nothing to do with the decline in the demand for West-European goods, since even before the seventeenth century crisis the peasants did not purchase them. A decline in demand by the nobles cannot be proved by a mere comparison of the size of their estates with the estates of the magnates. This would require more precise data, for a few wealthy magnates might have bought, to maintain their magnificent way of life and their princely residences, as many and even more luxury articles than all the minor nobility put together. The reduction in the urban market constitutes a weightier argument, though in this case too it may be a matter only of small groups of patricians.

To test Hobsbawm's views on the causes of the crisis of demand in the Baltic market, it is necessary to consider the effect of the Baltic grain-exporting countries on the West-European countries who bought their grain.

Verlinden and Scholliers have used archive material to study prices and wages in Flanders, Brabant and Antwerp[2] in the fifteenth and sixteenth centuries, and have provided figures which show the very great importance of imports of Baltic grain for the Netherlands, even in the sixteenth century. Agricultural productivity in the Netherlands was very high at that time—not far from the present level—but it could not keep pace with the growth of urban population. For this reason, Baltic grain constituted a considerable element in the total consumption of grain. Any reduction in imports of this grain at once caused a sharp rise in prices, and any complete cessation of such imports led to famine and a rise in the death-rate. What caused the reduction of imports of Baltic grain? In every case mentioned, the causes were purely *political*: closing of the Sound in consequence of war between Denmark and the Hansa, or events in Denmark itself.

---

[1] The export of landlords' grain should not be put on the same footing with the export of grain by the Teutonic Order, the Russian government, etc. It had a different basis.

[2] C. Verlinden, *Dokumenten voor de geschiedenis van prijzen en lonen in Vlaanderen en Brabant* (Bruges, 1959); E. Scholliers, *Loonarbeid en honger. De levensstandaard in de XVᵉ en XVIᵉ eeuw te Antwerpen* (Antwerp, 1960).

Even more significant evidence is assembled in Soom's work on the Baltic grain trade in the seventeenth century.[1] Though it relates mainly to Estonia and Livonia, it is nevertheless very relevant, since what interests us in this matter is not the volume of Baltic trade but the reasons for its fluctuations.

Soom establishes a direct link between hostilities in the Baltic region and the export of grain from this region. On each occasion, the victualling of the armies was a decisive factor, and to ensure this the Swedish government prohibited exports of grain. In 1615 this measure was applied in Reval, in 1618 in Pernau, and in 1622 throughout all the Baltic ports. These bans called forth protests by the grain-exporting nobles and merchants, whose incomes fell disastrously. For this reason, the government was obliged to manœuvre, now imposing bans and now lifting them. The years when the bans were in force, however, were much more numerous, right down to 1635, than the years free from them. Moreover, prolonged warfare disrupted the economy; production of grain declined in the Baltic region, together with the supply of grain from the Russian provinces, and so on.

The volume of imports into the Baltic region was directly dependent on all these unfavourable circumstances. The Dutch carried from Western Europe to the Baltic ports salt, wine, various types of cloth and apparel, luxury goods, haberdashery, and so on, only when they were able to bring back grain from these ports. Accordingly, though the demand for this grain was substantial all through the first half of the seventeenth century, it was possible to satisfy it only in favourable circumstances, that is, in the periods of peace. But how few these intervals of peace were!

Furthermore, from the middle of the seventeenth century onward a new phase began, characterised by a fall in the price of Baltic grain. In 1660–90 France ceased to need it, and German agriculture began to return to normal. These circumstances created an unfavourable situation for the Baltic exporters, which they tried to overcome by extending the cultivated area, so as to make up for the fall in prices by increasing the amount of grain they put on the market.

Very useful information of a similar kind is given in the books of the Polish historians M. Groch, M. Malowist and W. Czaplinski.[2] All three link the reduction in the export of grain from Poland which began about 1620 with

---

[1] A. Soom, *Der baltische Getreidehandel im XVII Jahrhundert* (Stockholm, 1961). See also V. V. Doroshenko's review of Soom, *Voprosy Istorii*, no. 10 (1963).
[2] M. Groch, 'A contribution to the question of the economic relations between the countries of Eastern and Western Europe at the turning-point of the Thirty Years' War' [in Russian], *Srednie Veka*, no. 24 (1963); M. Malowist, 'L'évolution industrielle en Pologne du XIVᵉ au XVIIᵉ siècle', in *Studi in onore di Armando Sapori* (Milan, 1957); W. Czaplinski, 'Le problème baltique aux XVIᵉ et XVIIᵉ siècles', *XIᵉ Congrès International des Sciences Historiques, Rapports*, IV, *Histoire moderne* (Stockholm, 1960).

the military operations in the Baltic region. France's trade in the Baltic was likewise undermined by the war.[1] Interesting material is to be found in P. Jeannin's detailed article on Baltic trade.[2] In the seventeenth century, after reaching its highest point in 1618, Baltic trade began to decline, with particular sharpness in the 1620s, Polish grain shipped from Danzig being the main commodity concerned. Though in 1622–4 harvest failures were to some extent responsible for this decline, the almost complete stoppage of grain exports in the following years was caused exclusively by the Swedish blockade of the mouth of the Vistula. Jeannin notes that the effect of war was no less potent in some later periods of the seventeenth century as well: for example, the invasion of Prussia and Poland by the Swedes in 1655–7 almost completely stopped the exportation of grain from Danzig.

Further, according to Jeannin's figures, the transition to a prolonged depression in Baltic trade took place only after 1650, despite the considerable decline in the 1620s.[3]

Thus, the evidence at present available enables us to take the view that the decline in Baltic trade that began in the 1620s was caused by war, and the acute deterioration that began in the 1650s was caused by a fall in demand for Polish and Baltic grain.

What is Hobsbawm's evidence for a crisis of demand in the seventeenth century in American and Asiatic markets? He starts from the proposition that until the Industrial Revolution exports to Asia were in general negligible, while Africa was valued by Europeans, right down to the end of the seventeenth century, mainly as a source of bullion.

The establishment of sea routes to Asia and the plundering of conquered countries greatly cheapened Asiatic products for Europeans, and the importation of gold and silver from America and Africa put substantial monetary resources at their disposal. Given these circumstances, Europe was able to derive very large profits from colonial plunder and Asiatic trade, but not from the export of industrial goods, which increased little. When this source of income was exhausted, a crisis began; the costs and overhead expenses of the colonial powers were greater than their profits.

Hobsbawm distinguishes three stages in the utilisation by Europeans of their American and Asiatic colonies: (1) a stage of easy profits (until the beginning of the seventeenth century); (2) a stage of crisis (apparently, until

---

[1] L. A. Boiteux, *Richelieu 'Grand maître de la navigation et du commerce de France'* (Paris, 1955), p. 319.

[2] P. Jeannin, 'Les comptes du Sund comme source pour la construction d'indices généraux de l'activité économique en Europe (XVIe–XVIIIe siècles)', *Revue historique*, CCXXXI (1964), 320–2 and table 7.

[3] Ibid. p. 323. On the importance of Jeannin's figures for the evaluation of the crisis theory as a whole, see below.

the 1680s); and (3) a concluding stage of more modest but, as against that, stable returns. On the Asiatic market, where high profits were due to monopoly in the trade in spices and similar goods, the crisis was probably caused by the steep rise in 'protection costs' in order to eliminate competition, as a result of which, for example, Portugal's spice trade barely paid its way. In the importation of precious metals and raw materials from America 'protection costs' played a smaller role, but in approximately 1610 the sources of gold and silver themselves began to dry up, and exports of these metals to Europe began to decline. A way out of the crisis was found by establishing large quasi-feudal estates in America, and in Asia by adjusting to the new level of overheads. In so far as the economic basis of the Spanish colonial system was broader than the Portuguese, the consequences of the crisis would be more far-reaching. Originally, emigration to America had stimulated the export of manufactured goods from the home country, but in proportion as production of these goods began in the colonies themselves Spanish manufacturers had to curtail their output. The effects in Spain of the influx of American precious metals are also well known.

From this evidence Hobsbawm deduces the collapse, as a result of the crisis, of 'the old colonial system'. This had an important consequence for Europe—a new system of colonial exploitation, based on increased exportation of manufactured goods to the colonies.

So far as the American markets and Spain are concerned it is possible to show that the phenomena mentioned by Hobsbawm considerably preceded the crisis period. The destructive effect of the 'price revolution' upon Spanish manufactories which had only just arisen was already fully felt in the first half of the sixteenth century. It caused the country to be flooded with cheap foreign goods which were exported through Spain to the American colonies, and also an increase in the export of raw material, particularly wool, from Spain to supply the manufactories of France and the Netherlands. In addition, the American market was of great importance for the development of French, Netherlands, German and even Italian manufactories not only in the first half of the sixteenth century but also in the seventeenth. It could even be said that the role of the American market was decisive, since manufacture in its early stage of development, when it has not yet created a large home market, depends above all on external markets and produces mainly for export, as Marx emphasised more than once.

To settle the question whether or not there was in the seventeenth century a trade crisis between Europe and America, we need abundant evidence which historians do not yet have at their disposal. Nevertheless, some recent works of research present evidence which contradicts Hobsbawm's conclusions.

Thus, in F. Mauro's book on the Portuguese colonies in America in the seventeenth century[1] figures are given that testify to the prosperity of trade between Portugal and America during that century[2] and to the fact that it consisted mainly of importing sugar from America and exporting Negroes thither.[3] In the Chaunus' extensive investigation of trade between Spain and America they show that its highest point came in 1580–1620 and that thereafter there was indeed a decline. But this was a decline in trade between Spain and America, not in trade between America and Europe as a whole. In the 1620s an important change took place in the economic situation: the Spanish Atlantic was transformed into the European Atlantic, Spain's role declined more and more, while the advanced countries of Europe became increasingly important. It is also significant that export of Negroes to the American colonies for the developing plantation economy was already very important at the end of the sixteenth century. Even more significant is it that over one-and-a-half centuries the export of European goods to America always exceeded imports from there (the latter consisting mostly of precious metals), that is, that the American market was sufficiently large.[4]

All this enables us to speak more in terms of competition between the countries of Europe for direct mastery of the American market (taking the place, in the 1620s, of the previous Spanish monopoly, under which non-Spanish goods could be exported to America only through Seville) than of a crisis of demand on the American market for Europe as a whole.

As regards the Asiatic market, Hobsbawm says nothing about a crisis of demand there for European goods. Perhaps his silence on this point can be understood in connexion with his view that Europe exported only slaves, furs, amber, and so on to the East, and that until the Industrial Revolution exports of European goods to Asia were not large. Hobsbawm mentions only the difficulties affecting demand for Eastern goods (spices) on the European market;[5] so that the crisis of demand in the East remains unsupported by any

---

[1] F. Mauro, *Le Portugal et l'Atlantique au XVIIe siècle (1570–1670). Étude économique* (Paris, 1960). See also Mauro's review of Hobsbawm's article, already mentioned (*Annales E.S.C.*, no. 1, 1959, p. 183).

[2] It is characteristic that there were no sharp variations in this trade during the century 1570–1670. The periods 1600–20 and 1640–70 were marked by slight depressions, while 1620–40 saw a considerable advance.

[3] Hobsbawm also notes the beginning of plantation economy in Northern Brazil already from the end of the sixteenth century onward.

[4] Huguette and Pierre Chaunu, *Séville et l'Atlantique (1504–1650)*, I–VIII (Paris, 1955–60).

[5] I note in passing that, according to the most recent evidence, the Iberian monopoly of the import of spices into Europe was abolished at the end of the sixteenth century by the Dutch, together with the English and French; that is, once again, competition went in favour of the advanced countries. (H. Kellenbenz, 'Autour de 1600: le commerce du poivre des Fugger et le marché international du poivre', *Annales E.S.C.*, no. 1, 1956).

evidence. Information does exist, however, showing that there was competition between European countries for domination of the consumer markets of the Levant and India. As with the Atlantic trade, losses by one country in this struggle meant gains by another.

Hobsbawm's idea of a collapse, as a result of the crisis, of the 'old colonial system' of plundering the colonies, and its replacement by a new system, with plantation economy and demand in the colonies for European goods, is very interesting. If this idea were to be substantiated, the middle of the seventeenth century would indeed mark an important turning-point in the development of Europe's economy, which would have been enriched with a new quality. However, the evidence mentioned above does not support Hobsbawm's view. Plantation economy made its appearance much earlier than the beginning of the crisis, and exports of European goods exceeded imports (of goods, as against precious metals) from the colonies, and were already important in the sixteenth century and the first half of the seventeenth. The collapse of the Iberian monopoly occurred as a result of the deadly competition from other countries, and not because of any exhaustion of the American and Asiatic markets affecting all Europe. For this reason it is hard to claim that a crisis of demand (we have seen that this is not supported by the facts) brought about this change in methods of exploiting the colonies. It would be more correct to say that a combination of direct plundering with plantation economy, accompanied by exports from Europe, was already in existence in the sixteenth century and continued to exist later on. As capitalism developed in the metropolitan countries, the features of colonial exploitation which were characteristic of fully developed world trade grew more important.

After analysing the crisis of demand on the Baltic, American and Asiatic markets, Hobsbawm proceeds directly to the home market. He does not discuss the situation on the West-European market as a whole, apparently because he looks upon the countries of this part of Europe as a single entity. Owing to this omission (in my view a very regrettable one), he has failed to observe something of great importance for understanding the economic situation in the seventeenth century, namely, the contest between the different countries of Western Europe for conquest of the consumer market in neighbouring countries. And since he also overlooks the question of competition for the overseas markets, he gives inadequate attention to the entire important problem of the *conquest* of consumer markets.

Hobsbawm begins his analysis of the crisis of demand on the home market by stating that very favourable conditions had been created for an extensive development of capitalist production in the sixteenth century, perhaps through the winning of overseas loot, or the growth of population and markets, and also the rise in prices. Rural industry of the putting-out type was widespread, not only in textiles but also in other branches of production. But this expansion came up against the obstacle presented by the feudal structure of society. The demand for agricultural produce, the rise in prices, and so on, might have led to the appearance of capitalist farming by gentlemen and the kulak type of peasants; yet the 'agrarian revolution' occurred only in England. In France, the nobles (some of them of bourgeois origin), like the urban merchants, went on exploiting the peasants in the feudal way; so that the investment of urban capital in the land did not give rise to agrarian capitalism. Even share-cropping, he says, was mainly nothing more than parasitism by the bourgeoisie, and together with state taxes it ruined the peasantry.

Two consequences followed from this. No improvements were made in agricultural technique, and demand for foodstuffs exceeded supply, which led to famines. Secondly, the country people, subject to the double oppression of landlords and townsmen (not to mention the state) suffered. Further, the more rapid rise of agricultural than of industrial prices reduced the profits of the manufacturers.

These conditions engendered a crisis of demand on the home market. The rural market shrank. As the history of France in the nineteenth century shows, the rich and middle peasants in general do not buy many industrial products; their money is spent in purchasing land and cattle, in building, and in celebrating traditional feasts. The needs of the towns, luxury markets and government temporarily concealed the fact that demand as a whole was growing less rapidly than production. Additional difficulties were created for the manufactories (perhaps in connexion with the stagnation in the town population) by the rise in labour costs. True, this phenomenon may not have extended to putting-out industries, because their workers were helpless to resist the merchant buyers-up who reduced their piece-rate wages. The depression in production was also fostered by the slackening of population increase and the stabilisation of prices.

Consequently, Hobsbawm substantiates his thesis about the narrowness of the home market due to the feudal structure of society as follows: except in England, the transition to capitalism did not take place in agriculture, and the country was sacrificed to the town. The ruined peasantry starved and died off, so their demand for industrial goods did not increase. The lowering of the real wages of the workers cut down demand in the towns as well.

The formation of a home market for capitalist industry is one of the most important factors in the establishment of capitalism. For this reason, clarification of the actual ways in which it develops historically is of paramount interest, and Hobsbawm's ideas on this deserve special attention.

He sees the fundamental reason for the narrowness of the rural market in the impoverishment and starvation of the peasants and in the high death-rate, phenomena which certainly strike one immediately. However, the view that the ruination of the peasantry reduces the effective demand of the population, and, therefore, the home market for capitalism, was refuted by Lenin, who showed in his work on the development of capitalism in Russia, 'that it is by no means the well-being of the producer that is important for the market, but his possession of money;...for the more such a peasant is ruined, the more he is compelled to resort to the sale of his labour-power, and the greater is the share of his (albeit scantier) means of subsistence that he must acquire in the market'.[1] Thus, the ruining of the small producers in the process of the formation of capitalist production leads to the creation and development of the home market, and not its reduction.

Emphasising the narrowness of the home market owing to the lack of effective demand on the part of the peasantry, Hobsbawm fails to see that the spread of the putting-out industries itself has a very direct connexion with the increase in the home market. Those peasants who became engaged in rural industry were drawn farther and farther into monetary relations with the market, and increasingly lost their previous passivity in relation to it. As will be shown later, Hobsbawm considers that the dispersed manufactory played an important part in overcoming the crisis of the seventeenth century, in so far as it disintegrated the social structure of the feudal countryside. It remains unexplained, however, why this (correct) idea does not also apply to the sixteenth century, for a wide extension of just this form of manufactory is a well-known feature of the very beginning of capitalist production, as Hobsbawm himself acknowledges when he describes economic progress in the sixteenth century. Nor does he take into account the expropriating influence of dispersed manufacture, or of share-cropping, which he sees as mere parasitism by the urban bourgeoisie, not perceiving that in fact it was a transitional stage towards capitalist rent.[2]

We must also note that evidence given in the works of French historians, based on posthumous inventories of the property of peasant families, testifies to the possession by well-to-do and rich peasants of a relatively large quantity of industrial products purchased by them.

Defining the economic processes which went on in the seventeenth century

---

[1] V. I. Lenin, *Sochineniya* [*Collected Works*], Moscow, 4th edition, III (1946), 26, 27 [English edition, 42].
[2] Lublinskaya, *Frantsiya v nachale XVII veka*, chapter I.

as a crisis of demand for the products of capitalist enterprises, and so as a general crisis of capitalism, Hobsbawm attributes to the manufactory stage phenomena which are inherent in developed industrial capitalism. But 'the laws which govern large-scale industry are not the same as the laws which govern manufacture'.[1] In particular, of course, manufacture in general is not capable of a radical transformation and conquest for industrial capital of the entire home market; it dominates national production only to a very incomplete extent.[2] Throughout the whole manufacturing period the number of large-scale centralised manufactories remains very small (along with a great extension in the same period of small ones, and still more of dispersed manufactories) and the amount produced by them increases comparatively slowly. Hobsbawm has also not taken into account the characteristics organically inherent in manufacture,[3] while ascribing to it features which are characteristic of mature capitalism.

How does Hobsbawm visualise the way the crisis was overcome? He considers that the crisis itself created the conditions which made possible the Industrial Revolution. Hobsbawm looks for the ways out of the crisis in the economic sphere (and not in the political sphere, as Mousnier does). However, he is at once confronted by the question: if the chief obstacles to the development of capitalism disappeared some time in the seventeenth century, why did the Industrial Revolution, which did not begin until the second half of the eighteenth century, still take so many decades to develop? It would seem that in England there were no further obstacles to a hastening of the process. In other countries, especially in France at the end of the seventeenth century, there were also signs of change, such as the agricultural innovations in Normandy and the south-western provinces.

Hobsbawm points to two types of obstacle in the way of the Industrial Revolution. The first was that the economic and social structure of society in that period did not leave enough scope. A sort of preliminary revolutionising was needed, which began long before the 1780s. The crisis of the seventeenth century accelerated this process. The second type of obstacle was that many branches of the economy, even among those which underwent rapid development between 1500 and 1800, possessed only primitive organisation and technique (the metal-goods producers of Birmingham, the gun-makers of Liège, the cutlers of Sheffield or Solingen). Of greatest importance was industry of a new type, such as the Manchester factories. What conditions

---

[1] Marx and Engels, *Sochineniya* [*Collected Works*], Moscow, 2nd edition, XXVI, part 2 (1963), 647 [Marx, *Theories of surplus value*, part 2: no English translation available. See Marx, *Histoire des doctrines économiques*, V, 176].

[2] Ibid. XXIII (1960), 758 [Marx, *Capital*, I, 1938 English edition, 772].

[3] See below, pp. 65–75.

in the seventeenth century favoured the growth, later, of Manchester industry?

Hobsbawm emphasises the difficulties confronting him which are rooted in the inadequate amount of work done on the economic history of the seventeenth century. The strong impression that 'somewhere about the middle of the seventeenth century European life was so completely transformed in many of its aspects that we commonly think of this as one of the great watersheds of modern history'[1] cannot be proved conclusively.

Nevertheless, he considers that the chief outcome of the crisis of the seventeenth century was a considerable concentration of economic power which prepared the way, both directly and indirectly, for the Industrial Revolution. Directly, by strengthening of dispersed manufacture at the expense of craft production and by speeding the process of capital accumulation; indirectly by providing a surplus of agricultural production, and in other ways. At the same time, the crisis also brought a partial regression, when considered from the standpoint of an eventual Industrial Revolution. Above all, if the English Revolution had failed—as many other revolutions failed in the seventeenth century—it is quite possible that the course of economic development would have been seriously retarded for a long time. On the whole, however, he thinks the crisis had definitely progressive results.

Hobsbawm considers that economic concentration took place throughout Europe, though in differing forms. In Restoration England and in the countries of Eastern Europe, the large landowners gained at the expense of the peasants and smaller owners. In industrial areas the craft-guilds were replaced by rural industry controlled by large-scale merchants, either native or foreign. A certain grouping of industries can also be seen as concentration: manufactories producing for nation-wide or foreign markets increased in certain areas at the expense of the widespread small manufactories which produced only for regional markets. Large metropolitan cities everywhere grew at the expense of other towns and of the countryside.

Let us consider these general ideas. It is possible to agree with some of them, others[2]—and, indeed, the author's conception as a whole—give rise to objections. In the first place, why must these phenomena be regarded as *consequences* of the crisis? Even if we adopt Hobsbawm's view that there was a many-sided economic crisis in the seventeenth century, any connexion between this and economic concentration seems doubtful. If we take into

---

[1] Hobsbawm, loc. cit. no. 6, p. 46. The quotation is from G. N. Clark, *The seventeenth century*, 2nd edition (London, 1960), p. ix.

[2] It must be observed, of course, that the view that all the social movements of the seventeenth century were 'unsuccessful revolutions' is without foundation (see chapter 2).

account that the only unquestionable fact is the crisis of demand for West-European industrial products on the Baltic market, such a connexion seems unfounded and brought into the argument rather speculatively.

Indeed, how could the decline in Baltic trade by itself hasten such funda-mental processes (among those considered by Hobsbawm) as the disintegra-tion of the social structure of the countryside, the appearance of technical improvements, and economic concentration, which in their turn hastened the development of dispersed manufacture, capitalist accumulation and the growth of agricultural production? If the outlet to one external market among many was hindered, why should this have led to such far-reaching conse-quences as the overcoming (and in a radical fashion) of obstacles to the development of capitalism generally? Even if we accept Hobsbawm's entire theory and extend the crisis of demand to all the external markets and the home market in every country, we cannot but ask exactly what causes brought about the eventual upturn in the economic situation, fostering an increase in demand and the end of the market crisis. What economic factors determined this turn, which is dated about 1680? Were the causes inherent in the capitalist mode of production in the manufactory period? Can we recognise in the crisis of the seventeenth century the consistent succession of phases, leading to a boom, which is characteristic of capitalist crises? Did it perhaps pass through some different phases? Hobsbawm does not ask these questions. Perhaps we are not yet in a position to answer them, but nevertheless such questions must be raised.

The main line of Hobsbawm's reasoning goes like this: (1) recognition that a crisis existed, (2) investigation of the reasons why it arose, (3) survey of the consequences of the crisis, general and particular, including those which, despite the overcoming of the crisis, continued to delay the arrival of the Industrial Revolution. Between the second and third points one has been left out, though concerned with a problem of no less importance (if not of the greatest importance of all), namely, description of the course taken by the crisis and the factors bringing about the turn. This omission, justified neither by logic nor by history, disrupts the causal connexion between phenomena, replacing this with a mere chronological sequence: *post hoc, ergo propter hoc*. While a number of facts are adduced to explain the reasons for the appearance of the crisis, no fact is given to enable us to understand the reasons why the crisis began to be overcome (so that it was succeeded in the 1720s by a boom which prepared the way for the Industrial Revolution of the second half of the eighteenth century), nor is this problem even considered. Therefore the causal connexion between the crisis and succeeding events remains undemonstrated, together with the reasons why the crisis was able to hasten the extension of dispersed manufacture, capitalist accumulation, the increase of agricultural production, and so on.

Leaving all these questions open, let us go on to look at the consequences of the crisis.

The results of the crisis for the development of agriculture in the West are not regarded by Hobsbawm as important. By 1700 the total cultivated area was hardly larger than in 1600, although maize, potatoes, tobacco and cotton had been introduced. Perhaps the provisioning of the biggest centres of population was effected partly through more intensive utilisation of the most fertile areas, and partly by 'poaching' on the preserves of other cities.

In Central and Eastern Europe the seventeenth century was a period of decisive victory for the new serfdom, or, more precisely, of the magnates over the lesser nobility. Whether this was a result of increased demand for grain on the external or internal market is of no significance in this case,[1] but the result is clear—a strengthening of the economic and political power of the magnates, that is, of the wholesale enserfers against whom even the absolutist monarchy could not measure its strength. In Prussia and Russia the price paid by the monarchs for their power was that they abstained from interfering with the absolute authority of the magnates on their own estates.

The triumph of the serf estate did not lead to any increase in the productivity of agriculture, but created a considerable marketable surplus of agricultural products, and in maritime regions stimulated the landlords to export grain.

But this could not radically solve the problem of the development of the economy, owing to the unproductiveness of forced serf labour, transport difficulties, and so on. There were already signs of a crisis of serf agriculture in the middle of the eighteenth century. However, Hobsbawm observes, it is important to note that the transfer to serf-estate economy coincided with the crisis of the seventeenth century and, perhaps, entered its decisive phase after the Thirty Years War, say about the 1660s. The crisis hastened this transfer because it weakened the peasants (being accompanied by such phenomena as war, famine, and increased taxation) and strengthened their exploiters.

Thus we have the right to conclude, if we follow Hobsbawm's theory, that both in the West and in the East of Europe the crisis had no impact on agricultural technique. As regards the structure of agrarian relations, in the West this remained unchanged (except in the Low Countries and England) while in the East the crisis hastened the transition to serfdom.

In so far as a long period—a century at least—is in question, the view that

[1] Here Hobsbawm modifies the sharpness of his initial opinion (see p. 47).

the agrarian structure of many Western countries remained unchanged cannot but give rise to doubt. In the era of primitive accumulation, the evolution of the countryside in the direction of capitalism, though slower than this development in the industrial sphere, must attract the historian's attention. In the countryside, complex and important processes of social and economic differentiation went forward among the peasants, with enrichment of the upper stratum and loss of land by the poorest, development of capitalist leasehold and share-cropping (which, as I have already said, was not a mere matter of parasitism by the bourgeoisie), the establishment of *de facto* ownership of land by peasants, and so on. Over the century between 1620 and 1720 all these phenomena spread and deepened considerably. In addition, there was an increase in agricultural production for the market, including peasant production. The increase in the intensity of agriculture in the fertile regions of France and other countries, which Hobsbawm mentions, testifies precisely to this. The cause, however, of these processes was not a crisis of demand for industrial products, but a whole complex of factors which operated in this period, and first and foremost the expropriation (in various forms) of part of the rural population and the formation of the home market.

I will not deal here with the debatable questions of the causes and phases of the 'new serfdom'. I will mention only one of the most questionable views expressed: the economic and political victory of the magnates at the expense of the lesser nobility (which, incidentally, is not true of Russia). The main problem is this: if the *transfer* to serf-estate economy took place simultaneously with the crisis, some time about 1660 (which, generally speaking, is dating this process too late), then how could the crisis in the West, characterised as it was by a general slump in all economic life, stimulate an increase in exports from the lords' estates? It would be natural to expect the opposite, that is, a decline in the export of grain and raw materials, since reduced industrial production could hardly facilitate increased demand for raw materials and foodstuffs.

The problem, raised by Hobsbawm, of the universal worsening of the position of the peasantry is a very important one. He considers that the crisis and its concomitant phenomena weakened the peasants and helped their exploiters to strengthen themselves. The fact that such a worsening did take place is beyond doubt. But it was not caused by the crisis as such. The process of primitive accumulation which was going on in the West broke up the peasantry into a rich upper stratum, possessing to a greater or less degree (depending on the general circumstances) the features of a rural bourgeoisie, an economically unstable middle peasantry, and a stratum of landless poor peasants from whom were recruited wage-workers for the towns and also, to some extent, for the rural areas. This process went forward in every economic situation, and such phenomena as a crisis of demand, wars, and so on, though they might quicken it, certainly did not start it.

Another group of causes operated in Eastern Europe, which I cannot discuss here. In any case, as stated above, any connexion between the crisis and the 'new serfdom' remains to be proved.

Most questionable, in my opinion, are Hobsbawm's ideas as to the effects of the crisis in industry. To them he ascribes the eliminating of the crafts and the craft-dominated towns from large-scale production, and the establishing of the 'putting-out' system in the countryside, controlled by men with capitalist horizons. The spread of this kind of enterprise in mining, metallurgy and shipbuilding is dated by Hobsbawm as the last third of the seventeenth century. Though 'putting-out' had appeared in the textile industry already in the later Middle Ages, the transformation of craft into 'putting-out' industries began seriously, he says, towards the end of the sixteenth century; in the middle of the seventeenth century a sort of watershed was reached, and this system was decisively established. The cheapness of its products assured it outlets when high-quality urban textiles lost their markets. The crisis encouraged the regional concentration of industries. The negative side of this process was the isolation of the self-sufficient towns with stagnant craft industries, the positive side was the more intensive disintegration of the traditional agrarian structure and the creation of conditions for a rapid growth of production, before the adoption of the factory system. In addition, 'putting-out' led to a considerable concentration of commercial and financial control.

To the extent that the entire paragraph about industry in Hobsbawm's article is devoted to dispersed manufacture alone (more precisely, to the putting-out system) and its significance for the growth of the volume of production and the break-up of the social structure of the countryside, the question of what effect the crisis had on centralised manufacture is left in the dark. One can only suppose that, if it developed as well, then this must have occurred less rapidly than the development of dispersed manufacture, and that its role was very much more modest. But Hobsbawm's silence on the matter provokes the question: why has this writer a blind spot for what was precisely the most advanced type of manufactory, where processes of division of labour which were of the greatest importance for this period were achieved, together with improvements in the instruments of production, and where the coming of machinery and factories was actually prepared? One is given the impression that dispersed manufacture, because it produced cheaper articles, is seen by Hobsbawm as a more important stage in the development of capitalism than the centralised kind. It is, in any case, the former that receives all his attention. It would appear that such a sharp distinction is historically unfounded, since everywhere (even in England) a combination of the two kinds was found, in a great variety of forms, with the putting-out system embracing not only the rural population but inhabitants of towns as well, in particular, workers who were outside the craft-guilds. A combination like this was usually determined by the technique of production itself which permitted part of an operation to be carried out by workers working on their own at home, or at any rate in the country. The cheapening of the articles produced resulted not only from the low wage-level of the workers who carried out the primary or simplest operations, but also from the division of labour in centralised workshops and the implementation of technical improvements (such as, for instance, fulling mills) which cheapened the production process. Subsequently, in the sixteenth and seventeenth centuries, centralised manufactories of this kind developed on a large scale, and, owing to their low cost of production (for instance, in the making of small metal articles), they completely conquered the market, ousting the craft-guilds and rural industry. The cheapness of particular articles was determined not so much by the type of manufactory as by the nature of the branch of industry. Needles, pins, and so on, were cheap, and were made in centralised manufactories (and were cheap precisely for that reason); clocks were dear, and were made in dispersed manufactories, and so on. The example quoted by Hobsbawm of the making of cheap 'new draperies' in contrast to expensive textiles has only a limited bearing.

Furthermore, the dating of the stages of development of dispersed manufacture is dubious. While the first date (later Middle Ages) is acceptable, the second and third (late sixteenth century and middle of the seventeenth) need to be made more precise. The extensive spread of dispersed manufacture took place in different countries at different times, and what is true of, say, Germany, does not apply to Spain, or France, and so on. The picture Hobsbawm draws is in general most significant for England, especially in relation to the craft-guild towns and the rapid progress of manufacture, and later of the factory system, outside old urban centres. It is applicable to other countries only with very substantial amendments. In France, for instance, the development of dispersed manufacture, not only in the countryside but also in towns (in the South, almost entirely in towns), was already taking place on a large scale in the first half of the sixteenth century and proceeded, at an increasing rate, all through the seventeenth, so the middle of the the seventeenth century was not a watershed.

Hobsbawm considers that the crafts were already ousted from the field of mass production by the putting-out system in the sixteenth century. This is partly true for England (though there too only with important qualifications), but is completely inapplicable to the Continent where for various reasons the craft-guilds were still showing themselves very tenacious of life even in the seventeenth century, and were very far from having surrendered their positions. An enormous quantity of small articles which were cheap by their very nature were made by the craftsmen for the home market. The relative weight of the craft-guilds in the total volume of national production declined, but in absolute figures their production was still capable of growth, all the more because—and this is most important—during the sixteenth and seventeenth centuries there was a marked tendency for the biggest and richest craft-guild workshops to be transformed into small centralised manufactories.

It remains for us to examine the last question relating to the consequences of the crisis of the seventeenth century—the accumulation of capital.[1] Hobsbawm's view is that at that time the problem of capital supply had two aspects. Probably, industrialisation generally required greater preliminary capital accumulation. Furthermore, it required investment in the right places. The maritime countries successfully used their foreign and colonial markets to accumulate capital, but even there this did not automatically eliminate misinvestment, the chief difficulty and a contributory cause of the crisis. The crisis led only indirectly to more effective capital investment, as a result of the encouragement by the absolute monarchies of enterprises which could not be developed without their aid, and in the maritime countries to a certain intensification of productive investment.

The problem of the accumulation of financial resources for capitalist production seems to me more complicated than that. It is quite probable that Hobsbawm's idea regarding the insufficiency of capital is correct. But means to overcome this difficulty were found even then. One can point to the considerable number of commercial and industrial companies of varying sizes and types, from those which were very large and operated regularly to those which united only a few people for very brief periods or even for the carrying out of a single order. I described such companies earlier;[2] here I would stress that this way of raising money and concentrating capital proved, as is well known, a successful one, and it had a big future before it. At the same time we must take into account what the sources of accumulation were. Not only in the sixteenth century but also in the seventeenth, part of the money invested in production was not as yet derived from capitalist

[1] Hobsbawm, *Past and Present*, no. 6, pp. 52–3.
[2] See p. 37.

profit. The latter (for reasons to be considered later) only grew at a slow rate in the manufacturing period. But the process of primitive (that is, non-capitalist) accumulation was going on at full speed, and furnishing money for investment in manufacture which was drawn from other sources (plundering of colonies, state subsidies, etc.) or represented merchant's profit and commission on banking capital, which had not yet been changed into elements of surplus value. In some countries, taxes on industry and trade were so heavy that sometimes part of the manufacturer's profit found its way into the unproductive sphere quite regardless of his intention and even directly contrary to it. In addition, where the bourgeoisie was itself the ruling power (as in Florence in the fourteenth century or Holland in the seventeenth), part of its income inevitably had to meet the needs of government, that is, it served the development of capitalist production only in indirect fashion. Finally, so long as the capitalist system had not become dominant in all or most of a nation's industry, and a bourgeois class had not been formed, the feudal framework could not but absorb a certain share of capitalist profit, thereby reducing the proportion available for extending production.

In concluding my analysis of the consequences of the crisis, I should point out that Hobsbawm does not say anything about how the crisis affected (if, indeed, it did affect) the process of expropriation of part of the rural and urban population and the transformation of landless peasants and ruined craftsmen into wage-workers in centralised manufactories, though in the seventeenth century this aspect of the process of primitive accumulation continued to be fundamental.

Hobsbawm defines the general conclusions of his work as follows.[1] The first stage of capitalist development took place within feudal society, which early capitalism was unable to burst, and in ways adapted to it rather than to modern capitalism. For this reason, at the first blow it received (whether by the reduction in the import of American silver or the collapse of the Baltic market), the entire unstable structure of capitalist production tottered. A period of economic crisis and social upheaval began, during which the transition took place from capitalist enterprises adapted to a feudal framework to a capitalism which transformed the world in its own image. The English Revolution was the most dramatic event in the crisis, its turning point and its most important result.

It is hard to agree with these conclusions; they are not supported by the facts to which I have referred in the course of my analysis of Hobsbawm's argument.

But there is another aspect of the matter, too, which must be given some

[1] Hobsbawm, *Past and Present*, no. 5, pp. 48, 49, and no. 6, pp. 62, 63.

attention, before going on to discuss the most recent works devoted to the theory of the seventeenth-century crisis. This is the question of what actually prevented a rapid development of capitalism in the period under consideration.

As we have seen, what underlies Hobsbawm's ideas is his sense of surprise at the very slow development of capitalism in the period between its beginnings and the Industrial Revolution.[1] In conjunction with his view that there was no obstacle to technical advance in that period, this surprise compels this author to seek the expression of the crisis and its cause in the decline of demand and in the feudal framework. Yet the slow course of capitalist development in its manufactory stage is not accidental or wholly due to the feudal framework, decline in demand, and so on. This characteristic was inherent in manufacture, to the same degree as the rapid rate of development was inherent in the capitalism of the nineteenth century, and was one of its typical properties. Engels speaks of the 'sluggish' progress of production in the period of manufacture,[2] in contrast to its rapid progress after the Industrial Revolution, Lenin of the comparative immobility of manufacture— likewise relative to factory industry.[3] The cause of this slowness lies in the retention throughout the entire manufactory period of the previous technical basis, that is, of production by hand.[4] Manufacture introduces into production by hand an extremely important innovation—the division of the labour process into detail operations, but in so far as production by hand is retained, the progress and deepening of the division of labour goes forward very slowly, and 'for whole decades (and even centuries) manufacture retains its form once it has been adopted'.[5]

Closely connected with this is the question of the skills of the workers in manufacture. Specialisation in the carrying out of detail operations by manual methods leads to a high level of virtuosity in the skill of each detail worker, and so the 'collective labourer' in a manufactory masters all labour practices with uniform skill.[6] At the same time, besides operations which require out-

[1] Dobb shares this surprise; he sees the cause of the slow development of capitalism in the slow rate of maturation of capitalist relations in the countryside, that is, in the last analysis also in the 'feudal framework' (Dobb, *The transition from feudalism to capitalism*, pp. 3–4, 9).
[2] Marx and Engels, op. cit. xx (1961), 271 [Engels, *Anti-Dühring*, 1934 English edition, 287].
[3] Lenin, op. cit. iii, 427, 428 [English edition, 428].
[4] Marx and Engels, op. cit. xxiii, 259 [Marx, *Capital*, i, 1938 English edition, 232]. 'Capital...is at first indifferent as to the technical character of the labour-process; it begins by taking it just as it finds it.'
[5] Lenin, op. cit. iii, 428 [English edition, 428]. Cf. ibid. 543, 544 [English edition, 542]. 'But production by hand remains, and on its basis, progress in methods of production is inevitably very slow.'
[6] Marx and Engels, op. cit. xxiii, 361, 362 [Marx, *Capital*, i, 1938 English edition, 341–2].

standing skill and dexterity, there are also other jobs to be done in manu-facturing production, which are carried out by unskilled workers. A hier-archy of labour power comes into being, with a corresponding ladder of wage-levels. However, it is the skilled workers, carrying out the principal cycle of productive operations, who always remain predominant, quantitatively and qualitatively. This means that the bulk of the workers have to be trained, and in so far as labour continues to be hand-labour, the mastering of a given skill, by apprenticeship, necessitates a long period of time (and corresponding expenditure). However, owing to a simplification of functions as compared with the craft era, this period is somewhat shorter than it was then.[1]

Owing to such inherent characteristics of manufacture as production by hand and a specific way of using labour-power, various obstacles arose in the way of its development which it was not itself able to overcome and which vanished only in the machine period. First, the predominance of skilled workers over unskilled kept up the expenditure necessary for wages and for the preliminary training of workers, especially for the most difficult detail jobs. Furthermore, although manufacture, through the breakdown of operations, made possible the recruitment of women and children for work, nevertheless entrepreneurs found themselves unable to carry this tendency very far owing to resistance by the adult male workers. Of great importance was the fact that the objective tendency inherent in manufacture, and the subjective striving by the entrepreneurs, to use female and child labour, lengthen the working day, lower the wages of skilled workers, and so on, came up against stubborn and, what is most important, successful resistance on the part of the workers. Marx notes that 'during the period between the sixteenth century and the epoch of modern capitalism, capital failed to be-come the master of the whole disposable working-time of the manufacturing labourers'.[2] For this reason, in spite of help by the state, the manufacturers managed to extend the working day of adult men in England only to a maximum of twelve hours, which in the middle of the nineteenth century, after its rapid increase in the age of large-scale industry, was in Massachusetts 'the statutory limit of the labour of children under twelve'.[3] The successful resistance by the workers to attempts to lengthen the working day, reduce

[1] Marx and Engels, op. cit. XXIII, p. 363 [Marx, *Capital*, I, 1938 English edition, 342–3]; cf. Lenin, op. cit. III, 429, 430 [English edition, 429, 430].

[2] Marx and Engels, op. cit. XXIII, 380 [Marx, *Capital*, I, 1938 English edition, 362]. 'Still, during the greater part of the eighteenth century, up to the epoch of modern industry and machinism, capital in England had not succeeded in seizing for itself, by the payment of the weekly value of labour-power, the whole week of the labourer' (ibid. 283 [English edition, 259]). There were only four working days to the week. Cf. the figures given by Mousnier, *Les XVIe et XVIIe siècles*, p. 255: in France there were 112 non-working days in the year before 1666, and 92 thereafter.

[3] Marx and Engels, op. cit. XXIII, 281 [Marx, *Capital*, I, 1938 English edition, 256–7].

wages, introduce female and child labour, and so on, is explained by Marx as being due to the fact that 'since handicraft skill is the foundation of manufacture, and since the total mechanism of manufacture as a whole possesses no framework apart from the labourers themselves, capital is constantly compelled to wrestle with insubordination of the workers';[1] he quotes complaints by contemporaries about the wilfulness and 'lack of discipline' of the most highly skilled workers, precisely those who were most valuable for the enterprises in which they worked.[2]

Manufacture's lack of any framework of machinery, independent of the workers (which meant that the proportion of constant capital was smaller and that of variable capital higher than in developed capitalism) made the skilled workers the entrepreneur's basic asset. The very existence of an enterprise depended on the presence of these skilled craftsmen. Migration of such workers was sufficient to cause manufacture to develop in a given country, or to leave it for another.[3] This is the explanation of many cases of the rapid disappearance of certain manufactories, or of their appearance seemingly from nowhere. This is the reason for the pursuit of skilled men by the manufacturers, the offer to them of all sorts of privileges, and so on. An entrepreneur was not able to dismiss skilled workers whom he found undesirable, and hire others, because often there were no others to be had: the labour market could be saturated only with untrained, unskilled paupers.

These internal causes, inherent in the very nature of manufacture, prevented manufacturers from obtaining substantial profits from their enterprises and held back the growth of the latter. But there were also other, external, factors operating in the same direction.

Hobsbawm talks of the transfer of production from the craft-guild basis to manufacture rather than of the struggle between craft-guilds and manufactories. Yet in the history of capitalism in any West-European country with a widespread craft-guild structure, this conflict developed with great violence, not only before the middle of the seventeenth century but also later. The policy of support for the craft-guilds, which nearly all governments adopted, together with subsidising manufacturers and granting privileges to them, contributed a great deal to prolonging this conflict. Craft-guild privileges concerned not only restrictions on the number of workers, but also preferential supply of raw material, the regulation of trade and of the quality of products in the interest of the craft-guilds, the hiring of skilled workers, and so on. Struggle against the rich craft-guildsmen, who usually operated closely

[1] Ibid. 380 [English edition, 362].
[2] Ibid.   [3] Ibid.

together in defence of their common interests, was therefore hard for the manufacturers, and they did not always succeed, especially in those cases when they were not able to beat their competitors down by purely economic means. Craft-guild and all other local privileges, internal tolls, and so on, were grave impediments in the way of the young bourgeoisie, and hampered the development on the home market of those principles of equality of opportunity for competitors without which capitalist production cannot expand freely.[1]

I mentioned earlier the significance of the home market for the development of manufacture.[2] We will here add one further comment. Among the intrinsic contradictions of capitalism is the fact that it destroys its own home market even as it creates this market. Destroying the basis for peasant domestic industry, capitalism ruins the peasants (who can no longer survive as peasants only), and, until they are transformed into wage-earners, their purchasing power is negligible.[3] This process goes forward fully, however, only in the era of developed capitalism, with its factories, etc. In the manufactory period, peasant domestic industry develops on a wide scale and constitutes an important help to the peasants, delaying their complete ruination and loss of land, so that they not only retain their former purchasing power (even though this was not large) but also increase it, to the extent that they are increasingly drawn into monetary relations. 'As soon as manufacture gains sufficient strength,' writes Marx, '...it creates in its turn a market for itself, by capturing it through its commodities.'[4]

The question of the world market calls for more detailed treatment, all the more because Hobsbawm, as already mentioned, puts his main emphasis only on the Baltic, not the colonial, market. I have pointed out how this opinion of Hobsbawm's fails to correspond with new evidence (not to speak of old evidence) obtained from abundant sources. Consideration of the problem of the external market enables us to look again at the part played by the production of luxury articles.

In conformity with the information available to them, which has been reinforced by more recent evidence, the founders of Marxism often pointed to the very great part played by the expansion of the world market as a result of the great geographical discoveries. For those countries where in the pre-

---

[1] Engels often refers to the obstacles to the development of the bourgeoisie presented by guild and other privileges. Cf. e.g. Marx and Engels, op. cit. xx, 107, 168, 279; xxi, 309 [*Anti-Dühring*, 1934 English edition, pp. 118–19, 185, 295; *Ludwig Feuerbach*, 1947 English edition, pp. 60–1].

[2] Cf. pp. 53–55.

[3] Marx and Engels, op. cit. xxxviii, 400 [Engels to Danielson, 22 September 1892; Marx and Engels, *Selected Correspondence*, 1934 English edition, 500].

[4] Marx and Engels, op. cit. xxv, part 1, 369 [Marx, *Capital*, iii, Foreign Languages Publishing House English edition, 331].

ceding centuries the break-up of feudal relations had already begun and where the level of craft-guild production was sufficiently high, one of the chief causes of rapid economic progress was 'the sudden expansion of the world market, the multiplication of circulating commodities, the competitive zeal of the European nations to possess themselves of the products of Asia and the treasures of America and the colonial system'.[1] Engels also defined very precisely the interrelation between different markets: 'Trade beyond the confines of Europe, which had previously been carried on only between Italy and the Levant, was now extended to America and India, and soon surpassed in importance both the mutual exchange between the various European countries and the internal trade within each separate country.'[2] In other words, external markets generally, and from the sixteenth century onward the new colonial markets in particular, were of primary importance for the rise and the initial phase of manufacture.[3] In these circumstances it was these markets, and not the slowly developing home market, that could offer the rapidly increasing demand that the previous craft form of production was unable to satisfy.

There are two other factors which I have already touched on in examining Hobsbawm's article. The first concerns the production of high-quality textiles and of luxury goods generally. According to Hobsbawm, the decline of manufacture in Italy was determined by the fact that it produced for a narrow circle of rich consumers. In countering this view I referred to the flourishing of the French luxury-goods industry. Here it must be emphasised that, serving mainly the external market, where high commercial profit was possible, this branch of industry was characterised by the fact that the merchant directly became an industrialist,[4] that is, transition to the capitalist mode of production took place by the shortest route, avoiding or shortening the stage of the putting-out system, in which the merchant's role is dominant.

My second comment relates to the rivalry between the countries of Europe for mastery of external markets, which Hobsbawm has not sufficiently taken into account. This rivalry operated from the very start, and played an important part in the rise of particular countries' foreign trade, at the expense of losses suffered by their competitors. In Marx's words quoted above,[5] this factor was mentioned as a direct result of the expansion of the world market.

---

[1] Ibid. 365. [English edition, 327].
[2] Ibid. xx, 106 [Engels, *Anti-Dühring*, 1934 English edition, 118].
[3] Cf. also Marx's words: 'Manufacture…arises where there is mass production for export.' (Marx, *Formy predshestvuyushchie kapitalisticheskomy proizvodstvu* (Moscow, 1940), p. 48). [*Pre-capitalist economic formations*, English edition, ed. Hobsbawm, p. 116].
[4] Marx and Engels, op. cit. xxv, part 1, 368 [Marx, *Capital*, III, FLPH English edition, 330].
[5] Cf. n. 1, above.

In the seventeenth and eighteenth centuries the conflict already took the form of trade wars between the nations of Europe,[1] wars which resulted, as is well known, in victory by the industrially developed countries over the merely trading nations.

Of great importance in considering the historical development of capitalism in particular countries and in Europe as a whole, is the relation between different types of manufacture, and between manufacture as a whole and the craft-guilds, and also the stages by which manufacture won mastery over different branches of production. This question is particularly important because manufacture is based on rural domestic industry and town craft industry, and is connected with them in a great variety of ways. It would be wrong to reduce the entire process of capitalist development merely to the evolution of large-scale centralised manufacture. This undoubtedly played the leading role, in that the division of labour within it led in the end to production by aggregates of workers ('the collective labourer') not only of consumer goods but also of means of production. However, for a picture of the general line of the development of capitalism and its successive stages, other types of manufactory must be taken into account as well.

It is well known that centralised manufactories in the pure form are comparatively rare phenomena, and that their weight in the total amount of national production was relatively slight, especially in the sixteenth and seventeenth centuries. But one cannot conclude from this that capitalist development as a whole was inadequate, owing to some such outside causes as a limited stock of currency, and so on. The clear predominance in nearly all countries of various forms of combination between centralised and dispersed manufactories was the result not only of the uniform basis of both manufacture and the crafts, namely, production by hand (the use of machinery in centralised workshops was sporadic; only large-scale factory industry was able to destroy, and actually did destroy, the craft industries of town and country), but also of firm production links between dispersed and centralised manufactories. For this reason it would be wrong to conclude that dispersed manufacture as such had (except in a very few branches) a conservative character *par excellence* all through the manufactory period (that is, before the nineteenth century), for a wide extension of manufactory production in the quantitatively and qualitatively most important branch of those days, the textile industry, was possible, as a rule,[2] only on the basis of combining

---

[1] Marx and Engels, op. cit. xx, 284 [Engels, *Anti-Dühring*, 1934 English edition, 300).
[2] Cf. Marx's view regarding the widespread existence of domestic industry (spinning and weaving) even in England and even as late as the first half of the eighteenth century (Marx and Engels, op. cit. xxvi, part 2, 646, 647). [Marx, *Theories of surplus value*, part 2; no English translation available. See Marx, *Histoire des doctrines économiques*, vol. v, 175.]

rural craft production with centralised workshops. I mentioned earlier a similar combination in the production of metal articles.[1] Such examples could be multiplied.

Combination of centralised workshops with rural crafts was not the only way in which such symbiosis took place. Urban craftsmen who were outside the craft-guilds, and even entire craft-guild workshops, were often drawn into the sphere of economic influence of a merchant-manufacturer. In such cases the organisational inter-relation assumed very varied forms, without, however, losing the chief feature of manufacture—that is, capitalist exploitation of the hand labour of wage-earning workers on the basis of division of labour in detail operations—no matter what guild or other signboards these workers were hidden behind.[2]

And so the normal picture of the organisational forms of production in the manufacturing period consisted of simultaneous, and in most cases closely interlinked, co-existence (and simultaneous development, right down to the rise of large-scale industry) of all types of manufactory, both in pure forms and in mixed. There also existed, right down to the end of the eighteenth century (and in some cases even later), craft-guilds whose sphere of activity was still very considerable; it embraced not only the making and sale of food products, clothes, footwear, etc., but also a multitude of small 'old-fashioned handicrafts',[3] which only large-scale industry annihilated, and by no means all at once.

The transition to factory production was accomplished, as Marx writes, through 'a medley of transition forms';[4] manufacture was by its very nature incapable of mastering all branches together to the same extent and fully, and still less capable of transforming the whole system of industry.

Other special features of manufacture follow from this: the small number of really large-scale units of capital and of large-scale capitalists; the need for the state to subsidise manufacturers not just once, when they were setting up their manufactories, but again and again; groupings in the form of trade and industrial companies, and so on.

That some already established manufactories required to be regularly subsidised is to be explained not so much by external causes as by the need for regular increase of constant capital. Inherent in the very nature of manufactory production is the principle of uninterrupted growth of capital, needed not so much for buildings, furnaces, etc., as for raw material, the amount of which needed grows faster than the number of workers. 'The

[1] See p. 36.
[2] Lenin, op. cit. III, 435, 438, 441 [English edition, 435, 439–440].
[3] Marx and Engels, op. cit. XXIII, 307 [Marx, *Capital*, I, 1938 English edition, 285].
[4] Ibid. 484 [English edition, 477].

quantity (of raw material) consumed in a given time by a given amount of labour increases in the same ratio as does the productive power of that labour in consequence of its division. Hence, it is a law based on the very nature of manufacture that the minimum amount of capital which is bound to be in the hands of each capitalist must keep increasing; in others words, that the transformation into capital of the social means of production and subsistence must keep extending.'[1]

Even more urgent was the need for subsidising certain branches of industry when they were in transition to manufacture. 'The minimum of the sum of value that the individual possessor of money or commodities must command, in order to metamorphose himself into a capitalist, changes with the different stages of development of capitalist production, and is at given stages different in different spheres of production, according to their special and technical conditions. Certain spheres of production demand, even at the very outset of capitalist production, a minimum of capital that is not as yet found in the hands of single individuals. This gives rise partly to state subsidies to private persons, as in France in the time of Colbert, and as in many German states up to our own epoch; partly to the formation of societies with legal monopoly for the exploitation of certain branches of industry and commerce, the forerunner of our modern joint stock companies.'[2]

I do not intend to discuss such special questions as the determination of the rate of industrial profit in the manufactory period by commercial profit, or the concentration of resources in merchant-controlled enterprises, the relation between profit and the rate of interest, and so on. I shall only observe that 'concentration appears earlier historically in the merchant's business than in the industrial workshop'[3] (which explains both the predominance of merchant capital and the merging in one person of the merchant and the manufacturer) and that the rate of interest is regulated by the general rate of profit,[4] so that the state can only legalise but not create a particular rate of profit.

The last question which we consider it necessary to say something about is the preparation of the Industrial Revolution. Hobsbawm expresses surprise at the fact that even in England, where after the bourgeois revolution there were seemingly no obstacles to a rapid development of industrial capitalism, the Industrial Revolution nevertheless took over a century to occur. He seeks the reason for this in the sphere of demand and considers that the Industrial Revolution was evoked by a gradual extension of markets, both home and

[1] Marx and Engels, op. cit. XXIII, 372 [English edition, 353–4].
[2] Ibid. 319 [English edition, 296].
[3] Ibid. XXV, part 1, 324 [Marx, *Capital*, III, FLPH English edition, 290).
[4] Ibid. 395 [Marx, *Capital*, III, FLPH English edition, 353].

overseas, especially colonial markets. From the middle of the seventeenth century a notable growth in the home market began in England, and with the eighteenth century exports also increased to the lands across the oceans where the new colonial system, that is, plantation economy, was taking shape.[1]

The internal—technical and economic—evolution of manufacture escapes Hobsbawm's notice. However, I regard it as essential to look at the fundamental processes taking place in manufactory production, which prepared the way for the Industrial Revolution.

As is well known, the division of labour into detail operations leads to something more than a high degree of specialised skill on the part of the detail workers. This high level of skill itself becomes possible owing to the progressive differentiation of the instruments of labour; the adaptation of these instruments for specialised purposes[2] leads to a situation in which a particular instrument operates to the full only in the hands of a particular detail worker. Manufacture helps forward the simplification, improvement and variegation of instruments of labour. The exceptional importance of this for the Industrial Revolution arises from the fact that, whereas in manufacture the starting point of the revolution in the mode of production was labour-power, in large-scale industry this role belongs to the instruments of labour.[3]

Marx particularly emphasised the point that the Industrial Revolution of the eighteenth century started from the machine as tool and not from the machine as motive power. Different forms of motive power, using the force of animals, water, wind, etc., were developed into machines not only during the manufacturing period but also long before it, but they did not revolutionise the mode of production; even the steam engine, in the form in which it was invented at the end of the seventeenth century and existed down to the 1780s, did not bring about the Industrial Revolution. 'It was, on the contrary, the invention of machines that made the revolution in the form of steam engines necessary.'[4]

For this reason, so far as preparation for the Industrial Revolution is concerned, the most important factor in the development of manufacture is the differentiation of the *making* of instruments of labour. 'Simultaneously with the differentiation of the instruments of labour, the industries that produce these instruments become more and more differentiated.'[5] Consequently,

---

[1] Hobsbawm, *Past and Present*, no. 6, pp. 54–63.
[2] Marx quotes as example the use of 500 varieties of hammer, for different detail operations (Marx and Engels, op. cit. XXIII, 353) [Marx, *Capital*, I, 1938 English edition, 333].
[3] Ibid. 382 [English edition, p. 366].
[4] Ibid. 386 [English edition, 370]; cf. also 384 [English edition, 368].
[5] Ibid. 365 [English edition, 346]. Marx quotes the example of the existence in Holland already in the seventeenth century of special manufactories making only weavers' shuttles (ibid. note 54). [English edition, 346, note 2.]

the centre of gravity gradually shifts from the various branches of industry producing consumer goods to that particular branch which to an increasing extent makes means of production. These instruments of labour were at first produced by purely manufacturing methods, that is, by means of the hand labour of 'the collective labourer'. Later, the framework of the working machine began to be made by machinery, though its operative parts (spindles, needles, saws, etc.) were still produced in manufactories (machine production of machine-tools began not earlier than the middle of the nineteenth century).[1] Thus, the technical basis for large-scale industry was at first provided by manufacture. 'Manufacture produced the machinery by means of which modern industry abolished the handicraft and manufacturing systems in those spheres of production that it first seized upon. The factory system was therefore raised, in the natural course of things, on an inadequate foundation. When the system attained to a certain degree of development, it had to root up this ready-made foundation, which in the meantime had been elaborated on the old lines, and to build up for itself a basis that should correspond to its methods of production.'[2] This process of gradual transition from the production of machines in manufactories to their production by machines established the revolutionary, constantly changing technical basis of large-scale industry, ousting the fundamentally conservative basis of manufacture. At the same time, steam engines made it possible to concentrate production in towns instead of scattering it up and down the country, as the water wheel had necessitated.[3]

The manufactory division of labour played an important preparatory role also in that the breaking-down of jobs into detail operations made possible the introduction of machines which at first also carried out these separate operations. Machines only gradually began to master complex operations as well.

There is another, no less important aspect to the matter. Machines as tools and as motive power were able to develop (and technical construction of them to be carried out) only because the manufactory period, with its strict division of labour, had prepared a considerable number of skilled mechanics.[4] Later on, this strict division of labour and specialised skill of the manufactory worker was transferred to the machine, and instead of a hierarchy of specialised workers a tendency developed to reduce them to the same level, abolishing the manufactory division of labour and opening up extensive

[1] Marx and Engels, op. cit. XXIII, 384 [Marx, *Capital*, I, 1938 English edition, 368].
[2] Ibid. 393, 394 [English edition, 378].
[3] Ibid. 388 [English edition, 372].
[4] Ibid. 393 [English edition, 377].

possibilities for use of female and child labour, lengthening of the working day, and so on.

This technical and economic progress, described by Marx, which took place within the manufactories themselves, was not only a complex process but also a prolonged one, for the changes accomplished in the sphere of the making of instruments of labour necessarily passed—being for a long time limited by the general slowness of development which was characteristic of manufacture with its hand labour—through a series of successive stages from production completely by hand to production completely by machinery. This was why it took such a long time not only to prepare for the first machine-tools but also for the Industrial Revolution itself, which was spread over several decades, until at last, in the middle of the nineteenth century the production of machines by machines began and the system of machine production was consolidated.

Mousnier's book and Hobsbawm's article have given rise both to direct reactions and to intensified interest in all aspects of seventeenth-century history.

An interesting contribution to the theory of the economic crisis of the seventeenth century was recently made by R. Romano.[1] While agreeing with Hobsbawm's conception, he also thinks it necessary to emphasise that, although the final transition to capitalism was prepared in the seventeenth century this was simultaneously a period of feudal reaction against the advance of capitalism. Romano dates the beginning of the crisis itself in 1619–22. Denying to the movement of prices the role of chief factor in the development of the economy, he regards this movement as merely a sort of index, a measuring instrument. The basis of the economic process was agriculture, which the author, in order to reveal the fundamental tendencies in it, analyses for the hundred years from 1560 to 1660.

Looking at the grain trade in the Baltic and in the Mediterranean, Romano notes the decline in the former after 1618 and in the latter after 1622.[2] For this reason he considers it beyond doubt that a turn for the worse, towards stagnation, set in about that time. However, he regards as groundless the view that the cause was war (especially the war between Holland and Spain that began in 1621). He does not believe those contemporaries who also put forward war as the explanation of the decline. The crisis of 1619–22 came at a critical moment. A contraction of industrial production had begun, as

---

[1] R. Romano, 'Tra XVI e XVII secolo. Una crisa economica: 1619–1622', *Rivista storica italiana*, LXXIV, part 3 (1962), and 'Encore la crise de 1619–1622', *Annales E.S.C.* (no. 1, 1964). These articles give a bibliography of the question of the seventeenth-century crisis for 1960–3.

[2] It must be observed that the figures quoted by Romano are very heterogeneous, show important fluctuations, and provide no basis for such a categorical conclusion.

also of the influx of precious metals from America, and in the latter case it was not a matter of exhaustion of the mines but of fall in demand: the stagnation that had begun in Europe had an effect on the decline in the production of silver.[1]

In the sixteenth century agriculture developed intensively under a régime of high prices and provided the basis for a general economic advance. In the seventeenth century the economic situation changed, which helped the feudal reaction that had begun in the countryside. It did not proceed everywhere in the same way, but everywhere it had a withering effect on the economy. As concrete examples, Romano refers to the activity of a company for the exploitation of mills at Cesena (Northern Italy), agriculture in Poland, and the creation of polders in Holland. In the first two cases he notes an onset of stagnation about 1620, but in the third case development took quite the opposite direction. But Romano sees Holland as an exception; all the other countries (France, Spain, Germany, to some extent England) followed the example of Italy and Poland. Their agriculture suffered, and this meant that commercial and industrial prosperity were out of the question, because if agriculture was going badly everything went badly.

The decline in prices for agricultural products throughout Europe after 1610 had a very severe impact on landowners and cultivators. In 1618–22 prices rose, but this could not improve the situation because the cause of the rise was harvest-failure. The rise in the cost of living made it necessary to increase the wages of town workers or else to reduce the scale of production. All this was accompanied by a currency crisis—a reduction in issues, a cheapening of credit. Therefore, says Romano, the usual cyclical crisis was transformed in 1619–22 into the beginning of a general economic crisis, marking the transition from an epoch of prosperity (the sixteenth century) to one of stagnation (the seventeenth century).

Romano estimates the profitability of agriculture in the sixteenth century as very high—15–30 per cent, judging by the general expenditure on the purchase of land and on improving it. Gradually, however, these high profits grew less in proportion to the capital invested in the land, and attained an average standard level of 3–5 per cent. The first generation which had invested money in land were satisfied, but their children and grandchildren had no grounds for satisfaction. A seignorial reaction took place, that is, a re-feudalisation, which Romano explains, on the social and economic plane, as

[1] Vilar puts forward a more convincing reason. The extraction of precious metals in America flourished through the use of cheap forced labour, together with technical improvements (amalgamation). In the seventeenth century revenue from the mines fell off sharply in connexion with a rise in costs mainly due to the catastrophic dying-out of the local population. (Vilar, loc. cit. pp. 32–3.)

a general death-agony of economic life. To the 'vital' sixteenth century he counterposes the 'sad' seventeenth, making an exception only for Holland, and to some extent for England.

Without repeating my argument about war as the cause of the contraction of the grain trade, I would point out Romano's inconsistency in his views about the role played by price movements. Denying price-movements the role of prime cause, and focusing all his attention on agriculture, he nevertheless puts at the basis of the successful progress which he sees in the sixteenth century precisely the rise in prices, bringing substantial profits to landowners. Thereby his range of investigation is restricted to this movement of prices, with currency circulation and the evolution of credit. The fact of feudal reaction in agrarian relations which Romano mentions, in itself unquestionably real and deserving attention, is put forward by the author in too general a form; for this reason the difference between France, on the one hand, and the countries of Central Europe, on the other, is blurred. The main point in Romano's concept—the primacy of agricultural development over that of industry, is unacceptable. The cradle of capitalism was industry, and industry influenced agriculture in the capitalist direction, to a greater or smaller extent.

In recent years, publications on the economic history of the seventeenth century have become so numerous, and the crisis theory has found so many supporters, that one of them, Pierre Chaunu, produced a short time ago an interesting article in which he was able already to draw some conclusions and to indicate the lines of future work.[1] The main propositions of his article amount to the following.[2]

Chaunu regards the problem of the sharp turn (the 'revolution') in the economic situation in the seventeenth century as very important. The most important thing is the movement of prices, taken, of course, not in isolation but as an index of the extent of industrial and commercial activity. It is from this standpoint that the author looks at the turn in the movement of prices at the beginning of the seventeenth century, which he tries to define more precisely for each of the large geographical regions (Mediterranean Europe, Northern Europe, America, the Far East). This enables him to note the chronological *nuances* in the process whereby the increase in prices came to an end, prices were stabilised, and then began to fall.

This process showed itself earliest of all—at the very end of the sixteenth

---

[1] P. Chaunu, 'Le renversement de la tendance majeure des prix et des activités au XVIIe siècle. Problèmes de fait et de méthode' in *Studi in onore di Amintore Fanfani*, IV (Milan, 1962), 219–55. The footnotes give an extensive bibliography.

[2] I leave aside the author's idea about a '*révolution intellectuelle*' between 1610 and 1680, by which he means the triumph of Cartesianism.

century—in Spain. In Italy it was complicated by four brief crises at the end of the sixteenth century and the beginning of the seventeenth, and the final turning-point came after 1620; it was about then that it came in Northern Europe also.

The general features of this conjuncture apply also to the colonies in America (though the Brazilian economy continued prosperous all through the seventeenth century)[1] and to the Portuguese possessions in the Indian and Pacific oceans. In the latter, however, a political factor enters into the situation; at the end of the sixteenth century the Dutch had already begun to take over from the Portuguese, and showed during the first decades of the seventeenth century a stormy and ever-growing 'youthful' vigour (*activités adolescentes*).[2] Therefore, it is not surprising that the general turn in the economic situation was considerably delayed in that region, and is indeed hard to recognise.

As a result of his survey of recent work, Chaunu considers that the existence of interdependence in the movement of prices (and along with this all commercial, industrial and colonial activity) has been proved for all the chief regions of the globe in the seventeenth century. The actual movement of prices was uneven: between 1586 and 1652 it passed through several cycles and affected different regions in a definite succession—first the Mediterranean and Spanish America, then Northern Europe, after which came, 'rather paradoxically', Brazil and the countries of the Indian Ocean. Chaunu particularly emphasises this chronological break, which had not previously attracted historians' attention.

Chaunu considers that it is as yet premature to try to explain all these complex phenomena. This will require extensive and many-sided work by many historians. The causes are seemingly rooted not in local, but in general conditions, and the author sees the main one as being probably what he calls *l'invention géographique*, that is the mastering by the Europeans of the whole surface of the earth. In the fifteenth to eighteenth centuries this process played, in his view, the same role that technical progress has played in the last 120 years. Demographic and climatic factors are also very important.

It is obvious that Chaunu ignores the development of capitalism. Whereas in the first part of his article, when he is analysing the movement of prices, one can suppose that he is assuming that this process is a well-known

---

[1] Chaunu analyses Mauro's book (see p. 52, n. 1) and considers that actually Brazil was not an exception; however, his conclusions are not very convincing. He attributes the prosperity of sugar production in Southern Brazil in the seventeenth century to its relatively youthful (*récent*) development in this area, which enabled it to remain at a certain level for a long period.
[2] Chaunu, *Studi in onore di Amintore Fanfani*, IV, 249. He calls the success of the Dutch '*extraordinaire et "scandaleuse"*' (ibid. 252).

phenomenon, the end of the article, where he discusses causes, removes all grounds for such an assumption. The 'scandalous' success of the Dutch in the Far East and the decline of Spain and Italy, etc. are not related by the author to the fundamental, pivotal process of the establishment and consolidation of the capitalist mode of production in some countries and its suppression in others. In addition, the very analysis of price-movements is undertaken in too general a form and, so to speak, 'adjusted' to the author's theory. In reality it presents a much more complex picture.[1] One is dubious too about the interdependence of price-movements and levels of commercial and industrial activity. For seventeenth-century France we have had occasion to show that the periods of low prices in the seventeenth century coincided with booms in trade and industry while, on the other hand, it is well known that the high prices in Spain in the second half of the sixteenth century coincided with a sharp decline in the level of Spanish industry. Many such examples could be quoted.[2]

Chaunu does not consider political events either. Only once does he bring in a political factor—the victory of the Dutch over the Portuguese in the Far East (though this was not a purely political event). War in Europe and its consequences for the colonies remain completely out of the picture.

Owing to these weaknesses, Chaunu's article is a merely formal analysis of prices generally, without making allowances for the peculiarities of the development of each separate country.

Moreover, the findings drawn from a critical analysis of the list of customs duties levied by Denmark on trade through the Sound, and also from other sources, do not confirm certain important propositions put forward by Chaunu and other supporters of the crisis theory. In Jeannin's article to which I referred when discussing Hobsbawm's theory, the sharp turn towards decisive decline in Baltic trade as a whole is ascribed to the period after 1650, and, consequently, there is a chronological discrepancy between the situation in the Mediterranean countries on the one hand, and that in the countries of Northern Europe on the other; the prolonged contrast between the two being more considerable than appears in Chaunu's account. Jeannin notes that the coincidence between these phenomena and the undoubted expansion of England and Holland was not at all accidental. Taking into account the important role played by Baltic trade in the crisis theory, one may conclude that the material used by Jeannin does not merely displace the starting-point of the crisis, it also indicates that the causes may be different from those recognised by the supporters of the crisis theory.

[1] See above, pp. 12–16.
[2] Some of them are quoted in Jeannin's article (P. Jeannin, *Revue historique*, CCXXXI, 323 ff., 336).

Craeybeckx[1] and Van Houtte[2] have produced interesting data and conclusions in articles devoted to the economic development of the Spanish
Netherlands, i.e. Belgium, in the seventeenth century. On the basis of extensive research these historians refute the traditional idea that industry declined
in that country after, and as a result of, the Netherlands Revolution. The
big towns of Flanders, and Antwerp, came to life again at the beginning of
the seventeenth century and successfully developed a number of branches
of production (various forms of textiles, the making of armaments, carpets,
lace, printing, etc.). It is characteristic that this prosperity came to an end
only with the end of the seventeenth century, and then not as a result of any
phenomena connected with a general economic crisis, but owing to the
protectionist measures adopted by France, which was the principal market
for Belgian goods. As a result of these researches we can extend the list of
countries which did *not* experience crisis phenomena in the seventeenth
century, adding Belgium to Holland and England. The data on the harmful
influence of French protectionism on Belgian industry are very important.
They confirm my opinion of the important role played by the conflict between individual countries for mastery of European markets.[3]

Thus historians have advanced a long way from earlier vague ideas about the
profound changes which were supposed to have taken place in the seventeenth
century, first put forward by the British historian Clark in 1929.[4] They are
now convinced that the facts at their disposal show unquestionably that there
was a crisis. Any modifications introduced into this thesis either deal with
the specific features of particular countries[5] or else are merely more precise
definitions. The theory of economic crisis as such is not subjected to doubt
or criticism. It has become a sort of axiom, a point of departure for all discussions, even in those cases where historians are not agreed on a particular
interpretation of particular economic and social phenomena or political
struggles.[6] It has made its way into more popular works.[7]

In analysing the views of the supporters of the theory of the seventeenth-

---

[1] J. Craeybeckx, 'Les industries d'exportation dans les villes flamandes au XVIIe siècle, particulière-
ment à Gand et à Bruges', in *Studi in onore di Amintore Fanfani*, IV (Milan, 1962).

[2] J. van Houtte, 'Déclin et survivance d'Anvers (1550–1700)', in *Studi in onore di Amintore Fanfani*,
V.   [3] See chapter 3.

[4] G. N. Clark, *The seventeenth century* (Oxford, 1929), (2nd edition, 1960).

[5] M. Roberts. 'Queen Christina and the general crisis of the seventeenth century', *Past and Present*,
no. 22 (1962). See the note on this article by A. S. Kan, *Voprosy istorii*, no. 2 (1963), pp. 197, 198.

[6] See chapter 2.

[7] In Méthivier's book (in the *Que sais-je?* series) on the *ancien régime* in France, the chapter on the
seventeenth century is called: 'Les fièvres économiques et sociales du "Grand siècle"', and the
opening paragraph of this chapter is headed: 'Le tumultueux XVIIe siècle', (H. Méthivier,
'*L'Ancien Régime*' (Paris, 1961).

century crisis I have principally endeavoured to check their reasoning and to evaluate the material used as the basis for their arguments. Taken as a whole, this theory cannot, in my view, be regarded as convincing. But this still does not settle the question of the existence or non-existence of a crisis, of its social and economic consequences (to which the following chapter is devoted), of the causes of stagnation and decline in the European economy as a whole. The negative conclusion drawn in this chapter is merely a first stage in the study of the problem of the peculiarities of capitalist development in the seventeenth century. I shall return in subsequent chapters to considering the causes of this slow rate of development.

CHAPTER 2

The theory of general political revolution in seventeenth-century Europe

THE historians responsible for the theory of the 'general crisis' of the seventeenth century concentrate their attention on two main themes—economic decline, and the role played by the state. Social relations, and political struggles in particular, sink, generally speaking, into the background. But writings do exist in which the chief role is assigned precisely to the political struggle, and in which a theory of 'general revolution' in the seventeenth century is set forth as the natural corollary of the theory of 'general crisis'.

In analysing the theory of the 'general crisis' of the seventeenth century, with special reference to Mousnier's book, I also touched on the problem of absolutism, in so far as the state is presented as the principal force which put an end to the crisis. I stressed, in this connexion, the *étatiste* nature of Mousnier's conception of absolutism and his tendency to gloss over class antagonisms. However, Mousnier does acknowledge the existence of absolute monarchy and of social antagonisms, and also the important part played by both in the social and political life of seventeenth-century Europe. I will now consider the theory of 'general revolution' in the seventeenth century, which is based upon a complete denial both of absolutism and of the class antagonisms characteristic of that stage in the development of state structure.

This theory comes from the Oxford professor H. R. Trevor-Roper, and was set forth by him in a long article[1] which gave rise to a lively discussion in

[1] H. R. Trevor-Roper, 'The general crisis of the seventeenth century', *Past and Present*, no. 16 (1959), pp. 31–64. The appearance of this article was preceded by a discussion devoted to the revolutions of the seventeenth century which was organised by the journal *Past and Present* in London in June 1957, and attended by about thirty historians. The participants focused their attention mainly on the English Revolution, and to some extent on the revolt in Catalonia ('Seventeenth-century revolutions', *Past and Present*, no. 13 (1958), pp. 63–72). The very fact that such a conference was held is extremely significant and shows that considerable interest in the subject exists. The articles in *Past and Present* dealing with various aspects of the crisis in Europe in the sixteenth and seventeenth centuries have been published in book form under the title: *Crisis in Europe, 1560–1660*, ed. Trevor Aston (London, 1965).

foreign periodicals.[1] The article, and the discussion it aroused, are of considerable interest as illustrating the methodological tendencies in contemporary historical work abroad. The writer endeavoured to present a fresh and comprehensive conception of the political crisis in the seventeenth century; his adversaries, teachers at the universities of London, Oxford, Cambridge, St Louis and Paris, rejected his fundamental ideas, and counterposed to them their own views.

Trevor-Roper examines the way this crisis manifested itself in the political sphere, pointing to the numerous 'revolutions' which broke out in the middle of the century, as a result of developments during the first half. Among these he includes the 'Puritan Revolution' in England, the Fronde in France, the *coup d'état* of 1650 in the Netherlands, the revolts in Catalonia and Portugal in 1640, the revolt in Andalusia in 1641, and the revolt of Masaniello in Naples in 1647–8. Each of these revolutions, if studied without relating it to the general crisis, appears to be quite independent of the others and due to purely local causes. If, however, they are considered as a group, they exhibit so many common features, he says, that they are seen to be constituent elements of a 'general revolution'.[2] An analysis of the spiritual and physical 'vulnerability' of West-European society, faced with this real epidemic of revolution, is the subject of Trevor-Roper's work. The writer is not so interested in the revolutions themselves (he ignores their actual course completely); but fundamental to Trevor-Roper's thesis is his view of the part played by political struggle, and of the state against which these revolutions were directed.

Trevor-Roper does not use the term 'absolutism' at all, for he refuses to accept this historical category. To take its place he employs the concept of the 'Renaissance state', headed by a monarch. Arising at the end of the fifteenth century, this political system continued to exist right down to the revolutions of the middle of the seventeenth century, and then came to an end, because these revolutions, whatever their outcome, compelled the governments to carry out reforms which led to the appearance of a new type of state, characteristic of the 'age of Enlightenment'.

Basic to Trevor-Roper's concept of the 'Renaissance state' is the idea of political power implemented by a monarch jointly with a bureaucratic machine; for this reason he denies the existence of autocracy, i.e. one-man rule. Nor is there, for him, any division of society into classes. In place of this Trevor-Roper gives us the idea of social structures which are either 'elastic' or 'rigid'. An elastic, working social structure protects society from revolu-

---

[1] 'Trevor-Roper's "general crisis"', *Past and Present*, no. 18 (1960), pp. 8–51.
[2] Trevor-Roper, loc. cit. p. 31. The writer develops ideas which were originally expressed in the book by R. B. Merriman, *Six contemporaneous revolutions* (London, 1938).

6-2

tion, whereas a weak or over-rigid structure will collapse. Trevor-Roper denies that the English Revolution was a bourgeois revolution (I shall return to this point later), and also denies the inevitability of revolution in general. Any revolution can be foreseen, he considers, and can be avoided by making the social structure more elastic.[1]

In his endeavour to justify his theory of the 'Renaissance state', Trevor-Roper stresses the unchanging nature of this state all through the sixteenth century and the first half of the seventeenth. This was an age which knew no political revolutions,[2] and even the turbulent convulsions of the Reformation and Counter-Reformation did not shake the pillars of aristocratic-monarchical society. The seventeenth century, however, proved unable to 'absorb' its revolutions. A decisive turn took place in the middle of this century, and the second half of it was markedly different from the first. Spiritually and politically there was a new climate. 'It is as if a series of rainstorms had ended in one final thunderstorm which has cleared the air and changed, permanently, the temperature of Europe.' In 1650–1800 we find a new general situation, the climate of 'the age of Enlightenment'.[3]

Thus, according to Trevor-Roper, it was precisely the universality of revolution in the middle of the seventeenth century that showed that, in the European monarchies which had successfully survived the wars and religious upheavals of the sixteenth century, profound structural defects had been revealed. These defects cannot be attributed to the Thirty Years War (more precisely, the wars of 1618–59); in the maturation process of the general discontent which eventually grew into revolution, the part played by war, though important, was by no means the most important.[4] Contemporaries considered that the weakening of the state was due to conflict between the government and the estates, the old-established representative institutions. The general line of government policies in the seventeenth century did indeed pursue the aim of destroying the 'mixed monarchy' of estates. It is necessary, however, to look into the question of what particular interests were represented by the revolutionary parties of that epoch, which gave strength to the estate institutions, since revolution, while unable to emerge from hopeless rural *jacqueries*, could do so from the protests of a *parlement*, a States-General, a Cortes, a Diet, and so on.

Trevor-Roper argues against those foreign historians, both Marxist and

---

[1] That the writer means any and every revolution is clear, since he offers as his example of an elastic social structure nineteenth-century England, which, thanks to this, was insusceptible to the 'epidemic of revolution' reigning on the Continent (Trevor-Roper, loc. cit. p. 34).

[2] For Trevor-Roper the Netherlands Revolution was merely one of the movements of the Reformation.

[3] Trevor-Roper, loc. cit. pp. 33, 34.   [4] Ibid. p. 32.

non-Marxist, who uphold the theory (which he regards as Marxist) that the general crisis of the seventeenth century was a crisis of production and that the chief role was played by the producing bourgeoisie, whose economic activity was hampered by the obsolete and wasteful, but jealously defended, productive system of 'feudal' society (the quotation marks are Trevor-Roper's). The crisis affected the whole of Europe, but since capitalism was sufficiently developed only in England, the revolution proved successful only in that country, leading there to the triumph of a new economic system. The other revolutions failed.

Arguing against Dobb and Hobsbawm, Trevor-Roper expresses the view that the theory of the English Revolution as a bourgeois revolution has not been substantiated by them,[1] and that this remains at best a mere hypothesis. According to him, Dobb and Hobsbawm still have to produce adequate evidence that the men who made the revolution were striving towards that end, or that what they were striving for was the real driving force of the revolution. They also still have to justify their view that the triumph of the capitalist system would have been impossible without a revolution. So long as such evidence is lacking, there is no reason to suppose that capitalism did not develop peacefully in England, and that the stormy 'Puritan Revolution' was otherwise than merely a religious affair, and was no more important in the country's history than, say, the Hussite–Taborite revolution in Bohemia —especially as the latter had many features in common with the English Revolution.

After making this criticism of the Marxist position, Trevor-Roper regards the field as sufficiently cleared to proceed with the exposition of his own ideas. I would like to dwell for a moment on his line of argument and, without anticipating either Hobsbawm's observations in reply (he took part in the discussion on Trevor-Roper's article) or my own views on the author's ideas as a whole, draw attention to a few points in it.

I have already dealt with the shortcomings which, in my opinion, exist in Hobsbawm's theory, and mentioned the reviews of Dobb's book in Soviet journals.[2] Without going over this ground again, let me stress that before criticising the Marxist point of view on the English Revolution, Trevor-Roper should have acquainted himself also with the large collective work on the subject by Soviet historians, and not have confined himself to describing

---

[1] It is typical that Trevor-Roper does not even mention the fundamental work by Soviet historians entitled *Angliiskaya burzhuaznaya revolyutsiya XVII veka* [*The English bourgeois revolution of the seventeenth century*], two volumes (Moscow, 1954), though this was reviewed in English by Christopher Hill in *World News*, II (1955), no. 30. Nor does he show awareness of the works of S. I. Arkhangelsky, V. M. Lavrovsky or M. A. Barg.

[2] See p. 5.

Dobb's book as a 'classic textbook of Marxist history',[1] which could imply it was representative. Moreover, Trevor-Roper's way of putting the question of the bourgeois character of the English Revolution is marked by over-simplification. As if it were merely a matter of whether men set themselves such-and-such an aim, or of proving conclusively that capitalism could not have developed without a revolution! Marxist teaching on the driving forces of bourgeois revolution in general, and in particular on the early bourgeois revolutions, totally escapes Trevor-Roper. He imagines that he has refuted the Marxist conception by declaring it to be an unproved hypothesis; in fact, his criticism clearly shows that he is familiar neither with Marxist teaching on the subject of bourgeois revolutions nor with Marxist works specially devoted to the English Revolution.

Let us now turn to the theory of 'the general revolution of the seventeenth century'. Trevor-Roper sees its cause in a crisis of relations between state and society. In spite of the great potentialities opened up in the sixteenth century, Europe's economic life remained basically unchanged. The political structure did not change either, for the 'Renaissance state' grew without breaking through its old integument, the medieval aristocratic monarchy. All that was new was the creation of the 'Renaissance court', a sort of political instrument which appeared following the destruction of the independence of the old centres of European civilisation, namely, the cities.

The antithesis of 'city' and 'court' (i.e. government) is set forth by Trevor-Roper in a very colourful way. It is a major element in his theory. He regards the city as the embodiment of order, rational economic policy and self-control, the cradle of early Renaissance culture. In contrast, the princes, standing at the head of their courts, embodied outrageous, spendthrift, irresponsible exhibitionism. After subjecting the cities and the church, and creating a new machinery of power, these princes extracted their revenue from the activity of the cities. After depriving the cities of their independence, the princes protected their trade and spent enormous sums on beautifying the capitals. The largest cities—Brussels, Paris, Rome, Madrid, Naples, Prague[2]— developed in the sixteenth century not as centres of trade and production but as the seats of luxurious courts. The princes' power derived from an alliance with the powerful machinery of government at their disposal.[3] Trevor-Roper defines this machinery as follows: a great and expanding bureaucracy, a huge system of administrative centralisation, the cadres of which were made up

[1] Trevor-Roper, loc. cit. p. 36.
[2] It is not accidental that this list omits such cities as London, Antwerp, Amsterdam, Marseilles Lyons, Hamburg, etc. And it should be mentioned that Paris also did not cease to be a major centre of trade and production.
[3] Trevor-Roper, loc. cit. pp. 38–42.

of courtiers and officers.[1] They were headed by great statesmen who were at the same time administrators, masters of a Machiavellian diplomacy, collectors and patrons of art. The middle and lower ranks of the bureaucracy imitated the way of life and the tastes of their leaders.[2] Salaries were not large, and the officials extracted everything they could from their offices, by semi-legal and illegal methods. Three-quarters of the cost of the bureaucratic machine was met, directly or indirectly, not by the government but by the country, in the form of various taxes and levies. The exchequer created and sold new offices, which were in the main quite unnecessary. During the sixteenth century, at a time of economic boom, an anomalous situation like this was bearable, but when, at the end of the century, symptoms of decline appeared, complaints began to arise thick and fast against the bureaucracy which had become a parasite on society and discontent with the government began to come to a head.

When the economy entered a phase of deep depression in the 1620s, hatred of the corruption of the bureaucracy and the luxury of the princes became widespread and took the form of Puritanism. Trevor-Roper extends the concept of Puritanism to cover absolutely all expressions of protest against the luxury of the 'Renaissance court'. This movement, he says, was complicated in different countries by different local factors: for instance, because in France the *noblesse* enjoyed exemptions from taxation, the tax burden fell mainly on the peasantry, and it was the peasantry who revolted. In England taxes affected everyone, and so the entire nation took part in the revolution; and so on.

Trevor-Roper refers a great deal to certain sources: various treatises, the demands presented by the Cortes, and so on.[3] The writers of these, he considers, all had one aim in view—liberation from the burden of centralisation. They advocated getting rid of this burden through abolition of superfluous offices and of the whole system of the sale and inheritance of offices, through reduction or abolition of indirect taxes which were of little profit to the state, and through other measures of the same sort.

Between 1620 and the 1630s (note these dates) the tensions between government and society increased, and a 'revolutionary situation' developed, he tells us. For this situation to become a revolution, however, a whole series of political happenings and political mistakes are needed. The distinctive features of these events are what to a certain extent accounts for the difference in the course taken by the revolution in different countries.[4]

[1] All participants in the discussion soundly criticised this definition (see below, pp. 91 ff).
[2] Trevor-Roper, loc. cit. p. 42.
[3] Among these sources we find the *Testament politique* of Richelieu, to which Trevor-Roper assigns the date 1629, or early in the 1630s, which is not correct.
[4] Trevor-Roper, loc. cit. pp. 50, 51.

Trevor-Roper considers that the best approach to the study of the problem is to study the measures which help to avoid revolution.[1] For this reason he proceeds to enumerate the reforms which not only might have saved but in many cases did save certain countries from a victorious revolution. 'On the one hand the parasitic bureaucracies must be cut down; on the other hand the working bureaucracy must be related to the economic capacity of the country.'

The first reform, being administrative in character, could be carried out quite peacefully, though it affected the interests of a class which, while parasitic, was nevertheless lively and powerful. The second reform, being essentially an economic one, was carried out through mercantilism, that is, the old and well-tried policy of the medieval cities, extended to the national scale.

The different ways whereby these reforms (i.e. the abolition of expensive state and ecclesiastical machinery and the adapting of mercantilism to the new conditions) were put through in different countries furnish, according to Trevor-Roper, the explanation of the national peculiarities assumed by the political crisis in each of the countries of Europe.

In Spain Trevor-Roper notes the many attempts by Olivares and Philip IV to reform the bureaucratic machine and suppress superfluous offices. These reforms remained ineffective, however, mainly because of war, which called for enormous expenditure and exhausted the country. In Castile there were no longer in existence any institutions capable of giving expression to protests against the excessively overgrown machinery of government, because the middle class (i.e. the bourgeoisie) was weak and penetrated by office-holders; the old Cortes had disappeared in the sixteenth century and the new was a purely aristocratic institution. The *ancien régime* survived, and lay as a heavy burden upon an impoverished land.[2]

In the Netherlands the Burgundian 'Renaissance court' had already been abolished in the sixteenth century, in the course of the revolt, though this was not aimed directly against the court. For this reason, no revolutionary situation developed there in the seventeenth century; society was healthy and the state machine had been reformed. Economic reforms were carried out in Holland, he says, not because a bourgeois revolution had taken place in the sixteenth century[3] but because the government had achieved a rational combination of old-time urban mercantilism with maritime trade. Amsterdam became a new Venice.[4]

The most interesting and significant example is provided by France. Both economic crisis and revolution (the Fronde)—though the latter was 'a rela-

---

[1] Trevor-Roper, loc. cit. p. 52.   [2] Ibid. pp. 54, 61.
[3] Trevor-Roper refers here to Dobb and Hobsbawm, who stress the feudal character of the Dutch economy in the seventeenth century (loc. cit. p. 55, note 24).
[4] Ibid. pp. 55, 56.

tively small revolution'—were overcome by the monarchy, which consolidated its position for another century and a half. The government adopted a mercantilist policy, and therefore, in spite of the 'failure' of the 'bourgeois' revolution (meaning the Fronde), industry, trade and science flourished under Colbert no less than in England, despite the 'success' of England's allegedly 'bourgeois' revolution. The reason was, Trevor-Roper explains, that the crisis in France was due not to the form of state administration, but to abuses which could quite well be corrected by means of the governmental reforms which were prepared, and to some extent implemented, as early as the reign of Henry IV (introduction in 1604 of the *paulette*) and the time of Richelieu (reform of the royal household). The French government had at its disposal a state machine which had undergone salutary reform, together with an army and substantial resources in money, obtained not from a politically active gentry (as in England) but from a scattered and inarticulate peasantry. Also to be taken into account is the political genius of Richelieu and Mazarin.[1]

The situation in England was different. The government there possessed no such political power as in France and Spain, and the taxes were borne by the gentry, strong in the counties and in Parliament. The kings and their closest advisers, especially Charles I and Buckingham, lacked political talent, and together with their 'Renaissance court' they resisted any attempt at implementing reforms. But economically England was far ahead of Spain. The Stuarts carried out a mercantilist policy, protected industry and shipping, secured external peace. They fostered the growth of capitalism on a scale unknown before. Unfortunately, this capitalist development 'entailed dislocation, claimed victims; and when political crisis increased the dislocation and multiplied the victims, the stiff and weakened structure of government could no longer contain the mutinous forces which it had provoked'.

It was characteristic that the leaders of the Long Parliament did not intend to change the economic policy of the Stuarts; they merely strove to put into effect the reform of the administration which had been planned long before by Salisbury. The monarchy was not in itself a hindrance to England's successful progress. The trouble was the monarchs: if James I and Charles I had possessed either the intelligence of Elizabeth or the docility of Louis XIII, the *ancien régime* in England would have adapted itself as peacefully to new conditions in the seventeenth century as it did in the nineteenth century. But these kings stubbornly defended their 'Renaissance court', and they were crushed. The blow was dealt, however, not by any bourgeois or 'mercantilist' revolution, for neither bourgeoisie nor mercantilists were enemies of the court. Another force won the victory—'the country', that is,

[1] Ibid. pp. 56, 57.

a non-political miscellany of men who were in revolt against the super-fluous, oppressive and parasitic bureaucracy. In the end, however, these men stepped down in favour of a restoration of the former dynasty, which continued to carry out its former mercantilist policy but did not revive the former abuses; the 'Renaissance court' had ceased to exist in England.[1]

Thus, Trevor-Roper concludes, in all the countries studied, revolutions were crises in political relations between society and the state. Only in Spain did the *ancien régime* remain unchanged, and this led to that country's decline. In Holland, England and France the crisis put an end to an entire epoch. It led to liberation from the burden of 'a top-heavy superstructure' and to return to a responsible mercantilist policy. The 'Renaissance courts' were so wasteful that they could flourish only in an age of general prosperity; the beginning of decline undermined them. In this sense the economic depression of the 1620s was no less important than that of 1929; in both instances, a temporary economic decline produced lasting political changes.

Trevor-Roper emphasises that all the governments appreciated that a crisis situation was threatening and some of them tried to find a way out of it. The reforms carried out in Holland and France contributed to restricting the scope of the revolution, but in England all attempts at reform failed owing to the Stuarts' fatal lack of political skill. Accordingly, 'the storm... struck the most brittle, most overgrown, most rigid court of all and brought it violently down'.[2]

Before proceeding to criticise this theory myself, I would like to draw attention to the replies to Trevor-Roper's article which have been published.[3]

It is clear that the most vulnerable aspect of the theory under consideration is the interpretation of the factual material, which is sometimes extremely strained. This is what has called forth most objections.

Mousnier has shown the complete divergence between Trevor-Roper's theory and the actual history of France in the first half of the seventeenth century.[4] It must be emphasised that the example of France is especially important for Trevor-Roper, because he uses it to demonstrate the effectiveness of reforms which are capable of softening the blow of revolution and causing it to fail. While pointing out that he was himself first in the field with

[1] Trevor-Roper, loc. cit. pp. 57–61.
[2] Ibid. pp. 61, 62.
[3] It should be noted that the comments made by Trevor-Roper's opponents are not co-ordinated, and they repeat each other to some extent.
[4] 'Trevor-Roper's "general crisis"', *Past and Present*, no. 18 (1960), pp. 18–25. As I have fully examined Mousnier's views in chapter 1, I here restrict myself to commenting on particular points.

the conception of a general crisis in seventeenth-century Europe,[1] Mousnier nevertheless attacks Trevor-Roper's presentation of the Fronde.

The popular risings of the first half of the seventeenth century, and the Fronde, were not at all revolts against the court and the bureaucracy. Members of the latter were themselves among the rebels, and played indeed a very important role in the Fronde. Rural *seigneurs*, royal officials and municipal officials, too, urged the peasants and the town populace to rise against the government. In most cases the relation of forces in France was such that the state machine, which according to Trevor-Roper was 'oppressive', considered itself to be, on the contrary, 'oppressed', and gained support in revolt from those social groups over which it had influence.[2] Consequently, Trevor-Roper's idea of a revolt of the country against the court and the state machine is not supported by the facts of French history.

Mousnier sees the cause of the discontent of the bureaucracy in the fact that its material and political interests were encroached upon by the government. The *intendants* deprived local institutions of all power, the officials were subjected to forced loans, and their salaries were cut. These facts also contradict Trevor-Roper's theory.

The French office-holders were not a socially homogeneous group and their material position varied. The bulk of them (the officials of middle and lower rank) lived modestly and imitated neither their senior colleagues nor, still less, the king. The incomes of the higher officials were principally made up of receipts from ground-rent, for these office-holders were at the same time feudal lords. Their salaries, and the wealth of the king's courtiers, could not have constituted an unbearable burden on the state budget[3] or on society, since in the first half of the seventeenth century the court absorbed only a small part of the state's revenue. Expenditure on the army, that is, on pay, supplies and billeting of the troops, was much greater. One can, of course, look upon military expenditure and prolonged wars as serving the interest of the court, but then one must first show that war was not waged in the interests of the nation as a whole, which would be difficult. On these

---

[1] It should be recalled that the first edition of Mousnier's book appeared in 1954, and that Mousnier had also written about the crisis in earlier articles. Trevor-Roper makes not a single mention of these works.

[2] I have written above about my disagreement with Mousnier's views as to the leading role played by nobles and officials in the popular risings of the seventeenth century (see p. 24). But in this instance we must note that, in his argument with Trevor-Roper, Mousnier correctly (for the given period) assigns the official caste to the camp of the political opponents of absolutism.

[3] Here Mousnier's ideas are fundamentally correct. At the same time, however, he overlooks the important conclusion which he himself has drawn, on the basis of a great deal of factual evidence, about the sale of offices as a form of state debt. Forced loans from office-holders signified an increase in the state debt, and the payment of interest on them fell in the form of taxation upon the masses. Consequently, in the last analysis, it was the people who paid for the bureaucracy.

points too, therefore, it seems Trevor-Roper's theory does not stand up to criticism.

The relation of social forces in the revolts of 1620–50 shows that they were directed not against the court and the bureaucracy but against commissaries sent out by the government (i.e. *intendants*), men who themselves came from the upper-official milieu. This struggle was between the bureaucracy and the court, rather than between the country and the court and its bureaucracy. In other words, Trevor-Roper's view of the court and the state machine as the object of attack by the whole country is refuted by Mousnier so far as France is concerned.[1]

In France the revolts which were most dangerous to the government took place at the court itself. The princes of the blood and the grandees wanted to adapt the monarchy to their own interests, to give it an aristocratic character. The provinces felt oppressed by their increasing subordination to the centre, and strove to recover their independence. The struggle of the grandees and the provinces against the king's Council was a struggle between feudal forces and the forces of progress.[2]

Trevor-Roper's view of mercantilism as a method of adapting the resources of a country to the burdens of centralisation is regarded by Mousnier as doubtful.[3] State mercantilism began as early as the reign of Louis XI and developed uninterruptedly thereafter. Laffemas, Richelieu and Colbert saw in it a means of ensuring French hegemony in external relations (which was especially important in a period of economic decline), and did not connect it more closely with tasks of internal policy.[4]

The attempt at revolution (the Fronde) does not constitute any sort of watershed in the history of France; political and social problems remained the same after it as they had been before. The process of social change began only at the end of the seventeenth century, and was unconnected with the events of the middle of the century.[5]

In general, Mousnier only accepts Trevor-Roper's recognition in his article of the problem of the crisis in political relations between society and

[1] I have had occasion, above, to argue against this notion of Mousnier's regarding the nature of revolts in seventeenth-century France, and I hope to return to the subject.
[2] I cannot but concur with this opinion of Mousnier's, though I do not regard the grandees as the most dangerous adversary of the government in the 1630s and 1640s. After the failure of Montmorency's rebellion in 1632, down to the *Fronde des princes*, the grandees remained in the background.
[3] Let us recall that Mousnier sees the mercantilist policy of the French government as the chief means for overcoming the economic crisis, i.e. in essentials his view is quite close to Trevor-Roper's.
[4] See above, p. 33, my views on mercantilism.
[5] Mousnier is quite right in assigning this date to the rise of the industrial bourgeoisie.

the state. He considers Trevor-Roper's attempt to solve the problem to be based on an inadequate analysis. The revolts and revolutions of the seventeenth century are still in need of careful and many-sided investigation.[1]

J. H. Elliott, of Cambridge, comes to similar conclusions, basing himself mainly on material from the history of Spain.[2] He points out that Trevor-Roper's very notion of a struggle between 'the country' and an extravagant court and state machine is inspired by English history. It cannot be extended to the continental countries, in particular not to Catalonia and Portugal. Though the evidence is not extensive, what there is testifies against rather than for Trevor-Roper's theory. In Spain, even in the peaceful year 1608, out of a budget of 7 million ducats, only 1·5 million were spent on the court and the salaries of officials, whereas the army and navy took 4 million. Since the sale of offices was less extensively developed in Spain than in France, the chief form assumed by the public debt was *rentes*. For this reason the problem of the diversion of resources into unproductive spheres has to be looked at in the light of 'the crippling difficulties that attended industrial development and commercial expansion in Castile'. It is undoubtedly true that the country was weighed down by the burden of maintaining the state bureaucracy, but the burdens imposed by war (depopulation of the Castilian countryside through recruitment of soldiers, army billeting, etc.) were equally heavy. Yet there were no revolts in Castile.

Trevor-Roper considers that the reason for this was the absence in Castile of 'effective organs of protest'. Elliott gives his attention to Portugal and Catalonia, which possessed such organs at that time. In reality, the difference was that neither Catalonia nor Portugal bore the burden of the state machine; they did not pay for the Castilian court and bureaucracy. As compared with Castile they paid very little, not even meeting the cost of their own defence. Throughout the period between 1599 and 1640 the government received from the Catalan Corts the sum of one million ducats, together with a few minor taxes (which did not even cover the cost of the Viceroy's administration), while in this same period Castile was paying more than six million

---

[1] Mousnier suggests that this problem be tackled in an international way. He himself intends to contribute to the work through the activity of a commission based on the Sorbonne and headed by him, the *Centre de recherches sur la civilisation de l'Europe moderne* (see *Past and Present*, no. 18 (1960), p. 25). There recently appeared a very detailed list of subjects and problems for researchers, drawn up by Mousnier ('Recherches sur les soulèvements populaires en France de 1483 à 1787', *Revue du Nord*, no. 174 (April–June 1962), pp. 281–90). This questionnaire of 53 points is divided into three sections: (1) historiography and work on sources; (2) social, economic and spiritual circumstances of the risings; (3) course taken by the risings; (4) classification of the risings; and (5) their consequences (economic, social, spiritual, etc.).

[2] 'Trevor-Roper's "general crisis"', *Past and Present*, no. 18 (1960), pp. 25–30. See also J. H. Elliott, 'The decline of Spain', *Past and Present*, no. 20 (1961), and his book *Imperial Spain, 1469–1716* (London, 1964).

ducats every year. There was no selling of offices in Catalonia, nor any parasitic bureaucracy.

In other words, Elliott shows that revolutions occurred precisely in those countries of the Iberian peninsula which lacked in general those reasons for protest which are emphasised by Trevor-Roper. The real cause of revolution was that the reforms of Olivares were designed to obtain resources for war, not to reduce the luxury of the court, pensions, offices, etc. After the war began, in 1621, expenditure on the army immediately more than doubled (not including naval expenditure), and this was only the beginning. Later on, the Spanish army increased to twice the size of the one Philip II had had at his disposal. The enlarged scale of war faced the government with problems of corresponding scale; for this reason the reforms of Olivares were dictated by the needs of war, which called for a thoroughgoing reorganisation of the Spanish fiscal system. The increasing need for money drew the Spanish government into conflict with Portugal and Catalonia, which revolted not against a bureaucracy but against increased expenditure on war and the growing exploitation of their resources by Castile.

Other governments too, Elliott points out, ran into trouble in carrying out similar, very difficult tasks of extracting revenue from under-taxed provinces. Richelieu was more successful in this than Olivares, but their experience had many common features. Both of them came to power with the best intentions for reform, but war obliged them to put these plans aside. They were compelled to increase the burden of taxes and thereby unwittingly precipitated revolution. Their attempts at reform in the 1620s did not have the aim of avoiding revolution. On the contrary, they brought the government into conflict with those who until then had enjoyed special liberties and immunities; it was, therefore, precisely these reforms that brought revolution nearer. The clue to understanding the revolutionary situation of the 1640s is to be found in the decision of the Spanish and French governments to exercise fuller control over all parts of the state although neither government as yet possessed the administrative means, or the fiscal resources, to exercise such control. The decision was dictated by the strong and imperious demands of war.

Elliott's argument is very interesting. He shows convincingly that Trevor-Roper's theory is not valid for the Iberian peninsula, either. After the Fronde, the Portuguese and Catalan revolts are removed from the list of seventeenth-century revolutions which can be seen as protests by society against the cost of bureaucracy.[1] These revolts turn out to be different in nature. Elliott's

[1] In the list of revolutions which he gives at the beginning of his article, Trevor-Roper also includes the revolt in Andalusia in 1641 and the Neapolitan revolt of 1647-8, but thereafter says nothing about either of them.

94

conclusions in this field are sound; so is his comparison between the policy of Olivares and Richelieu's work. Though the general line of Richelieu's tax policy has as yet been far from adequately studied, nevertheless it seems clear that he endeavoured—not always successfully—to unify the tax system and to impose tax burdens on the privileged provinces (generally speaking, those which were on the frontiers and which had been incorporated comparatively recently, not before the fifteenth century) in proportion to their size and the part they played in the national state. Many revolts were caused precisely by these measures. In his comparison between Spain and France, and in putting such decided stress on the demands of war (with which also one must agree), Elliott overlooks, however, one very important circumstance. Portugal and Catalonia occupied a special place in the system of the Spanish monarchy, and they cannot be compared in this connexion with the frontier provinces in France. Portugal could look back on centuries of independent existence as a state, based on solid territorial, ethnic, linguistic and other foundations. Its inclusion in the Spanish realm in 1581 had no lasting basis, and so this was reversed; in 1640 Portugal recovered its sovereignty, which has remained unshaken down to our own day. The revolt in Catalonia had a clearly expressed separatist character, conditioned by the previous history of this large province; this feature has to some extent continued down to the present time. In its social composition and driving forces it was very complex and does not lend itself to a simple explanation. The government's victory was due to many factors, the chief of which was, in my opinion, that, given the way sovereign national states had to be organised, conditions were not favourable in the seventeenth century for those countries which in the past had possessed only regional autonomy to achieve complete autonomy.[1] The protectorate of France over Catalonia could only be illusory (the separatist-minded cities and nobles took this into account), but just for this reason it did not constitute for the French government an important and permanent interest, and France made use of the Catalan revolt only to the extent that this was necessary and advantageous in time of war. Thus, the revolts in Portugal and Catalonia were fundamentally different phenomena, resulting from the peculiarities of the process of the formation and development of national states in the Iberian peninsula. On this plane, the success of the Portuguese revolt was as 'normal', as much to be expected, as the defeat of the revolt in Catalonia.

[1] I include in these concepts the totality of the social, economic and political history of the separate regions (and not merely the history of their status as territories) which were gradually merged into the system of a nation-state community.

In its application to England, Trevor-Roper's theory has been criticised by Lawrence Stone, of Oxford.[1] He considers that the principal misfortune of the English government was not that its machinery was large; on the contrary, it was too small. There was no standing army, there were no paid officials in the counties, and the central bureaucracy, which was not numerous, was badly paid. The bulk of the gifts, pensions, monopolies, and so on, with which the Crown was lavish, went only to a few peers. The total amount of taxation was considerably less than in France and Spain; for example, in 1628 Normandy alone paid as much as all England. After Buckingham's death the cost of the court was greatly reduced, so that if this was the cause of the country's discontent, the revolution ought to have broken out in the 1620s, not the 1640s. The increase in discontent among the gentry was due, in Stone's view, to the fact that the government began vigorously to levy enclosure fines from them and to demand from them a higher payment than before for the upkeep of a less costly state machine. The collapse of the government is to be explained by its moral isolation, economic harmfulness and financially burdensome nature. It had no resources for waging a successful struggle. The administrative structure of the English court was weak, and so it collapsed.

Though limited in scope, Stone's argument is based nevertheless on indisputable facts which Trevor-Roper had to recognise[2] in his reply. But it must be pointed out that, by shifting the centre of attention mainly to the gentry, Stone largely avoids dealing with the fundamental causes of the English Revolution.

Hobsbawm's remarks in the discussion also relate to England, but are unfortunately too brief.[3] He agrees with Trevor-Roper's concept of the Western revolutions of the seventeenth century as a crisis of the *ancien régime*. He finds the weakest point in Trevor-Roper's argument the view that the 'right' economic policies could not be carried out under James I and Charles I. Tacitly rejecting the explanation of the opposition to these policies as being due to the stupidity of the kings concerned, Hobsbawm quite correctly notes that such 'right' policies required the overthrow of the *ancien régime*; after the revolution a very different situation came into being. In other words, Hobsbawm considers that this turn took place not merely after the revolution but because of it. Trevor-Roper wishes to show that

[1] 'Trevor-Roper's "general crisis"', *Past and Present*, no. 18 (1960), pp. 31–3. Cf. other articles by Stone, in particular one on the English social structure of the sixteenth and seventeenth centuries ('The inflation of honours, 1558–1641', *Past and Present*, no. 14 (1958)).
[2] 'Trevor-Roper's "general crisis"', *Past and Present*, no. 18 (1960), p. 38.
[3] Ibid. pp. 12–14.

an internal reform of the *anciens régimes* would have produced the same result; but he does not prove that it did so.[1] The fundamental question that interests Hobsbawm is how favourable conditions for the Industrial Revolution were established. It was from this standpoint that, in his own article, he looked at the economic crisis of the seventeenth century, giving most of his attention to the homeland of this revolution, England. In Holland, he considered, the 'feudal business economy' did not permit the Industrial Revolution.[2]

As regards the incentives of those who took part in the revolution (that they did not consciously set themselves the aim of developing capitalism is a point which has become quite 'classical' in the writings of bourgeois historians), Hobsbawm observes that the gap between men's intentions and the social consequences of their actions is wide. In conclusion he objects, with justification, to the ascribing to Marxism of the view that *all* fundamental social transformations must necessarily, regardless of circumstances, take the form of violent revolutions of the classical type. He also expresses doubt whether any Marxist has maintained the view, ascribed to Marxists by Trevor-Roper, that the revolutions of the seventeenth century were 'bourgeois' and 'capitalist', successful in England and unsuccessful elsewhere.

Hobsbawm's argument is certainly quite convincing to any historian who is sufficiently familiar with the economic history of England between the sixteenth and eighteenth centuries. It was rejected, however, by Trevor-Roper in his reply to the discussion,[3] as being unproved. Thus the dispute between the Marxist and the bourgeois historian was reduced to a demand for evidence.

Professor Hexter, of St Louis University,[4] made a very interesting contribution. He congratulates Trevor-Roper on rejecting the old tradition which ties the mid-seventeenth-century crisis merely to the rise of the bourgeoisie.

---

[1] It would be more correct to say that Trevor-Roper wants to use the example of Colbert's successful mercantilist reforms to demonstrate this point—that if such reforms could be put through in France after an unsuccessful revolution, then they could have been put through in England as well, and thereby could have prevented a successful revolution from occurring. Quite apart from the unscientific nature (pointed out by Hobsbawm) of the question raised by Trevor-Roper, of how revolutions 'could have been avoided', it must be stressed that reforms such as Colbert's were already insufficient to satisfy the English bourgeoisie and gentry of the 1640s. By that time they needed something immeasurably more than an active protectionist policy on the part of their government. England at the time of the revolution and France under Colbert cannot be compared so simply, for English capitalism had considerably outstripped capitalism in France.
[2] I cannot agree with Hobsbawm's view about the 'feudal' economy of Holland. Dutch manufactories were very well developed in the seventeenth century.
[3] 'Trevor-Roper's "general crisis"', *Past and Present*, no. 18 (1960), p. 40.
[4] Ibid. pp. 14–18. [Professor Hexter is now at Yale.]

In his examination of these problems, Trevor-Roper gives 'a fuller content' to such concepts as mercantilism, Puritanism, court, country, and so on. These concepts, with their full 'European' resonance, must serve as structural elements in further study of Early Modern history (i.e. the sixteenth and seventeenth centuries). However, Trevor-Roper's picture is too general, so that instead of illuminating matters he rather obscures them, not to mention the fact that he simply ignores much that does not fit into his conception.[1]

Hexter's view is that war, both external and civil, was much more costly than the court and bureaucracy, in all countries. To refute this, Trevor-Roper would have needed to provide figures. Hexter does not agree, either, that the Reformation and the religious wars of the sixteenth century were less important than the revolutions of the seventeenth century. Trevor-Roper supports his argument with the fact that in the sixteenth century these wars did not bring about thoroughgoing social changes; but behind this lies the assumption that only social movements possess really profound significance. Both of these propositions are of dubious validity. We cannot, in the age of nuclear physics, regard only *social* revolutions as significant; nor is it possible to ignore the Reformation, which caused the monasteries to be suppressed, with important social consequences. The civil wars in France hastened the decline of the nobility. It seems to Hexter that, in the course of his argument, Trevor-Roper changes, without noticing it, the way he sees the problem: having begun with statements about the existence of a crisis as the cause of revolutions, he ends by considering revolutions from the standpoint of their influence on the crisis.[2]

Hexter's remarks are to a great extent justified,[3] but his positive views (except for his reasonable thoughts about the part played by war) are modest, and, apart from a few special themes (the family, science, the adaptability of society), he contributed nothing new to the discussion.

Professor Kossmann, of London University, approached the problem more comprehensively,[4] though he too presented his argument in the form not of a general critique but of an examination of particular questions. Nevertheless, the nature and scope of these questions are such that they fundamentally undermine the theory criticised. They are as follows.

The date of the onset of the crisis is left vague. First, Trevor-Roper alleges

[1] Among such omissions Hexter includes the growth of modern science, the stability of the patriarchal family, and the adaptability of society to changes in the economic and ideological spheres.   [2] I deal below with Trevor-Roper's reply.
[3] He is, of course, right in his evaluation of the dissolution as regards its social consequences, which Trevor-Roper denies.
[4] 'Trevor-Roper's "general crisis"', *Past and Present*, no. 18 (1960), pp. 8–11. See also his book on the Fronde (E. Kossmann, *La Fronde*, Leyden, 1954).

that the 'climate of the Renaissance' continued down to the middle of the seventeenth century. Later it turns out that as early as 1620 a depression had occurred which was as serious as that of 1929 (Kossmann notes the implausibility of this analogy), and Europe had entered the Baroque period.

First, Kossmann points out, the existence of a general crisis is demonstrated, then it turns out that this was not so, since, in so far as the crisis was caused by abuses, it had been overcome in Holland already in the sixteenth century, in Spain no attempt was made to overcome it, and in France these attempts had brought redress. In the end we find that one country alone suffered from this crisis: England.

Why enumerate revolutions and revolts, Kossmann asks, if you consider that in the Netherlands and France they lacked real importance? Trevor-Roper regards the Fronde as 'a relatively small revolution', albeit more profound than the Wars of Religion in the sixteenth century, despite the fact that the latter went on six times as long.

Such terms as 'court', 'country', and so on, are incomprehensible. What does Trevor-Roper mean by opposition 'to the court'? If he means by 'the court' the entire machinery of government, what can we make of the French *parlement*, i.e. the bureaucrats, revolting against 'the court'? Does he mean that the Fronde was a conflict between the *parlement* (part of 'the court') and the government (also part of 'the court')? In fact the Fronde was a very complex affair, and only *inter alia* was it a conflict between the 'court' and part of the bureaucracy (and not between 'the court' and the bureaucracy on the one side and the country on the other).

Kossmann doubts, with justification, whether the French 'court' was reformed. There is every ground for supposing that the economic, social and political situation in France in the 1640s was very much worse than in England.

One cannot account for the comparatively harmonious development of Holland in the seventeenth century merely by the absence there of a 'court', says Kossmann. How then is one to account for the position of the French government in 1649 and the Dutch in 1650 in relation to the oligarchy of office-holders? The latter considered that with the coming of peace the strengthening of the central authority necessitated by war must be halted. The dispute ended with a temporary defeat for the governments, but they soon afterwards gained the upper hand. Consequently, neither in Holland nor in France did the events of mid-century signify any sort of turning-point. These were conflicts not between 'court' and 'country' but among the ruling groups; in France the conflict sparked off a civil war which had quite different causes.

Kossmann does not try to present a different theory about the crisis and revolutions of the seventeenth century, but, by exposing the internal contradictions of Trevor-Roper's argument and casting doubt on his basic thesis of the antagonism between 'country' and 'court', he essentially deprives this concept of all foundation. That was why Trevor-Roper, in his reply[1] had to deal especially with his comments. He claimed that Kossmann was asking for a degree of precision in the dating of the crisis that no historian could possibly provide.[2] At the same time, however, Trevor-Roper was obliged to admit the inadequacy of his definitions and of his reasoning—due, according to him, to the brevity of the article. Thus, he considered it necessary to make clear that after 1620 the crisis became perceptible throughout the entire state system of Europe (he admitted that Holland must be excluded from this generalisation). Economic changes were brought about by the depression of 1620, military and political ones by the Thirty Years War.

Trevor-Roper agreed that his terminology—'court' ,'office', and so on—was vague. Under offices he includes all ecclesiastical offices as well as secular ones, on the grounds that the church was in those days part of the bureaucracy, and its influence over the masses helped to strengthen the shaken position of the court.[3] Answering Hexter, he denied that the dissolution of the monasteries had any social significance, since, he claimed, their land continued to be managed in the same manner as before. The dissolution was important only in so far as it prevented the creation of new, reinvigorated, regular orders in the Protestant countries.

Trevor-Roper also admitted the importance of war. He was even disposed to attribute the major role to it. War, however, cannot be separated from the form of society. For Spain, for instance, it was an expedient to remedy a disease which had already manifested itself in time of peace.

He formulated his fundamental argument in reply to his critics thus: there was a general crisis of structure,[4] but transition from this to revolution required definite political occurrences.

He agreed that the 'court versus country' antithesis was an over-simplification, as Kossmann and Mousnier had objected. It needed to be specified that social crises are stimulated not by clear-cut conflicts between mutually exclusive interests but by conflicts of interest within one body. 'Court' and

---

[1] 'Trevor-Roper's "general crisis"', *Past and Present*, no. 18 (1960), pp. 34–42.
[2] Let us recall that, in point of fact, he gave 1620, precisely, as the year when the depression began.
[3] This is especially important to him, so as to be able to show the burdensomeness of the state machine in Spain.
[4] Another objection arises here. At the beginning of his article, Trevor-Roper speaks of the elastic or rigid structure of *society*. Later, however, when he examines the English Revolution, he concerns himself only with the rigid structure of *government*.

'country' are not contradictory concepts, but constantly overlap each other. However, by accepting this, Trevor-Roper abandoned his fundamental thesis.

One may therefore conclude that he was unable to meet the objections to this thesis, which found no support among his colleagues. They objected to his baseless and arbitrary interpretation of facts. With all courtesy, and with compliments to Trevor-Roper's brilliant and picturesque style, they nevertheless severely criticised his bold but unfounded conception.

They omitted, however, to deal with the methodological basis of Trevor-Roper's theory. Only Hobsbawm opposed it from a different methodological standpoint, and no-one undertook to analyse the idea which constituted his initial premise—the very existence of a number of contemporaneous 'revolutions'. Yet this initial premise, from which all his other propositions are derived, is the most vulnerable aspect of Trevor-Roper's theory. In my view, the theory in question, which is both reactionary and of no value for historical work, is an attempt to 'create' a number of revolutions in order to 'destroy' them all. I say all, because, as he presents it, even the English Revolution turns out to be a miserable and momentary consequence of some curious stupidity on the part of the early Stuarts. Revolutions, it seems, are quite unnecessary and—if one knows how to foresee them and paralyse them by means of reforms and adequate political flexibility—they are not to be feared, because the great majority of them will fail. All these 'revolutions' were needed by Trevor-Roper, not for the purpose of investigation and comparison, but in order to demonstrate that they were predestined to failure.

To enumerate under the single heading of 'revolution' such essentially different phenomena as the English bourgeois Revolution, the restoration of Portuguese independence, the rising in Naples against Spanish rule, and, finally, the complex web of different movements which is called the Fronde, testifies first and foremost to the fact that the very concept of 'revolution' is being used in an unscientific spirit. The only basis for comparing them is their simultaneity (which is also more apparent than real); but this is not analysed in Trevor-Roper's article. He refuses to discuss individual peculiarities, examination of which would have led to elimination from the set of seven 'revolutions' of every one except the English Revolution, declaring that what matters to him is what they have in common. In his search for common features he has got into a blind alley, for what he regards as common—the struggle between 'the country' and an oppressive state machine—turns out to be literally non-existent in every one of the 'revolutions' on his list.

By looking at the seventeenth century from a frankly *modernisant* standpoint (hence his analogies with nineteenth-century England and with the depression of 1929), Trevor-Roper prevents himself from understanding the peculiarities of class structure characteristic of the different countries of Europe, which were at different stages in the development of capitalism. His division of European history into the epochs of the Renaissance (1500–1650) and the Enlightenment (1650–1800) collapses at the first critical touch, for in none of the Continental countries he studies was the year 1650 any kind of turning-point, and in England it was indeed a moment in the beginning of the bourgeois political system, but certainly not of the Enlightenment. Trevor-Roper's rejection of the concept of absolutism proves to be particularly formalist in character, since he insists that it was precisely the absolute will of the (stupid) Charles I that opposed the reforms which had been planned, and did not allow them to be put into effect. Has anyone ever conceived of absolutism in such a simple way, without seeing social forces backing up the absolute ruler? In short, the very basis of Trevor-Roper's theory is unsound.

The positive answer to the problems of seventeenth-century society, the state, the nature of the state system, reforms, and so on, which Trevor-Roper has raised, will be considered in relation to France in the subsequent chapters of this book. Let me remind you that it is France that occupies a special place in Trevor-Roper's conception, and that he locates the start of all his crisis phenomena in the 1620s, the years which are central to my exposition.

CHAPTER 3

Fundamental features of
French economic development between
1610 and 1629

THE economic history of France in the first half of the seventeenth century is known only in general outline. It may be that, even in the future, after fresh sources have been made available for study, it will not become known in sufficient detail. This view is suggested by the local studies, both old and new, whose authors note the very scattered and in many respects random nature of the sources which have survived, and which improve only after the middle of the seventeenth century.[1] In any case, as regards the period which concerns us, scholars do not have the facts needed to make it possible to provide a detailed description of the growth or stagnation of industry, trade, agriculture, and so forth. At best we can merely note a tendency in the movement of economic affairs. However, if this tendency is reflected more or less uniformly in a group of sources of a particular sort, which not only confirm each other but also do not contradict what is known about other spheres of activity, we are justified in feeling confidence in these indices and using them to define the special features which are characteristic of the period being studied.

The treatises, pamphlets and memoranda of various kinds constitute such a group of sources; they mostly express the demands and aspirations of special interests, whether corporate or individual. These always include a more or less extensive section describing the state of trade, production, finance, and so on. For a number of reasons which are discussed below, economic matters begin to assume greater importance in sources of this kind, precisely in the second decade of the seventeenth century. This was the period of the awakening, so to speak, of French economic thought. Kept in the background until then by the acuteness of the political and religious struggles which in the sixteenth century had engrossed most of the attention

---

[1] See, for instance, Goubert's work on the Beauvaisis, magnificent in its thoroughness and precision (P. Goubert, *Beauvais et le Beauvaisis de 1600 à 1730, Contribution à l'histoire sociale de la France du XVIIe siècle* (Paris, 1960)).

of thinkers and statesmen, the economy began to become an object of interest to various sections of French society.

First and foremost we have Montchrétien's treatise, unusual for the period in its size and scope, which first appeared in 1615 and which was reprinted in 1889.[1] It has frequently been the subject of special studies by historians and economists[2] and has been widely used in works dealing with France at the beginning of the seventeenth century, and also in works on the history of political economy. In short, it is a famous source of its kind, and all the more so because the expression 'political economy' first appeared in the title of this treatise.

In their analysis of Montchrétien's work, French economists have always thought in terms of the economic problems and theories of their own time. While considering the author one of the pioneers of the theory of mercantilism, that is, assigning him a definite place in history, they have nevertheless sought in his writings for more or less clearly formulated definitions of value, price, profit, the market and other categories of nineteenth-century economic science. Reading in the title of Montchrétien's treatise the words *œconomie politique*, they have tried to see it as a sort of code of economic concepts, which they modernise, turning the author into something like a direct forerunner of the classical bourgeois political economy of the eighteenth century. Historians have used it as a source from which to draw large handfuls of abundant, reliable and wittily presented material. Montchrétien's treatise still awaits both an up-to-date edition with commentary and a comprehensive analysis.

In the most recent studies of Montchrétien, and especially in the article by Marcel Rudloff,[3] the author's plan for the 'industrialisation' of France is examined. Rudloff does not hide the fact that his interest in this particular subject was aroused by its topicality in relation to the under-developed countries, and emphasises that the remarkable topicality of Montchrétien's treatment of it results from the circumstance that, like present-day economists, he is preoccupied with finding ways and means to bring about an economic 'take-off' (*décollage*) and to eliminate obstacles standing in the way of this.[4] Rudloff finds in Montchrétien a 'theory' of development which

---

[1] Antoyne de Montchrétien, *Traicté de l'œconomie politique dedié en 1615 au roy et la reyne mère du roy*; with introduction and notes by Th. Funck-Bretano (Paris, 1889).

[2] J. Duval, *Un économiste inconnu du XVII° siècle: Antoyne de Montchrétien* (Paris, 1868); G. de Vaudichon, *Montchrétien (1575–1621)* (Amiens, 1882); P. Dessaix, *Montchrétien et l'économie politique nationale* (Paris, 1901); P. Lavalley, *L'œuvre économique d'Antoine Montchrétien* (Caen, 1903).

[3] M. P. Rudloff, 'A. de Montchrétien et les problèmes du développement économique', *Revue d'histoire économique et sociale*, XL, no. 2, (1962).

[4] Rudloff finds a similar situation in the Germany of the 1840s, and draws a parallel between Montchrétien and Friedrich List (loc. cit. pp. 148, 149).

he regards as the most important and original part of the treatise. Its author had the correct intuition that the road to economic progress lies through production; what he calls 'increase in the number of manufactures', in contemporary terms, industrialisation. At the same time he does not sacrifice the interests of agriculture, and, though he acknowledges the importance of foreign trade, he considers it to be secondary. Rudloff regards Montchrétien as more of an 'industrialist' than a mercantilist, in so far as he subordinates foreign trade and navigation (i.e. colonial expansion) to national economic development.

Rudloff sets forth Montchrétien's theory of industrialisation as follows. The chief factor in economic development is man and his work, in workshops and manufactories. Therefore the worker must be given technical training[1] and inculcated with love of work and work skills. This is the best method for eradicating unemployment and idleness; as for those who are idle out of malice, to them the severest measures must be applied. In so far as man is born to productive labour, technical training is a necessary condition for this, and labour itself is the chief social value.

Montchrétien sees manufactories as the embodiment of the division of labour which reigns in human society, and the principal source of wealth for both people and state. He goes further than his predecessors (in France, Laffemas), in that he lays down a plan for encouraging industrial development in a definite sequence.[2] One must begin with the production of metal (*forge*); then must come textile and leather production, printing, and the glass industry. All these branches are in need of technical improvements which will make the production process easier, quicker and cheaper. The state must not only help the progress of native industry by directing it along the right path, but also protect it from foreign competition. In connexion with the latter task, Montchrétien's attitude is aggressive, his thinking on economic matters being permeated with nationalism and *étatisme*. The important role assigned to the state is due to the author's view of all economic development on a broad national scale and his ascribing greater significance to political measures than to the attractive power of profit. His address to the prince leads him into the realm of mercantilist thought, but what he expects from the government is not that it should organise the economy so as to expand foreign trade, but that it should give direction to the country's economic development. In addition, the state must ensure justice, provide technical

[1] On this question Rudloff sees a complete correspondence between Montchrétien's ideas and present-day theories about the economic take-off of under-developed countries (loc. cit. p. 153).
[2] Here also Rudloff sees a complete analogy with the works of present-day writers who have analysed the great difficulties in the way of industrialising the under-developed countries (loc. cit. p. 158, note 35, and p. 174).

training, and maintain an appropriate fiscal and financial system and administration—in short, be responsible for order and social stability. But the most essential conditions are internal and external peace, for civil and external wars bring with them innumerable losses and calamities.[1] Montchrétien sees protectionism as a necessary means for safeguarding the internal market, native manufactures and agriculture from the foreigner, for the national economy must be protected from the anarchy of unregulated trade; such anarchy limits the possibilities for profitable investments in industry. In order to free the country from dependence on others and to enhance its power to compete, a national merchant navy must be created, and likewise trading companies on the model of the Dutch East India Company. When this has been done, bright prospects will open before France of developing and settling the richest parts of America, and the country will leave its rivals behind.

Rudloff's main conclusion is that Montchrétien anticipated two present-day ideas, and that this constitutes the originality of his theory: (1) his approach to the economic process is based on a voluntarist conception of man and a desire to increase social welfare, and (2) he puts the industrialisation process at the centre of economic development as he conceives it.[2]

It is not difficult to see that Montchrétien's views have here been substantially modernised, though it is not European countries that Rudloff has in mind. In many respects, as will be seen, this approach leads to a strained interpretation and even a distortion of Montchrétien's ideas. Let us now turn to the original.

We know little about the author's life. He was born in 1575 and received some education in the humanities. In his work he refers from time to time to the authorities of Antiquity, at the same time criticising them where their views were not borne out by the economic situation in seventeenth-century France. Montchrétien owned an iron-manufactory, and he visited England and Holland, so that he had observed for himself the economic life of more advanced countries. He was an excellent observer, with a keen and penetrating eye. He died in 1621 while recruiting soldiers in Normandy for the rebel Huguenots. It may be that he was himself a Huguenot, though there is no direct proof of this.

Montchrétien's work is distinguished from similar documents, that is, from treatises, memoranda, pamphlets, and the like, devoted in almost every case merely to particular economic or financial questions, not only by its size (in Funck-Brentano's edition it runs to nearly 400 pages), but also by the breadth of the subject-matter. Separate chapters are devoted to manu-

---

[1] Rudloff, loc. cit. pp. 161-4.   [2] Ibid. p. 174.

factures, trade, navigation and colonies, and, finally, 'politics', that is to say, the taxation system of the kingdom of France.

The treatise is saturated with the rich experience of an intelligent practical man, and his reflexions on the economic life of France, Holland and England. The latter provides him with a peerless example of the role of protectionism. Montchrétien frequently makes comparisons between the trade, industry and colonial policies of these three countries. As a rule, these comparisons prove unfavourable to his own country, and, as a sincere patriot, he writes with bitterness about the shortcomings and backwardness of France. Nevertheless, the whole treatise is filled with a rare optimism and faith in the great future of France, a country generously endowed by nature, with a people industrious, skilful and inventive in every matter and possessing an acute and versatile intelligence.[1]

Montchrétien undoubtedly had a practical aim when he wrote his book. It is dedicated to Louis XIII and Marie de Médicis and constructed in the form of an address to them. With all proper respect, the author advises Their Majesties to undertake a multitude of steps of different kinds which, in his opinion, are needed for the revival and strengthening of the economy, and, consequently, for the enrichment and greatness of the kingdom of France and the monarchy. One can hardly suppose that the author seriously reckoned on attention being given to his counsels by a fourteen-year-old boy or by a Queen Mother who was indifferent to economic questions. It is more probable that the treatise was aimed at the members of the king's Council, and especially the *intendants des finances*, to whom it could be particularly useful in connexion with the debates about government finance and taxation in the States-General.[2]

Proceeding to analysis of Montchrétien's main ideas, we note first of all that his acquaintance with the life of Holland and his admiration for its economy affects in a very pronounced way his appreciation of the social structure of France. The third estate (*le populaire*) is for him the most important and fundamental part (*le premier fondement*) of society. It consists of peasants, craftsmen and merchants, very closely linked together in their activity, which is in no way less honourable or important than the work of the liberal arts, for it serves the needs of men.

Montchrétien is convinced that the government should actively influence the economic life of society; princes are mistaken when they suppose that it is something which arranges itself. This is not true, for the art of politics is dependent, even though indirectly, on the economy (*œconomie*), and proper

---

[1] Montchrétien, op. cit. pp. 24, 33, 34.
[2] A mention of the forthcoming meeting of the States-General appears in the text (ibid. p. 148).

management of the latter is beneficial both for the state as a whole and for each of its members. Of great importance is a wise distribution of people between the different branches and occupations. The king must give every attention and care to the common people (*partie populaire*), by regulating already existing manufactories and establishing new ones, giving encouragement to decaying navigation and reviving declining trade.[1]

Montchrétien sees the question of manufactories as really the main one, and he discusses it in great detail. However, his ideas on this subject, and his demands, bear little resemblance to the abstract notions about man, labour, industrialisation, and so on, which Rudloff attributes to him.

Man is born to constant labour, and the interests of society require activity (*action*) above all. For this reason the state cannot and must not tolerate idlers, especially since there is work for all. In France the gifts of nature and human skill are found in abundance in every province, and each of them supplies the country with grain, wine, salt, cloth, wool, iron, etc. France is also rich in people. Accordingly, manufactories can and ought to exist everywhere, all the conditions needed for them being present. How then is the undoubted decline of the French economy at this time to be explained? First and foremost by the lack of order and ability to use people to the best advantage.

The measures which Montchrétien proposes in order to eliminate these shortcomings are remarkable. They show that study of Dutch experience in the sphere of manufactory production had enabled him to formulate a number of concrete proposals, based upon a clear notion of the type of work done by the worker in a manufactory.

'Whoever succeeds', writes Montchrétien, 'in using properly this living instrument, this motive tool (*cest instrument vivant, cest util mouvant*) which is capable of every skill and every operation, can congratulate himself on having organised his household in the best possible way.'[2] In France they do not know how to use people correctly, and therefore many are obliged to go abroad to find employment (to Spain, Flanders, Germany, etc.), while others tramp about without work or occupation, crowding the cities and main roads as vagabonds. Work must be given them: for this purpose, workshops to serve as training centres must be set up in every province, on the Dutch model, where training of workers will be carried on by skilled foremen. These must be nurseries of workmen for the manufactories, and this will

---

[1] Montchrétien, op. cit. pp. 12–16. It is this view of the state's role in the organisation of the economy that explains the term used by the author in the title of his work—*œconomie politique*.
[2] Ibid. p. 25. As examples of this skill Montchrétien quotes the northern peoples (i.e. Holland and England); and Cato, who spared no effort in training his servants, and even made of doing this a sort of trade (*mestier et marchandise*).

bring great wealth to the country. Whoever does not want to work will have to be forced to.[1]

We see here the classic picture of the age of primitive accumulation and the classic demand that the government should introduce compulsory labour. What is significant, however, is that the writer conceives the fundamental measure for putting an end to unemployment to be technical training, since this will provide the manufactory owners with already-trained workers and thus reduce their costs of production. We note that the organisation of training workshops and all the expenditure connected with these are to be the government's responsibility. Montchrétien proposes to employ compulsory (and therefore unskilled) labour not in the manufactories but in workhouses for inveterate vagabonds and beggars.[2]

It is quite clear that, in recommending these measures, the writer proceeds from a situation in which there are a large number of unemployed while at the same time the manufactories are short of skilled labour-power, and not from any abstract notion about man, endowed with the capacity for labour, as a factor in the economic process.

Of great interest are Montchrétien's ideas regarding the need for a rational organisation of labour in manufactories, with maximum use of every single worker. He makes the interesting observation that French workers are by nature very capable, but that 'they have a fault, which is less theirs than ours [Montchrétien has the entrepreneurs in mind], namely, that most of us do not know how to discern their abilities', and that 'they do not follow a suitable order of proceeding in their work (*ils ne procèdent pas en leurs travaux avec trop bon ordre*), which fact undoubtedly hinders very seriously their natural industriousness'.[3] Montchrétien sees as the way out of these difficulties the establishment—by royal permission, with, of course, grant of all valuable and honourable privileges—of numerous manufactories, situated in different provinces and engaged in making some of the articles most widely in demand. The direction of these manufactories should be entrusted to men who are sufficiently capable and experienced to know how to divide the work intelligently among their workers, in accordance with the abilities, natural or acquired, of the latter. The result will be splendidly skilful work.[4] It is more than probable that this proposal was suggested to Montchrétien by his observation of how work was organised in the Dutch manufactories, where at this time an advanced division of labour into separate operations was already practised.

Montchrétien regards the protection of men who can be of use in manu-

---

[1] Ibid. pp. 26, 27.
[2] Ibid. pp. 106, 107.
[3] Ibid. p. 30.
[4] Ibid. p. 38.

factories as very important: 'If Your Majesties wish to help inventive persons (*beaux esprits*) and extend your hands to them to draw them out of the crowd (*la foule du peuple*) in which they are caught, hidden and held back by misfortune of fate, Your Majesties will thereby discover and open up a thousand perennially active springs of profit, glory and usefulness.'[1] But innovations must be kept from foreigners, for it is necessary to look after one's own people first and foremost. In this connexion it would do no harm if the French were to copy something from the practice of the English. The rights and privileges of foreigners residing in France should be curtailed, the only exceptions being those who are teaching Frenchmen some profitable branch of production.

Then Montchrétien embarks on the central part of his chapter on manufactures, and enumerates the various branches of production. Rudloff considers that he is here pointing the way to the development of national industry, laying special stress on metallurgy and metal-working (*forge*), which should also give us cause to see in him the perspicacious author of an 'industrialisation plan'. This view of Rudloff's represents a modernisation of Montchrétien, not only because an importance is ascribed to metal-working, this supposed heavy industry of the beginning of the seventeenth century, which in fact it did not possess at all, but also because, carried away by his idea, Rudloff has overlooked a great deal. Why does Montchrétien actually begin with *agriculture*, and not with metal-working? Why does he proceed, immediately after the latter, to the making of hats and caps? Why does he then set out the remaining branches in the following order: the making of linen, woollen fabrics, silk fabrics, leather articles, printing, glassware? This hierarchy seems a strange one, especially if one looks upon it as an 'industrialisation plan'. In fact it has its own logic, being based mainly on the degree of utility and benefit to the state and the manufactory-owners of particular branches of production.[2] Nor must we lose sight of the writer's principal aim, namely, to draw the government's attention to the need actively to influence the economic life of the country, in the direction desired by the entrepreneurs.

This is the reason why Montchrétien begins with agriculture, which supplies the means of life and the raw material for production. For France, agriculture is of primary importance and the source of all wealth. Yet it is in poor condition and is threatened by even worse misfortunes if urgent measures are not taken. Landowners do not manage their land themselves; in pursuit of profitable offices they prefer to lease it out. It is badly cultivated, for the leaseholders try to get as much out it of as quickly as possible. The peasants are very poor, mostly having no land of their own, but working for others.

---

[1] Montchrétien, op. cit. p. 35.   [2] Ibid. p. 46.

It is understandable that they have no inclination to work hard, and that the land becomes exhausted and overgrown with weeds. Yet these are the chief suppliers of food to the entire country, and it is they who pay the bulk of the taxes. Their money maintains the army, the garrisons, the magazines; their money fills the treasury. The peasant should be sustained, not loaded with burdens. When the prince protects the peasants from excessive burdens he is acting in his own interest; the peasants are the feet of the state, and when they slip, the head and the other members suffer.[1]

Montchrétien's analysis is more profound and more acute than the views of his contemporaries. In 1614 the States-General were about to be convoked. Many publicists called for reduction in taxation and lightening of the load on the peasants, pointing to the possibility of disorders breaking out. These appeals were repeated by the deputies who attended the sessions of the States-General.[2] But none of them showed the other causes of the peasants' poverty besides high taxation. Montchrétien saw more than that—the neglect of their land by noble landowners, the expropriation of the peasants, the exhaustion of the soil. At the same time, he had no other measure to propose but the one which was put forward by literally everybody, and which was the only one possible in the conditions of the time, namely, reduction of taxes.

If however, on methods of improving agriculture, Montchrétien was not distinguished from his contemporaries, on the question of industry, a sphere of activity close to his experience, he showed incomparably greater resourcefulness.

At the beginning of his discourse on this subject he particularly stresses, like any other mercantilist, the need to produce everything within the boundaries of one's own country, so as not to be dependent on anyone for anything.[3] Then he begins to talk about metal-working. He sings its praises most poetically, to the best of his ardent and graphic imagination: 'This art of arts,[4] the common element in all of them...the first instrument of invention...the moving force and organ of movement (*le mouvant et l'organe du mouvement*).'[5] Special attention must be given it, for it supplies the weapons which make the king's enemies tremble.

[1] Ibid. pp. 40–5.
[2] See A. D. Lublinskaya, *Frantsiya v nachale XVII veka (1610–1620 gg.)* [*France at the beginning of the seventeenth century, 1610–1620*], (Leningrad, 1959), chapter 4.
[3] Montchrétien, op. cit. p. 46. It is characteristic that, in considering agriculture, he says nothing about this principle, because it was clear that France not only satisfied all her requirements with her own products, but also exported a great deal of grain, wine, salt, fruit, and so on.
[4] He uses the term 'art' because in the sixteenth and seventeenth centuries the crafts and industry were often called *arts mécaniques*.
[5] Montchrétien, op. cit. p. 47.

More than 500,000 Frenchmen live by this craft ('like salamanders in the fire') and, in addition, it is used in many other crafts. Neighbouring countries (England, Holland, Flanders) have in their time borrowed a great deal from France, through Huguenot emigrants,[1] in the field of the making of weapons, locks, knives, and so on. As yet, though, they have not surpassed their teacher. Germany is famed for its metal wares, but the French products are not inferior.

Thus, it would seem, the position of this branch of industry is good. No, answers Montchrétien, it is bad; but it ought to be good. The foreigners should be eliminated and the French helped to take into their own hands the entire production of iron and steel. The importing of hardware into France should be prohibited. Such imports mean the ruin of thousands of people in the towns, and whole provinces, which are occupied in making these goods. Enormous harm is done by the importation of scythes and sickles from Germany and Lorraine. These goods are in themselves very much needed in France, but the trouble is that French-made sickles and scythes cost twice as much as imported ones. Out of poverty, the French peasants are forced to go for cheapness, and they buy the imported tools in spite of their poor quality, which is the reason why, walking in the country, one hears 'the complaints of the poor labourers, disappointed in what they have bought'. These scythes are so fashioned that you cannot make out whether they are of iron or steel; they are sold not in the cities[2] but in the markets of villages and country places (sometimes in large quantities, 100,000 units at a time) and then retailed throughout the provinces. More than 800,000 *livres* find their way abroad every year in payment for scythes and sickles alone, while French craftsmen remain without work. Furthermore, the entrepreneurs in France do not introduce technical improvements and machinery (*engins*) to speed up and ameliorate the production of metal articles, because they are not sure of an outlet for large categories of their goods. Yet if only one skilful and courageous man were to come forward, many would follow his example.[3]

Let us recall that Montchrétien was himself the owner of an iron-working manufactory, and we must presume that he had considerable competence in this matter. For this reason his observations and demands seem to us to present substantial interest. First, they quite conclusively disprove the view (which we mentioned earlier) that the French peasants bought extremely few metal articles or even tools, preferring, through poverty, to make do with

---

[1] This observation is very interesting, if one takes into account that what was involved was the production of weapons and metal articles.
[2] Supervision of the quality of merchandise was carried out in urban markets.
[3] Montchrétien, op. cit. pp. 51–6.

wooden ones. Secondly, Montchrétien reveals the precise cause of the importation of scythes and sickles: though worse in quality, they were cheaper than the French-made ones, and, moreover, became much cheaper still after the Dutch had begun to bring them in by sea, thus cutting down transport costs. French scythes and sickles were dear because they were of good quality, which the makers were not permitted to lower on pain of being forbidden to sell them (*decry*). Finally, it is very important that Montchrétien does not draw a static picture, but describes the decline in the French iron-making manufactories which had begun comparatively recently as a result of the importation by the Dutch, in their own vessels, of articles produced in Germany and Lorraine. The cheapness of goods imported without control, and therefore of poor quality, stifled[1] the high-quality French production of these goods.

Montchrétien's proposal for reviving French metal-working does not consist of mere prohibition of imports. He asks that control over the quality of goods be abolished; then French scythes will become as cheap as German ones and at the same time will still be better than these. They will conquer the markets for themselves and oust the imported ones; confidence in the possibility of unhindered sales will make possible the revival of former manufactories and saturate the market with their products, because for manufactory production an assured market is the only thing to be taken into account. 'Nothing brings cheapness so much as plenty, plenty comes from the work of many men, and there can be no shortage of work for many men if the goods they produce sell well.'[2]

France can all the better afford such a measure because it possesses for its own manufactories an abundance of raw material, suitable sites with timber and water available, and skilful workers. Moreover, if foreign goods disappear from the French market, then an influx of foreign workers into France will begin (because there will be no work for them at home), and the French can learn a lot from them. They must be attracted and welcomed, 'for there can never be too many workers in a country'—on the contrary, the state suffers from the lack of them.[3]

This plan of Montchrétien's is very significant. The ousting of foreign competitors from the internal market would not only give French manufacturers the monopoly of sales in France but would also supply them with highly skilled workers ready-made, so to speak. The work of these foreigners would in turn reduce the costs of production (high level of skill = intensified division of labour = cheapening of the product) and would make it possible to

---

[1] Montchrétien actually used this word (*estouffer*).
[2] Montchrétien, op. cit. p. 54.   [3] Ibid. pp. 56–7.

extend production. We have seen that the connexion between these phenomena was quite clear to Montchrétien and that he correctly perceived in them the possibility of a better and quicker development of manufactory production. Very interesting also is the fact that Montchrétien asks so little from the government. In this instance he asks merely for abolition of quality-control. Here is one of many instances of the inconvenience caused to the manufactory-owners by the age-old regulation of production of goods for the internal market, which deprived them of the principal condition for success, namely, equality of opportunity in competition between their goods and imported ones.

Let us now draw some conclusions about this 'heavy industry of the seventeenth century'. As we have seen, the author is still very far from any sort of plan of 'industrialisation', though he understands the importance of metallurgy and of the production of metal articles for all branches of industry (but this, one must suppose, was appreciated long before Montchrétien). For us his ideas have a two-fold interest. His sharp eye, trained perhaps by the example of the more developed Dutch manufactories, saw with exceptional acuteness not only the backwardness of French practice but also the way to get rid of this backwardness by purely economic means. In addition, the facts he quotes provide irrefutable proof of the negative effect of Dutch trade and industry on the development of French manufactory production. Bitter rivalry, both commercial and industrial (and not merely commercial, as, for example, there had been at one time between Genoa and Venice), had already become the norm in relations between the countries which had taken the path of capitalist development.

Montchrétien begins his section on the textile industry, not without purpose, by dealing with the production of felt hats and caps from the fur of beavers and rabbits. The point is that the French have no competitors in this branch: 'it has fully and wholly remained ours'. It is very prosperous. (Thereafter, Montchrétien arranges the other branches mainly in order of decreasing prosperity.) Why is this so? 'Our heads change their shape too often, and this inconstancy prevents the foreigner from profiting in the matter.' In other words, the capriciousness of French fashion (which the French had already at this time begun to impart to other nations) guards the monopoly of the home market for these goods, and this market is continually expanding, for 'the merchant dresses like a nobleman'.[1] However—and here the writer becomes petitioner—measures are needed for checking the quality of the Spanish wool imported by the Flemings, which is full of grease, sand and stones.

[1] Montchrétien, op. cit. pp. 60, 61.

Montchrétien regards the production of linen as the most widespread branch of industry in France, giving employment to a multitude of people—men, women and children. In this trade France has left all her competitors on the foreign market a long way behind because of the high quality of her linen. Although the Dutch misrepresent their linen and canvas as French, putting French customs marks on them, nevertheless they do not stand up to comparison, since the French linen is bleached in fresh water, whereas the Dutch is bleached in semi-salt water. Especially considerable and profitable is the export of French canvas to Spain. The Spanish ships are rigged with French sails, and not with Dutch, Flemish or German ones.

The trouble is, though, that the Dutch have penetrated into the very heart of this important and profitable industry. They have set up their manufactories in France; there they bleach the linen they have imported from Holland, and thither they lure French craftsmen by offering big wages. They also buy up unbleached fabric.[1] The Dutchmen must be expelled, and the sale and export of linen and canvas made a monopoly for Frenchmen. In other words, the king is asked to take very serious steps, and once again they are to be directed against the Dutch.

The French clothing trade, formerly prosperous, is in a very depressed condition. It is scattered all over the country, and everywhere there is good-quality raw material available for it. But the French skill in this work has ceased to be a national secret. Who does not know that the English have mastered this skill, thanks to French emigrants, and that today the sound of French speech is heard in English manufactories? The French market is flooded with English cloth, mostly of poor quality in respect of material, preparation (it shrinks in the rain) and dye (indigo, forbidden in France, is used instead of woad). True, the demand for cloth has fallen off a great deal owing to the fact that many more people have begun to wear silk. Nevertheless, it is necessary to support French cloth production, because many people are employed in it. The government should ban the importation of English goods, as has already been done by the Flemings, by Hamburg, and others.[2]

Silk production and the making of silk fabrics (satin, velvet, brocade, taffeta, etc.) and stockings are seen by Montchrétien as very profitable and having good prospects in France. So much silk is made in the country that there should be no need to buy any abroad, and the French know how to weave it. Why should such a lot of money be spent on imported silk fabrics and stockings (for stockings alone 3 million *livres* being spent every year)?

[1] In the production of linen, work at home (preparation of the flax, spinning, weaving) was combined with operations carried out in centralised workshops.
[2] Montchrétien, op. cit. pp. 70–5, 82–3.

The king should either forbid superfluous indulgence in silken clothing, or else extend the production of silk fabrics in France to a level at which it can completely satisfy demand.[1]

This point is of interest for several reasons. It is beyond doubt that in France at this time demand for silk fabrics and various articles made of silk (stockings, ribbons, silk lace, etc.), which had already become firmly current not only among the nobles but also among the rich and well-to-do strata of the citizenry, greatly exceeded the resources of the French silk industry. Though the efforts of Henry IV, Sully and Olivier de Serres had achieved certain positive results, they had not succeeded in eliminating the principal weakness, namely, the shortage of raw material. It is typical that Montchrétien does not even mention the desirability of a ban on imports of silk fabric. The measure which he had asked to be adopted regarding English cloth would evidently be inappropriate to this case. He probably remembered the failure of Henry IV's attempts to stop these imports. He would hardly have had much confidence, either, in the effectiveness of decrees against luxury. The main difficulty, it must be supposed, was that the French silk industry was still really underdeveloped, owing to shortage of raw material, and the most important measure to be taken to foster it must bear upon that shortage—that is, larger quantities of raw silk must be obtained. The prospects before this branch of industry depended (and, indeed, this view was fully confirmed as time went by) on the existence of a long-established and continually expanding demand on the home market, while the reputation for skill of the French craftsmen, already well established abroad, guaranteed a wide expansion in foreign markets as well.

As regards English fustian, Flemish camlet and other lightweight fabrics, Montchrétien confines himself to noting that these are all made in the French style and are none the worse in quality for that; in order to sell their fabrics at home the English merchants even pretend that these are French. Their importation into France hinders the development of French industry. Nowadays the French tailors, the best in the world, find themselves faced by competitors, even within France itself. Scottish and Flemish craftsmen have mastered French fashions, and work, helped by countrymen of their own, in the principal cities of France.

The leather industry is also in a bad way, though formerly it was numbered among the most profitable, because not less than three-quarters of the population of France wear leather shoes (the rest wear shoes made of wood or rope). Home-produced raw material is insufficient, and hides are imported from Barbary, from the Cape Verde Islands, and so on. Nor are there

---

[1] Montchrétien, op. cit. pp. 76–80, 223.

sufficient craftsmen, so that it is necessary to make do with Flemings. Leatherwork and the quality of footwear is deteriorating, and steps should be taken to combat these abuses.[1]

Passing on to the 'noble art of printing', Montchrétien finds himself once more on familiar ground—in this case, as a writer who has published his own work—and devotes much attention to this art, on account of its great profitability and extremely wide diffusion. True, it is now established in all countries, and so cannot provide such high profits as formerly, when only a few peoples knew its secrets and exported their books to the rest. Also, demand is not what it was: many libraries have been established, and, more-over, a book is a commodity that lasts and does not wear out as clothes do. All the same, with intelligence one can make plenty of money in this trade too, proof of which is to be seen among the Flemings, who have a very sharp nose for profit.

Montchrétien describes very graphically the method whereby the Flemings make high profits from printing, and we quote his actual words, because they offer a basis for estimating the difference between Flemish and French printing-works and thereby the level of development of the French printing trade at that time.

In many cities of Flanders there are numerous printing-works 'where poor people of the locality work for very low wages, but where the journeymen-compositors themselves are paid fifteen cents [a cent being one-hundredth of a gulden] more than the French, who only get twenty-five cents, and where they do correspondingly more composition. Thanks to this greater amount of work done (*tasche augmentée*) they [i.e. the Flemish book-publishers] sell their books at approximately half the price that our own can afford to charge, and they send us many books which are in very wide demand and therefore sell very readily. By this means they deprive our printers and booksellers (in whose opinion the best books are not those which are the best printed but those which sell most quickly and most profitably) of a field of activity which was theirs and even the mediocre profit that they used to make.'[2]

The importation of foreign books should be forbidden, thereby bringing aid to French printing, which gives work to 50,000 people; and this is all the more desirable in that by their content the imported books do harm to good morals and seduce people from their allegiance to lawful authority. The privilege of copyright ought not to be conceded for more than four to six years, after which all publishers should enjoy equal rights in the publishing and sale of books. Export of French paper and type should also be forbidden.

[1] Ibid. pp. 85, 86.   [2] Ibid. pp. 90, 91.

Then foreigners would be obliged either to have their books printed in French printing works or else to buy French books. At present they print harmful books on French paper with French type, and sell them in France; things have even reached such a state that some Englishmen have acquired paper mills in France and process English rags in them.[1]

Thus, neither abundance of good paper, nor the availability of such valuable equipment as printers' type, nor the multitude of printing-works and skilled craftsmen, has preserved French printing at the beginning of the seventeenth century from inability to compete with the Flemings, and this for purely economic reasons. The cheapness of imported books—almost as little as half the price of French ones—is first and foremost determined by the higher productivity of the Flemish printing-works and their more intense division of labour, as a result of which many detail operations can be carried out by less skilled or even unskilled workers for low wages. Moreover, the Flemish printers supply an extensive demand, their books (prayer-books, pamphlets, etc., being chiefly meant here) are printed in large editions and are quickly bought up owing to their cheapness and the absence of a censorship.

Owing to the skill of Italian craftsmen resident in France in glass-making, and to the excellent quality of the raw material, the making of glass, and of glass and cut-glass ware, flourishes on the estates of the nobles.[2] This branch of industry must be encouraged, and the nobles' monopoly of it maintained, with no further grant of privileges.[3]

After completing his survey of the branches of manufactory production,[4] Montchrétien goes on to draw the conclusions which arise from the situation he has described.[5] It seems to him beyond doubt that industry ought to be developed. The country's wealth is based precisely on industry, which is indeed the beginning and end of it (*premier vivant et dernier mourant*).[6] The prince can have peace of mind only if all his subjects possess the means of subsistence, and this is provided by industry. Otherwise, dangerous popular disturbances are inevitable.

[1] Montchrétien, op. cit. pp. 91–95.
[2] In France the nobles had long possessed the right to conduct glass-making workshops without losing thereby their exemptions from taxation, which they forfeited if they engaged in any other form of production.
[3] Montchrétien considers this measure a good reward for those noblemen who had loyally served the king in the civil wars of the sixteenth century. These *gentilshommes-verriers* numbered not fewer than 2,500 (op. cit. p. 97). This argument, curious in the mouth of a manufactory-owner, is to be explained by the fact that such noblemen need not be given pensions.
[4] It is typical that his list does not include the manufactories producing guns, gunpowder, carpets and some other articles, which were mostly state-owned enterprises, and enjoyed special attention on the part of the authorities.
[5] Montchrétien, op. cit. pp. 103–28.
[6] Ibid. p. 99.

What measures must be taken so that from little settlements large, rich towns may grow, such as Holland, Zeeland and Friesland are full of? Workers must be trained, for skilled craftsmen are very much needed. Idleness must be stamped out, and manufacturers encouraged by showing them the way to make profits and win honourable privileges. Such measures serve at once the interests of private individuals and the public weal. Schools must be set up for the children of the poor, where they can be taught crafts. Women too must be trained, for they also should work. In Holland the children of vagabonds and beggars are housed in special asylums, boys and girls separately, and trained to different kinds of work in the manufactories. When they grow up, they marry (among themselves) and work in the same asylums, but for wages. Such asylums would be built by French manufacturers, too, if they knew that the products of their enterprises were guaranteed a market through the prohibition of foreign imports.[1] Wilful vagabonds and beggars must be compelled by the severest measures to do the heaviest work, in correctional workhouses.

Montchrétien's idea is perfectly clear, and arises from the need to have trained workers in the manufactories, as well as from the endeavour to make use of the labour of women and children. However, he puts the burden of expenditure for technical training upon the government. The manufacturers were agreeable to meeting the charges connected with this only if a children's home was transformed into a sort of manufactory and the children living therein were bound to them till the end of their days.

The next point is the need to reduce the cost of manufactory production. Why are the Dutch able to sell their goods so cheaply? 'There, the most subtle minds, the richest and most successful of men, regard it as most worthy to seek and advantageous to find some ingenious and useful way whereby the practice of the commonest and most necessary arts may be made easier and more rapid. From this they gain great profit, especially because by machines and mechanical tools they lighten the work of men and thereby reduce the costs of production (*frais de la besogne*). This, more than the abundance and skill of their craftsmen, is what enables them to sell us goods at such low prices—all the more so because now, when they have gained possession of our market, they concern themselves not so much with good quality as with large quantity, and devote their industry rather to prettifying (*farder*) their goods, so as to sell them at higher prices, than to making them really good.'[2]

It follows that measures ought to be taken to prevent possible overproduc-

---

[1] See also Lublinskaya, *Frantsiya v nachale XVII veka*, pp. 26, 27.
[2] Montchrétien, op. cit. p. 119.

tion, as this reduces profits. In order to avoid the inconveniences resulting both from dearth of goods and from excessive plenty of them, the government should seek means of establishing a wise balance between the one and the other.

The last conclusion, and in Montchrétien's view the most important, is the vital necessity of protection—the first and most essential condition for the prosperity of French manufacture is the prohibition of imports from abroad. The prosperity of England and of Flanders is based on such prohibition.[1] There is nothing more advantageous to the state than a rich and varied industry, supplying all demands—the prince has the same responsibilities in relation to this as the architect has in relation to the building of a house.[2] Not in vain does the government in Holland come to the aid of private businessmen (*la main publique aide à la particulière*) and set up new manufactories.[3] 'Have courage, then, Most Christian Majesties,' Montchrétien concludes, 'and carry through this great task, making glorious your reign thereby.'[4]

This appeal for courage was not accidental. While goodwill on the part of the government, expressed in its orders, was sufficient to ensure the training of workers, the introduction of technical improvements, the avoidance of overproduction, and the provision of subsidies, for the carrying out of a consistent policy of protection real courage was needed, and this in the field most difficult for France at that time, namely, international relations. Montchrétien understood this quite well, and, in order to see his call for protection realised he sets out a number of ideas relating to diplomacy.

At the time that he wrote his treatise, that is, in 1614, the civil wars had only just entered their initial stage and it was hard to foresee all their subsequent development. The prospect of the convocation of the States-General inspired many hopes for a peaceful settlement of the conflict which had begun, and for the realization of reforms. Nevertheless, the international situation in Western Europe that had taken shape since the death of Henry IV was clear enough. Montchrétien gave his advice to the king in full awareness that it would encounter serious resistance from the king's ministers, who were conducting a very cautious foreign policy.

The commercial treaties concluded by Henry IV with England, Spain and Holland granted equal rights to French merchants. But after the king's death in 1610 these rights were increasingly violated, to France's loss. The government preferred to put up with this encroachment without making any serious protest, for in a period of weakened central authority and mounting civil strife it was very interested indeed in retaining even the passive support of

[1] Montchrétien, op. cit. pp. 112–14. [2] Ibid. p. 123.
[3] Ibid. pp. 118, 119. [4] Ibid. p. 128.

just those countries—England, Spain and Holland—with which it would have had to quarrel if it had taken the road of systematic defence of French merchants and manufacturers. This interest on France's part in keeping up political alliances was shamelessly exploited by her neighbours in order to create favourable conditions for their trade. Despite the commercial treaties in force, they increased their import duties on French goods and in all sorts of other ways put the French merchants who visited them in an unequal position. The freedom of action of foreign merchants in France has already been mentioned.

For this reason Montchrétien asks two fundamental questions. Should the neighbouring countries be asked to fulfil their treaties conscientiously? If France possesses all she needs, has she any need of foreign trade?[1] Answering the first question affirmatively, he is thereby obliged to explain in great detail his view that a developed foreign trade is necessary.

Montchrétien demonstrates this by proceeding both from the state's need for money and from the experience of history and of his own time, which gives his argument a twofold interest: the development of mercantilist theory on the one hand, and, on the other, the discussion of the history of the French economy of the sixteenth and early seventeenth centuries, in close connexion with world economy (allowing, of course, for the limited validity of this term in the period in question). The last-mentioned aspect is very important for us, as it clearly shows the categorical necessity of studying the economic development of any country in Europe, beginning in the sixteenth century (to some extent, even in the thirteenth century) not as a self-contained entity but as a part of the extensive and closely interconnected complex of the countries of Europe.[2]

Montchrétien proposes that correct fulfilment of the commercial treaties be secured without straining relations with allies in whom France is interested. A stand must be taken on the basis of law, that is, of the articles of the treaties, and an effort made to ensure that the merchants of all countries enjoy equal rights.[3] There should be no monopolies in trade.[4] Yet French merchants find themselves placed in an extremely difficult position in certain countries.

England systematically increases her import duties on French goods, even resorting to downright prohibition of the importation of some of them, and also bans exports of her own raw material. French merchants are subjected to all manner of humiliations in that country. Montchrétien quotes a conversation, which he claims to be typical, between French and English merchants.

[1] Ibid. p. 130.
[2] Mousnier, Hobsbawm and others pay insufficient attention to this aspect of the problem of the development of capitalism in the seventeenth century.
[3] Montchrétien, op. cit. pp. 130–7.   [4] Ibid. p. 256.

The Frenchman asks: 'Why do you treat us so badly?' 'Because you are foreigners', comes the answer. 'But we do not treat you like this in France.' 'Because you are unwise, do we have to be stupid?'[1]

Montchrétien considers that export duties should be increased on French goods exported to England (grain, wine, paper, fruit, and various articles) and English merchants in France placed in the same conditions as French merchants have to endure in England.[2] Such vigorous measures were determined, we must suppose (this is clear from what follows), by the facts that England was not France's direct neighbour, that she prized very highly French good-quality wines, wheat, paper, luxury articles, etc., and, finally, that political alliance with her was not so important as alliances with other countries.

The situation is different where Holland is concerned. France has done so much for her—and this quite recently[3]—that the Dutch ought not to treat French merchants badly, especially as they import only wine into Holland, while exporting linen, serge, camlet, soap, butter and cheese. The French need to learn from the Dutch; that is the greatest benefit they can obtain from dealings with them. The Dutch like France, they are under great obligations to her, and they will be glad to help the French.[4] From these considerations of Montchrétien we can conclude that, in his opinion, the government is in a position to curtail the rights of the Dutch as regards their hitherto unrestricted activity inside France. The government must stick to the principle that the rights of foreign merchants in France cannot be greater than the rights of French merchants.

The latter, says Montchrétien, need defending in Spain as well. Spanish merchants freely carry on their business in France and freely travel to all parts of the country, whereas direct trade with the Spanish colonies in America is closed to Frenchmen. The Spanish government obtains a huge revenue from taxing the trade carried on with America by other countries, especially France, which supplies the bulk of the manufactured goods and foodstuffs sent over there. French merchants pay exorbitant duties in Spain (on the average, up to 40 per cent of the value of the goods, excluding grain), whereas Spaniards (and other foreigners) pay not more than 2·5 per cent in France. The Spaniards seize French vessels sailing to America, kill French colonists, and so on. The rights of French and Spanish merchants must be equalised.[5] This aspiration, too, could be regarded as realisable, since

[1] Montchrétien, op. cit. pp. 194–205.   [2] Ibid. p. 206.
[3] He means the truce between Holland and Spain, concluded in 1609 as a result of vigorous support given to Holland by France.
[4] Montchrétien, op. cit. pp. 144, 207, 208.
[5] Ibid. pp. 209–20.

France had quite recently (in 1612) concluded a political alliance with Spain, and so could obtain concessions from her.

Accordingly, in Montchrétien's opinion, the international situation in 1614 was such that the French government could proceed to follow a sufficiently strict protectionist policy and bring about restoration of that equality of rights for French merchants which had been violated by neighbouring countries.

At that time these views were to a considerable extent justified. Subsequent events, however, made such a policy, which was indeed most necessary for the development of the French economy, impracticable for the time being. The failure of the reform programme in the States-General, the flare-up of civil war in 1615–20, the military campaign against the Huguenots in 1620–9, in short, the extremely unstable political situation inside the country, together with the beginning (though, so far, outside the frontiers of France) of the Thirty Years War, put it beyond the power of the government either to grant extensive subsidies to manufacturers or to press upon allies (Spain still being included among these) demands for changes in customs tariffs. But as soon as the situation improved, in 1626 (it turned out to be only a short breathing-space), Richelieu immediately undertook a number of measures.[1]

Having shown the government not only the necessity but also the possibility of protection, Montchrétien goes on to consider the importance of external trade. Internal trade is very useful and necessary for the normal life of the country, but profit—even though attended by risk—is to be got only from external trade. It is the best and quickest means of enrichment, and wealth furthers the might and prestige of the state. It provides money, and 'we live today by gold and silver... they supply the needs of all men... Money is the sinews of war... One cannot make war without men, maintain men without pay, find pay without taxes, levy taxes without trade.'[2] For this reason merchants are necessary and useful to the state. True, they are more concerned about their own profits than about the public interest, but this is understandable and tolerable: without their thirst for profit they would not take on themselves the risks they assume on land and sea. They are not for that reason to be struck out of the list of honourable citizens and treated like

[1] On the events of 1615–20, see Lublinskaya, *Frantsiya v nachale XVII veka*; on those of 1620–6, see the following chapters of this book. It is characteristic that domination of the French market by Dutch merchants continued right down to Colbert, and only the Franco-Dutch 'trade' war of 1672–80 put an end to it (see e.g. H. Enjalbert, 'Le commerce de Bordeaux et la vie économique dans le bassin aquitain au XVIIᵉ siècle', *Annales du Midi*, LXII (1950).
[2] Montchrétien, op. cit. pp. 141, 142. The idea that the principal revenue of the state came from taxes on trade and that therefore it was most necessary for the state that merchants should be rich, was widespread at that time. (L. A. Boiteux, *Richelieu 'Grand maître de la navigation et du commerce de France'*, (Paris, 1955) p. 216.)

helots.[1] Limits must be laid down for profit; a respectable profit is as legitimate in trade as in any other occupation. In Italy merchants have first place, they are greatly esteemed in England, in Holland they dominate in everything. In general, Holland is a splendid example of how trade can enrich a country. How rapidly this small country has come to dominate the trade of the whole world! The Dutch combine the industriousness of the French with the ability to conduct business (*ménagerie*) which is characteristic of the English.[2]

France can and must follow the example of Holland, and all the more so because this will not mean anything new, but only the restoration of the previous state of affairs.

Thus, his line of argument leads the author to the need to make a brief excursion into the history of French foreign trade in the sixteenth century and to look for the reasons for its decline in the second decade of the seventeenth. All this is of considerable interest for the economic history of France and in relation to the problem of the relations between the countries of Europe on the world market at the beginning of the seventeenth century.

Before the Discoveries, Spain and Portugal were poor, Montchrétien observes. Now they are rich in gold and silver, and in a position to satisfy their demand for grain by buying it in France, which in this way obtains much precious metal. But the main reason for the former prosperity of French trade in the Iberian peninsula was that in the first half of the sixteenth century (beginning in the reign of Louis XII) French merchants themselves freely sold their goods in Spanish and Portuguese ports and exported gold and spices from there. In fact they held the monopoly of trade with America through Spain in both directions; Holland and England were in those days unable to challenge their rights. Under Henry II this monopoly was the condition for the extraordinary prosperity of Franco-Spanish and Franco-American trade. Nobody hindered the French, their commercial connexions were successfully and firmly established, they freely sailed the seas and gained great profit. The civil wars which then broke out in France dealt a heavy blow to trade, but even in that period long and fairly successful voyages were undertaken. On the whole, however, the civil wars grievously ravaged the country and undermined trade, since it is merchants who are the first to be ruined by wars. During that period England and Holland gained strength, and with the end of their wars with Spain (in bringing which about Henry IV rendered a great service, reconciling Spain first with England and then with

---

[1] Montchrétien refers here to the position of the merchants in France.
[2] Montchrétien, op. cit. pp. 137–44.

Holland) they began to oust the French from the Spanish and American markets. While Henry IV lived this was not particularly felt, and France, as in former times of peace, supplied Spain with grain, linen, cloth, hardware, and other goods. After the king's death the situation markedly worsened, and the interests of French merchants were encroached upon. Besides the high import duties already mentioned, they suffered by the fact that Spanish merchants themselves brought American goods into France (hides, ginger, dyes) and sold them cheaper than French merchants could who imported them from Spain, because they did not have to pay the 10 per cent duty charged; under similar favourable conditions they bought linen in France. Thanks to this they made 23–25 per cent more on French goods sent to America than French merchants were able to make.[1]

Further heavy loss was inflicted on the French everywhere by the English and Dutch, whose exports increased sharply. In the sixteenth century there were no Englishmen in Turkey or Barbary, and the merchants of Marseilles supplied the English with oriental goods. Now they have their own trading companies operating there, and the English ambassador in Constantinople is disputing with the French for the privilege of trade with the Levant.[2] The Dutch have also appeared in the Mediterranean, and with those people it is enough to appear in some place for them to get control of everything and push the French out. The reason is the cheapness of their goods, especially at first, when they want to get control of a trade, and so they sell their goods at half-price, even at a loss to themselves. This happens because, through the proper use of their workers (*par l'exact employ de leurs hommes*), they produce a large quantity of goods of all kinds and, in addition, they draw a very large profit from the freighting of their innumerable ships.

[1] Ibid. pp. 155–66, 189–90.
[2] Montchrétien considered France's trade with the Levant to be unprofitable. Through Marseilles alone there passed every year to Turkey and Persia more than seven million *écus*, two-thirds of this in Spanish currency obtained from the sale of French goods in Spain. Imports from the Levant consisted mostly of raw silk. It was very dear owing to high duties (up to 14–15 per cent), and in addition, what was especially deplorable, it mostly did not remain in France to be made into silk fabric but was exported to Genoa, Lucca, Milan and other Italian cities, from which France then later imported expensive silk textiles, on which, moreover, export duties had to be paid in Italy and also in the Swiss passes. 'Everyone who wears silk clothes', writes Montchrétien, 'pays more than twelve *livres* in tribute to foreign rulers' (op. cit. pp. 221–3). This view of the Levant trade, though rather widely held at the time, was mistaken. Later, Richelieu became convinced of its falsity. In fact, France needed imports of raw silk. These imports provided French silk manufactories with their raw material; the export of their products brought a 100 per cent profit, and the duty paid on them enriched the state treasury. Nearly 25,000 families were employed in these manufactories. The gold paid for raw silk in the Levant came not from France itself but from Spain, where French merchants disposed of the goods of various kinds they brought from the Levant. They also sold some of the raw silk in Italian ports. The whole of the trade was in the hands of rich merchants of Marseilles, who had ousted Venice from it. (Boiteux, op. cit. pp. 315, 320.)

The Dutch have squeezed French trade out of Senegal and Guinea and have already appeared in Canada. They have enticed experienced French captains on to their boats. Owing to the Dutch, the French have already nearly lost their profitable oceanic herring fisheries, and the Dutch have grown rich from them. The French fishermen still retain the very profitable cod fishery, which gives employment to 600 vessels and 15,000–20,000 Norman and Breton fishermen. The merchants make 30–50 per cent profit from this trade, and it is essential that it be reserved for the French.[1]

The picture drawn by Montchrétien of progress in French trade and industry down to the middle of the 1550s, then decline down to the beginning of the seventeenth century, a fresh big advance in 1600–10, and then another decline after 1610, coincides broadly and in many details with what we learn from other sources. No contemporary penetrated so deeply into the meaning of these changes.[2] Of course, many phenomena and their hidden significance escaped Montchrétien, for the most acute man of those days could not divine the laws of capitalist production, then taking shape.[3] Nevertheless, the principal conclusions which follow from Montchrétien's argument are sound: (1) France's foreign trade, flourishing in the first half of the sixteenth century, then suffered decline, chiefly owing to the civil wars in France; with the coming of peace it revived, but now its progress was hindered by competitors; (2) French merchants were the losers in competition with their Dutch, and to some extent also with their English rivals, owing to the comparative dearness of their goods; (3) because of the weakening of the central authority in France, and the consequent decline in the international prestige of the French government, French merchants found themselves in an unequal position in all foreign markets (and even, as shown earlier, in their own home market); (4) a strong government can remove this obstacle through diplomacy and protectionist measures, and a cheapening of the products of French

---

[1] Montchrétien, op. cit. pp. 226–35. In 1614 the return from the cod-fisheries was calculated at ten million *livres;* half of the fish caught were exported to Spain, Italy and Germany.

[2] To be more precise, none of the writers whose works were written in those years and have come down to us. In the business correspondence of merchants we come upon ideas similar to those expressed by Montchrétien. It is quite possible that among them such views were fairly widespread.

[3] I must mention the following curious argument of Montchrétien: although, as a result of the deluge of American gold, prices had markedly risen, nevertheless *la valeur essentielle des marchandises est immuable*, in contrast to the accident of price, which may for one reason or another either rise or fall, so that what is dear today may later on become cheap (op. cit. p. 257). The 'price revolution' of the sixteenth century had taught contemporaries the accidental nature of price-formation and undermined their notions about a connexion between the value of a commodity and its price. Montchrétien raises this disparity to the level of dogma: value is fixed, price is accidental. And yet he makes valuable observations on this very question of the non-accidental nature of price-formation, pointing to the reasons for the cheapness of the products of the Dutch manufactories and the declining cost of Dutch goods.

manufactories must be secured through technical training, bans on imports, etc.; (5) the best way of developing foreign trade, which has excellently proved its worth in England and Holland, is the organisation of large-scale trading companies.[1]

Montchrétien himself nowhere speaks of the *political* reasons for the commercial and industrial prosperity of Holland, though he knows very well that there 'merchants are dominant in all things' (it is typical that, while mentioning more than once the huge profits obtained by the Dutch from their shipping, he nevertheless gives first place to Dutch industry, Dutch manufactures).[2] Absolutist England is for him almost as magnificent an example of the prosperity of trade and industry, achieved through the protectionist measures of Elizabeth Tudor. Because of this, his expression of loyal feelings and confidence in the government rings true. He evidently believed sincerely that a similar prosperity of the economy of absolutist France could be achieved if only his proposals were put into effect.

In this connexion Montchrétien did not stint his advice on many other matters as well. He gave a great deal of attention to the circulation of money, to taxation, and to colonial expansion.

He described in detail the extremely confused currency situation in France, which caused much suffering to the mass of the people. Stocks of gold and silver coins of full value were disappearing from the country, clandestinely exported by foreign merchants, in spite of all the official bans and the controls at the frontier, to Seville, Lisbon, London, Amsterdam, etc. Often these foreigners obtained money from French merchants as loans, because the Frenchmen, finding it impossible to invest their capital in trade, sought any available sphere of investment for it.[3] The outflow of good

[1] Montchrétien sets out in detail the structure of the Dutch East India Company and warmly recommends the government to set up such companies in France (ibid. pp. 252–60).

[2] Cf. Marx on the great importance of the Dutch manufactories (Marx and Engels, *Sochineniya*, 2nd edition, xxv, part 1, 365 note 49). [Marx, *Capital*, Foreign Languages Publishing House English edition, iii, 327 note 49.]

[3] In this connexion Montchrétien again vividly describes the difficulties experienced by French merchants as a result of the predominance of foreign merchants in France itself. (In a memorandum from the financier Charlot, presented to Richelieu in 1626, it was stated that in Rouen alone there were resident sixty rich foreign merchants; in the entire country they numbered 200,000; see Boiteux, op. cit. p. 191.) Having no opportunity of getting even a 'respectable' profit, because trade has become unprofitable, French merchants prefer to invest their money in loans, land, offices, and so on (Montchrétien, op. cit. pp. 168, 169). This interesting observation shows that it was not only because the French bourgeoisie were being bled by taxes that they tried to find shelter for their capital in the non-productive sphere. This phenomenon is to be explained first and foremost by the fact that in the given circumstances investment in French trade and industry was simply *unprofitable*. According to Du Noyer de Saint-Martin, whose statements relate to 1613–14, ownership of land by the French bourgeoisie was so considerable that it brought them an income of more than six million *livres* a year, while their investments in Dutch and Venetian trading companies exceeded twelve million *livres* (see Boiteux, op. cit. p. 194).

currency was accompanied by an inflow of bad from across the frontier;[1] the Flemings maintained in France special money-changers to operate this sort of exchange, and drew big profits from it (up to 25 per cent a month, according to Montchrétien). The country was flooded with bad copper money, while there was a shortage of silver and gold. Everybody suffered as a result, and especially the ordinary people, who were driven to despair by it (*un desespoir pour le peuple*).[2] Montchrétien's characteristic style in expounding his views, full of strong feeling, easily and naturally passing over at times into irony and sarcasm, reaches its climax in these pages of his book. He writes of the many tragic occurrences resulting from the disorder in the currency situation, and on behalf of the people implores the government to establish order as soon as possible in this field. The circulation of foreign coins (other than Spanish ones) must be prohibited, the ratio between gold and silver must be exactly fixed,[3] payments must be formulated in money of account,[4] good coins for small change must be issued, and a vigorous struggle undertaken against law-breakers who take French currency abroad, especially against smugglers, etc.

The information Montchrétien gives about the confused currency position is very useful. It supplies many additional features for a description of the economic decline of France after 1610: the withdrawal of capital from trade and industry, the difficult conditions of the mass of the people, and so on. There were two fundamental causes for the disorderly state of the currency. The establishment in Henry IV's reign of a good-quality French gold and silver coinage, together with the abundance in France of equally good Spanish coins, led to the smuggling of this good money out of the country, as a result of which France was flooded with foreign coins of worse quality and much valueless small change. This injured both the population and the state. It was no new phenomenon. In the sixteenth century Spain had

---

[1] The reference is to foreign coins with a lower content of gold and silver than French or Spanish coins (the latter being plentiful in France). Montchrétien estimated that from the silver coins worth a quarter-*écu* (15 sous) the Flemings minted coins worth 16·5 sous, i.e. they gained six sous from each *écu* (60 sous), or in other words, 10 per cent profit (op. cit. p. 172). Cf. similar statements in Isaac de Razilly's memorandum of 1626 (L. Deschamps, 'Un colonisateur du temps de Richelieu: Isaac de Razilly. Biographie, mémoire inédit', *Revue de Géographie*, XIX (July–December, 1886), 459–60).

[2] Montchrétien, op. cit. p. 175. The tax collectors insisted on being paid in good money. In addition, the abundance of brass money for small change facilitated an increase in the prices of articles of primary necessity.

[3] The traditional ratio between the two precious metals (1:15) had been upset during the sixteenth century in favour of gold, especially after 1545, when American silver poured into Europe. In the second half of the sixteenth century and at the beginning of the seventeenth (Sully's currency reform of 1602) a new ratio was fixed by law on more than one occasion, but never for long, because reality demanded continual adjustments and re-adjustments.

[4] I.e. showing payment in *livres* and not in specific coins.

experienced a similar 'flight' (*fuite*) of good money into other countries, leaving Spain with an acute shortage,[1] which disrupted economic life. Montchrétien's treatise shows us that in his day France had begun to be threatened by the same fate. The country was losing a certain quantity of the precious metal which reached it (according to the example given by Montchrétien, the loss amounted to 10 per cent), without receiving any equivalent, and part of the French currency was draining away uselessly. The second cause of the trouble was that these losses were due more to political than to economic circumstances. Not being safeguarded by an adequate protectionist policy (in so far as, after 1610, France's commercial treaties with other countries were being violated by them to the disadvantage of French trade and industry), the French economy was suffering all along the line. The smuggling out of good money had gone on under Henry IV, too, but on nothing like such a scale as after the king's death, when foreign merchants began to feel free to do as they pleased in France, and civil strife increasingly disrupted the country's normal existence. The measures proposed by Montchrétien in this connexion cannot be regarded as sufficient in themselves. They were capable of good effect only if combined with all other protectionist measures.

Montchrétien's proposals regarding taxation are very interesting. For France this question was a particularly burning one not only on the financial but also on the social and political plane, and it was therefore being vigorously discussed in connexion with the forthcoming assembly of the States-General.[2] It must be said that, of all the projects of reform, Montchrétien's was the most radical.

He proposes to make an income tax the fundamental form of taxation, and for this it would be necessary to compile every five years a cadastral survey, based on declarations to be submitted, stating property and income. This way of distributing the load of taxation, besides being more just and less burdensome to the mass of the people (and therefore strengthening the social structure), would also bring a great advantage in that the survey returns could also provide exact information about the size of the population, its age-groups, and the conditions and occupations of the inhabitants.[3] It would be possible to calculate how many men should be recruited into the army, how many sent to the colonies, and so on. The government would

[1] Henry IV had good reason to say that there were more Spanish gold pistoles in France than in Spain itself (Montchrétien, op. cit. p. 160).
[2] See Lublinskaya, *Frantsiya v nachale XVII veka*, chapter 4.
[3] Montchrétien discourses eloquently on the need to escape from all sorts of storms (*orages et tempestes*) by welding together the upper, middle and lower strata of society, which could be achieved by uniting the interests of men of different social position (op. cit. p. 239).

129

know the kind and quantity of goods to be produced, which of them and in what amount could be exported, what branches of the economy to stimulate, and so forth.[1]

Montchrétien proposes that the farming out of the salt-tax (*gabelle*) be stopped and that the internal trade in salt be made as free as any other trade (*tirer le sel en liberté comme une autre marchandise*).[2] At the same time, there should be a substantial increase in the export duty on salt, which France supplies to many countries and regions.[3] The Dutch, for example, draw such large profits from their trade in salt fish precisely because they get salt so cheaply from France. The profit from free internal trade in salt, alone, could amount to ten million *livres*.[4]

The duties charged upon foreigners for the export of other principal items of French exported goods must also be raised—on grain, wine, cloth and linen. Even if, in consequence of these measures, exports were reduced, this would do no harm: these goods would become cheaper on the home market, and that would please the people. A state is rich not in abundance of gold and silver but in all the necessities of life; whoever has more of these is the richer by it (*qui plus en a, plus a de bien*). This opinion is worth noting. The writer adds that in France there was now more gold and silver than in the fifteenth century, yet the French were not the richer for it, nor even merely better off.

An increase in export duties was all the more necessary because these had already been increased for French merchants in Holland and England; there could therefore be no objection to this measure, which merely restored the former equality of rights. Furthermore, French wine was so highly valued abroad that foreigners would continue to buy and export it, like salt, grain and linen, in spite of the increased duty. In order to get money, 'which is not produced in France', exports were necessary, but the country ought not to export raw material and import finished goods. In addition, the export of grain should be strictly regulated, so as not to deprive the provinces of their supplies of food. Internal trade ought also to be strictly regulated.[5]

---

[1] Montchrétien, op. cit. pp. 345–56.
[2] Furthermore, the Dutch must be deprived of their right to transport salt by river from Brouage into Normandy and Picardy. By this means alone they made 180,000 *livres* a year in freight charges, because their vessels carried the goods more cheaply than the French. Montchrétien insists that this practice be banned for the additional reason that it affected 'a great multitude of poor people who must be kept from committing excesses, for the sake of public order' (op. cit. pp. 185, 186).
[3] Montchrétien names Holland, Germany, Savoy, Switzerland, Geneva, the Grisons, Valais, Orange, and the Comtat-Venaissin (op. cit. p. 236).
[4] Ibid. pp. 235–7.
[5] Ibid. pp. 239–69. Montchrétien here gives very interesting information about the large-scale purchase of grain and wine from the peasants by big wholesale traders who then sold this produce

Montchrétien's final proposal in the sphere of finance is for the redemption of Crown property. It must be redeemed, and not simply confiscated, because the prince cannot treat with contempt the interests of private persons and destroy public confidence. This measure was being urged at this time by very many others besides Montchrétien; it was not an original idea. The redemption of Crown property later came to occupy the central place in the financial reform plan of the Assembly of Notables in 1626, and I shall consider it in detail in the appropriate chapter.[1]

As a whole, Montchrétien's plan of fiscal reform was particularly significant for the commercial and industrial bourgeoisie. The plan abolishes the tax privileges enjoyed by certain estates of the realm, since it introduces an income tax to be paid by the entire population. Abolishing the salt-tax farm and allowing this product, so important in everyday life, to circulate freely like any other, meant at the same time the abolition of a tax which bore very heavily upon the people, namely, the *gabelle*. He proposes to increase state revenue by increasing the export duties to be paid by foreign merchants, because this increase would fall upon goods (grain, wine, salt, linen) which Holland, Spain and other countries could not do without, so that there were no grounds for fearing that such a measure would undermine the French export trade and deprive France of the money earned from exports. The latter might decrease a little, but if this happened it would mean that the goods affected would become cheaper on the home market.

The purely bourgeois character of Montchrétien's plan is further underlined by the fact that he has not invented anything, but merely suggests that use be made of the experience of the (bourgeois) Dutch Republic. He wants to introduce a bourgeois fiscal system into feudal France and to cut with one blow the Gordian knot of unresolved contradictions between the increasing expenditure of the absolutist state and the increasing poverty of the bulk of the tax-payers; between the threat to the property-owning classes from the discontent of the masses, unbearably burdened with taxes, and the many fiscal privileges enjoyed by certain estates of the realm; between the state's need to encourage foreign trade which brought money into the country, and the high taxes weighing upon the French bourgeoisie, which deprived the latter of a substantial share of their profits and made them unable to compete; and so on and so forth. Montchrétien's plan was completely unrealisable

abroad. The poor peasants could not get out of debt; hardly had they gathered in their harvest than they were obliged to surrender almost all of it, and then buy grain and siftings at a high price, in order to feed themselves somehow or other till the next harvest. They ate bad bread, which made them ill and weakened them (ibid. pp. 261–3). Cf. above, p. 55, my remarks on the purchasing power of the poor peasantry.
[1] See chapter 6.

in absolutist France. The abolition of the *gabelle* and estate privileges had to wait till more than a century and a half later. Even such a modest measure as the redemption of Crown property came up against insuperable obstacles in 1626. The only practicable—and actually realised—part of his plan was the raising of customs duties.

However, Montchrétien had one more piece of advice to offer, something which he regarded as very important indeed—that colonial expansion in America should be reinforced. The example of neighbouring countries showed how advantageous this was, and France should hasten to catch up with them.

France was densely populated, its population having increased especially rapidly during the period of peace.[1] Part of the population should be sent to the colonies, there to found 'New Frances'; rebels, idlers and criminals should be chosen for this fate.

Montchrétien speaks of the Indians with respect. Though European crafts were unknown to them, they were by nature intelligent, generous and just, they honoured courage and valued freedom highly. They held their land in common without dividing it, and they cultivated it only sufficiently to provide their sustenance, so that they were not notably industrious (*peu laborieux*). If the French could succeed in imparting their own virtues to the Indians without infecting them with their vices, the natives would prove worthy people (*braves hommes*), and all the more because they hated their oppressors, the Spaniards and Portuguese, while being friendly towards the French.

In order to develop colonies, large-scale expenditure was needed on the fleet, on the construction of ports, and so on, but all this would soon be repaid a hundredfold. Colonies were an inexhaustible source of wealth. Permanent and many-sided commercial ties must be created between them and the mother country. To the colonies one could export linen, cloth, leather goods, hats, footwear, hardware, knives, nails, tools, cauldrons and metal pots, earthenware and glassware, fishing tackle, haberdashery, rosaries and many other things. From the colonies could be obtained gold, silver, copper, silk, cotton, aromatic and medicinal herbs, gum, saffron, sandalwood, furs and hides, dyes, valuable species of wood, flax and hemp, pepper and spices—in short, everything that was then exported from the East and from the Northern countries. In the colonies one could raise vines, plant olive-trees, cultivate sugar-cane, ginger, all kinds of grain, rice, peas, vegetables, fruits, and the mulberry, and one could rear cattle and catch whales, as well as cod and other fish.

[1] Montchrétien gives interesting facts about the mass emigration of French people to Spain, where they brought land under cultivation which had remained deserted since the expulsion of the Moriscos; rent was lower there than in France. (Montchrétien, op. cit. pp. 315–18.)

The advantages of trade with the colonies were beyond question. It would be exclusively in the hands of French merchants, who would be free of the obligation to pay heavy duties and levies to foreigners. The export of manufactured articles to the colonies would greatly expand production in the home country and give work to many people.

A voyage to the West Indies took only six weeks. There was a good climate and a fertile soil there, and along the coasts were many islands, where ports could be built. From the West Indies attempts could be made to seek a passage leading into the Pacific Ocean; such a route to China would be shorter and easier than the difficult route round Africa. In fact, the only thing needed was for the government to take the initiative with colonial expeditions.[1]

These plans and arguments are very interesting. Permeated with the bourgeois spirit of the epoch of manufacture, they concentrate on eliminating those obstacles which were hindering the French bourgeoisie in its competition with the merchants and manufacturers of other countries. Colonies are seen as being, first and foremost, outlets for the products of the mother country—outlets closed to all competitors. They are to become sources of raw material only in so far as this is needed in order to extend production at home. Furthermore, colonies are to be settled with emigrants from France, they are to be 'New Frances'. This is their socio-political significance—to draw off socially dangerous elements from the home country: Montchrétien's stress on the colonisation of America as such is typical of him. He is not preaching either ruthless pillage (this explains his favourable attitude to the Indians) or a plantation system with use of slave labour. In other words, he emphasises precisely that aspect which is missing from Hobsbawm's conception, namely, the reproduction on American soil of those features of the French economy which seemed to him the best, for these would be free in America from the hindrances which obstructed the development of manufacture and agriculture in France itself.

It may be that detailed investigation of archive material will extend, correct and render more precise the information contained in Montchrétien's treatise. At present it is an important source for the study of a wide range of subjects connected with the economy of France at the beginning of the seventeenth century and with vital questions of the manufactory period as a whole. Many of the concrete facts given in this source confirm the propositions which Marx formulated mainly on the basis of British and Dutch evidence.

The treatise is also of particular interest in relation to a critique of the crisis theory. It bears witness to the decline of the French economy. But this

[1] Ibid. pp. 273–333.

did not manifest itself in 1620–30 (the period to which the sponsors of the crisis theory assign its beginning), nor did it result from a market crisis, falling prices, declining population, the feudal agrarian structure, etc. The significance of Montchrétien's observations is that French industry was declining because of competition, too severe for it to withstand, from the more highly developed manufactory production of Holland, and, to some extent, of England. Under these conditions protectionism really was the only way to create, by political, that is, forcible means, an artificial situation, closed to competitors, within which the French bourgeoisie could thrive and gather strength for successful competition later on. In this particular case, the link between the development of manufactory production and a strong state power stands out very clearly. This, however, provides no justification for saying that the state itself created this form of economy.

It seems to me that these considerations are essential for estimating the different types of protectionism and the different scales on which it was applied in particular countries.

Montchrétien's treatise also testifies to the desperate economic struggle that was being waged in the markets of Western Europe itself (not to mention the Baltic, Levant and American markets) between the merchants and manufacturers of different countries. He writes that the Dutch and English showed 'remarkable, incomparable diligence in ferreting out in every corner of this kingdom that which they seek'—i.e. profits.[1] This fundamental motive operated in other cases too. All the markets known to the Europeans in those days were cockpits of furious competition, where gain by one party meant loss by another, and a crisis in one nation's trade meant success for the merchants of rival nations.

Montchrétien's mercantilism is different from a mercantilist state policy.[2] He represents, so to speak, a bourgeois variant of mercantilism, such as was very unusual at that time. Money interests him chiefly from the angle of the state's needs: it is required in order to pay the army, and so on. What is fundamental for him is production and the cheapening of products, and his aim is to expand production so as to saturate the home market, first and foremost. It may be that this tendency in his thinking is explained by his occupation, but in any case this is what gives his conceptions their special *nuance*. Moreover, his occupation enabled him to perceive the development of a bourgeois economy in terms of its autonomous movement, whereas 'state' mercantilism assigned to it merely the role of a means for the country's economic advance and the enrichment of the absolutist state, which was

---

[1] Montchrétien, op. cit. p. 161.
[2] Rudloff rightly notes this difference (see above, pp. 105, 106).

feudal in its political basis. This is what explains the interesting point that, in his plan for fiscal reform, Montchrétien does not trouble himself with reflexions on whether such a radical break with the past was possible, given the contemporary social and political structure of France. He proclaims what the bourgeoisie needs for its economic growth, and clearly perceives the obstacles blocking the way for this growth. He says nothing about the social and political obstacles, either because of the immaturity of the political thinking of the French bourgeoisie in his day—which seems to me the most likely explanation—or else for some other reason which has escaped my notice. In any event, it is important to observe that he demands from the government not only a great deal more than it was in a position to give at the beginning of the seventeenth century, but also more than a feudal-absolutist France could in general give to the bourgeoisie. He wants to see established those conditions for the completely unhindered development of his class which could appear only after a bourgeois revolution.

We must also note that Montchrétien provides us with very interesting material relating to the manufactory-owners' needs for trained and skilled workers. Even in France, which one would think was rich in such qualified people—a multiplicity of crafts of many kinds had existed there over a long period, with their system of thoroughgoing technical training—capitalist production felt an acute need for skilled labour-power.

To what extent did the ideas expressed by Montchrétien echo the aspirations and sentiments of the commercial and industrial bourgeoisie of France? About this there can be no argument: on the most fundamental points the coincidence was complete. We can judge of this by the instructions to deputies (mandates) to the States-General of 1614–15 and by the pamphlet literature of that period. Remember that Montchrétien's treatise itself was a sort of 'individual' mandate, and a work of propaganda intended for a wide public. It is not without significance that he conforms to the usual pattern for this kind of writing at that time—a statement that an 'illness' exists, followed by methods for 'curing' it. Montchrétien's work is distinguished among the numerous pamphlets published in 1614–15 by the wide scope of his 'diagnosis' and the well-thought-out nature of his 'prescription', but it is essentially the same kind of work as the others.

The mandate of the third estate of the province of Anjou put forward the demand for abolition of the existing salt-tax (*gabelle*), which should be replaced by a single tax on salt to be paid by everyone. We find the same thing in other mandates too, and also in the composite mandate of the chamber of the third estate at the States-General. The section of this document dealing with trade reads as though it had been copied from Montchrétien, although in fact, of course, this was not so. The difficult situation of the French merchants and manufacturers was a generally known and recognised fact. Everyone sought escape from this by the same means, namely, an intensification of protection.[1] I should like to remark at this point that these considerations render pointless, in my view, the question whether or not Richelieu read Montchrétien's treatise. Merely to put the question in this way seems unfortunate. It is not a matter of whether or not he read it, the point is that he could not but have known about it. None of the leading statesmen of that time could be unaware of the reality which Montchrétien discusses; it was discussed to the same extent as purely political affairs.

By what means could the difficult position of the French economy be changed for the better? In what forms and to what extent could that multitude of proposals be put into effect which had been stimulated by the convocation of the States-General, with the hopes it engendered for the realisation of reform?

There could be two roads towards implementing these proposals: the appropriate measures ought to be taken by the government, and at the same time considerable efforts ought to be put forth by the merchants and manufacturers themselves. It should be stressed that, in spirit and temper, the French trading and industrial bourgeoisie (especially the Huguenots among them) were not very different from their successful competitors, the Dutch, English and others. They had their sufficient share of audacity, adventurousness and enterprise. The trouble was that their efforts were too individualistic in character; with the exception of the Huguenots and of the Marseilles merchants, trading companies were short-lived and feeble, and the competition between different provinces, and even towns, hindered the economic consolidation of the rising class.[2] Finally, the very fact of the division of the French bourgeoisie into a Huguenot section and a Catholic section (of which the former possessed at that time the lion's share of privileges and profits) was a marked peculiarity of France, setting a unique imprint on the process of the formation of the bourgeois class as a whole, and slowing down the course of this process.

The bourgeoisie's power of initiative was shown especially in the way it unremittingly urged the government to adopt the measures which it needed. The number of petitions, memoranda, and so on, addressed to the king

[1] See for more detailed treatment, Lublinskaya, *Frantsiya v nachale XVII veka*, pp. 148 ff.
[2] The discord between the towns of Brittany and Normandy was typical. The Marseilles merchants were distinguished by their unusual solidarity and had a special organisation of their own (*les députés du commerce*), a sort of trading company which dealt quite independently with the king, with French ambassadors, and even with foreign states, zealously defending their interests, often at the expense of the commercial interests of France as a whole (Boiteux, op. cit. pp. 199, 326).

and members of his Council was very large. Furthermore, the bourgeoisie undertook a great deal itself, carrying out its tasks without seeking authority from above. Even in the very inauspicious sphere of foreign competition it again and again tried to find a way out of the existing situation. Essentially, the bourgeoisie everywhere and in every way marched ahead of the government, and demanded from it more than it could give, not because it hoped thereby to obtain more, but in consequence of the very nature of its activity. It needed adequate scope for its development, and it sought to achieve this with appropriate vigour.

Among the governmental measures carried out between 1610 and 1625, that is, before Richelieu had taken up in real earnest questions of trade, the navy and navigation, the following may be mentioned. In 1616 a *Chambre générale du commerce* was set up, at the request of the merchants, being a reformed version of the consultative commission on questions of trade and manufacture which had been established in Henry IV's time.

Some measures were taken to protect French maritime trade, with two main aims in view: defence of the ports and coasts against attack by pirates, which were very frequent along the Mediterranean shore, and struggle against the pirates of the high seas. In 1612–21 several plans were drawn up for the creation of special maritime orders of chivalry, with their own fleets (*Chevaliers de Saint-Louis, Ordre de Saint-Louis*, etc.), similar to the Knights of Malta, in order to hunt down pirates and to escort French merchant ships. In 1624 Richelieu proposed that private persons undertake responsibility for convoys, and after several schemes had been discussed, a contract was concluded with the big tax-farmer Lagrange, who undertook to construct and maintain, over a period of nine years, forty ships for the defence of the coasts; after which these ships would become the property of the state. The contract was ratified by the king's Council, but was evidently not carried out, since only a few years later Richelieu had come to the conclusion that it was necessary to protect maritime trade and the coasts by means of a state fleet.[1] Even before then, however, the government had more than once tried to protect French merchants in conflicts arising abroad.

A number of large trading companies were formed: in 1611 (reorganised in 1618) the *Compagnie de Montmorency pour les Indes Orientales*,[2] in 1620 the *Compagnie de Montmorency pour la Nouvelle-France* (i.e. Canada). In structure, the latter was an example of the 'mixed company' which later became very widespread. The capital was provided by shareholders most of whom were big merchants and shipowners directly engaged in the trade. The manage-

---

[1] Ibid. pp. 47–51.
[2] Montmorency was at that time admiral of France (see chapter 6).

ment of the company was in the hands of a *Collège de Directeurs* and of an *intendant* appointed by the admiral (later, by the king's Council).

In Dieppe some merchants organised a company for trade with Senegal and Gambia; it was headed by the big Rouen shipowner Rosée, but other Rouen merchants were hostile to it.[1]

Nearly all of these companies, just like many of their successors, proved not sufficiently viable. They needed constant oversight and support, and frequently had to be reorganised.

The main reason for their weakness was the generally unfavourable situation in which France found herself on the European and overseas markets; to surmount these obstacles, active governmental support was needed. A very important factor, too, was the antagonism between the rich import-merchants in the major ports—Marseilles, Bordeaux, Rouen, and the rest. This was due to the fact that the organisation of companies with monopoly rights in a given market meant injury to their already long-established private commercial connexions, and infringement of their interests. I have mentioned the hostility of the Marseilles and Rouen merchants to the companies.

Economic and technical conditions had considerable bearing on the problem. Shipbuilding was much more costly in France than in Holland and England.[2] Some of the materials were partly imported from Holland, at great expense, because direct trade with the Baltic countries was difficult for the French.[3] Owing to the fact that the French ports were mostly somewhat shallow, vessels were of small tonnage, not exceeding 200 tons, whereas for ocean voyages vessels of 800–2,000 tons were then needed. For this reason French vessels had only a small carrying capacity, and this shortcoming could not be counterbalanced by their advantages of speed and manœuvrability. The more capacious English and Dutch ships needed only half as large a crew and half as much store of provisions (though the latter were much worse in quality than on French ships), and with the same size crew as a French ship these English and Dutch ships could carry as much as three times the amount of freight. France was famed for its good seamen, but discipline aboard ship was weak, and there were many foreigners among the captains and even among the ratings (Scots, English, Irish, Flemings, etc.).[4]

Thus, as regards shipbuilding and navigation, France was also very much behind her competitors, and this had a severe effect on the state of French trans-oceanic trade (trade with the Levant was in better shape).

[1] Boiteux, op. cit. pp. 79–81, 334.
[2] Later on, Richelieu often preferred to order ships from Holland.
[3] See chapter 6   [4] Boiteux, op. cit. pp. 203–11.

Returning to the measures taken by the government, it must be emphasised that in its main features the internal policy pursued in 1610–25 was rather favourable to the bourgeoisie. The régime of economy in government finance introduced by Luynes in 1617, and the abolition of the *paulette* (on which bourgeois circles had also insisted strongly), were both to the advantage of the bourgeoisie. The victorious struggle against the great nobles, together with the struggle waged everywhere and in every way against Spain, also had the effect of clearing the road for freer development of the bourgeoisie. In the last analysis, the struggle against the Huguenots and the suppression of their special political organisation tended in the same direction, even though as a result of the defeat of the Huguenots La Rochelle lost its wealth. In other words, the general line of the policy of the absolutist government after 1615 was in no way opposed to the requirements of the development of capitalism in France. This is the principal and decisive consideration which must determine one's overall estimate of the government's activity.

Nevertheless, very many specific demands put forward by the bourgeoisie could not be satisfied. The tax system was not reformed in the least;[1] there could, of course, be no question of the radical reform proposed by Montchrétien. The war with the great nobles, and then with the Huguenots, had its debit side as well—it did harm to the country both through the devastation caused by the armies and through the increased taxes and expenditure which it necessitated. There was a similar negative side to the indirect war (*guerre couverte*) against the Habsburgs.

As early as 1610 and the immediately following years, French trade was suffering from the privileged position of the Spanish merchants. The increase in protectionist measures in Spain in the 1620s (the new customs law of 1623, the creation in 1624 of a privileged trading company based on Seville, etc.) closed the Spanish and American markets to many French goods (only grain, linen and haberdashery were exempted). This was a new and heavy blow to the French economy, because sales in those markets brought big returns. Very important consequences also followed from the deflation which was beginning in Spain. The profitability of French exports to Spain, and through Spain to America, was founded, all through the sixteenth century and at the beginning of the seventeenth, on disparity between prices. In France prices were lower than in Spain, and so the cost of producing the French goods was less. By selling them at the high prices prevailing in Spain, the French obtained extra profits. As, however, the flow of precious metals into Spain declined, prices began to fall in that country, and the difference

[1] See chapter 6.

in price-levels, so advantageous to the French, began to be evened out.[1] It was characteristic that, for the same reason, in the 1620s a decline began in the seasonal (and also more lasting) emigration to Catalonia of French pedlars and of craftsmen and land-workers in search of work. This emigration had been going on for a long time, and down to the 1620s was of great benefit to the French, since prices in Catalonia were higher than in France.[2]

The war which began in 1621 between Spain and Holland also did much damage to French maritime trade. The Spanish government replied to the aid given by France to the Dutch[3] by putting all sorts of obstacles and difficulties in the way of French merchants, even confiscating ships carrying grain.[4] This explains the attempts made by the French merchants to find a way out not so much by restoring their previous Spanish trade (they approved of war with Spain, for political reasons) as by winning fresh markets in the Baltic region, in Russia, in the Near and Far East, and more especially in North Africa and America. Significant in this connexion are such facts as the voyages of Norman and Breton merchants to Java and Sumatra in 1620–3,[5] the association formed by Norman merchants for trade with Senegal, the activity of French Catholic missionaries (Capuchins) in the Near East, which was closely linked with the commercial interests of French merchants,[6] and, finally, a certain intensification of colonial and maritime expansion.

To help us appreciate this tendency, there is a source available which is in its way no less interesting than Montchrétien's treatise. Typically, it came into being in similar circumstances.

In the last months of 1626, in connexion with the forthcoming convocation of the Assembly of Notables, at which economic questions were to be discussed,[7] Richelieu received a number of memoranda relating to French trade and navigation.[8] In part, their appearance must be ascribed to the interest

[1] J. Meuvret, 'Circulation monétaire et utilisation économique de la monnaie dans la France du XVIe et du XVIIe siècles', *Études d'histoire moderne et contemporaine*, I (Paris, 1947), 27.
[2] J. Nadal and E. Giralt, *La population catalane de 1553 à 1717. L'immigration française et les autres facteurs de son développement* (Paris, 1960).
[3] See chapter 5.
[4] See data in H. Hauser, *La pensée et l'action économiques du cardinal de Richelieu* (Paris, 1944), pp. 54 ff.
[5] W. Coolhaas, *Generale missiven van gouverneurs-generaal en raden aan heren XVII der verenigde Oostindische Compagnie, Deel I: 1610–1638* (The Hague, 1960).
[6] See Hauser, op. cit. pp. 36 ff.; G. Vaumas, *Lettres et documents du Père Joseph de Paris concernant les missions étrangères (1619–1638)* (Lyons, 1942). See also G. Zhordaniya, *Ocherki iz istorii franko-russkikh otnoshenii kontsa XVI i pervoi poloviny XVII veka [Studies in the history of Franco-Russian relations at the end of the sixteenth century and in the first half of the seventeenth]*, part II (Tbilisi, 1959). I hope to return to the subject of French policy in the Near East in the 1620s.
[7] See Chapter 6.
[8] L. Deschamps. 'La question coloniale au temps de Richelieu et de Mazarin', *Revue de Géographie*, XVI and XVII (Paris, 1885), 367.

which the government had shown in these matters in the immediately preceding years,[1] together with the fact that the *Compagnie des Cent Associés de Morbihan* had just been founded and Richelieu himself appointed *Grand Maître et Surintendant Général du Commerce et de la Navigation*. To some extent these memoranda owed their appearance to the initiative of their writers, who were directly concerned with their subject-matter by reason of their own activities. The situation at the end of 1626 strongly recalled that at the end of 1614, on the eve of the meeting of the States-General. Plans for all kinds of reforms, and rumours of such plans, gave birth, just as twelve years earlier, to much pamphleteering.

One of these memoranda, not printed at the time,[2] but dated 26 November 1626, was signed by a man already known to the cardinal and who later became one of his confidential agents. This was Isaac de Razilly (1580–1637), knight of the Order of Malta, who had sailed a great deal in the Mediterranean and in the Atlantic. He later became vice-admiral and viceroy in Canada. His brother François de Razilly was one of the leaders of a big French expedition to the mouth of the Amazon in 1612–15. Isaac de Razilly wrote his memorandum on the basis of a full knowledge of his subject, reinforced by a wealth of personal experience.

Razilly's memorandum is constructed on the usual plan of those days, and in this respect too is similar to Montchrétien's treatise: first of all, establishment of the fact that a very unsatisfactory situation exists, then enumeration of the measures needed to put it right. But his naval interests cause him to devote much attention to the political consequences of the dismal situation caused by France's lack of a navy, and in particular, the defencelessness of her shores. He stresses that the operations by the Huguenots in 1625, when Soubise seized the mouths of the Loire and the Gironde, together with the islands along the Atlantic coast,[3] damaged not only French trade but also the international prestige of the French government, especially in the eyes of the English.[4] At the same time he lists all the natural advantages of France relevant to the development of navigation: numerous ports, a favourable arrangement of waterways, a sufficiently dense population, plenty of foodstuffs grown in the country, to serve to supply expeditions to distant places, the splendid qualities of French sailors as fighters and as seamen, and so on.[5]

[1] See above, and also the constitutions of the Dutch trading companies, published in the semi-official *Mercure françois* in 1623–4.
[2] It was published only at the end of the nineteenth century. See L. Deschamps, 'Un colonisateur du temps de Richelieu...', *Revue de Géographie*, XIX (July–December 1886).
[3] See Chapter 4.
[4] Richelieu could not remain indifferent to these observations, since the possibility of English aid to the Huguenots greatly worried him (see chapters 4 and 6).
[5] We have shown above that in reality the situation was not so hopeful.

In the second part of his memorandum, entitled *Articles pour persuader ung chascun de risquer sur mer et trouver fonds pour la navigation*, the warlike aspect of the question is also predominant.[1] Razilly considers in detail the types of vessel needed, their equipment for war, and the organisation of coastal defence against pirates. He also deals with the financial and organisational aspects of the establishment of large-scale companies for the conquest of territory in Africa and America. He urges that all the monied sections of French society be drawn into the financing of them, from the courtiers and the financiers to the cities, with the king himself setting the example, along with Richelieu and their entire entourage. Razilly also advises that resources be raised by introducing new taxes on iron, linen, tobacco and so on, and by a saving in military expenditure, through the disbandment of the garrisons of fortresses other than those on the frontiers.[2]

Razilly also considers the use of a well-armed navy from the standpoint of defending and helping French trade (without, of course, excluding the possibility of using it for warlike operations generally, in particular against the Huguenots). This aspect deserves special attention. The writer constantly takes into account the fact that wherever the French have shown themselves as merchants or colonists, they have everywhere encountered resistance from the Spaniards, the Dutch and the English. For this reason they stand in need of strong naval support from the mother country.

After surveying (still from the same standpoint) Africa, Asia and America, Razilly comes to conclusions which are of interest in relation to the questions we are concerned with. First, however, let us consider his views regarding European trade. He considers it as being regulated (that is, sufficiently organised) and sees its principal purpose as being the extraction from neighbouring countries of the maximum quantity of gold and silver with the minimum loss by France of money paid for inessential foreign goods. For this reason he condemns imports from the Levant and from Holland[3] and commends French grain and linen exports to Spain. This opinion testifies to the primitiveness of his position as compared with Montchrétien's. Actually, it is hard even to call him a mercantilist in the strict sense of the word. In accordance with the ideology of a small nobleman[4] Razilly belongs

---

[1] Deschamps, 'Un colonisateur du temps de Richelieu...', *Revue de Géographie*, XIX (July–December 1886), 453–64.

[2] There was at that time much talk of this reform (see chapter 6).

[3] Like Montchrétien (see pp. 127–8) he shows the harm done by the currency speculation carried on by the Dutch. Deschamps, 'Un colonisateur du temps de Richelieu...', *Revue de Géographie*, XIX (July–December 1886), 459–60.

[4] This aspect of the document is well underlined by R. Mandrou in his introduction to the Russian translation of Razilly's memorandum which appeared in *Srednie Veka*, XX (Moscow, 1961), pp. 327–9.

much more with the advocates of the monetary theory which assessed profit only in terms of the money obtained from other countries in exchange for the home country's goods. However, as we have observed, the essence of his memorandum, unlike Montchrétien's, is not to be sought in its economic analysis.

Africa attracts Razilly because of its west coast: Morocco, Senegal, Cape Verde, Guinea, these are the regions he specifies. One could send them iron, glass and spirits and obtain in exchange hides, wax, gum, ivory, musk, gold-dust and Barbary horses. The profit amounted to nearly 30 per cent, and the trade was a reliable one in so far as the Portuguese did not present too much danger to the French.

The situation was different in Asia and the East Indies. The Spaniards and Dutch did not allow the French to enter there. The only suggestion Razilly can make is that direct trading relations be established with Persia, avoiding Turkey by means of an ocean voyage round Africa and up to the Persian Gulf. Franco-Persian trade would bring substantial returns, since the high duties exacted by the Turks would not have to be paid.[1]

Razilly's greatest enthusiasm is excited by America (cf. Montchrétien) and especially by the eastern shore of South America. He regards the establishment of colonies there as a most advantageous and most urgent matter. What wealth was to be found in El Dorado alone! The French should show the greatest perseverance and application in colonising these paradisial regions. Large companies must be formed, and the maximum number of colonists sent there. Then neither the Spaniards nor the Portuguese would be able to oust the French.

It is typical that Razilly assigns the chief role in colonisation not to merchants but to leaders of expeditions, that is, to military and political authorities. Merchants, in his view, only chased after quick profits and did not concern themselves with the future. This opinion is noteworthy in that it provides further evidence of the insufficiently profitable nature at that time of American trade and colonisation, unless supplemented by systematic plundering of American territory and, in particular, of precious metals. It is typical that throughout this memorandum Razilly utters not one word about this; a contest with the Spaniards on this issue was quite beyond the strength of France, and a strong privateering fleet would have been needed to plunder the gold and silver obtained by Spain in the New World by sea, in the English fashion.

Is this perhaps the reason for the failure of the attempts at colonisation

[1] *Revue de Géographie*, XIX (July–December 1886), 460. Richelieu tried to reach Persia by a shorter route, through Russia (see Zhordaniya, op. cit.).

and trans-oceanic trade made by the French in the following years? It cannot be regarded as accidental that later on Richelieu concentrated his attention not on America (and certainly not South America) but on the regions Razilly rather despised—Persia, and the Near East generally. With his usual sound and balanced realism, the cardinal sought those routes which could be utilised as soon as possible, with the least expenditure possible and the maximum possible results, not only economic but also political. Therefore, as soon as he was convinced of the incorrectness of the view that the Levant trade was unprofitable (this view was held by both Montchrétien and Razilly), which happened soon after 1626, he chose to direct his efforts along this path, which was already a well-trodden one, and to get from it many and various advantages.

What is the principal factor in the general tendencies which emerge from the sources we have analysed? Without anticipating the conclusions to be drawn about the existence or otherwise of an economic crisis in the seventeenth century, let us for the moment merely note what can be said about the state of the French economy in 1610–29, as I have described it.

There can be no doubt that France in 1610, possessing fairly well-developed manufactories and an extensive trade, and endowed with great natural resources and a population which was dense by the standards of that age, nevertheless found herself in considerable difficulties. The capitalist element in the economy should have been developing, if not faster, then at any rate no slower than under Henry IV, in 1598–1610. Yet even the possibility of maintaining production and trade at the previous level was being called in question.

Equally well established is the fact that one cannot put all the blame on the civil war. At the time when Montchrétien wrote his treatise this had only just begun; yet the economic *malaise* was already quite plain to him. Later, in 1615–29, internal and external wars did, of course, deepen this *malaise*.

The most important factor was the backwardness of France, as compared with Holland and England, in the level of capitalist development in industry. Of course, the connexion between industry and agriculture, as regards the development of capitalism as a whole, is very important indeed, and there is no need to insist upon this. Nevertheless, it seems to me that it is necessary to devote attention to the lag in the development of what was the principal sphere of production at that stage.

France lagged behind her competitors in respect of all the important indices. The division of labour in French manufactories was at a lower level; the shortage of skilled workers did not allow the entrepreneurs to establish an adequate hierarchy of wage-levels. State subsidies, which were absolutely necessary at that time, were casual and sporadic, and small in amount, while accumulation of money was not on a large enough scale; France was excluded from that direct plundering of colonies which nourished primitive accumulation in Holland and Spain, and indirectly in England as well.

The consequence of all this was that French industrial products were comparatively expensive. As a result, the French commercial and industrial bourgeoisie was unable to compete successfully with the Dutch and the English in its own home market, and to some extent also in foreign markets. It was obliged to use its capital in other ways, and this capital either flowed directly into the sphere of state credit, through loans and tax-farming, or was employed for the purchase of offices, that is, indirectly made its way into the same unproductive sphere. The purchase of land had the same effect. Now and then, French merchants even lent their money to Dutch and Spanish merchants. Consequently, even those profits which were obtained directly from trade and production were not entirely devoted to the expansion of bourgeois economy.

French shipbuilding and navigation, and therefore also French trans-oceanic trade, was behind English and Dutch, technically and economically. The urban particularism of the merchants was very strong in France, too. That was why the trading companies which arose spontaneously, without being organised by the government, were usually small, which made it still harder for them to compete in overseas markets.

For all these reasons, the French bourgeoisie was very interested indeed in increased protection, and the government of France endeavoured to meet its needs in this respect. But first it was necessary to solve a number of very important problems in the sphere of internal politics, in particular to put an end to the Huguenot 'state within the state' and to restore the health of government finance.

CHAPTER 4

The suppression of the Huguenot 'State within the State'

THE strengthening of French absolutism in the first half of the seventeenth century did not serve the interests of the ruling class alone. Without a strong state power it was not possible to solve the country's most important economic problems or to ensure the maintenance of national sovereignty. The political premise for fulfilling these progressive tasks was victory by the central authority over the grandees. In 1620 the king's army triumphed on the battlefields, but this was only the first stage in the political annihilation of the grandees. The next stage was to destroy the Huguenot 'party', which provided them with a powerful military and political reserve force.

The struggle against the Huguenots, with the aim of abolishing their political independence, extended over a long period and took the form of a succession of military campaigns.

In 1620, as a result of the expedition to Béarn, the government strengthened its position on the frontier with Spain, in the Huguenots' rear.

In 1621, a campaign was fought in the Huguenot provinces of the southwest—Poitou, Saintonge, Guyenne—and about sixty Huguenot cities and fortresses were taken. These regions were overcome, with the exception of the most important Huguenot base, La Rochelle—which, nevertheless, was cut off by the construction near it of some large royal forts. An attempt, however, to capture Montauban, the key to Languedoc, proved unsuccessful.

In 1622 military operations were transferred to Languedoc itself; it capitulated to the king and was occupied by the royal forces. Thus, the Huguenot South was brought to heel. All that remained was to conquer La Rochelle; but that required a fleet. In 1625 the Huguenots, preparing to resist the inevitable siege of La Rochelle, seized the islands which protect the city on the seaward side. At the beginning of 1626, however, a victory by the royal army restored the *status quo*.

In 1627–8 the siege of La Rochelle took place. The city was not only blockaded, but also completely cut off from the Huguenot 'mainland', whose resources were in any case to a great extent exhausted as a result of the earlier campaigns. Together with the absence of aid from the English, this circumstance was decisive in determining the fall of La Rochelle. In 1629 the last centres of Huguenot resistance in the mountainous areas of Languedoc were crushed.

Even this brief enumeration of stages shows that they had a recognisable sequence and correlation. They signified a gradual increase in the success achieved by the government, and its ability to carry through a definite strategical plan. The special importance of the campaigns of 1620–2 deserves to be emphasised. They are always depicted in writings on this period as having been unnecessary and fruitless, and even as bringing shame on the government.[1] But this estimate does not correspond to reality. As I shall show, despite partial failures, the campaigns of 1620–2 were absolutely necessary, and on the whole successful from the government's point of view. It would not have been possible to undertake and carry through a siege of La Rochelle and put an end to the existence of the Huguenot political organisation without first capturing important positions in the south-west.

To justify this view I shall pay particular attention to the campaigns of 1620–22, and deal with them in rather more detail than with the well-known events of 1625–9.

The reign of Louis XIII (1610–43) has long been divided by French historians and, generally speaking, by all foreign historians, into two main periods: before Richelieu's accession to power (1610–April 1624), and the administration of Richelieu (1624–December 1642).[2] The first period is usually disposed of very briefly. In the second, the six years between 1624 and 1630 are sometimes specially picked out as those in which Richelieu's influence was gradually growing, until in 1630 he triumphed over all the parties at court.

This neat and superficially satisfactory chronological division of the reign is derived from the principal facts in the life-story of the chief minister. Up to a point it is justified by the circumstance that these biographical facts correspond in some degree to the stages in the process of consolidating French absolutism. But this correspondence is only partly valid, and the date for which it is least valid is 1624, the year of Richelieu's entry into the king's Council.

If we study the history of France in that period not from the standpoint of the biography of Richelieu, waiting through 1620–4 for the moment to strike, and preparing for it by working on public opinion to promote his own

[1] See below, p. 152.
[2] Louis XIII survived Richelieu by only five months.

interests, but from the standpoint of the tasks which confronted the government in its internal and external policies, it becomes clear that the turning-point occurred not in 1624 but in 1621 (or, more precisely, in the second half of 1620), immediately after the victory of the king's army over the army of the nobles at Ponts-de-Cé, that is to say, while Luynes was still chief minister. It was then that the road towards the strengthening of absolutism was taken, a road which Richelieu followed thereafter with increasing success. Even at this early date the government was in a position to undertake a number of important tasks, the first and foremost of these being the political unification of the country, that is, the suppression of the Huguenot 'state within the state'. This task, of really urgent importance, was beyond the capacity of Henry IV in the twelve years of his reign when peace prevailed (1598–1610), though it undoubtedly figured in his plans.

For this reason, the new period in the history of France in the first half of the seventeenth century begins not in 1624 but in 1620, and it concludes in 1630, when, as a result of the external war, the country was faced with problems of a different order. For nearly a decade, with interruptions, a desperate civil war was raged between the government and the Huguenots, who eventually suffered defeat. This war involved nearly all those who held the most important government posts in those days, being passed on by each of them to his successor like the baton in a relay-race. It dominates the history of this decade, and the government looked upon it as the most important state task, to which all others were subordinated. It was not Richelieu who began this war, though it was he who brilliantly concluded it.

An exposition of the events of 1620–9 will show whether this view of the decade can be regarded as justified. First, however, we must give some attention to analysing the traditional view of the four years 1620–4 which preceded Richelieu's accession to power, because this is especially significant in relation to this particular question.[1]

The cardinal himself devoted considerable effort to denigrating and defaming his predecessors. In the *Testament politique* their activities were described as disastrous, bringing the country to complete collapse: we find the same point of view in the *Mémoires* which he inspired. This detraction is expressed very sharply in the numerous pamphlets with which Richelieu was directly or indirectly associated, and these views were repeated in many works published between the seventeenth and nineteenth centuries. In the

---

[1] Let us recall the basic facts in the history of 1620–4. Luynes's administration lasted until 14 December 1621; then, until February 1624, came the administration of the Brûlarts, father and son (Chancellor Sillery and Secretary of State Puisieux), who were succeeded for a few months by the *surintendant* La Vieuville. While the latter was still in the saddle, Richelieu entered the king's Council, on 29 April 1624; La Vieuville was dismissed on 13 August 1624.

second half of the nineteenth century, however, they were called in question by Cousin and Zeller.[1] Criticising Richelieu's pamphlets and *Mémoires* on the basis of documents from the archives, they undertook a sort of rehabilitation of the policy of Luynes, examining it more objectively. Even for them, however, Richelieu remained the chief hero of those years, although he was still obliged to work in secret, and the theme which most interested them was his gradual advance to power.

The views of Cousin and Zeller had only slight influence on the conception which had become traditional, and which received fresh support in the biography of Richelieu in several volumes, written by Gabriel Hanotaux, which began to appear in the 1890s;[2] for a long time (to a large extent this is true even now) it determined the opinion generally accepted in historical writing and among the public at large.

Hanotaux contrasted the strong rule of Richelieu with the vacillating and unsuccessful policy of the mediocre and cowardly Luynes and his equally unimpressive immediate successors. Hanotaux's fundamental position was that Luynes, in contrast to Cardinal Richelieu's guiding principle of *raison d'état*, was guided by purely personal considerations, endeavouring to retain at any cost his unique position and the confidence of the king. Because of this he neglected the grandeur of France and its prestige in international relations, submitted to the influence of the papal Nuncio, conducted a Catholic and pro-Spanish policy, and so on.[3] Yet the situation in Europe was such that France could have assumed the role of arbiter, and her vigorous intervention could have prevented the development of the war then beginning, which, as a result of the passivity of France in those years, flared up later on and raged for many years, with terrible consequences. Hanotaux considered that not only the destiny of France but also that of all Europe depended on the line to be taken by Luynes.[4]

Luynes, in Hanotaux's opinion, proved unequal to the task, which demanded exceptional breadth of political understanding and a gift of foresight, based on an analysis of the over-all situation and a weighing of all the possibilities. Luynes did not grasp the situation which had taken shape. 'At the very moment when a vigorous intervention in European affairs would have ensured the preponderance of France, the wretched favourite reopened

[1] V. Cousin, 'Le Duc et Connétable de Luynes', *Journal des Savants* (Paris, 1861–3); B. Zeller, *Richelieu et les ministres de Louis XIII de 1621 à 1624* (Paris, 1880).

[2] G. Hanotaux, *Histoire du cardinal de Richelieu*, I–VI (Paris, 1893–1947). The four years which interest us are studied in Volume II, which appeared in 1896.

[3] Here Hanotaux repeats closely the arguments of the pamphlets of 1619–21 directed against Luynes (see below, pp. 155–6, 195).

[4] Hanotaux, op. cit. II, part 2, 357, 358, 382, 383, 386.

the period of civil strife, and soon afterward that of the wars of religion.'[1] This is how Hanotaux judges Luynes's decision to begin the war against the Huguenots. Luynes, as he sees it, was faced with a choice—either to fight the Huguenots or to fight the Habsburgs. Because he did not realise that it was imperative to choose the second alternative, he chose the first.

Hanotaux's fundamental thesis is clear enough, but he subsequently becomes entangled in insoluble contradictions. He cannot but admit that the Huguenots really did threaten the national unity of France, that they strove to exploit the weakness of the royal authority after Henry IV's death to enlarge their privileges, going so far as to ally themselves not only with Protestant states but also with Spain, and so on.[2] Moreover, he comes to the conclusion that, essentially, Luynes had no choice, that the Huguenots, 'by their fatal and unaccountable insolence' directly compelled him to move against them,[3] that his decision was in accord with the traditions of French national policy, the chief aim of which was the internal unity of the country.[4] Thus, his condemnation of Luynes for choosing war against the Huguenots is virtually cancelled out.

Hanotaux's judgments on the foreign-policy tasks of France are no less contradictory. A moment earlier, as we have seen, he was blaming Luynes for his decision not to intervene in arms in the affairs of Europe. But almost on the very same pages Hanotaux declares that what was needed was not to choose between internal and external war, but to follow two lines simultaneously: to hold the Huguenots in check, and to strike at Catholic Spain. For this, however, qualities of dexterity and strength were needed, genius of the highest order, qualities which Luynes lacked.[5] Finally, he sets out the general line of policy which, in his opinion, should have been adopted, which Luynes failed to follow, and which the cardinal was later to carry through—a sort of 'mission' entrusted to France, a 'truly French' policy. It was necessary to remain aloof from the wars between the Protestant (northern and republican) powers and the Catholic (southern and monarchical) ones and to oblige them to exhaust themselves in conflict with each other. Then France would be able to establish in Europe an equilibrium favourable to her own interests.

Hanotaux used comparatively few sources—the despatches of Italian ambassadors; memoirs, including Richelieu's; some archive material—but these nevertheless influenced to a certain extent the final views of this writer, obliging him to deviate somewhat from his preconceived opinions, so that

---

[1] Hanotaux, op. cit. II, part 2, p. 405.
[2] Ibid. pp. 407–14.
[3] Ibid. pp. 405, 432, 440.
[4] Ibid. p. 486.
[5] Ibid. p. 416.

he was forced into this contradictory position. Moreover, there is an arbitrariness of interpretation in Hanotaux's ideas about the problems of foreign policy facing France in this period. In reality, a country weakened by seven years of civil war was in no position to claim the role of arbiter in Europe. The causes for the prolongation of the Thirty Years War must be sought first and foremost in Germany itself. As was shown by the course of the war, the resources at the Habsburgs' disposal were very substantial, and could not be eliminated by a single successful campaign. Even Richelieu, with his 'genius of a high order', was unable to remain aloof from the *mêlée* and take advantage of the mutual exhaustion of the combatants; France had to enter the war, and was victorious neither at once (far from it) nor without paying a heavy price. Finally, Hanotaux seems to forget that only after the capture of La Rochelle did Richelieu launch the campaigns of 1629–30. Until then the cardinal steadily restricted himself to diplomatic *démarches* in his dealings with the Habsburgs, that is, he behaved very much as Luynes had behaved.

Hanotaux sees the government's policy in 1622–4 almost exclusively from the standpoint of Richelieu's approach to the realisation of his cherished aim, entry into the king's Council. He fails to make a genuine analysis of the events of those years, in his haste to reach as soon as possible that date, 'ever memorable' for the cardinal, 13 August 1624, when at last the glorious personal rule of Richelieu began. Hanotaux merely mentions that the Brûlarts (Sillery and Puisieux), who were in charge of affairs in 1622–3, procrastinated endlessly, never deciding on any active step against the Habsburgs.[1] After their dismissal the *surintendant* La Vieuville went over to a more determined policy, but took fright at the difficulties confronting him and turned for help to Richelieu, who within three months brought about his dismissal.[2]

Tapié, the author of a recent work of a general character on France under Louis XIII and Richelieu, entitles the short chapter he devotes to 1617–24 'Louis XIII et la cause catholique', and this title defines Tapié's fundamental conception very well. He accords little significance to the government's internal policy in the period between the death of Henry IV and the rise of Richelieu, considering that the events of those years affected the interests of only a few people and that the main road of history lay elsewhere, in profound changes taking place in the life of France, the results of which made themselves felt later on. No substantial changes were to be observed in the economy in those years, he thinks, but such changes did occur in the realm of ideology. These amounted to a renaissance of Catholicism, 'a rejuvenated

[1] Ibid. pp. 506–10, 528, 532–5.   [2] Ibid. pp. 549, 550.

Catholicism...at once coherent in doctrine and multiform in operation, which was able to penetrate the most varied sections of society and everywhere to modify ways of thought and ways of life', a Catholicism whose clergy 'could be said to be shaping a new society'.[1] This Catholicism exerted great influence on the naturally pious king and even more on Luynes, who proved to be merely a puppet in the hands of the *dévots*, an influential group composed of prelates and certain courtiers.[2]

As Tapié sees it, the king and Luynes failed to understand the tasks before France in both internal and external policy. Europe at the beginning of the seventeenth century was being torn apart by the tendency to form national states, on the one hand, and, on the other, the tendency to defend the traditions of former medieval unity—now identified with the hegemony of the Habsburgs. The Catholic church, with its ideal of spiritual unity, worked to promote the latter tendency. 'In general, Europe vacillated between the idea which it had formed of living together in unity, and fear lest this unity be effected by violence, with sacrifice of the sovereignty of states and of everyone's individual right to control for himself his way of life, his thinking and his business affairs.'[3] At this critical moment of acute vacillation France could, says Tapié, by active intervention have considerably changed the course of events. But the men at the helm lacked bold initiative, strong will and prudence, and they did not grasp the significance of the situation that had come about; their acts were governed by routine, frequently they avoided taking definite decisions, and so on.[4] Faced with the need to choose, they were incapable of discerning where France's fundamental interests lay. They thought that a struggle with Spain would strengthen the Protestants of Europe, who were a menace to royal thrones everywhere and allies of rebels inside France itself—that is, that it would strengthen the Huguenots. The mistake made by Luynes and the king in going to war with the Huguenots lay in the fact that the latter in reality presented no danger either to the monarchy or to the national unity of France. The Catholics asserted that the Huguenots were working to establish a republic in the Dutch style, but this was false. Furthermore, many Protestant grandees stood aloof from the struggle. Only two regions rebelled—the provinces along the Atlantic coast, and Languedoc. The two years of war with the Huguenots (1621–2) brought the king little glory and insignificant results, and during this same period Spain so greatly strengthened its position that French diplomacy was rendered impotent. The change of ministers in the first half of 1624 was

---

[1] V. L. Tapié, *La France de Louis XIII et de Richelieu* (Paris, 1952), pp. 100, 101, 109.
[2] Ibid. p. 145. [3] Ibid. p 123.
[4] Ibid. pp. 122, 139, 142, 143, 145, 158.

caused by the personal antagonism between members of the Council and the unsuccessful financial policy of La Vieuville; then, at last, Richelieu took the helm.[1]

As we see, Tapié's views are very similar to Hanotaux's. He lays even greater stress than his predecessor on the religious factor. The difference between them lies in Tapié's denial that a 'Huguenot danger' existed. I shall show later the incompatibility of this view with Richelieu's subsequent actions, but here let me point out that the reason for Tapié's view, which I think mistaken, is his lack of attention to the significance of the social and political struggle waged in France during the 'interregnum' between Henry IV and Richelieu. This is why he does not estimate properly the real possibilities before the government. Shifting the centre of gravity to the foreign-policy aspect he, no less arbitrarily than Hanotaux, discusses what the government ought to have done, rather than analyses what steps it actually took and why.

The year 1620 was a turning-point in the internal policy of the French government not because the latter ventured for the first time to take determined measures (such measures had been taken earlier, for instance in 1616–17), but because these measures were crowned with success. It was precisely then, when the revolt of the grandees and the *noblesse d'épée* attained its widest scope, when the area embraced by the troubles covered almost half of the entire country, when the Huguenots were furnishing effective support to the leader of all the forces opposed to the 'tyrant' Luynes, namely, the Queen Mother Marie de Médicis—it was at that critical moment that the true source of the government's strength was fully revealed: the support given to it by the towns. In 1620 the towns took decisive steps. They hit out at the nobles and, despite the noble garrisons occupying their citadels, opened their gates to the small royal army. Thanks to this support, the latter advanced much faster than had been expected by the grandees, who had counted on the king being preoccupied with sieges of the towns of Normandy while the provinces along the Loire and the Huguenot areas completed their armament. The towns disrupted these plans for a long-drawn-out defence of Normandy. That was why, at the battle of Ponts-de-Cé, the king's army was faced by only part of the enemy's forces, because the rest had not had time to concentrate. This victory for Louis XIII was made possible by the support of the towns.

The peace concluded by Marie de Médicis and the king (actually, by Richelieu and Luynes) deprived the party of the grandees, both Catholic and

[1] Ibid. pp. 139, 148, 151, 160, 161.

Huguenot, of leaders, of watchwords, and of the support of the *noblesse d'épée*. The seven years' civil war came to an end.[1]

This swift and brilliant success brought out the best in the nineteen-year-old king. The warlike valour he showed in this first campaign stood out all the more vividly beside the military mediocrity of Luynes. Louis XIII personally participated in the marches, sieges and battles, conversing with his officers and soldiers. The army for the first time saw its king, framed in the aura of his father's soldierly glory, and appreciated, with unfeigned admiration, his fortitude, his cool courage, his self-control, and his simplicity of manner. But among those who were close to the king, and later also in wider circles, a rumour began, and was gradually confirmed, that Louis was not capable of governing in person. Experienced members of the royal household and statesmen avidly sought in the modest and brief-spoken young man (he stammered, and tried to speak as little as possible) the features of his father, that outstanding commander, politician, diplomat and wit, the fascinating and lively 'Béarnais'. They sought them but did not find them. The age was favourable to the early development of the individual generally, and in particular to the early manifestation of talent. In the seventeenth century, as in the Middle Ages, childhood and adolescence ended early; the young generation of every stratum of society began to stand on their own feet not later than the age of fourteen or fifteen. Louis XIII proved to be a fine officer, but no general. He had neither much intellect nor much shrewdness.[2]

Several good inclinations were observed in him as a child. He was a quick, cheerful, bright boy, and adored music. He was brought up strictly, and attempts were made to correct, by beating, his worst defect, extreme stubbornness; but without success. He grew up in the palace of Saint-Germain, outside the capital, among his numerous brothers and sisters, stepbrothers and stepsisters (all Henry IV's children, legitimate and illegitimate alike, were brought up together). He soon showed a sense of his personal dignity, and jealously defended his special position as the Dauphin, the future king of France, refusing to acknowledge as equals his elder brothers the Vendômes (sons of Henry IV and Gabrielle d'Estrées). After the tragic death of his father

---

[1] See A. D. Lublinskaya, *Frantsiya v nachale XVII veka (1610–1620 gg.)* [France at the beginning of the seventeenth century, 1610–1620] (Leningrad, 1959), pp. 286–90.

[2] In the twentieth century several works appeared in which the writers tried to 'rehabilitate' Louis XIII, pointing out, to counterbalance the picture drawn by Dumas and Hugo, that he had many positive qualities. Using a great deal of material from the records they really did show that the king was not stupid, weak-willed or small-minded; at times he was even capable of acting more or less independently. But, of course, all these 'corrections' could not show that Louis XIII possessed political talent. (See L. Batiffol, *Le Roi Louis XIII à vingt ans* (Paris, 1910) and *Richelieu et Le Roi Louis XIII* (Paris, 1934); P. Erlanger, *Louis XIII* (Paris, 1936); Ch. Romain, *Louis XIII, un grand roi méconnu* (Paris, 1934); L. Vaunois, *Vie de Louis XIII* (Paris, 1944).

he spent some unhappy years. His mother did not love him; he was re-membered only when there were official ceremonies to be performed. Seven years of neglect and disregard caused him to become reserved, two-faced and self-possessed to a degree unusual for his age. At sixteen he took part along with Luynes in a secret conspiracy, and carried out a palace revolution, giving his assent to the murder of the favourite d'Ancre and the disgracing of his own mother.

He continued to act as he did at nineteen. But he knew how to recognise and appreciate other men's brains and talents. Richelieu found in him one who really was *le meilleur maître qui fût jamais*—a serious man with a strong will and a high sense of the duty laid upon him by his position as king. He was unaffected and had no concern for etiquette. Hunting, to which, like Henry IV before him, he was enthusiastically devoted, enabled him to spend many days in the heart of the woods and in modest country houses, far from the court, which he often found a disagreeable place. Frequently, during campaigns and progresses, he had occasion to meet the common people; like his father, he did not shun them. He did not permit looseness in speech or behaviour around him, and was himself diffident. His piety was sincere.

In the period under review, Luynes was his only close friend. Being twenty-three years older, he guided the king in all matters. The first three years of his administration (1617–20) were fortunate. After the Assembly of Notables at Rouen at the end of 1617 Luynes introduced some reforms (abolition of the *paulette*,[1] reduction in the nobles' pensions, disbandment of some regiments) which effected a certain saving in expenditure, and so on.[2] The revolt of the grandees in 1619, when they tried to exploit the discontent among the *noblesse d'épée* caused by Luynes's reforms, was put down with very few concessions on the part of the government. The campaign of 1620 ended in a brilliant victory. Luynes ruled on his own, sometimes accepting the counsel of those ministers of Henry IV who were living out the last days of their long lives, and not replacing those diplomats already in posts. He did not allow any of the grandees to take part in high politics, and entrusted all responsible missions to his brothers. He became extremely rich, and linked himself with the great house of Rohan by marrying the beautiful Marie de Montbazon (later Duchesse de Chevreuse). The king left everything in his hands, but sometimes, when 'unburdening his heart' to those around him, he would humorously complain to them of 'King Luynes' (just as he did later on in relation to Richelieu). The grandees hated Luynes; in the pamph-lets they inspired, his name was dragged in the mud; he was jeered at and

---

[1] On the *paulette* see below, pp. 181–2.
[2] *Documents d'histoire publiés par E. Griselle*, I (Paris, 1910), 41.

foul witticisms were showered on him on account of his origin from among the petty nobility. Some of the courtiers, among whom there were many intelligent and perceptive men, regarded Luynes as a man of mediocre qualities, but adroit and tactful. They esteemed him for his simple and courteous manners, his fidelity in many ways to the as yet patriarchal customs of the court of Henry IV. Provided they were not themselves Huguenots, they praised his diplomacy and his policy directed towards destroying the political power of the Huguenot party.

The triumph over the nobles in the summer of 1620 put point-blank the question of the future policy to be followed by the government. It could decide to be satisfied with what had been achieved and rest on its laurels. It could continue the campaign, directing this against those still unbroken allies of the Queen Mother, the Huguenots. It could go over to an active policy in the field of international relations. Luynes chose the second of these three policies; to attack the Huguenots. The reason for his decision must be explained in some detail.

From the first years of its appearance, that is, from the 1560s, right down to the Edict of Nantes in 1598, the so-called Huguenot party (the union of Huguenot grandees, nobles and cities) maintained the initiative in armed struggle against the government, in order to defend the freedom of the Calvinist religion and also the numerous privileges which it managed to secure for itself in the course of nearly forty years' existence. At the time of the promulgation of the Edict of Nantes these privileges—military, economic, financial, political—were very great.

After 1598 and down to 1620 this defensive struggle (which, as we shall see later, was quite inevitable) was carried on mainly by legal means, within the framework of laws provided by the Edict of Nantes. From 1620 onward the initiative in the struggle passed to the government, which settled accounts by force of arms with the Huguenot 'state within the state'.

Thus we can observe three periods: 1560–98, 1598–1620, and 1620–9— periods respectively of strength, of the beginning of decline, and of the destruction of the Huguenot party as such.

Certain features of the party's situation in 1620 were important in relation to subsequent events. On the whole, its situation was already far from satisfactory. It had been bad in 1600–10 and had continued to deteriorate since then. The government of Henry IV was not at all concerned to fulfil the Edict of Nantes with precision. The king did not infringe the freedom of conscience of his former co-religionists, but without making any fuss and, so to speak, without warning, he endeavoured to encroach on the political rights which they had been given, not by the Edict itself but according to its supplementary articles, granted 'by the king's grace' for eight years, and thereafter more than once renewed. The payment of the garrisons was cut by half and allowed to fall into arrears. Fortresses whose commanders became converted to Catholicism were not restored to the Huguenots. Permission was not given for repairing the fortifications of Huguenot cities. Access to offices was made, in practice, very difficult for Huguenots.[1] Finally, the militant Counter-Reformation, feeling its growing strength, carried on active missionary work in several provinces.

Instead of their original fairly widespread extension over the whole country, the Huguenots were now in a position where their predominant, or considerable, power was confined to a few south-western provinces: Poitou, Saintonge, Guyenne, Gascony, Languedoc, Béarn, together with the Dauphiné. The basic block of Huguenot areas in the south-west was linked with the outlying Dauphiné to the east through the Vivarais district (on the right bank of the Rhône, between the river and the Cévennes), which consequently possessed great strategic importance.

These were mainly maritime and mountain areas. Many of the towns in these areas (about a hundred) were Huguenot fortresses (*places de sûreté*), with permanent garrisons. It was supposed that these fortresses would merely guarantee places of refuge to the Huguenots in the event of possible persecution by the Catholics. To a certain extent this was indeed so, but only to a certain extent. In practice these towns were outside control by the royal authority. In the larger centres power was in the hands of the city councils, and in the middle-sized and smaller ones in the hands of Huguenot grandees and nobles, who acquired these places by inheritance.

There were about 800 Calvinist communities (*églises*) in all in the whole of France, uniting 350,000–400,000 families, that is, about 7–8 per cent of the total population. Of these, 70–75 per cent were in the south-western provinces and the Dauphiné, and about 15 per cent in Normandy and Brittany. In the other provinces Calvinist communities existed only in ones and twos.[2] To the north of the Loire the Huguenots had no fortresses.

In many places in the Huguenot provinces Catholic worship had already disappeared in the 1560s, while in others, mainly in large towns, small Catholic communities continued to exist. Here and there, small groups of Catholics assembled in chapels outside the city boundaries. There was, of course, even in the very heart of 'Huguenot territory', one stronghold of

---

[1] H. de Rohan, *Mémoires. Collection Michaud et Poujoulat*, 2nd series, (Paris, 1837), 494.
[2] C. Malingre, *Histoire de la rébellion excitée en France par les rebelles de la religion prétendue réformée depuis le restablissement de la foy catholique en Béarn en l'année 1620 jusques à l'an 1622* (Paris, 1623), pp. 3, 149.

Catholicism, the city of Toulouse, and also some large Catholic towns, such as Bordeaux and Grenoble, and fortresses in the hands of Catholic grandees and other nobles. But these did not determine the overall situation in the provinces concerned.

At the beginning of the seventeenth century the Huguenot party was noticeably shrinking. Conversion of Huguenot nobles to Catholicism took place on a substantial scale, especially in those provinces (Brittany, Provence, Burgundy, Champagne) where the Huguenots possessed no cities or fortresses.[1] The government and the local authorities did a great deal to encourage it.[2] Frequently the initiative actually came from them, for renunciation of Calvinism in the great majority of cases was related not only to religious beliefs but also, and even primarily, to material interests. Huguenots went over to Catholicism in those instances where they were offered pensions, offices at court or military appointments, and where the church property they had seized during the civil wars of the sixteenth century was bought back from them or exchanged for other property. Officials were awarded titles of nobility, ministers were given pensions and financial compensation.[3]

The Huguenot nobles learned from the examples set by the behaviour of their grandees. Marshal Châtillon, the grandson of Admiral Coligny, left the Huguenot party. In 1621 the leader of the Huguenots in the Dauphiné, the Duc de Lesdiguières, turned his coat, receiving in return the constable's sword, that is, the highest military appointment. The Huguenots were persecuted most severely and unrelentingly in the 1620s by the Prince de Condé, son and grandson of the chief leaders of the French Calvinists in the sixteenth century. It must be remembered that when any prominent Huguenot nobleman (not to mention a grandee) went over to Catholicism he was followed in this move by all his family and his noble *clientèle*.[4] As a result, the number of members of the Calvinist communities grew smaller and smaller; for those who remained, the cost of maintaining the community became very burdensome.[5]

Among other grandees, such respected old leaders as Bouillon, Sully and others, remained neutral, in the political sense. For the Huguenot party as a whole this was only a little preferable to actual renunciation of Calvinism by these men, since it was already impossible to count on their aid and influence.

---

[1] Malingre, op. cit. p. 3.
[2] By rallying to the Catholic faith they would 'rally more closely to the king's service', for their Calvinism 'to some extent estranges them from that complete obedience and devotion which subjects owe to their lord'. (*Documents d'histoire*, I, 408.)
[3] Ibid. I, 403–6; II, 372, 373.   [4] Ibid. I, 399, 408.
[5] Malingre, op. cit. p. 3.

The only real leader, and the soul of the entire party, was Sully's son-in-law, the duke and peer Henri de Rohan, Prince de Léon (1579–1638), one of the greatest aristocrats of France. Proud in the distinctively Breton way, the first duke in his ancient family (which displeased his mother, since the family's motto proclaimed: *Roi ne puis, duc ne daigne, Rohan suis*), not a very highly educated man, but intelligent and steadfast, an excellent politician and demagogue, and a talented general and organiser, Rohan was undoubtedly an outstanding person, *un grand personnage*.[1] The *Mémoires* and treatises he wrote tell us of his political and religious *credo*. The Huguenot party, with its organisation and military strength, was for Rohan not only a 'sacred cause' but also the chief basis for the power of the grandees of *both* religions. As we shall see later, this opinion was shared by the Catholic grandees as well. Objectively it was a sound one. The events of 1610–20 showed clearly that in the conditions of that time grandees could achieve a certain degree of success only if all of them joined forces, regardless of religion. The tragedy of Rohan's activity was that with tremendous energy he again and again strove to restore the crumbling unity of the Huguenot party, trying to revive the fire from the burnt-out ashes. Michelet called him an *amateur des causes perdues*.

In his life and manners Rohan conformed to the strict and plain ways of his native Brittany and of the Huguenots of the sixteenth century. A small man with a harsh, unattractive face, he was a tireless, unpretentious and brave warrior, accustomed both to the frosts of the mountains and to southern heat. There is no reason to doubt the sincerity and profundity of his religious sentiments.

Rohan appeared at the head of his party only with the campaign of 1621. Until then, the highest authority among the Huguenots was wielded by the last companions of Henry IV, the dukes of Bouillon and Sully, and Duplessis-Mornay. But in the period 1610–20 he persistently pushed forward towards his aim, attracting attention by his energy and the consistency of his actions. In 1612 he captured an important strategic town in Saintonge, St-Jean-d'Angély, covering La Rochelle from the landward side, but the principal arena of his activity was the mountainous regions of Upper Guyenne and Upper Languedoc.

His closest relatives and coevals, his brother the Duc de Soubise and his brother-in-law, Sully's son, the Duc de Rosny, were not distinguished by any talents, and Soubise, inconstant and fussy, hindered more than he helped. Rohan's real assistants were his retinue of Huguenot noblemen, who were nearly all talented and courageous officers. But, to his sorrow, this cohort

---

[1] G. Tallemant des Réaux, *Historiettes. Texte intégral établi et annoté par A. Adam* (Paris, 1960), I, 620–1.

dwindled before his eyes, through losses in battles and sieges. Richelieu, who was a good judge of people, later took many of Rohan's companions into the king's army, as he took Rohan himself after the destruction of the Huguenot party.

And so, a shrinking territory and dwindling numbers gave the Huguenot party cause for alarm. As abandonment of Calvinism occurred most frequently among nobles and grandees, the military power of the Huguenots was also on the decline, a circumstance which proved fatal to them in the wars of 1621-9.

The Huguenots' standing army was quartered in cities assigned to it for this purpose. Garrisons which were large for that time, and in relation to the towns where they were stationed, were distributed among the strategically most important centres: in towns along the Loire, covering the approaches to the Huguenot provinces of the south-west: Saumur (364 men) and Jargeau (180 men), and also in the fortresses of Poitou: at Thouars (165 men), Niort (210 men), Châtellerault (197 men), and Fontenay-le-Comte (87 men). In small towns the garrisons were also small, but these towns were very numerous, scattered along all the chief rivers and roads of Guyenne and Languedoc and also the mountain passes of the Cévennes. The total number of the soldiers making up these garrisons was 4,000; they were paid by the state, in accordance with the supplementary articles of the Edict of Nantes.[1]

The citadels in the Huguenot towns were, as a rule, in good condition and capable of accommodating considerable additional forces. The citizens were to a certain extent trained to arms, and possessed arms. In the larger towns they constituted a substantial reserve force (in La Rochelle, for instance, 7,000-8,000 foot). The towns' fortifications, however—walls, towers, moats—had been neglected during twenty years of peace. During this period the towns had acquired suburbs which also needed to be fortified. The most up-to-date technique of fortification required large-scale earthworks—bastions, crown-works, counterscarps, and so on—which extended far beyond the walls, partly screening them from the enemy and making it more difficult to bombard the town or to storm it. These fortifications had to be erected afresh almost everywhere. Only a few of the Huguenot towns had always kept their fortifications in good order. At La Rochelle there were twelve large bastions, revetted with trimmed stone, double moats and embankments in front of the walls; inside the city there were 150 pieces of artillery, not counting culverins.[2] Some other towns also had guns. Bergerac and Clairac (Clérac), important towns in Guyenne, were well fortified.

[1] Malingre, op. cit. pp. 151-6.
[2] Ibid. pp. 259-60.

Besides the garrisons and town militia, the Huguenot party could also count on armed detachments under the command of grandees, and on troops specially hired by them and by the towns in case of emergency, which were maintained with money raised from the towns by assessment.

Thus, the armed forces of the Huguenots were concentrated not only in the hands of grandees and noblemen but also in those of big towns where the grandees did not rule. And the money needed for war was provided by the towns. This military and financial organisation formed a stout shield defending not only freedom of worship but also the material and political interests of the Huguenots: the privileges and autonomy of the towns, and also the possession of the church property seized by the nobility and the ministers (in part also by the citizens) in the sixteenth century.

The Huguenots retained their republican organisation within the French kingdom. This combination of republican forms with military power, within the boundaries of a more or less sharply defined territory, gave grounds for talking of a 'state within the state', which did not mean a monarchy within a monarchy. There was a sort of co-existence of a republic with an absolute monarchy.

In 1620 the Huguenot provinces were grouped in a number of *cercles*. At the assembly of the *cercle*, held every three years, or more often if necessary, deputies were elected to the general assembly, where the condition of affairs was discussed, *cahiers* were drawn up for presentation to the government, and plenipotentiaries (*députés-généraux*) were chosen to attend upon the king, for observation of the fulfilment of the Edict of Nantes. Despite all their efforts, the Huguenots were unsuccessful after the death of Henry IV in extending their privileges and rights (for instance, securing additional fortresses, increasing the size of garrisons, etc.). They managed only to establish, without authority to do so, these *cercles*, which gave them greater freedom of action within the limits of their territory and introduced greater cohesion into the separate provinces.

The church organisation of the Huguenots was likewise republican. To a certain extent it was analogous to the structure of the Calvinist congregations in Holland in the early stage of the Reformation and the struggle for independence, while the republican form of state was not yet fully developed and the organisation of the church was preparing the way for it. The Huguenot ministers were at the same time important political figures, standing at the head of the territorial units, the church congregations, of the Huguenot organisation. In the assemblies and in the party generally they played a very important role, directing those elements which contemporary Catholics called *les plus factieux*. The Huguenot grandees (Bouillon, Lesdiguières) strove to weaken the influence of the ministers, who reduced their relative weight in the party, and often came into conflict with them, denying their right to constitute a separate group in the assemblies, alongside the nobles and the towns.[1] Many houses and benefices which formerly belonged to the Catholic church had been in the possession of ministers for half a century.

To understand the internal situation in the party properly, it is most important to grasp the interrelation of social forces within it. Between the towns, on the one hand, and the grandees and the nobles generally, on the other, unity was never particularly firm. They were kept together by community of faith and the need for a united organisation to defend their privileges. But in every other respect their interests were frequently quite different.

In the period of the civil war of 1614-20 the Huguenot grandees and nobles, combining with their Catholic fellow-feudalists in an alliance directed against the government, found themselves unable to draw the Huguenot towns into their quarrel. These towns were royalist in outlook and did not favour disturbances. Their economic interests linked them with the central authority, provided only that their fiscal privileges and rights of self-government were safeguarded.

Thanks to these privileges, some large towns (La Rochelle, Montpellier, Montauban, Nîmes and others) still maintained their independence as city republics. At the same time, they derived considerable advantages from forming part of a large centralised state the government of which in some degree took account of their interests in both its internal and external policies. In combination, these conditions were very favourable for the development of the Huguenot bourgeoisie. Very significant in this respect was the brilliant prosperity enjoyed by La Rochelle precisely in the period between the end of the sixteenth century and 1628. The city paid none of the king's taxes;[2] its customs régime admirably fostered the growth of trade, for duties on exports did not exceed 1·8 per cent and on imports they were even lower. Goods belonging to Rochelais merchants themselves were free from all duties.[3]

But the Huguenot towns were torn by internal social conflict, and the bigger and richer the town the more acute was such conflict. Examples of this were the towns of Languedoc, about which more anon, and La Rochelle itself, 'queen and mistress of all' the Huguenot towns.[4]

The city council of La Rochelle consisted of a hundred members: the

[1] *Documents d'histoire*, I, 576, 581.　　　　[2] Malingre, op. cit. p. 259.
[3] E. Trocmé et M. Delafosse, *Le commerce rochelais de la fin du XVᵉ siècle au début du XVIIᵉ siècle* (Paris, 1952), pp. 24, 44.
[4] Malingre, op. cit. p. 258.

mayor, forty-eight 'peers' (the most outstanding citizens) and fifty-one 'bourgeois'. This was an oligarchy of the richest merchant-shipowners. Until 1610 their power in the town was complete. Then a strong opposition party was formed, calling itself *les francs bourgeois*, headed by a group of comparatively recently enriched merchants who were excluded from the ruling oligarchy. They based themselves on the masses of the people, hostile to the oligarchy, masses which, as in any large port, included many manual labourers, stevedores and so on, whose position was always very insecure. The masses of the townspeople were in general practically kept out of municipal affairs and deprived of rights. A few radically minded ministers also joined the opposition. The latter achieved substantial successes. It had its representative in each parish and was able to get half a dozen of its members on to the city council, with the titles of 'syndics' and 'tribunes'; they were elected and changed by the people every year. This large and rich town (there lived in it more than 120 merchant-shipowners, with a capital of 100,000 *écus*, a huge sum for those days) was in the grip of bitter internal conflicts.[1] A similar situation, only slightly less acute, was typical of all the Huguenot towns.

The conflict between the nobility and the towns, the conflict inside the towns between the bourgeoisie and the masses—all this was known to everyone in France who was interested in politics, and in the first place, of course, to the government.

But before examining the events of the war, I must explain how paradoxical the existence of the Huguenot republic within the French kingdom in the circumstances of early seventeenth-century Europe really was.

By that time the Reformation had almost completed its advance, and the Counter-Reformation had achieved its partial successes. The religious map of Europe had assumed fairly definite outlines, which broadly continued to prevail thereafter. These outlines cannot be entirely identified with the outlines defining capitalist development in Europe, and still less can they be taken as a basis for studying the international relations of the time. Particular care is needed in analysing the situation in those countries where considerable masses of the reactionary nobility and ruling princes were drawn into the Reformation, whether Lutheran or Calvinist. With all these reservations it remains absolutely essential to take account of the religious factors. This

---

[1] Ibid. pp. 258, 259. The Guards officer Fontenay-Mareuil, who visited La Rochelle in the summer of 1620, remarked that in fact the freedom of this city was illusory, for between the municipality and the people there was no agreement on anything, and each side ceaselessly kept suspicious watch on the other (Fontenay-Mareuil, *Mémoires. Collection Michaud et Poujoulat*, 2nd series, v (Paris, 1837), 154.)

11-2

is most important in relation to political struggles and to the situation of religious minorities in the different countries.

The Calvinist states (Holland, Scotland, Geneva, and some German principalities) refused to tolerate the Catholics. Anglican England was also not a country where religious toleration existed. The Lutheran countries (Denmark, Sweden, some German principalities) refused to tolerate either Catholics or Calvinists.

The Catholic countries (Austria, Spain, the Spanish Netherlands, the Italian states other than Venice, Poland, Bohemia after the Battle of the White Mountain, some German principalities) refused to tolerate any Protestants. Only Hungary was distinguished by a certain degree of toleration.

In Switzerland and Germany, countries without religious uniformity, the independence of particular cantons and principalities was combined with refusal to tolerate other religions on the given territory. Nevertheless the political federation of the Swiss cantons was very stable (for only thereby could the independence of Switzerland as a whole be maintained), while the two federations of German principalities—the Catholic League and the Protestant Union—were very unstable, not possessing political independence, as Switzerland did, and, moreover, being opposed to each other. The ties that bound them were in both cases based on a common purpose, but this was to achieve and maintain the political independence of each separate principality, and was not directed towards the strengthening of the federation itself.

France thus really offered an unprecedented example of the co-existence not only of two religions but also of two forms of state structure within the frontiers of a single political organism, and this in a period of intense development of the internal market and of the formation of the French nation out of two 'nationalities', North and South. French Calvinism had set up its characteristic republican organisation on a considerable territory with a population of mixed religious composition, where the power of the absolute monarch was very much restricted owing to the political and military power of the Huguenots which had been recognised by law. This entire complex of phenomena was described by one contemporary, Pasquier, as 'monstrous' (*prodige*), and this opinion was shared by many.

The striving for religious and political uniformity which was so characteristic of the European states of that age is to be explained by no means only by religious factors, though these were very important. Adherence to a particular religion involved also the presence or absence of certain privileges. It involved also in many cases a certain political or national orientation. The religious fanaticism of the masses and of the clergy was rooted in these circumstances, which excluded toleration not as a matter of principle (as a principle, statesmen liked to make a parade of it from time to time, presenting it as the basis for their actions) but as an everyday practical reality. In France after the Edict of Nantes, compulsory toleration was foisted on the people, but underneath this official façade the passions that had been revealed in the sixteenth century still slumbered, and in the wars of 1621–9 they broke out into the open again.

As regards the 'monstrous' co-existence on the political plane, this can best be understood by analysing the programmes of the two sides, the Huguenots and the government.

The programme of the Huguenot party after the Edict of Nantes, and especially after the death of Henry IV, with whom they had had personal ties, amounted fundamentally to extending their territory and their rights, with the further aim of getting these extensions endorsed by a new edict, more favourable to them than that of Nantes. They sought to obtain from the government, either peacefully or through civil war waged jointly with the Catholic grandees, new strategic points of importance to them, in Poitou, in Languedoc and to the north of the Loire. In this they failed, apart from Rohan's capture of St-Jean-d'Angély in 1612. On the other hand they extended their church organisation to embrace the Calvinists of Béarn (as explained below) and improved their political organisation, grouping the provinces into *cercles*. But for the discord between their towns and their nobles, the Huguenots might perhaps have succeeded in achieving more than this. This discord, however, was no accidental phenomenon.

What lay behind the striving to extend the Huguenot territory, secure more fortresses and strengthen the political organisation? What would have happened if they had been successful?

The inclusion of the Calvinists of Béarn in the church organisation of the Huguenots (and this church organisation was closely interwoven with the political organisation) signified more than merely an extension of the Huguenot territory; it brought that territory down to the Spanish frontier along nearly the entire extent of the Pyrenees, a fact which made this development particularly alarming for the French government. New towns brought within the borders of the Huguenot provinces would have made their territory more compact, as well as enhancing their military power. The frontier of the Huguenot republic would have become more clearly defined, extending along the Loire and the line of the Cévennes to the shores of the Mediterranean, and then along the Pyrenees to the Atlantic and up to the mouth of the Loire. Obtaining fortresses to the north of the Loire would have strengthened the position of the Huguenots in the other provinces and checked their tendency to drift away from the religion of their fathers.

Contemporaries evaluated these tendencies very soundly. Numerous instances could be quoted from the sources of the view, widespread at the time, that the Huguenots intended to set up an independent republic similar to the 'United Provinces', that is, to Holland. 'The Huguenots want to establish themselves (*se cantonner*) in the kingdom in the Dutch fashion'; '...their purpose is to set up *estats populaires* in the style of the United Provinces of the Netherlands, and themselves make the laws governing them. Their fathers showed them the way; the delight that they find in democracy may move many of them to these fresh aspirations.'[1] 'The Huguenots intend to proclaim themselves a free union of cities on the model of Flanders,[2] inviting Count Henry of Nassau into France to command their army.'[3] One contemporary mentioned the 'popular' (*populaire*) character of the Huguenot state: 'The mayors of the cities and the ministers wield all power, the nobles having only the outward show of a share in it. Consequently, if their plans [i.e. the plans of the Huguenots] are realised, the French state will be transformed into something like Switzerland or Flanders [i.e. Holland], which will bring the aristocracy and nobility to ruin.'[4] In one pamphlet the aim of the Huguenot revolt is defined as the establishment of 'un gouvernement populaire...auquel ils visent y a longtemps à l'exemple de nos voisins.'[5] The Nuncio also wrote that the Huguenots' aim was to organise *un gouvernement populaire*, directly opposite in kind to the temporal monarchy, just as they had organised an ecclesiastical administration which was directly opposite to the spiritual monarchy of the Catholic church.[6] 'From much evidence, it was clear that the Huguenot leaders, and especially Rohan, had a long-prepared plan': gradually to acquire all sorts of privileges, 'to free themselves little by little from subjection to the king, and eventually to set up a republic similar to the Dutch', in which Rohan was ready to play the part of the Prince of Orange.[7]

It must be pointed out that the terms *estats populaires, gouvernement populaire*, were used at that time to mean rule by the bourgeoisie.

The objective significance of the Huguenot programme corresponds to the opinion held by contemporaries. Much of it was confirmed by the course of events in 1621–9. For this reason one cannot simply brush aside the republi-

---

[1] Malingre, op. cit. pp. 2, 140.
[2] At the time this name was used sometimes for the entire Netherlands and sometimes only for the united provinces in the north, i.e. what we now call Holland.
[3] *Documents d'histoire*, II, 355.
[4] G. Saulx-Tavannes, *Mémoires. Collection Michaud et Poujoulat*, 1st series, VIII (Paris, 1837), 233.
[5] *La justice des armes du roy* (s. l., 1622).
[6] See G. Hanotaux, op. cit., II, part 2, 415, note 1 (this note also gives similar quotations from other sources).
[7] Fontenay-Mareuil, op. cit. p. 156.

can, i.e. bourgeois tendencies which were undoubtedly present in the party, corresponding to the ambitions of the rich Huguenot bourgeoisie. These tendencies were considerably strengthened by the separatism which had still not disappeared in the South (showing itself strongly in the civil wars of the sixteenth century) and which was characteristic of the entire population of these provinces.

However, these were only tendencies, and they were countered by other, more powerful forces. One of these was the progress of the national development of France. This process, based on the growth of an economic community, gradually overcame the separatist tendencies, and the abolition of the Huguenot political organisation marked a very important stage on the road to the unification of the country. Another aspect of this process was that France as a whole was developing in a bourgeois direction, and there were no insuperable problems in the relationship between the Huguenot bourgeoisie and the absolute monarchy, which was then in its progressive phase. Furthermore, the situation in France was radically different from that in the Netherlands in the second half of the sixteenth century, when the Calvinist bourgeoisie, striving to achieve its economic and national aims, waged uncompromising war against the alien power of feudal and Catholic Spain, which was doomed to decline. Finally, there was also a difference between Holland and the Huguenot republic as regards the balance of social forces within each. Though Rohan, by virtue of his personal qualities, was perfectly well suited for the role of Prince of Orange, the presence in the Huguenot provinces of a mass of *noblesse d'épée* had no analogy in Holland. These nobles, based on the backward feudal agrarian order existing in the mountains and forelands of the Huguenot territory, formed a powerful counterweight to the bourgeois elements in the party. At times the social conflict in the towns assumed, for a number of reasons considered below, a special colouring; the movements of the popular masses were utilised successfully by Rohan and the nobles, so that the bourgeois circles were left without support.

Thus, in the political programme of the Huguenots, as in the whole life of the party, there was a curious combination of the interests of the bourgeoisie with those of the nobility and the princes, that is, of the interests of estates which were essentially antagonistic to each other. In the circumstances of France at the beginning of the seventeenth century, this deprived the party of lasting unity and made its programme unrealisable.

The government's programme in relation to the Huguenots was quite clear, though not completely consistent owing to lack of money and to the international situation. It intended to suppress the military power and the political organisation of the Huguenots. Regardless of the demands of Rome and of many French leaders of the Counter-Reformation, revocation of the Edict of Nantes was not yet on the agenda. It was a matter of abolishing those rights which the Huguenots had obtained under the supplementary points of the Edict, which had been granted for eight years only, and later renewed (also for limited periods) by Henry IV and by the Regent Marie de Médicis. These rights had been granted by the king as a 'grace' and could be withdrawn at the end of the period for which they were granted —in the event of insubordination, even before then.

The Huguenots had shown such insubordination during the civil wars of 1614–20. Their grandees and nobles had waged war against the government jointly with the Catholic grandees and nobles, in 1615–16 and in 1620. The Huguenot assemblies convened in that period had often adopted a rebellious attitude; though, to be sure, the Huguenot towns had been royalist and had prevented the entire party from opposing the government.

However, the government's decision to bring the Huguenots to heel was based on considerations of a more general nature. In 1620, when the civil wars ended with the triumph of the king's army, the government could not but draw conclusions from this. These conclusions were drawn not only by Luynes, the king and the members of the king's Council but by all who were engaged in politics in one way or another.

The years of civil war had shown that those successes which had been temporarily won by the grandees and nobles during their armed conflict with the government were due to definite causes; the chief of these (leaving aside the international situation, aid from abroad, etc.) was the possession by the grandees of large armed forces and of effective slogans which appealed to the public. These slogans were sometimes very useful to the rebels. Thus, in 1615–17, the grandees waged their struggle for power under the slogan: 'For the king and against d'Ancre!', a very popular slogan with all sections of society, including the people, who attributed all the burdens of the ruinous civil war to the hated foreign favourite. This slogan, however, had two parts, and the former, 'For the King!' was just as important for everyone, except the grandees, as the latter. For this reason, as soon as d'Ancre had been killed, the slogan 'For the king!' turned against the grandees, and at once deprived them of even a vestige of popularity.

Their slogan in 1619–20, 'For the king and against Luynes!' was incomparably less effective than the slogan 'For the king and against d'Ancre!' To the initiators of the revolt alone, along with the nobility who followed them, was Luynes a 'tyrant' who had excluded the princes from participation in the king's Council and the nobles from pensions and military appointments. In other sections of society—among the bourgeoisie, the officials, the people—his policy met with a sympathetic response, both for its own sake and because it was backed by the king's authority. The counterposing of the king to Luynes in the slogan of the grandees found no echoes outside their own circle.

It was different with the armed forces of the grandees. The fact that in 1615–16 Condé and his army appeared in the Huguenot territory and found support there could not but be disturbing. A still more alarming situation occurred in 1620, when the main forces of the rebels were concentrated in the Huguenot provinces and the Huguenot grandees and their noble followers almost all rallied to the party of Marie de Médicis, when the fortresses and armed forces of the Huguenots were placed at the service of the reactionary programme of the grandees.

Consequently, abolition of the armed might, and so of the political organisation, of the Huguenot party appeared as the most urgent task before the absolute monarchy in its further struggle with the grandees as a whole, regardless of their religious affiliation. This was clearly appreciated by contemporaries. The Venetian ambassador wrote to the Seignory: 'By taking their fortresses from the Huguenots, the king will thereby put an end to their military power, and without this all the troublemakers...will find themselves deprived of a solid support that they could have relied on.'[1] This opinion was shared by many.

A favourable circumstance for the government was the mass transfer in 1620 of nobles from the army of the grandees into the royal regiments. Beginning his attack on the Huguenots immediately after the victory at Ponts-de-Cé, the king retained thereafter this valuable military force, which enlarged his cavalry arm substantially. Nevertheless, nine years (with breaks) were needed before the final victory, and the struggle was a desperate one.

The international situation prolonged the war. The struggle against the Huguenots had to be carried on in circumstances in which the conflagration of the Thirty Years War was gradually building up. The situation in western Germany and northern Italy compelled the French government to suspend or postpone its actions against the Huguenots more than once; but not through any intervention by the Protestant allies of the Huguenots, who had frequently aided them in the sixteenth century. In this period the Protestant rulers were largely paralysed, because their own situation was very complicated, and often extremely difficult. As a result, they particularly needed help from France in their struggle with the Habsburgs, and were interested in the strengthening of French absolutism. The Thirty Years War prevented the

[1] B. Zeller, *Le Connétable de Luynes. Montauban et la Valteline* (Paris, 1879), p. 86.

Huguenots from obtaining help from outside, and they were left to their own resources. Contemporaries observed that it was specially advantageous for the government that the European Protestants 'remained in that situation until the king had settled accounts with the Huguenots, and recovered only when he needed them to prevent the House of Austria from subjecting the whole of Germany and thereafter the rest of the world'.[1]

The French government was hindered in its struggle against the Huguenots especially by Spain, whose rulers watched closely all internal developments in France and exploited the slightest opportunity to strengthen their positions in northern Italy and on the Rhine. England also took advantage of the situation, though much less—at first clandestinely and later openly supporting the Rochelais. These external interventions gave the Huguenots temporary breathing-spaces which they employed for preparing their next campaign, building fortifications around their towns, and so on.

The second reason for the prolongation of the war was that the Huguenots possessed a considerable armed force. Their principal towns—La Rochelle, Montauban, Montpellier—were well fortified and large enough in extent for besieging them to call for a big army and no small military skill. The king's army was, especially at the start, not very large, and without experience. The government's constant lack of money and its various financial difficulties were also important factors.

Why did the government begin with an expedition to Béarn?

Like the other Pyrenean provinces (Navarre, Bigorre, Comminges, Foix), Béarn occupied at that time a quite special position in the structure of France.[2] These mountain provinces were very backward in their social and economic development. Calvinism, which had triumphed there among the greater nobles, the petty nobility and the townspeople, had special characteristics in this region, resembling in many ways the Calvinism of Scotland. These provinces were the domain of Henry IV as king of Navarre, and enjoyed so many privileges that for practical purposes they were independent. No innovation could be made without the agreement of the local States, in which the Calvinist nobility predominated.

At the beginning of the sixteenth century the entire southern part of Navarre was seized by Spain, and the independent kingdom survived only on the northern slopes of the Pyrenees (which covered only one-fifth of the former territory of Navarre), thanks to the pro-French orientation of the ruling dynasty of Albret, which was related to the French royal family

[1] Fontenay-Mareuil, op. cit. p. 160.
[2] A good outline of the history of Béarn will be found in a little book which, though popular in character, is based on independent research: P. Tucoo-Chala, *Histoire de Béarn*, Paris, 1962.

(Henry II d'Albret married Francis I's sister Marguerite, Jeanne d'Albret married Antoine de Bourbon, Henry III d'Albret married Marguerite de Valois). Queen Jeanne d'Albret abolished the Catholic religion in the 1560s; the confiscated property of the church became a royal possession, a large proportion of it being later sold or given away.

When Henry III of Navarre became king of France in 1589, as Henry IV, he gave Navarre and Béarn (i.e. the bulk of his domain) to his sister Catherine, Duchesse de Bar, and after her death he annexed to France only Foix, Bigorre and the southern parts of Languedoc. He was unable to deal with Navarre and Béarn in the same way owing to the opposition shown there to such a change. The point was that, if they were absorbed into France, the provisions of the Edict of Nantes would apply there, and, consequently, the secularised property of the Catholic Church would have to be given back. However, Henry IV did restore Catholic worship in a few towns.

After his death, the Calvinists of Béarn attended the Huguenot conferences in 1611 and 1616; fearing a change for the worse in the government's policy, now that there was no longer a king who came from Navarre, they tried to enlist the political support of the Huguenots. And they succeeded in this. They continued to object to annexation, and their attitude encountered increased opposition in France. Thus, at the States General in 1614 the Third Estate included in its *cahier* a demand for the ending of the independence of Navarre and Béarn and in general of all 'sovereign' provinces, which thereafter should become part of the kingdom of France.

The position was complicated by the fact that in Béarn and Navarre the Salic Law prevailing in France, whereby women and their descendants were excluded from the succession to the throne, did not apply, and the crown of Navarre descended by the female line as well as by the male. If Henry IV's sons had had no direct heirs, the dominions of the house of Albret (and we must remember that they occupied almost the whole Pyrenean frontier of France) would have passed to the Duc de Rohan (through his grandmother, Isabelle d'Albret). Before the birth of the Dauphin (the future Louis XIII), Rohan was regarded as the heir presumptive to the kingdom of Navarre. All these circumstances show the importance of the Béarn question in 1610–20. The retention of political independence by the Pyrenean provinces, and their adhesion to the Huguenot territory, not only rounded off the latter but also put at the disposal of the Huguenots all the southern frontier provinces, facilitating communications with Spain and aid from her in case of need.

In the following years the ties between the Béarnais and the French Huguenots were finally consolidated, politically and ecclesiastically. In

answer to this, in June 1617 the king's Council issued a decree on the unification of Navarre and Béarn with France and the restoration of Catholic
worship and return of church property there, which meant the extension to
these provinces of the provisions of the Edict of Nantes. The losses suffered
by owners of secularised property were to be compensated out of the royal
domain. This measure deeply offended the material interests of the population[1]—ministers, citizens and especially nobles.[2] The States of Béarn
vigorously opposed its implementation. The commissioner sent by the king
for this purpose was ignominiously driven away. The Huguenots demanded
the rescinding of the decree, and under the conditions of the conflict with the
greater nobles in 1619-20 the government was unable to put its decision into
effect.

The victory at Ponts-de-Cé decided the fate of Béarn. At the same time
the international situation developed unfavourably for the Huguenots. The
treaty of Ulm, concluded at that time through the mediation of France,
brought about the localisation of war within the borders of Bohemia; even
the German Calvinists, the nearest neighbours of the Czechs, could not
help them.

Louis XIII marched south with his entire army, and at Pau, on 20 October,
in his presence, the Supreme Council of Béarn confirmed the edict of
unification, and the deputies of the States took an oath of allegiance to the
king. The local militia (about 8,000 men) was dissolved, and a henchman of
the king was appointed commandant of the strong fortress of Navarrenx.
When the king returned to Paris on 7 November he was received there with
enthusiasm. Later (in 1624) a royal *parlement* was established at Pau.

The expedition to Béarn was a great success for the government. The
Spanish frontier had been occupied and a wedge driven into the Huguenot
rear from the south. During its march to Béarn the royal army had taken
some Huguenot towns in Poitou and Guyenne, leaving garrisons behind it;
that, is, it had consolidated positions which were important both in themselves and for future campaigns.[3]

Predictably, as soon as the king had left, troubles began in Béarn. Protests
against the recovery of secularised church property were especially vigorous;
many defended their possessions by force of arms,[4] including ministers,

---

[1] G. Hanotaux, op. cit. p. 425, note 2. Tapié considers that under this decree only ministers were
obliged to hand back church property, but he gives no evidence for this interpretation (Tapié,
op. cit. p. 120).
[2] Sale and distribution of secularised church property mainly benefited the nobles (P. Tucoo-Chala,
op. cit. pp. 62, 66).
[3] Fontenay-Mareuil, op. cit. p. 158.
[4] H. de Lagarde, *Le Duc de Rohan et les protestants sous Louis XIII* (Paris, 1884), p. 21.

'who were losing one of their chief strongholds'.[1] The Duc de la Force, one of the Huguenot leaders and governor of Béarn, fearing to lose his position as independent ruler of this territory, sought to restore the *status quo ante*, and prepared for armed conflict, strengthening fortresses and raising troops. To suppress him an army of 5,000 men was sent to Béarn, commanded by the Duc d'Epernon, and La Force was driven out of the province. The governorship was conferred on Marshal Thémines. Fierce repressions began. D'Epernon acted in warlike fashion, expelling ministers, destroying Calvinist cemeteries, handing Calvinist churches over to the Catholics.[2]

Seeing by the example of Béarn the fate in store for them, the Huguenots began to organise local assemblies at which they elected deputies to a conference of all the Huguenots, held at La Rochelle. Preparation for war began; the raising of troops, collection of money from the towns, seizure of money from royal tax-collectors, and so on. Religious hatred, which had temporarily died down, flared up again. In Montauban and other Huguenot towns, persecution of Catholics began.[3]

The assembly at La Rochelle, opening on 28 November, assumed supreme authority and became the permanently functioning leading organ of the Huguenot party. Special committees were set up, measures taken to secure the most threatened fortresses along the Loire, and a special organisation for war worked out. To head each of the eight territorial *cercles* a grandee was appointed: in Upper Guyenne and Upper Languedoc, Rohan; in Lower Languedoc and the Vivarais, Châtillon; in Lower Guyenne, La Force; in Béarn, his son; in Brittany and Poitou, Soubise; in Dauphiné and Provence, Lesdiguières; in Normandy, the Ile-de-France and Sedan, Bouillon; in Saintonge, with La Rochelle, the assembly itself. The supreme command was assigned to Bouillon. None of the commanders had the right to make peace, or even a truce, without the consent of the assembly at La Rochelle, which 'ruled like a republic over the grandees who carried on its war, recognising no one higher than itself, and keeping in its own hands all the threads of administration and absolute power,'[4]—which did not prevent it from officially acknowledging the king as sovereign (its seal was engraved with the words: *pour Christ, roy et le peuple*).[5] Later the assembly issued regulations regarding the conduct of the war, the levying of money and trade

[1] Fontenay-Mareuil, op. cit. p. 155.
[2] Ibid. pp. 155, 157; Lagarde, op. cit. p. 21.
[3] Fontenay-Mareuil, op. cit. p. 155; Malingre, op. cit. p. 85; B. Zeller, *Le Connétable de Luynes*, pp. 26, 27.
[4] Malingre, op. cit. p. 142.
[5] Ibid. p. 342.

by sea and land, and requisitioning of vessels sailing on the Garonne, Charente and other rivers.[1]

However, Bouillon refused the supreme command and remained passive, merely defending his own principality of Sedan. Lesdiguières and Châtillon soon went over to the king's side and proceeded to renounce Calvinism. La Force took no very active part in the military operations. Only the Rohan brothers remained: the Duc de Rohan and Soubise. This alarmed the assembly greatly and even shook its courage. But on 27 February a popular movement broke out in La Rochelle. A mob broke into the town hall and forbade the city council to begin negotiations with the king.[2]

The government also got ready for war. But among the members of the king's Council, and in influential circles in the capital, there was much disagreement. The king, Luynes, Condé and the *surintendant* Schomberg considered war inevitable, for only by smashing the armed might of the Huguenots could the military base of the rebellious aristocrats be destroyed.[3] This view found a large echo among the Catholic population of the towns, who considered that the Huguenot towns should be reduced to submission,[4] that is, that the rights of all the towns of France, whether Huguenot or Catholic, should be equalised. This demand for equality, both economic and political, was very characteristic of the Catholic bourgeoisie of France at that time.

The advocates of war took into account the fact that it might entail a certain weakening in the position of France in the international arena, in so far as all forces would have to be concentrated on the struggle against the Huguenots, which Spain would not fail to exploit. Nevertheless, they refused priority to the tasks of external policy, all the more so because any military intervention by France in the European war while the Huguenot power continued to exist within the country threatened to bring about an attack by this power against the government: the Huguenots would lose no time in utilising for their purposes a departure of the king's army beyond the frontiers.[5] It should be added that the advocates of war with the Huguenots

[1] Malingre, op. cit. pp. 160–231. These illegal levies on trade were collected even from English merchants, whom for political reasons the Huguenots should have spared (letter from Viscount Doncaster to Soubise, from Bordeaux, 23 December 1621; Saltykov-Shchedrin Library, Leningrad, Avt. 72, no. 19).

[2] L. Anquez, *Histoire des assemblées politiques des réformés de France (1573–1622)* (Paris, 1859), p. 336.

[3] '...la rébellion et la désobéissance ayant tousjours trouvé sa retraicte et son azyle et seureté dans les armes de ceux de la religion prétendue réformée' (Malingre, op. cit. p. 251).

[4] J. Gassot, *Sommaire mémorial* (Paris, 1934), p. 324.

[5] 'There is also one Thing which does and will hinder us always from doing anything considerable out of France, and that is the Fear we have of some commotion within the Kingdom, upon the account of Religion.' (*Perroniana* (Cologne and Geneva, 1669), p. 151 [English translation, *The miscellaneous remains of Cardinal Perron, etc.* (London, 1707), p. 42].)

were at that stage convinced that the campaign would be a swift one, as the enemy's resistance would be overcome without particular difficulty.

There was another opinion, pro-Huguenot in tendency, which was widespread among the grandees. It was determined not by sympathy with the Huguenots as such but by realisation that abolition of the military power of the Huguenots would mean danger to the higher nobility as a whole. According to this point of view, the Huguenots should be left in peace, and their claims should even be satisfied, that is, the positions of the grandees strengthened. Then, given internal peace, more attention could be paid to external affairs, and the danger from Spain dealt with.[1]

The government could not accept this programme. Ever since the end of the civil wars, that is, since the 1590s, its main task had been struggle against internal foes, namely, the grandees, in order to strengthen absolutism in the country. Only diplomatic methods could for the moment be employed in foreign relations. For this reason, then, Luynes opted for war on the Huguenots.

Luynes began military operations against the Huguenots only after thorough diplomatic and financial preparations, which he carried through in the first four months of 1621.

The international situation at the beginning of 1621, in the third year of the Thirty Years War, was becoming more and more complicated. After the imperial victory at the White Mountain, on 8 November 1620, French diplomacy was confronted with three main problems: more precisely, though these problems had existed even before the imperial victory, they now became extremely acute.

Expansion of the Spanish dominions in northern Italy, at the expense of Savoy, Venice, Mantua and other small states, and seizure by Spain of the passes through the Alps, could not be allowed to take place. It was necessary to safeguard the Rhenish provinces (the Palatinate, Juliers, etc.) from the Spanish forces stationed in Flanders, under Spinola's command, and from those of the Catholic League, commanded by Tilly. A diplomatic struggle had to be waged against the emperor, so as to prevent him from becoming any stronger.

France was particularly sensitive to any variation to Spain's advantage, however slight, in the situation in northern Italy. At the most difficult moments of the struggle with the princes in 1610–20 the government had still taken care to check attempts made by Feria, the governor of Milan, to extend his territory and get control of the passes into Switzerland. Control

[1] B. Zeller, *Le Connétable de Luynes*, p. 13.

of these passes guaranteed the Habsburgs' vitally important communications between Milan and Austria, through the Tirol (also, through Genoa, between Austria and both Spain itself and the Spanish possessions in southern Italy) and between Milan and the Habsburg possessions on the western frontiers of Germany (Franche-Comté, Alsace, Luxemburg) and in the southern Netherlands. Through these passes Spain could safely and quickly switch her troops from south to north or from north to south. The Swiss passes were needed also by Venice, for access by her mercenaries from across the Alps.

In 1620–30 the Valtelline, the narrow valley of the River Adda, descending from the east into Lake Como, which was in Milanese, that is, Spanish territory, was the arena of an intense diplomatic and military conflict between France and Spain. Through the Valtelline ran the routes leading to the source and upper course of the Inn (along the valleys of the Upper and Lower Engadine) and to the Rhine. The valleys of these rivers provided routes into the Tirol and into south Germany, the Valtelline was the nodal point of these routes, and control of it meant control of them.

Down to the beginning of the sixteenth century, the Valtelline, an Italian-speaking area, belonged to the Visconti rulers of Milan; then it passed under the authority of the Grisons, the south-eastern part of Switzerland occupied by the three 'Grey Leagues' which did not belong to the confederation of Swiss cantons. Whereas Zwinglian Protestantism had triumphed in the Grisons, the Valtelline had remained Catholic. Francis I of France, when he ruled over Milan, and as a result of his alliance with the Swiss cantons, proclaimed the Valtelline a French protectorate. Henry IV in 1603 renewed the alliance with the Grisons, and obtained for France and her allies (which meant Venice) the freedom of the passes, whereas these were to be closed to Spain. This meant that Milan was cut off from the Tirol and from south Germany. The governor of Milan, Fuentes, then built on the shore of Lake Como, just at the starting-point of the routes which had been closed to him, Fort Montecchio (also called Fort Fuentes), and tried to oblige the Grisons to grant him the same rights as were enjoyed by France and Venice. The Grisons suffered diplomatic pressure from all the interested states. Each of these had its supporters there, at enmity among themselves. The struggle proceeded with fluctuating fortunes, favouring in turn whichever group was linked with the country that was strongest at a given moment. In 1619, taking advantage of the civil war in France, Spain seized the Valtelline, on the pretext of protecting its Catholic inhabitants from the Protestant Grisons.

Thus, before beginning the war against the Huguenots, the French government had to restore the situation in Italy at least to the *status quo ante*, that is, to ensure that the Valtelline was brought back under the authority of the Grisons and that the Alpine passes were closed to Spanish troops.

At the beginning of 1621, Luynes sent his brother (who shortly afterwards received the title of Duc de Chaulnes) to England to negotiate with James I, who was much concerned to help his son-in-law Frederick, the Elector Palatine and 'winter king' of Bohemia, who had fled from his kingdom after the battle of the White Mountain. The French proposed to James that they bring joint pressure to bear on Spain to compel her to give back both Frederick's possessions in the Upper Palatinate, which had been occupied by Spinola, and also the Valtelline. At the same time, Louis XIII requested James not to give aid to the rebel Huguenots. There was also talk of a match between the future Charles I and Henry IV's youngest daughter Henrietta, a matter which had already come up more than once in Anglo-French diplomatic discussions.

Of these proposals, only the first was important to the English government, and at that time it was preparing to achieve the desired result by way of a marriage alliance with Spain.[1] Moreover, envoys from the assembly of La Rochelle were persistently asking for aid from England, and influential bourgeois circles in London, having business ties with La Rochelle, were backing these appeals. For these reasons, James I confined himself to vague assurances.[2]

Having failed with England, Luynes turned to direct pressure on Spain. At the end of January he sent to Madrid the prominent diplomat and general Bassompierre, with instructions to act vigorously in order to make Philip III give back the Valtelline. By so doing he broke with the previous very cautious policy of the old ministers (Villeroy, Sillery, Du Vair, Puisieux) who, in conditions of almost continuous civil war in 1610–20, had leant over backwards to be cautious in relations with Spain, manœuvring in order to weaken Spain *insensiblement et par des moyens qui ne causent ni d'aigreur ny de l'altera-tion aux esprits.*[3]

After the victory over the grandees, Luynes considered the government's position to be stronger, and intended to act more decisively. Henry IV's old counsellors did not approve, however, any more than they approved of war against the Huguenots. Without denying that it must come, they nevertheless considered that France should go on playing for time.

---

[1] For this purpose the Prince of Wales, accompanied by Buckingham, later spent some time travelling incognito through France and Spain; but their romantic adventure came to nothing.
[2] B. Zeller, *Le Connétable de Luynes*, pp. 24, 25; Fontenay-Mareuil, op. cit. p. 157.
[3] Letter from Puisieux to Léon, 7 August 1619. (Saltykov-Shchedrin Library, Leningrad, Avt. 106, no. 66).

At the moment when Bassompierre was sent off to Spain, the French government had not yet received the news that the Grisons, with the consent and agreement of Venice, had seized by force the Bormio pass, in the upper part of the Valtelline, thereby re-establishing their communications with Venice and severing Milan's link with the Tirol. After this, the Spanish governor of Milan, Feria, yielded to the Grisons to a certain extent: he gave back the Valtelline, but on condition that the Spanish forts which had been built there should remain for another eight years, and that the passes should be open to the Spaniards as well. In other words, Spain retained military control of the valley, and Venice remained as before under the threat of Spanish invasion.

Meanwhile, Bassompierre had been instructed to allow no alliance to be made by the Grisons, either with Milan or with Venice. Consequently, the French ambassador had, on his arrival in Madrid, not merely to declare France's disapproval of such alliances, but also to try to put an end to the alliance already concluded between the Grisons and Milan. Venice, France's ally in the struggle against Milan, was striving hard to secure an alliance with the Grisons, because only in this way could she make sure that the mercenaries she hired, and who were absolutely essential to Venice in the event of military operations, would be able to march unhindered into her territories. This situation gave rise to clashes between Venice and France, because the latter often needed to recruit mercenary troops in the same countries as Venice—in the Rhenish provinces, in Switzerland, in Liège and elsewhere. On this account, relations between these allies, who were also competitors, sometimes became strained, and they would take certain steps without notifying each other, after which they would exchange reproaches of mutual duplicity.

This was the situation on the present occasion. When, therefore, at the beginning of March (after Bassompierre had departed and news had reached Paris of the secret agreement made behind France's back between the Grisons and Venice), the Venetian ambassador proposed to Luynes that a coalition be formed between France and the northern Italian states for military operations in the Valtelline, Luynes rejected this proposal. He even went so far as to express to the Venetian his strong disapproval of the fact that Venice had made an alliance with the Grisons without consulting France, and also that Venice was obstructing French interests in Turkey in various ways. Relying on the success of Bassompierre's mission, Luynes declined to accept the plan for war in the Valtelline; he needed to keep his hands free for the war against the Huguenots. It is significant that during this discussion between Luynes and the Venetian ambassador, the chancellor said that if the French army which had already been assembled was sent out of the country, so giving freedom of action to the Huguenots, Spain would incite the latter to rise in revolt and would supply them with funds. This statement is worth noting; it was not made without good grounds, and, as we shall see, it proved correct.

Having arrived in Spain, Bassompierre easily and rapidly carried out his task. The position was that Philip III was dying, and the treasury was empty. At the same time, the period of truce with Holland had come to an end, and the prospect of renewed war with her was looming up. In mid-March the following proposal was put to the French ambassador: Spain would make concessions in Italy (that is, would hand back the Valtelline), if the French would undertake not to hinder Spanish activities in Germany. In other words, the Valtelline would be traded in exchange for a free hand on the Rhine.

Before his death, on 30 March 1621, Philip III enjoined his successor to return the Valtelline to France. Within a fortnight, on 15 April, it was done, by the Treaty of Madrid. Did this signify that France had actually purchased the Valtelline at the price of non-interference with Spanish policy in Germany?

There are no grounds for such a supposition. If the Valtelline question was of first importance, the situation of Germany was not far behind it. To give Spain the chance of dominating the Rhine would have been an almost suicidal act on the part of the French government, since it would threaten to eliminate the German Protestants, France's allies, as an anti-Habsburg force.

This is confirmed by the fact that, when he despatched Bassompierre to Spain, Luynes did not leave him to his own unaided resources. France backed his determined attitude by open preparation for war. This was in a situation in which war was undesirable for Spain, owing to the expected death of Philip III and the inevitable difficulties that would arise, when the sixteen-year-old Philip IV came to the throne, in the forming of a new government (Olivares became the chief minister only in 1623).

This war-preparation was all the more opportune, as a means of supporting diplomatic pressure on Spain, because its results could be directed with equal facility either into a campaign in Italy, for the Valtelline, or into an internal campaign against the Huguenots.

On 31 March Luynes was appointed constable of France, that is, com-mander-in-chief, receiving his sword of office on 2 April from the hands of the king. This nomination to the highest military appointment of a man who had in no way distinguished himself in the military sphere was received by the court with discreet murmurings and by the Parisians with incredulity and derision. The grandees especially felt wounded to the quick; every one of them had a claim to the title of constable, and, furthermore, Luynes, by being invested with it, had been placed above them in the army, so that their privileges of precedence over him vanished. The actual command of the armed forces was to be entrusted to an experienced general, Lesdiguières, who received the appointment, next in rank after that of constable, of *maréchal de camp général*.[1] But for the present he did not want to fight against his Huguenot co-religionists, and advised that war be declared against Spain instead. His view became widely known, and so his appointment confirmed the impression that France was preparing for external rather than internal war.

At the end of March the government was still vacillating, or rather, putting on a show of vacillation: should the king go to Lyons, which would mean a campaign of the Valtelline, or into Poitou, which would mean a campaign against the Huguenots? On 5 April the king moved to Fontainebleau, but by stopping there left open the question of his ultimate destination. Only on 28 April did he proceed to Orléans;[2] and only on 5 May from Orleans down the Loire into Poitou. The campaign against the Huguenots had begun.

I have drawn attention to these dates because they provide grounds for considering that the delay could not have been accidental. The war with the Huguenots was decided on after receipt of the news of the signing of the Treaty of Madrid (15 April).[3] Three weeks, from 15 April to 5 May, was a more than sufficient lapse of time for news to travel from Madrid to Orléans, from where the king could have proceeded either to Lyons or against the Huguenots.

The news of the Treaty of Madrid made it possible to begin the campaign against the Huguenots. Under this treaty the Valtelline was to be given back to the Grisons and all the forts erected there since 1617 were to be demolished. France and the Swiss cantons were to guarantee the fulfilment of the treaty. Its provisions were so favourable to France that Bassompierre feared that the treaty might be merely a device to gain time; after all, it would be possible to put off its actual implementation on one pretext or another—and the Valtelline was so very necessary to Spain. For this reason he advised

[1] The Huguenot grandees and the assembly of La Rochelle were so seriously alarmed by the rumours of Lesdiguières' appointment, which must inevitably entail his renunciation of Calvinism, that in the middle of March they set up a special 'committee' with the task of either dissuading Lesdiguières or else of organising opposition to him.
[2] Malingre, op. cit. p. 146.
[3] This date appears in all the documents. Yet Hanotaux (op. cit. p. 442) erroneously gives 25 April, as also does Tapié (op. cit. p. 159). The date 25 April does not, or course, offer the possibility of comparison with the date when the expedition against the Huguenots began.

Luynes to wait until the Grisons had taken possession of the disputed territory, and only after that to move against the Huguenots.

But Luynes could not wait. In Béarn rebellion was about to break out at any moment, and in the Vivarais war between Huguenots and Catholics had been going on for half a year already with varying fortunes. Religious antagonism had blazed up in several cities. Bloody clashes between Catholics and Huguenots occurred in mid-April in Tours and Poitiers. In Tours the Calvinist church was burnt down. The judge sent by the king sentenced a number of Catholics to death for this, but it proved impossible to carry out the sentence. A crowd of small craftsmen and workmen tried to release the condemned men, and the armed city militia had difficulty in dispersing them.[1] Around Toulouse, Montauban, Castres and the towns of Lower Languedoc the Huguenots occupied fortresses, plundered Catholic property, and seized the cash-boxes of the tax-collectors in this area.[2] The assembly of La Rochelle was preparing for open war, and refused to submit to the order to dissolve sent by the king in the middle of March. It was important for the government not to allow the Huguenots sufficient time to erect new fortifications around their cities; even without that, the start of the campaign had been delayed owing to the need to wait on the outcome of Bassompierre's mission.

The Treaty of Madrid ensured a favourable international position. At the same time, financial measures were also taken to muster the resources needed for the support of a large army of 40,000 foot and 6,000 horse.[3]

In his financial policy, Luynes followed the line of his predecessors, the old ministers of the time of Henry IV and the Regency. Like them he endeavoured to avoid any large increase in the taxes falling on the mass of the people. Now, as before, the government turned mainly to the privileged orders, specifically to the officials and the clergy.

The circumstances under which the new conditions for the *paulette* (the special levy introduced in 1604, in exchange for payment of which the officials were guaranteed the inheritability of their offices)[4] were formulated, were characteristic. The *paulette* had been abolished in 1617 but then, on 31 July 1620, restored for a period of nine years (1621–9); at the end of 1620 new conditions to govern it had already been worked out.[5] It was now made to apply not to all officials but only to those who at the end of 1620 and beginning of 1621 would pay a levy equivalent to 5 per cent of the price of their office;

[1] The execution took place at the beginning of May, when the king was passing through Tours (Malingre, op. cit. pp. 120–4).
[2] Ibid. pp. 128–9. [3] Ibid. p. 132.
[4] On the *paulette*, see A. D. Lublinskaya, *Frantsiya a nachale XVII veka (1610–1620 gg.)* (Leningrad, 1959), pp. 65, 66, 288.
[5] R. Mousnier, *La vénalité des offices sous Henri IV et Louis XIII* (Rouen, 1945), pp. 256–9.

in subsequent years this levy was reduced to 1 per cent. In other words, this was a forced contribution from the officials at the rate of 5 per cent in 1621 and 1 per cent during the following eight years—over the whole nine years, 13 per cent of the price of their offices. Taking into account the enormous amount of capital invested in offices (it is not possible to state the total sum, but it certainly came to not less than 500 million *livres*), the contribution was bound to bring in substantial sums every year, and especially at the beginning of 1621.

Under the new conditions, only *premiers présidents* and *procureurs-généraux* of the *parlements*, that is, a few dozen persons, were to be exempt from paying the *paulette*. In addition, from now on the *paulette* guaranteed to all the other members of the higher courts only the value of their offices, and not the right to dispose of them, as the king intended himself to fill posts left vacant by death, paying the dead man's heir the price of his office, at the official, not the market rate (that is, a price considerably less than what the heir would get if he could sell the office). Property in the form of offices was thus encroached upon.

As soon as these conditions became known, an avalanche of protests poured down upon the government, both in the capital and in the provinces. In response to them, the government announced that, since the new conditions were not liked it would again abolish the *paulette*. This determined attitude was due to the victory just won over the grandees; in 1620 the *paulette* had been restored on the eve of the military campaign in order to placate the officials and confirm their royalism; after victory had been secured it was possible to encroach on their interests a little. But the officials did not want to part with their money. On 15 December 1620 the Paris *parlement*, revolting against the new conditions for the *paulette*, adopted a resolution of protest. As usual in such cases, bargaining began between the government and the *parlement*. The king went as far as to concede, in the declaration by the king's Council on 22 February, that the new conditions for the *paulette* were not to be applied to the entire body of higher officials. These were exempted from payment of the contribution; in return, the text of the *parlement's* resolution of 15 December was torn out of its register. The contribution was made obligatory for all other officials, including the financial ones.

This meant that the most powerful officials had betrayed the interests of their junior colleagues. The fruits of the six months' struggle, in which the higher dignitaries had been supported by all the officials, had gone to them alone. In 1621 the split between the higher strata of French officialdom and the rest was intensified. The most influential sections of the *noblesse de robe* had in fact won themselves immunity from forced 'loans' (*prêts à jamais rendre*).

In April a loan of 2,000,000 *livres* was raised from the financiers, of which 1,500,000 went into the treasury and the rest was used to meet old loans. In order to pay the interest of the loan (6½ per cent), an edict was issued increasing the price of salt (by four sous per *minot* of salt), which was expected to bring in 100,000 francs a year.[1]

Large demands were presented to the clerical estate. The government wanted to obtain from them a million *livres* for the war against the Huguenots. The clergy did not want to hand over any cash, and would agree only to maintain 6,000 foot soldiers. The government insisted, and threatened a partial secularisation of church property.[2] After prolonged altercation, the clergy were obliged to submit.

Thus, the resources for the war against the Huguenots were raised mainly from the officials, the clergy and the financiers. The increase in the salt tax was comparatively slight.

Before describing the campaign of 1621 I must say something about the important difference between the two armies which took part in it, the Huguenot army and the king's army.

The principal theatre of operations in 1621–2 was the South—Upper Guyenne and Languedoc. For this reason, the part of the Huguenot army which played the leading role in this campaign was the section commanded by the Duc de Rohan; the most important forces of the Huguenot party were concentrated under his leadership, the rest being dispersed to serve as garrisons in the cities.

The Huguenots possessed a great advantage in having a commander like Rohan, whom the royal forces could not rival. Rohan displayed to the full his military and organising gifts in the campaigns of 1621–9, perhaps just because he had to overcome serious difficulties. The peculiar features of the Huguenot region, the limited resources at his disposal, and the general situation in the country, were all against him.

He had to recruit his forces from a comparatively small region, mainly in the Cévennes. The Upper Cévennes area was able to supply not more than 2,500 soldiers, the Lower Cévennes not more than 5,000 or 6,000, but these included good officers with experience of war. Like Switzerland, Scotland and other mountainous regions, the Cévennes supplied mercenary soldiers to a number of Europe's armies. The young people of the Cévennes could not

---

[1] B. Zeller, *Le Connétable de Luynes*, pp. 46–50.
[2] Beginning in the middle of the sixteenth century, partial secularisation of church property took place in France on not less than nine occasions; the church estimated that, as a result, it was deprived of more than a third of its property.

make a living in their native hills,[1] and this compelled them to emigrate in order to seek their fortunes. It should be mentioned that the figures given represent the total number of soldiers that could be recruited in the Cévennes; the majority of these, however, were not professional soldiers. The professionals were recruited from among the members of the young generation who found themselves redundant in the mountainous conditions of their home district. The bulk of Rohan's highlanders, however, were brave and self-reliant but poorly trained volunteers. Sometimes they were armed with nothing better than ancient arquebuses and muskets. They found it hard to spend a long time in the plains in an unfamiliar climate; for many of them, Montpellier was almost the edge of the world.

Rohan was not able to recruit his co-religionists whose homes were outside the Huguenot areas (more will be said about this later); nor could he hire foreign mercenaries (Swiss, *lansquenets*, etc.), as the government had taken steps to prevent this.

Thus, Rohan had no standing army in the strict sense of the word. His limited means compelled him to disband nearly all his troops at once when a campaign came to an end. His army lacked artillery; the Huguenots' guns were dispersed among the cities, where the garrison commanders not only owed obedience to Rohan but had also to reckon with the municipal councils, who did not always recognise his authority. On the other hand, he possessed, as already mentioned, an excellent body of officers.

All these circumstances, together with the topography of Upper Guyenne and Languedoc, forced upon Rohan particular forms of strategy and tactics. He had to avoid pitched battles with the king's army, which was large, made up of regular soldiers, and equipped not only with siege artillery but also with field-guns. He could succeed only through speed and mobility, good knowledge of the terrain, and skill in making use of mountain conditions. So long as he was operating in the Cévennes, he was master of the situation. At that time, this area possessed no real roads, but only tracks along which the highlanders, who knew them well, were able to move, with their little group of officers headed by Rohan, at a pace that astonished the commanders of the king's army. To defend the cities of Upper Guyenne and Languedoc, that is, the provinces which shared between them the ridge of the Cévennes, Rohan used the latter as a sort of corridor for rapid movement of troops. If needed, he could be in the east of the region, at Alais (Alès) and Anduze, or in the west, at Castres and Milhau (Millau). His headquarters were in these last two towns, so that they were especially important to him, and he exerted all possible efforts to keep control of them.

[1] *Documents d'histoire*, II, 364.

Rohan had to draw not only his men but all his resources from the same restricted territory. In order that the cities should be able to withstand sieges successfully (and it was to besieging and capturing cities that the royal army applied itself), they had to be kept supplied with large stocks of munitions and foodstuffs. To ensure this, the rural areas had to be protected from the devastation systematically carried out by the royal forces. That was why Rohan continually moved about Guyenne and Languedoc, supplying and defending the cities *from without*, bringing them fresh reinforcements, munitions and provisions and hindering the activities of the king's troops. He was elusive and indestructible.

The king's army consisted of the permanent nucleus of what were called the *vieux régiments*, complemented by experienced French professional soldiers, and of foreign legions and new regiments of volunteers. Though the cavalry, made up of noblemen, was excellent, and the artillery adequate, neither of these was of much use in the mountains and foothills against small detachments of the enemy who well knew how to conceal themselves. In many places the stony character of the soil made it hard to dig trenches or to lay mines under the walls of cities. The royal army's ability to man-œuvre was limited. The direction of operations was dispersed between different commanders, who had grown used to doing as they pleased, and neither Luynes nor the young Louis XIII was capable of changing this situation.

The king's army fought with the aim of wearing the enemy down, and operated where it could expect to succeed, that is, it laid siege to the cities of the plains, the wealthiest and most important centres of the Huguenot South. This military task was dictated by a political aim. These cities were not only military objectives; their subjection to the king would mean the undermining and eventually the collapse of the Huguenot political organisation.

Before leaving Paris, the king issued a declaration to the effect that the government had no design on the religious rights of the Huguenots but was merely fighting to put down rebellion. This declaration was a very shrewd move. It guaranteed to Huguenots who refrained from taking part in the rebellion the enjoyment of all their rights and the inviolability of their property. The result was that in the provinces to the north of the Loire (that is, outside the limits of the Huguenot territory) all the Huguenots stayed at home, and their co-religionists in Guyenne and Languedoc were left with insufficient numbers. The southerners were not only unable to raise an army adequate for military operations, an *armée en campagne*, as in the sixteenth century, but they found themselves with insufficient men even to make up garrisons in all their cities.[1] A little later, when religious discord became more intense, the government disarmed the Huguenots in Normandy, Brittany and Picardy, and many of them left France, emigrating to England and Holland.[2]

The capital was left in the care of Luynes's father-in-law, the Duc de Montbazon, while Condé was sent into Berry and the Bourbonnais to recruit troops and make sure of Sancerre and the other Huguenot cities along the Loire.[3]

At the beginning of May, the king moved westward from Orléans, and a substantial part of the king's army, which had wintered as garrisons in the cities of Poitou and Guyenne, was concentrated in the direction of Saint-Jean-d'Angély, which the men of La Rochelle had hastily fortified. There the war began: officers of the king's army began a skirmish with the enemy without having been given any order to do so, *comme par une inspiration*.[4] Such irresponsible actions, which sometimes did considerable damage to the plans of the king's generals, occurred on a number of subsequent occasions. Each officer regarded himself as having the right to command his unit at his own discretion.

In order to close the route across the Loire into Poitou completely, and, having secured his rear along the Loire, to be in a position to move more quickly down to the South, where the Huguenots had not yet managed to fortify those cities in Guyenne and Languedoc which were in a bad state of defence, the king put a large garrison into Saumur, a Huguenot fortress of great strategic importance. There were reports that the assembly of La Rochelle itself intended to send substantial forces there, and the governor of Saumur, Duplessis-Mornay, one of the last of the veterans of the civil wars of the sixteenth century and one of the last of the Huguenot political writers, would not be the man to prevent this. He was removed from his post for the duration of the campaign, and not reappointed at the end of it, and he died soon afterwards. His death was a great loss to the Huguenot party, for he possessed high standing among his co-religionists and also enjoyed consideration at court, where his opinion was respected.

The king made the journey from Saumur to besiege Saint-Jean-d'Angély between 17 May and 1 June. During these two weeks, all the Huguenot cities situated on or near his route opened their gates, and others proclaimed their allegiance to the government. Some of the Huguenot grandees (Castelnau, Trémouille and others) assured the king of their loyalty and thereby kept the cities they governed. The start of the campaign was hopeful,

[1] Fontenay-Mareuil, op. cit. p. 158.   [2] Malingre, op. cit. pp. 246–9.
[3] Ibid. pp. 329–37.   [4] Fontenay-Mareuil, op. cit. p. 158.

resembling the king's expedition into Normandy in 1620. At Saint-Jean-d'Angély, however, the royal army encountered serious opposition. The city had been in Rohan's hands since 1612, and had a large garrison which the Rochelais had reinforced with about five hundred men, commanded by Soubise. But they had not succeeded in fortifying the city according to the new system, that is, by erecting large earthworks around the suburbs. Rohan was not near, having gone south to prepare for defence the great cities of Upper Guyenne and Languedoc and then send new forces from there to help Soubise.

The king's army blockaded Saint-Jean-d'Angély, and the city's supplies of munitions were cut off.[1] Soubise refused the demand that he surrender, because he expected aid would be coming from Rohan. And so the siege began: assaults, sorties, skirmishes, sometimes of a desperate character. The king's army contained many noble volunteers who were in quest of glory and longing for battle. They continually hindered the operations of the regular army by their attempts to storm particular strongpoints on their own, even when expressly forbidden, and rushing in mobs to wherever a fight was beginning. They caused a great deal of trouble and embarrassment to the high command.

The king and Luynes counted on a quick siege. Then they would be able to fall upon the South not later than June or July, and conclude the campaign by the autumn. However, the siege dragged on for more than three weeks, and this had considerable effect on later developments.

Though the city was comparatively small, and was invested on every side, the siege presented great difficulty. The king's army did not yet know how to conduct regular sieges,[2] rapidly overcoming the bastions and crownworks projecting from the walls. It included only one single military engineer, the Italian Gamorini, and his advice was not always followed. The artillery operated poorly; it was commanded by Sully's son, the Duc de Rosny, whose conduct aroused misgivings. The government was badly prepared for war. Luynes had imagined that the mere presence of the king would suffice for every city to open its gates.[3] This lack of foresight had to be made up for as the campaign proceeded. At the end of May Lesdiguières joined the forces in the field and took the needful measures.[4] In place of Rosny he appointed to command the artillery Luynes's brother, the Duc de Chaulnes. A fierce bombardment of the city began; communications were severed between Saint-Jean-d'Angély and La Rochelle, and Soubise could no longer look

[1] B. Zeller, *Le Connétable de Luynes*, p. 67. [2] Fontenay-Mareuil, op. cit. p. 160.
[3] B. Zeller, *Le Connétable de Luynes*, pp. 71, 72.
[4] The siege of Saint-Jean-d'Angély is described in great detail in Malingre, op. cit. pp. 292–325.

forward to aid either from La Rochelle or from his brother, for he was blockaded on all sides. Nor did intervention by England prove successful; the king rejected the protest conveyed by a special envoy from England, and the latter had to leave without having achieved anything.

Artillery bombardment did very severe damage to the city, leaving not a single building intact. On 23 June it was followed up by an assault, and the fortified suburbs were taken. The following day saw an intensified bombardment, and the city walls were breached in several places. Soubise's position was hopeless, and on 25 June he surrendered. He was allowed to leave the city with his troops. Saint-Jean-d'Angély was sacked and all its privileges abolished; the city's sources of revenue were incorporated in the royal domain, their management being assigned to royal officials. A royal garrison was stationed in the city for the period needed for the fortifications to be demolished, and all the inhabitants were obliged to take a hand in these works. The city was transformed into an unfortified settlement, its walls and bastions levelled with the ground, its moats filled in. Contemporaries commented on this as *le spectacle le plus nouveau que nous ayons peu voir en nos jours.*[1] Similarly thorough measures were subsequently taken with every city that surrendered. Those that were small were turned into mere *bourgs* after their walls had been knocked down. Louis XIII said that his aim was to allow fortified towns only on the frontiers of the kingdom.[2]

The fall of Saint-Jean-d'Angély greatly perturbed the Huguenots. The city had been regarded as impregnable; in 1569 (after the battle at Moncontour) it had withstood a long siege and surrendered only with reservation of all its privileges. After this defeat the Huguenots retained only three reliable fortresses: La Rochelle, Montauban and Clairac. The gamble on English diplomatic intervention had failed, and there were no grounds for hoping for aid from Germany. Holland, in expectation of renewed war with Spain (the truce concluded for twelve years in 1609 expired on 25 March) was interested in obtaining help from the French government, and had no intention of helping the Huguenots.

Nevertheless, though the fall of Saint-Jean-d'Angély was a heavy blow to the Huguenot cause, the king's army had been held up by the siege almost to the end of June, a delay which was vexatious to the government both in itself and because of complications in the field of external relations. Every event on the civil war front at once found an echo outside France, and especially in that region where Spain was striving to achieve her ends by any and every means, namely, northern Italy. As soon as it became clear that the royal army was held up before Saint-Jean-d'Angély, Feria lost no time in occupying

[1] Malingre, op. cit. p. 326.   [2] Ibid. p. 400.

all strategic points along the Adda and in the valley of Chiavenna. While political considerations basically dictated this move, of course, he took as his pretext the need to protect the Catholic people of the Valtelline from persecution by the Protestants of the Grisons.[1] The Valtelline became a Spanish possession, the Treaty of Madrid being crudely trampled on.

After the capture of Saint-Jean-d'Angély, the road to La Rochelle was open, but at that stage the objective of the campaign was not La Rochelle but the South. For this reason the government restricted itself to cutting communications between La Rochelle and the South, leaving d'Épernon in Saintonge with an army of 12,000 men. Soon, moreover, his presence was required in Béarn, and only a small force was left behind in Saintonge.

The army was moved to the South, to Sainte-Foy on the Dordogne and Clairac on the Garonne, with the aim of proceeding from there to Montauban in order to lay siege to that city. The royal commanders were confident in their artillery, thanks to which the resistance of Saint-Jean-d'Angély had been overcome. Additional guns were to be brought up from Toulouse, and munitions from Paris and Champagne.[2]

During the seven weeks' march from Saint-Jean to Montauban (27 June to 17 August) the king mastered all the Huguenot towns—and there were some important ones—along his route, in Saintonge and Guyenne; they all, with one exception, opened their gates to him, even though among them were some, such as Bergerac, which were strongly fortified and had large garrisons. The example of Saint-Jean had shown that resistance would be useless.

The single exception was Clairac. Its situation was a particularly important one, blocking the road to Montauban. This strong fortress, with its numerous garrison (4,000 men), was capable of holding up the royal army and giving the people of Montauban time to get ready for the siege which seemed inevitable. If Clairac held out for a month and a half, the entire campaign would be spoiled, for autumn was a late time to be starting a siege of Montauban. For this reason a number of members of the king's Council advised that a detour be made around Clairac, even though this would also take time. Relying on the power of his guns, however, the king decided to attack the city; the army suffered heavy losses, but within a week Clairac fell.

Thus, the campaign was proceeding favourably for the government, but much more slowly than had been expected. The army reached Montauban, the chief fortress in the South, only in the middle of August. Crowning

---

[1] This pretext deceived nobody. Even the Nuncio wrote, in December 1621, that 'religion is a cloak under which the Spaniards hide their designs upon Italy'. (B. Zeller, *Le Connétable de Luynes*, p. 229).

[2] Malingre, op. cit. pp. 379, 380.

success now depended on the length of the siege. If they proved able to take the city quickly, all Languedoc would have to submit, and the war in the South would be over. Only La Rochelle would remain to be dealt with. A prolonged siege meant loss of time and failure of the campaign, because in the existing conditions it was not possible to carry on the war in late autumn and winter.

A prolonged siege also entailed a danger of complications externally. As early as June, when representatives of the Swiss cantons met French envoys in Lucerne, the Protestant cantons declined to serve as guarantors of the fulfilment of the Treaty of Madrid, giving as their reason the French government's war against the Huguenots. Naturally, in these circumstances Feria would not give up the positions he had occupied. The Valtelline remained in his hands, and all France's allies in Italy were in danger, as before.

In the light of these facts we can understand the dispute that broke out in the king's Council immediately after the taking of Clairac (4 August) on the question of what to do next—to advance on Montauban, or to go directly into Languedoc? One might send part of the army to Montauban, to cut it off from the other areas, while sending the bulk of the army into Languedoc, where the towns had not yet managed to complete their fortifications. Receiving no aid from anywhere, Montauban would have to surrender. As against this plan, one might besiege Montauban with the entire army, since it was the key to Languedoc; so long as it remained in the Huguenots' hands the other towns could not be taken, because they could receive help from the Cévennes.[1]

The king insisted on besieging Montauban, counting on the destructive effect of his artillery, the fall of Clairac having strongly confirmed him in this view. Luynes had hopes also of internal discord in Montauban, where he had supporters (*intelligences*) whose task would be to incline the city towards submission to the king. At that time Luynes concentrated all power in his hands. Already constable, he became also Keeper of the Seals after the death of Du Vair, at the beginning of August. This 'innovation', without precedent in the history of the French monarchy, the union in one person of supreme power in both military and civil matters, occurred because at that moment Luynes had no man of his own to whom he could entrust the post of Keeper of the Seals.[2] Military and official circles were intensely irritated by this development. The king lent an ear to their protests and to their malicious jokes, in which they repeated that Luynes was a good constable only in peacetime and a good Keeper of the Seals only in wartime, thus insinuating

---

[1] Fontenay-Mareuil, op. cit. p. 161.   [2] B. Zeller, *Le Connétable de Luynes*, p. 94.

that he was fit for neither post. But Louis did not reverse his decisions. The army headed for Montauban, arriving on 17 August.

Even before this the Duc de Mayenne had taken Nérac and other fortresses to the south of the Garonne; recalled from before La Rochelle, d'Épernon advanced into Béarn.[1] As a result, Montauban found itself isolated from the west and the south, and the principal approaches to it by river, along the Garonne and the Tarn, were closed.[2]

Montauban, situated on a high bank of the Tarn, was regarded as the best fortress in France after La Rochelle. Besides walls and moats, its defences included two large fortified suburbs. But at the beginning of the campaign it was not ready for a siege, and the garrison was small. In June Rohan, in whose territory it was included, arrived there and began feverish preparations. The garrison was strengthened, and additional fortifications were hastily erected, according to plans drawn up by Rohan and under his supervision. The entire male population was drawn into service, divided into thirty battalions and given military training under the command of experienced officers. Then Rohan handed over his command to La Force while he himself, in the middle of July, having established himself at Castres (to the south-east of Montauban, on the western slopes of the Cévennes), began collecting money from the cities and recruiting soldiers from all the neighbouring districts: Gévaudan, Rouergue, Albigeois, Foix, Lauraguais, and especially from the Cévennes. From those mountains warriors came down who were armed with ancient arquebuses and carried Calvinist psalters. They were led by captains from the nobility. The place of assembly was Rohan's second headquarters, Milhau, on the upper Tarn. Thus, Montauban's communications with the north and east were controlled by Rohan.

The king's army invested Montauban on three sides, leaving free (because of the terrain) precisely the north-east corner. It was divided into three large corps, called *quartiers*, under the command of Lesdiguières, Mayenne and Bassompierre. The city was so large that not only could this great army not close the ring around it but also the three sections were so distant from each other that even the shortest path between them took an hour's uphill horse-riding to traverse.[3] This meant that the army was inadequate for the siege of Montauban. Relying on his secret agents within the city, Luynes declined the help of a force of 6,000 men recruited by Vendôme in Brittany;

[1] Ibid. p. 80.
[2] All the circumstances of the siege of Montauban are described in great detail by Malingre, writing from the government point of view (op. cit. pp. 473–559), and from the Huguenot point of view by an anonymous citizen of Montauban, in *Histoire particulière des plus mémorables choses qui se sont passées au siège de Montauban* (Leyden, 1623).
[3] B. Zeller, *Le Connétable de Luynes*, p. 96; Fontenay-Mareuil, op. cit. p. 162.

it was the lack of such a force that prevented Montauban from being invested on all sides. Meanwhile, the activities of Luynes's men in Montauban were exposed, and they were hanged. Now everything depended on the contest of arms.

They began to construct earthworks—approaches, trenches and the rest. The most vulnerable spot in Montauban's system of fortifications was the hill of Saint-Denis. They had not realised that they should have captured it at once, and so they had to lead trenches up to it. Owing to bad administration in the king's army, this took a great deal of time; the enemy managed to strengthen their bastions so that 'it would have needed a whole century to take them'.[1] Mayenne twice attempted to take them by assault, without adequate preparation, and was beaten back; he himself was killed in a skirmish (17 September). Both sides suffered heavy losses, mainly from cannon and musket fire. The king lost many distinguished officers, and great numbers of soldiers. Lesdiguières conducted the fortification works so badly that the defenders succeeded in exploding a mine in the middle of his trenches, so that they were able to cut off and capture a fort he had constructed. The king's artillery did not live up to the hopes that had been placed upon it. The guns had to fire from a great distance, and the cannonade failed to do serious damage to the large and strongly fortified city.[2]

In short, all the defects in the royal army which had been felt in some degree already during the siege of Saint-Jean-d'Angély manifested themselves now to their full extent. The king ordered a new levy of 10,000 men, summoned the noble volunteers to join him before Montauban, and called for money from Paris. Although it was already nearly the end of September, he did not want to raise the siege; there were reports that, despite the successful defence, or rather, as a result of it, the citizens of Montauban were frightfully exhausted and worn out. There was no unity in the city. A peace party, composed mainly of rich bourgeois, had been formed. During his stay in Montauban, Rohan and the pastors struggled hard against these people; now, in the moment of crisis, they acquired such an ascendancy that the citizens sent a deputation to the king to notify him of their desire to submit, if only Rohan would agree. The latter, though all this time carrying on secret negotiations with Luynes (who was related to him by marriage), would not agree to the proposed separate peace. What he needed was a *paix générale*, that is, a new treaty between the government and the Huguenot party as a whole, guaranteeing all their rights and privileges. For this reason the initiative of the citizens of Montauban failed to attain the desired results.

[1] Fontenay-Mareuil, op. cit., p. 162.
[2] B. Zeller, *Le Connétable de Luynes*, p. 99.

The essential question now was whether Rohan would be able to bring help to the besieged city. Only success in this task could strengthen the duke's position. He hastily despatched all the men he could collect in the time, about 1,500, and on 28 October half of these got into the city. The rest either fell or were taken prisoner. Montauban was now in a position to continue its defence, and Rohan broke off his negotiations with Luynes.

Difficult days came upon the royal army. Epidemics spread, the continual failures demoralised the soldiers, and large-scale desertion began. The fugitive soldiers became bandits, plundering the population of the surrounding area.[1] At the beginning of October, Montmorency brought 5,000 men from Languedoc, reinforced with another thousand from Toulouse. But disease and desertion had done their work: the army was visibly melting away. Within a few days only, a mere third of the force from Toulouse remained.[2]

After three months, on 10 November, the siege was lifted. Nevertheless, even at that moment the government possessed a number of advantages. Despite the failure before Montauban, the king now held eighty Huguenot cities and was master of Poitou, Saintonge (except La Rochelle), Lower Guyenne, Gascony and Béarn. In addition, the small Huguenot towns in Normandy, Picardy and Berry, which were not included among the *places de sûreté*, had been taken. The royal forces had also had some success in the Vivarais—the Huguenots retained only Upper Guyenne, Languedoc and the Dauphiné. This meant that their territory had been reduced by two-thirds. Although it had not proved possible to capture Montauban, positions had been taken which were important for the campaign of the following year. However, the government also faced some serious difficulties.

When the news of Mayenne's death reached Paris, the fanatical Catholics (let us recall the popularity of the Guise family in Paris in the period of the League) set fire to the Calvinist church at Charenton and killed several Huguenots, together with some Catholics who tried to prevent the killings.[3] Marie de Médicis tried to exploit this outburst of fanaticism, wilfully entering the capital and inciting against Luynes the grandees who were living there. As has already been mentioned, the war against the Huguenots was very unpopular among the higher nobility. A number of pamphlets appeared in which Luynes was censured and impudently mocked not only for his failure before Montauban but also for his entire policy—his war against the Huguenots, his pushing aside of the great nobles, his 'connivance' with Spain in the Valtelline and the Palatinate, and so on.

The situation in the ill-starred Valtelline was very alarming. The failure

---

[1] Ibid. p. 135. [2] Fontenay-Mareuil, op. cit. p. 163.
[3] B. Zeller, *Le Connétable de Luynes*, p. 116.

of the siege of Montauban reinforced still further Spain's determination to remain mistress of the Alpine passes. Spinola occupied the Upper Palatinate and Juliers. In this connexion the Pope also took up a more pro-Spanish attitude. He offered to help France in the Valtelline if she would abandon her Dutch allies (who had just lost Juliers), that is, he repeated the proposals which Philip III had put to Bassompierre before the signing of the Treaty of Madrid. As before, the Spanish government was playing a double game. In its official declarations it condemned the acts of its governor of Milan, but in fact it approved and encouraged them. In September and October Feria erected two more forts in the Valtelline, against Venice, and tried to make the Grisons sign a treaty by which the Valtelline would be incorporated in the Milanese and Spain would obtain the exclusive right to use the passes. The position was menacing: the Grisons could not repel Spanish aggression with their own unaided forces, Venice was in jeopardy, and France was faced with the loss of all her rights in the passes. Immediately after the lifting of the siege of Montauban, the Venetian ambassador told Luynes that it was absolutely necessary to fight Spain, because otherwise she would not give up the Valtelline; and this time Luynes offered no objection to the organising of a Franco-Italian coalition against Spain.

All these considerations counted for a great deal in the government's decision to call off the siege and return to Paris.[1] At the same time, the programme for further struggle against the Huguenots in the following year remained in force, and the king continued to show confidence in Luynes; at the beginning of December, at Toulouse, the king's confessor, the Jesuit Arnoux, was dismissed for speaking against the constable.

On the way from Toulouse to Paris it was necessary to take again by force the towns of Monheurt and Sainte-Foy, which had been recovered by the Huguenots, as otherwise the road to the north would have been closed to the king. In anticipation of the next campaign and in order to hold firmly the positions which had been won, nearly all the standing army was distributed for the winter as garrisons in the towns of Guyenne. The greater part of it, under Marshal Saint-Géran, was stationed around Montauban. Another part, concentrated around Sainte-Foy, was commanded by d'Elbeuf, one of the Guise family.

At that time Luynes fell ill, and on 15 December 1621 he died. Is it necessary to discuss the question of what would have become of him if he had not died so unexpectedly? To contemporaries it was of burning interest, as rumours that the king was turning against him had been circulating for some time, and many people connected the war against the Huguenots

---

[1] B. Zeller, *Le Connétable de Luynes*, pp. 233, 234.

mainly with Luynes's influence. The whole of the higher nobility longed for his dismissal. Most historians, echoing sources hostile to Luynes, have considered that Luynes died as his star was setting. The important thing, however, is not his personal fate as such but the political line associated with him. Did this change after his death?

Luynes's enemies, who were numerous at court, expressed the hope, some in writing (in memorials) and others by word of mouth (as we learn by the reports of memoirists and the despatches of foreign ambassadors), that with his death everything was bound to change. They did not, of course, fail to note some words spoken by Louis XIII which showed his lack of respect for the remains of the man who not long before had been his friend. One well-established fact is well known, being recorded by the very accurate writer Fontenay-Mareuil: on Luynes's coffin the lackeys escorting it played cards, while their unharnessed horses grazed alongside.

But we must also take other facts into account. More than once, later on, the king spoke of Richelieu in similar and even sharper terms of condemnation, and more than once the cardinal found himself in a very critical situation, expecting to be dismissed, yet in his case too, only death 'dismissed' him from the leading position in the government. The flood of pamphlets directed against him was sometimes even more imposing, and their tone incomparably sharper, and yet they changed nothing. Returning to Luynes, it must further be observed that the king allowed his brothers to retain all the wealth accumulated by the family, depriving them only of those offices which were of political importance.

But the most important fact, which has not been mentioned by historians, was that even after Luynes's death the output of pamphlets directed against him did not cease, while their tone became even sharper. The biggest and harshest of these pamphlets, *La France mourante* and *La Chronique des favoris*, were attacks on a man already dead. In both of them, personalities were accompanied by a consistent critique of Luynes's policy, a defence of the claims of the higher nobility (the Princes of the Blood, Marie de Médicis, and so on) to participate in the king's Council, and a condemnation of the war against the Huguenots. The combination of these themes was not accidental: I have already mentioned why the grandees did not wish to see the power of the Huguenots destroyed. Why, then, did they trouble to mention the dead favourite? In order to attain two aims: to remind the reader of the failure of the military campaign, and to turn the government against a continuation of this policy.

The government, indeed, though Luynes was no longer alive, continued the war against the Huguenots into the following year, 1622. This same line was maintained even later, and it was taken up in 1624 by Richelieu. I have shown earlier why it was necessary for the consolidation of absolutism. For this reason it seems most probable that, had Luynes lived, nothing would have altered; that is, the war with the Huguenots would have continued, together with cautious manœuvring from time to time in the field of foreign policy.

Before passing to the campaign of 1622, I must briefly touch on La Rochelle and related questions. Up to now it had remained in the background, though many people (and especially the Catholic clergy) considered that this hotbed of heresy should have been dealt a decisive blow at the very start. The Rochelais lost no time in making the best of the circumstances. Though the king's army blocked their communication with the interior, the sea was at their disposal. As the government had no fleet, they were undisputed masters of the coastal waters, seizing the islands of Oléron and Ré and also the port of Blaye, up the Gironde, and hindering the trade of Bordeaux. A fleet was absolutely necessary if they were to be overcome, but enormous sums would be required in order to bring this into being. Luynes's financial policy, however, was a markedly cautious one. The sources drawn upon to cover extraordinary expenditure—forced loans from officials, the sale of new offices, subsidies from the clergy, borrowing from financiers—showed how much any increase in taxation was dreaded, because of the danger of embarrassments caused by possible popular revolts. Great restraint was observed even in extracting contributions from the privileged orders; the government hesitated to face them with more extensive demands. Both methods—squeezing the church and the officials, and increasing taxes—seemed dangerous. Under these conditions it appeared impossible to build a fleet, and this circumstance prolonged for several years the threat from La Rochelle.

After Luynes's death the awkward question came up of how the government was to be composed, or, more precisely, of who was to be at the head of it. There was no-one in the king's entourage who could take Luynes's place and enjoy so much of the king's confidence. Louis XIII was in general not given to showing confidence in people, particularly statesmen, but, on the other hand, once he had become convinced of someone's worth, he did not waver in his attitude to that person. This was shown with especial clarity later on, in his relations with Richelieu.

That it was not possible to trust Marie de Médicis had been proved by the whole preceding half-decade, 1615–20. True, behind the Queen Mother could now be seen the figure of Richelieu (as yet only Bishop of Luçon), who had already attracted the special attention of such shrewd and discerning diplomats as the Venetian and Tuscan ambassadors. Over him, however, lay the shadow of a past disagreeable to the king: in 1616–17 Richelieu had been a minister in the government of the favourite d'Ancre, who was later assassinated by order of Louis XIII, and in 1619–20 he had been Marie de Médicis' adviser during the armed revolt of herself and the higher nobility against the government. Nobody doubted his talents. Everyone knew that it was he who conducted the entire diplomatic game of his protectress, and did it with success. He was already beginning to be feared in court circles, all the more so because his former ingratiating and flattering manner was increasingly replaced by a cool composure and an ever more assertive ambition. He wanted to be a cardinal, and the Queen Mother worked hard on his behalf. The king and Luynes gave her official backing through the French ambassador in Rome, but in conversation with the Nuncio and in secret correspondence with the Pope they warned that it would be undesirable to confer the cardinal's hat upon the Bishop of Luçon. This high ecclesiastical dignity would give him an important place not only in the French church but also, what was incomparably more dangerous, in the king's Council, which was what Marie de Médicis was hoping for. At the moment, the first place in the Council, as regards rank, was held by Cardinal de Retz, but Richelieu undoubtedly aspired to this place.

Louis XIII respected his father's old counsellors, and trusted them. But their ranks had become thin. The most important of them, Villeroy, had died in 1617. The *président* Jeannin, who enjoyed a deserved reputation as an experienced politician, was eighty, and had few years before him. Of the same age was the Keeper of the Seals, De Vic, who was appointed to this post after the death of Luynes, and himself died within a few months. Chancellor Sillery was no younger. The secretaries of state, apart from the Chancellor's son Puisieux, were, for all their knowledge and experience, second-rate figures. The old generation of high dignitaries was leaving the stage, and there were no successors in the wings.

The head of the king's Council, Cardinal de Retz, a modest man, known for his piety and Christian virtues, had no views on his own on state affairs and played only a decorative role, not a leading one, in the Council. There remained two men—the Prince de Condé and the controller-general of finance,[1] Schomberg.

[1] After Sully's dismissal in 1611 the office of *surintendant* was, for political reasons, temporarily abolished (cf. Lublinskaya, *Frantsiya va nachale XVII veka*, pp. 106–7, 109). Until the appointment of La Vieuville (see p. 222), Sully's successors were officially entitled controllers-general of finance, heading what was called the *direction des finances* (cf. the *règlement* of 5 February 1611, in Mousnier, 'Les Règlements du conseil du roi sous Louis XIII', *Annuaire-Bulletin de la Société de l'histoire de France, Années 1946–7* (Paris, 1948), p. 128). Nevertheless, contemporaries continued as before to refer to them as *surintendants*, which accounts for the varying descriptions of these officials in the sources.

The latter was an interesting figure. Like Sully he was a general who at the same time managed the state's finances. Count Henri de Nanteuil de Schomberg (1575–1632), son of a German captain who became a naturalised Frenchman, married the daughter of the Duc d'Halluin, whose title later came to him. His great career began in 1616, when Richelieu, as minister in the government of d'Ancre, sent him to Germany, where Schomberg retained numerous connexions. There his task was to convince the Protestant princes not to place any hopes on the agitations of the French grandees, who were fighting against the government.[1] Though the king long remained suspicious of everyone who had been associated with d'Ancre, in 1619 Schomberg was named controller-general of finance and *grand maître de l'artillerie*. It is hardly to be doubted that the second of these appointments, for which he was well fitted, brought the other one with it. War with the grandees was about to begin, and war expenditure should be under the control of whoever was in charge of the artillery, just as Sully in his time had similarly occupied these two posts. The dignity of constable being left unfilled after the death of Luynes, Schomberg was almost the most important person in the French high command (he became a marshal in 1625). He enjoyed the reputation of an able and cautious commander and an absolutely honest man, something that was rarely found in the management of state finance. But he had no outstanding talents, and he was not quick-witted.[2] His principal function was to procure the means for carrying on the war. He was obviously not suitable for the leading position in the government.

The Prince de Condé had a tempestuous past behind him. Between the death of Henry IV and his arrest in 1616 he headed the princely opposition and fought against the government. His alliance with the Huguenot grandees enabled him, after the campaign of 1615–16, to become, by the treaty of Loudun, head of the king's Council, pushing aside Henry IV's old ministers who had ruled during the regency of Marie de Médicis between 1610 and 1616. But this triumph of the great nobles and their leader lasted only about a month. Condé was arrested and locked up in the castle of Vincennes. Later on, in the period of the struggle against the grandees allied with Marie de Médicis, Luynes released Condé and brought him into the Council in the modest capacity of a counsellor. This move was dictated by a desire to deprive the great nobles of a specious pretext for opposition: the first Prince of the Blood was allowed to take part in state affairs and had no grounds for com-

[1] See Lublinskaya, *Frantsiya v nachale XVII veka*, p. 246. It is interesting to note that Schomberg's father was in 1571 sent by Charles IX to the princes of Germany with the mission of strengthening their friendly attitude to the French government (*Lettres de Henri III, publiées par M. François*, 1 (Paris, 1959) p. 181, note 2).

[2] B. Zeller, *Richelieu et les ministres de Louis XIII*, p. 32.

plaint. For similar reasons the Queen Mother, too, was admitted after 1620 into discussions of state affairs. And, indeed, Condé did not take up arms again in opposition to the government; but he had reasons of his own for this.

Down to the birth of Louis XIII in 1601, Condé had been, under Henry IV, who had no legitimate sons until then, the heir apparent to the throne, because he was the king's nearest relative in the male line. Now, in 1622, the situation might be repeated. Louis XIII had no children, and the heir to the throne was his brother Gaston. Thus, only the latter stood between Condé and possible succession to the throne, and he calculated that he had a better chance than Henry of Navarre had had in his time of succeeding, as in the end he did, his three childless cousins. These hopes drew Condé away from his earlier role as leader of the higher nobility. They also inspired his desire to settle with the Huguenot party as soon and as drastically as possible, so as to ensure for himself thereafter a prosperous reign. That was how he explained his behaviour to a contemporary who, like many others, was amazed by its strangeness,[1] for Condé, son and grandson of Huguenot leaders of the sixteenth century, was in his hatred of the Huguenots more thorough-going than any *dévot*.

All this was well known to the king, and for this very reason Condé could not be put at the head of the government. From his father's old ministers and from Luynes the young king had learnt to be careful and circumspect, to weigh up the real possibilities in a situation. The failure of the siege of Montauban in 1621 had been another instructive experience for him. Besides, he had to reckon all the time with the international situation. I have already shown that at certain moments he was capable of exerting influence, even decisive influence, on the government's policy. It was characteristic that Condé was not with the king before Montauban; he had been sent off to operate in Berry and the Bourbonnais.

After Luynes's death, the king decided to rule in his own person, and desired to be informed of the progress of absolutely all matters, so as to be able to give decisions on them independently. However, as the court foresaw, this experiment proved unsuccessful. The young man revealed all his qualities and his limitations. He grasped the problems of politics, was filled with desire to make France great, as his father had done, and was persevering. But he lacked that equipment for the fulfilment of 'the office of a king' which his son and successor, Louis XIV, possessed through the splendid training he received from a statesman of such calibre and skill as Mazarin, who had himself been trained by Cardinal Richelieu. Louis XIII's endeavours led only to a situation in which the chancellor and the secretaries

---

[1] Fontenay-Mareuil, op. cit. p. 167.

of state began to ask the king's sanction for everything they did. The king was overwhelmed by the range of tasks confronting him, especially in the field of foreign policy, and the many and various difficulties which called for unceasing thought and consideration. He abandoned this role once and for all.

In these circumstances the actual management of affairs (with the approval of the king, a condition which Louis XIII always insisted upon) could be undertaken either by some new member of the king's Council (such as the Bishop of Luçon might become, with the support of Marie de Médicis) or by one of its existing members. Setting aside those members who were unfitted for this role—the Queen Mother, Retz, Condé and Schomberg—there remained only the Brûlarts: chancellor Sillery and his son Puisieux, who was in charge of foreign affairs and who possessed already in Luynes's time considerable authority and initiative. Louis XIII did not want to admit Richelieu into the Council, and there were no other candidates besides the Brûlarts. As early as the end of December 1621 they strengthened their position by getting their kinsman, *commandeur* de Sillery, appointed ambassador to Rome. In the approaching conflict with Spain over the Valtelline this diplomatic post was of particular importance, and the Brûlarts had to have a reliable man of their own close to the Pope.

It has already been mentioned that the king did not change the decision to proceed with the war against the Huguenots. The Brûlarts had to follow this line of policy which, it must be stressed, enjoyed great popularity in Paris, despite the protests of the great nobles. Even leaving aside the circles of *dévots* at court and elsewhere, consisting mostly of Jesuits and other clergy, and demanding complete eradication of heresy in France and throughout Europe, the entire Catholic population of northern France (and in the South this was even more so) were hostile to the Huguenots. Memoirs and pamphlets in great number testify to this. The Huguenots were condemned for separatism, for endeavouring *se cantonner à la manière de la république*, for disobedience to the king. Though 'bad subjects' they nevertheless enjoyed great advantages and privileges (how much did not their tax exemptions alone cost!), and the war against them was carried on with the money collected from 'good subjects' who lacked these privileges. Bourgeois circles in the capital and in the provinces hailed a policy which aimed at abolishing the special position held by the Huguenots. As was shown by events in Tours, Poitiers and Paris, the urban masses were disposed to give very clear expression to their hatred of Protestants. For this reason, a decision against continuing the war might (quite apart from the fundamental factors already mentioned) have the effect of undermining to a certain extent the government's prestige, something to which the Brûlarts could not agree.

But they had to overcome the resistance of Marie de Médicis and the princes. These circles, besides their steady opposition to the war against the Huguenots, were now pointing to the danger from abroad.

Spain was exploiting her success in the Valtelline and Chiavenna. Continuing to act as though on his own initiative (which enabled the Spanish government to disavow him in case of need), Feria took complete control of the approaches to the Splügen pass. At the same time, Archduke Leopold consolidated his position in the Upper Valtelline and the Upper Engadine, where he established garrisons. By the end of 1621, all the strategic points were already in the hands of Spain and Austria, and the Grisons were forced to sign a treaty giving the Valtelline to Milan. A diplomatic effort by France to prevent the signing of this treaty was unsuccessful. Matters had taken such a turn that armed intervention had become absolutely unavoidable for France. But to undertake this would endanger the campaign against the Huguenots.

The Spanish ambassador in Paris was officially informed of Louis XIII's intention to go to Lyons, and thence, after making an alliance with Savoy and Venice, into Italy.[1] Troops began to concentrate upon Lyons during March. On 12 March, however, it was suddenly decided to send them westward, that is, once more against the Huguenots. This decision was caused by the behaviour of the latter.

After the king's return to Paris at the end of 1621 the Huguenots began urgently to prepare for the campaign of the following year. Their preparations consisted not only of collecting money, recruiting soldiers and fortifying towns. It was of great importance to them to win back those towns which in 1621 had been taken by the king. This was especially true of fortresses which were strategically important. Sainte-Foy, Tonneins, Clairac, Royan (which covered the entrance to the Gironde from the sea) passed back into Huguenot control. In Nègrepelisse and Saint-Antonin the citizens massacred the royal garrisons.

Rohan in particular was in a hurry, wishing to exploit as fully as possible the great increase in his prestige after his successful aid to Montauban. He endeavoured not only to get Upper Guyenne and Languedoc ready for war, but also to strengthen his personal power, shaking off the inconvenient supervision exercised by the assembly of La Rochelle and by that of the *cercle de Languedoc*. His relations with these assemblies became more and more strained. It was the bourgeoisie and the pastors who were predominant in these representative institutions of the Huguenot party. It was typical

[1] Lyons could also, however, serve as the starting-point for an advance down the Rhône into Languedoc, that is, into the Huguenot areas.

that the assembly of La Rochelle resolved to take decisions by majority vote of all the members and not of the orders (as was the normal practice at that time in all representative institutions based on the estates of society, where each 'chamber' had one vote only), a resolution which gave decisive predominance to the bourgeoisie. The same situation existed in the *cercle* assemblies too. Not without reason did Rohan, at a meeting of the Languedoc assembly, angrily denounce its members as republicans, and declare that he would rather preside over an assembly of wolves than over an assembly of pastors.[1]

The assemblies looked upon the Huguenot grandees and other nobles mainly as their military arm, obliged to subordinate itself to their decisions. Rohan, however, wished to be not merely a military commander but also a political leader, that is, he wanted to decide all questions himself, to conduct the war at his own discretion, disposing of financial resources, putting forward conditions for peace negotiations, and so forth. It was natural, therefore, that the assemblies should maintain a very guarded attitude towards him, even though they appreciated his services and his abilities. Still greater (and, as things turned out, quite justifiably so) was their suspicion of certain other Huguenot grandees, mainly Châtillon and Lesdiguières, who actually did change soon afterwards to Catholicism and the king's service. Already in September 1621 the assembly of Languedoc removed Châtillon from the post of general commanding Lower Languedoc and the Vivarais, choosing an obscure nobleman to replace him.[2] At the end of the year, however, after the lifting of the siege of Montauban, Rohan took over this post. At first all power continued to reside with the assembly, who controlled finance, issued orders, and the rest, only delegating matters of minor importance to decision by Rohan's army council. But at the beginning of 1622 Rohan, on his own initiative, assumed the title of *chef et général des églises réformées du royaume ès provinces de Languedoc et Haute Guyenne et gouverneur de Montpellier*, deprived the assembly of all its power, and himself began to impose taxes on town and country alike (in the towns he extracted forced loans from the most comfortably off citizens),[3] and to allot responsibility for definite quotas of soldiers to each area, while he himself chose the members of his army council, and so on. When the cities and the assembly protested to the assembly of La Rochelle, he ignored them. In January the assembly of La Rochelle authorised him to enter into peace negotiations with the king, but he paid no attention to their instructions. Increasingly he adopted a

---

[1] Lagarde, op. cit. p. 54. [2] Ibid. pp. 55–60.
[3] A. Cazenove, 'Campagnes de Rohan en Languedoc', *Annales du Midi*, nos. 55, 56 and 57 (Toulouse, 1902–3). (See here, no. 56, p. 498.)

policy of coercing the cities, which aroused resistance on their part. I have mentioned that there was always a yearning for peace in certain bourgeois circles in the large towns. The example of Montauban in 1621 had shown that, given suitable circumstances, this mood could even lead to readiness to deliver up a city to the king if acceptable terms were offered; sometimes only Rohan's presence in a particular city prevented its surrender.

The situation in the smaller Huguenot towns was even more complicated. Their garrisons were, as a rule, very small[1] and their fortifications in a poor state. Rohan could not increase the size of these garrisons; indeed, he took soldiers from them. Consequently, these small places were left defenceless, at the mercy of fate. They were in danger of attack by the king's army, but also, and especially, by Catholic nobles who found no difficulty in seizing and pillaging them. Essentially, Rohan's policy was systematically to sacrifice these smaller towns in order to preserve the large ones. From the military standpoint this was inevitable, but it did him much harm politically.

The campaign against Rohan began even before the king's departure. As early as February three armies were making their way into Languedoc. From the west came Montmorency, from the Dauphiné (through the Vivarais) came Lesdiguières, and from Provence came Guise. These lines of march, together with the king's intention to go to Lyons, from where he could take either the route across the Alps or down the Rhône to Languedoc, show that, as before, conquest of the Huguenot South remained the government's principal aim. Warlike operations began in March. Lesdiguières captured the towns along the Rhône, thereby severing the Dauphiné from the main Huguenot territory and ensuring free use of the Rhône by the king's army for bringing up munitions and food supplies. Montmorency occupied some towns around Montpellier. The situation was developing unfavourably for Rohan, and he withdrew into the Cévennes.[2]

At the same time things were happening in Poitou. Counting on the king's being delayed in Lyons and on difficulties in the external sphere, Soubise occupied the island of Oléron and the towns of Royan and Les Sables. Making a sortie out of La Rochelle with 3,000 men, he tried to break the blockade of the city on the landward side and strengthen his hold on the neighbouring localities. This development forced the king to leave Paris on 20 March for Nantes. If Soubise succeeded in his plan, the government would have lost in Poitou and Saintonge all the positions won in 1621, and

---

[1] For example, in the diocese of Uzès in 1622, there were stationed in nineteen towns (not counting Uzès itself) only 356 men and in four towns only did the garrisons amount to fifty men. In the other towns they numbered only between five and ten. (Ibid. no. 55, p. 349.)

[2] Ibid. no. 56, pp. 492–4.

occupation by the Huguenots of towns along the Atlantic seaboard would make it easier for them to receive help from England. It was the Prince de Condé who advised the king to make haste. He took this good advice; a small army under Condé, drawn from the royal garrisons, advanced rapidly and inflicted a defeat on Soubise on 15 April. Condé's military reputation rapidly increased, and this fortified still further his opinion that an immediate and complete military suppression of the Huguenots was essential. Other results also followed from the quick victory over Soubise. First, the king could proceed at once to the South, where the Huguenot cities of Guyenne and Languedoc were not ready to defend themselves. Secondly, Poitou and adjoining areas were still at the government's disposal, and in order to prevent further attempts by the Rochelais, a strong fort (Fort-Louis) was quickly erected near the city, so as to block their communications on the landward side. A very large garrison was put into this fort. A few months later galleys arrived at Bordeaux from the Mediterranean ports; these were to be employed in cruising near La Rochelle to obstruct its maritime trade. However, the ocean proved to be too rough for these galleys, which showed once again that it was impossible to do real damage to La Rochelle without a sailing fleet.

After the victory over Soubise the king moved quickly to the South. Once more Royan, Sainte-Foy and Clairac were taken. Nègrepelisse and Saint-Antonin paid heavily for the slaughter of their royal garrisons; they were thoroughly sacked and then burnt to the ground. All the small towns of Guyenne opened their gates to the king. The king made a detour round Montauban and proceeded to Toulouse and Carcassonne, and on 18 June arrived at Béziers. The objective of the campaign was Montpellier, a key position in relation to the whole of Languedoc; he was carrying through the plan which in 1621 had been set aside in favour of the siege of Montauban. The king's rapid and successful advance put an end to the negotiations which had begun between Lesdiguières and Rohan. The latter insisted on the complete fulfilment of the Edict of Nantes, that is, the return of all the cities, but the government refused to relinquish them. Furthermore, it placed great hopes on the growing discord between Rohan and the cities of Languedoc, which were increasingly showing their *mauvais vouloir*. At the end of May there was even a revolt in Nîmes against Rohan, but he pacified the city and arrested its governor.[1] Instances of Rohan's officers going over to the king became more frequent. In July Rohan executed one of these deserters, whom he had captured, but this did not help matters.[2] He spent June and July in feverish activity in Montpellier, Castres and Milhau, preparing these cities for defence.

[1] A. Cazenove, loc. cit. no. 56, p. 497.   [2] Ibid. no. 56, p. 504.

The campaign developed very quickly, much more quickly than in the previous year. Nevertheless, the government encountered great difficulties. From the military point of view, it was well prepared and more experienced, but its financial situation was serious. The royal edicts for raising revenue met with protests by the *parlement*, and had to be registered at a *lit de justice*, that is, in the presence of the king himself. Loans from financiers (secured on the receipts to be obtained through the new edicts, and the next year's revenue) were obtained only with difficulty, and the prospects for further loans were not promising. These financial difficulties seriously hampered the government's operations. Even the king's guards in the Louvre did not get their pay, and expressed discontent.[1] The army's pay fell into arrears, and the soldiers grumbled. The king was frequently told that Schomberg had shown himself unfitted for the post of controller-general of finance, that he had little understanding of money matters and let the financiers do as they pleased. The last charge was justified, but Schomberg had no alternative. The state budget had shown an increasing deficit for several years; loans had to be raised with the minimum delay, and, therefore, on unfavourable terms. Feeling the precariousness of his position, Schomberg sought support from Condé and backed his programme of war for the complete crushing of the Huguenots.

This programme was not fully approved, however, by the king and the Brûlarts. Like Luynes in 1621 they had all the time to take into account the international situation and co-ordinate their operations with changes in that sphere. Puisieux dealt with foreign relations himself, reporting only to the king, excluding Condé and the other members of the Council.

The external situation was as follows. As soon as it had become clear, in March, that the campaign against the Huguenots was beginning, Spanish diplomacy immediately sprang into activity. Although wanting to retain at all costs the Valtelline and the Alpine passes, Spain feared to start an open war in northern Italy, and tried to hide her aggression under some plausible pretext. For this reason she put forward the proposal that the Valtelline be temporarily transferred to papal rule. This meant that the Spaniards would continue as before to be masters of the situation, but France would be deprived of any excuse for armed intervention. France demanded one thing only, fulfilment of the Treaty of Madrid, and at the same time threatened to ally with Venice, Savoy, Switzerland and the Grisons in order to wage war for the return of the Valtelline to the Grisons.[2] In May, however, it became clear that internal affairs were absorbing most of the French government's attention and the bulk of its financial resources. Vigorous action abroad was

[1] B. Zeller, *Richelieu et les ministres de Louis XIII*, pp. 64, 65. [2] Ibid. pp. 76, 79–94.

beyond its power, and so diplomatic moves were likewise of little effect. Then the government resorted to other methods. Secret envoys of France incited the Grisons to take up arms, promising them aid from the Dauphiné, to be brought by Lesdiguières, who would be acting 'irresponsibly' like Feria in Milan. The Grisons did attack the Spaniards in the Valtelline, and denounced their treaty with Feria, by which the Valtelline had been given to Milan. The Grisons were cleared of Spanish and Austrian troops, and all that remained was to wrest the Valtelline from Feria and thrust the Archduke Leopold back into the Tirol. Lesdiguières was instructed to aid the Grisons 'irresponsibly', so that they might at least hold on to the territory they had already occupied. At the same time, Sillery and Puisieux considered it would be rash to attack Spain openly, without previously securing allies. This attitude was resedted by the nobles, for whom war in Italy was always a particularly alluring prospect; they crowded round the king, crying: 'Sire, to the Valtelline!'[1] However, the king did not change his plans, and the campaign against the Huguenots went forward. Louis XIII had now some further good reasons for not leaving France. Just at this time Count Mansfeld had appeared with his forces on the borders of Champagne and Lorraine.

Mansfeld was one of the German *condottieri* of the period of the Thirty Years War, a Lutheran, and at the moment fighting against the emperor, but ready if need be to take service with anyone at all. After the flight of Frederick V to Holland and his loss of the Palatinate, Mansfeld prepared to seize this territory from the Spaniards who had occupied it, and to this end concentrated a large army in Alsace. At the end of 1621 the truce between Holland and Spain expired, and, in expectation of renewed warfare, the rulers of the Spanish Netherlands sought to win Mansfeld to their side. The French government tried to do the same, carrying on negotiations with Mansfeld in February–March 1622 (through third parties) in which they offered to make him a colonel, *maréchal de camp* and *général des Flammans*.[2] At the beginning of May, being promised forty thousand *écus*, he offered France his army of 20,000–25,000 men for a campaign in the Valtelline or in Germany, asking for a quick answer, since, if the king did not want these troops, 'I must offer them to someone else, for without war I cannot live'.[3] Evidently the king declined this offer; Mansfeld, after some success in the

---

[1] B. Zeller, *Richelieu et les ministres de Louis XIII*, p. 98. Despatch of the Venetian ambassador, 4 July 1622.
[2] Letters from Mansfeld to Louis XIII, 11 February, 11 and 18 March 1622 (Saltykov-Shchedrin Library, Leningrad, Avt. 5, nos. 59–61.)
[3] Letter from Mansfeld to Puisieux, 3 May 1622 (ibid. no. 64); similar letter to Louis XIII, same date (ibid. no. 62).

Palatinate and Hesse, remained in Alsace and fought against the Archduke Leopold and Tilly. It must be recalled that in June 1622 the Spaniards and Imperialists were still far from victory on the Rhine; the situation changed only after Leopold had driven Mansfeld and his allies out of Alsace, when the latter passed through Lorraine to the borders of Champagne. Bouillon, who was at Sedan, called on Mansfeld to enter France, calculating that the need to protect the eastern provinces from these soldier-bandits would hinder the royal army's operations outside Montpellier, since part of the army would have to be transferred northward. However, Mansfeld could hardly accept, since his purpose in approaching the French frontier was to bring pressure on the king to give him money to maintain his army.[1]

Nevertheless, Mansfeld's appearance so near to Champagne alarmed the government (part of the king's Council was in Paris), and an army was raised to defend the frontier. Mansfeld did not stay there long, but moved off to help the Dutch in Bergen, besieged by the Spaniards, and then to Breda. This meant that the Huguenots' hopes of a diversion of the royal army from the south were not fulfilled.

The main strategic task of the government's forces was, without repeating the mistakes made the year before during the siege of Montauban, to blockade Montpellier as completely and extensively as possible, that is, to occupy the whole surrounding area within a big radius, seizing the neighbouring cities, so as to make it impossible to bring help. Montpellier was cut off from the Cévennes after the capture of Marsillargues, Lunel and Sommières to the north and Saint-Gilles to the east. Châtillon surrendered Aigues-Mortes to the king, thus depriving the Huguenots of the possibility of receiving supplies by sea (already in July it cost Rohan much trouble to obtain powder and shot).[2] The fall of Saint-Geniès de Malgloires severed the Huguenots' communications between the Cévennes and Nîmes. At the beginning of August the royal army concentrated around Montpellier and began the siege. However, the army, which had suffered losses in the course of the operations in Guyenne, the Vivarais and Languedoc, and which had had to find garrisons for all the towns it had captured, was not immediately capable of surrounding a large city. Vendôme's troops were urgently sent for from Brittany, and Lesdiguières was despatched to the Dauphiné to fetch reinforcements. Part of the army which had been raised to resist Mansfeld had to be assigned to the siege of Montpellier. At last the blockade ring was almost complete.

The king's army consisted of four 'old' (that is, standing) regiments, the royal guard, and eight regiments recruited in the South; it had forty-three

---

[1] Fontenay-Mareuil, op. cit. p. 170. Evidently the money promised him in May had not been paid.
[2] Cazenove, loc. cit. no. 56, p. 503.

guns and a large force of cavalry. Quite a number of Huguenot noblemen had come over to the king, attracted by presents and pensions. The army was well supplied, from the Rhône. Nevertheless, under Condé's command, the siege was badly managed. The assaults which he mounted, against the king's judgment, were unsuccessful, and the army sustained severe losses. Heavy rain hindered the making of trenches and approach-works. Condé's prestige declined, and it was necessary to relieve him of the supreme command. In its time the appointment of Lesdiguières to be constable had had precisely this purpose, but in renouncing Calvinism he had made the condition that he would never fight against his former co-religionists.

The garrison of Montpellier consisted of six regiments of regular troops and three of city militia. They were commanded by Argencourt, who was expert in the art of fortification (*un des plus grands remueurs de terre et des plus entendus aux fortifications de son temps*)[1] and conducted the defence in an able manner. But the city could not hold out for long without help. Such help might come from two quarters: from Rohan, or as a result of complications in the international situation.

Rohan's position was more difficult than in the previous year. His links with the cities of Languedoc had been cut. His army was melting away, because many recruits—poor peasants from the foothills—went off in June to seek employment, as was their custom, as day-labourers in seasonal agricultural work.[2] Rohan found it hard to raise 4,000 men from the Cévennes, and it took him five weeks instead of the ten days he had allowed for. Nîmes supplied, instead of the expected thousand, only forty men. Money from the cities came in slowly, and he was short of munitions. But he had promised help to Montpellier, and the city, relying on this, held out stubbornly all through September, hoping that the king would decide to abandon the siege, as he had done in 1621 in the case of Montauban. At the beginning of October Rohan led his army down from the Cévennes into the plain of Montpellier, as far as strongly fortified Corconne, but the royal forces barred any further advance. He would not take the risk of throwing his raw recruits into battle with the king's regular troops, for defeat would mean the fall of Montpellier and of the whole South; provided he kept his army intact and exploited the international situation, Rohan could count on obtaining acceptable conditions of peace.[3] He offered to meet Lesdiguières for negotiations;

[1] Fontenay-Mareuil. op. cit. p. 170.
[2] Cazenove, loc. cit. no. 56, p. 514.
[3] As early as August he had entered into peace talks with Lesdiguières, but these had been broken off. The king laid down as an indispensable condition that he should enter Montpellier, Nîmes and Uzès with his army, but these cities would not agree, fearing that no matter what the terms of capitulation might be, the army would plunder them. Condé had declared publicly that he

the meeting took place, and very quickly (18 October) resulted in the signing of a peace treaty.

Before looking at the articles of the treaty I must clarify the conditions under which it was signed. The situation outside Montpellier was such that the king's army was capable of continuing the siege, while Rohan was not in a position to bring help to the besieged city. However, autumn was approaching, and if Montpellier held out for even another six weeks, the siege would have to be lifted, and then the government would be obliged to quit the South again, without having achieved any better success than in 1621. Rohan's position was not one of weakness; on the contrary, given these circumstances, he could even lay down certain conditions. At the same time, however, the government's military strength was increasing, with troops approaching Montpellier from every side. Both parties were thus far from having exhausted their resources.

Why did both parties wish to make peace? Rohan needed a breathing-space. He could achieve this while retaining certain advantages which he held. His readiness to halt military operations and secure these advantages does not therefore require any special explanation. The government's position was different. To understand it we must see how matters stood beyond the frontier, and in particular in the unfortunate Valtelline. The pope's secretary, Agucchi, had reason to write that on this little piece of land the armies of many states were concentrated, and every ruler in Christendom was involved in its affairs in one way or another.[1]

In August and September 1622, when the siege of Montpellier was on, the Spanish government hoped that the French king's army would be held up there as long as in the previous year outside Montauban. Despite numerous promises to clear out of the Valtelline, Spain continued to regard it as her territory. At the end of September the Archduke Leopold defeated the Grisons, and Spinola made a further advance in the Palatinate. The Lower Engadine and eight districts were taken from the Grisons and annexed to the Austrian Tirol; the remaining forts of the Grisons were occupied by Austrian garrisons. All this signified the establishment of unimpeded communications between the Spanish possessions in Italy, on the one hand, and the Netherlands and Austria on the other. In other words, the French government's war against the Huguenots had enabled the Habsburgs to achieve a great success. Venice was isolated, and was obliged to accept the

would allow his soldiers to plunder, as he had done at Lunel, in violation of the surrender terms. (Cazenove, loc. cit. no. 56, pp. 511–15; B. Zeller, *Richelieu et les ministres de Louis XIII*, pp. 126, 127.)

[1] Despatch of 9 August 1622. See B. Zeller, *Richelieu et les ministres de Louis XIII*, p. 142.

conditions of Feria's agreement with the Grisons, concluded in Milan. Should Louis XIII hasten into northern Italy, the Archduchess Isabella was to send Spanish troops to the French frontier and order them to invade France.

In October it seemed obvious that France could not hope to evict Spain and Austria from the Valtelline.[1] But Louis quickly made peace with Rohan and then went to Lyons, near the frontier. Evidently, the government calculated the advantages of making peace with Rohan as follows: certain successes must be achieved and consolidated in a treaty, but this must be done as quickly as possible, so as to be able then to transfer the army to the frontier and threaten Spain with an invasion of northern Italy. It is from this standpoint that we must look at the terms of the peace of Montpellier.

The published articles of the treaty consisted of confirmation of the Edict of Nantes, demolition of newly erected fortifications, restoration of Catholic worship everywhere except in La Rochelle and Montauban. The Huguenot cities were to admit the king with some regiments within their walls. An amnesty was proclaimed. Under the secret articles, La Rochelle[2] and Montauban retained all their fortifications, and at Nîmes, Castres, Uzès and Milhau they were to be only two-thirds destroyed. Those fortresses which at the time of signing the treaty were held by the Huguenots were to remain theirs for three years. Those which had been captured by the king's army or which had submitted to the king were to remain in the government's hands and cease to be Huguenot *places de sûreté*. The citadel and new fortifications of Montpellier were to be razed to the ground, and henceforth the city's consuls—one Huguenot and one Catholic—were to be appointed by the king. Rohan was made governor (but without garrisons) of Nîmes, Castres, Uzès, and the Cévennes, and allotted a pension of sixty thousand *écus* as compensation for the governorship of Poitou, which was taken from him.

How can the results of the campaign of 1622 be summed up? Undoubtedly it constituted another success, though an incomplete one, for the government. The latter now controlled not merely a few dozen small and medium-sized Huguenot cities; the cities still remaining to the Huguenots (La Rochelle, Montauban, and those assigned to Rohan) could be counted on the fingers of one hand. The Cévennes remained outside the sphere of the king's authority. Royal garrisons were introduced into the cities of Langue-

---

[1] B. Zeller, *Richelieu et les ministres de Louis XIII*, pp. 142–7.

[2] In spite of the strong protests of the Rochelais, Fort-Louis, which barred La Rochelle's communications on the landward side, was not demolished, and continued to be occupied by a strong garrison. (Fontenay-Mareuil, op. cit. p. 171.)

doc. Consequently, the incompleteness of the king's success (which was clear to all, both in France and abroad) should not hide the fact that, except for a mere five places (though these were very important ones) and the Cévennes, the Huguenot South had been conquered by the government.

The Huguenot garrison left Montpellier at once and the soldiers went home. The king entered the city and spent a few days there. Two regiments (4,000 men) were left as a garrison to remain until the fortifications had been demolished. Another four or five regiments and three squadrons of light cavalry were disposed around the city. Lower Languedoc had not merely been conquered, it was occupied by the government's forces.

No open struggle against the Huguenots took place in the remainder of 1622 or in 1623-4. It broke out again only in 1625. This interval was due to the following reasons. The international situation, and, even more, the fierce struggle for power within the government, made it impossible for a time to proceed to the next and final stage of the struggle against the Huguenot party, namely, the subjection of La Rochelle. To capture this Huguenot citadel would be a very difficult and costly enterprise, and the government was fully aware of it. During 1621 and 1622 many important pre-conditions for the siege of La Rochelle had been realised, namely, the almost complete isolation of the city on the landward side, through the occupation of Poitou and Guyenne in 1621 and that of Lower Languedoc in 1622. In these circumstances even the independence of Montauban, confirmed by the peace of Montpellier, lacked the importance it had possessed in 1621. Only the fall of La Rochelle was needed now for the complete collapse of the Huguenot power in the south-west. This task was still on the agenda, and must be carried out as soon as it became possible.

There remained, however, one more task besides this most important one, namely, that of consolidating the government's authority in the occupied territory.

Peace was established only with difficulty. Many cities were dissatisfied with the terms. Rohan had much trouble in persuading them to submit to what they found the most painful article of the treaty, the demolishing of their fortifications. This work was to be undertaken at the expense of the cities themselves, and the municipalities concerned dragged it out as long as they could, excusing themselves by reference to the shortage of labour and money. The razing of the fortifications of the larger cities (Montpellier, Uzès, Nîmes, etc.) proceeded extremely slowly. Significantly, the grandees who were in command of the royal garrisons and the units of the king's army stationed around the cities connived at these delays. They were alarmed at the prospect of the destruction of the political power of the Huguenots, because this would mean a strengthening of the royal authority and a weakening of the power of the higher nobility.[1] Once again we here come upon a fact which is essential for the understanding of the political struggles of this period. For the higher nobility as such, without distinction of religious belief, the political power of the Huguenots, and especially their fortresses, garrisons and artillery, was an important political and military reserve force in their own struggle against the strengthening of absolutism, which as yet they did not at all regard as having finally failed. It was this very circumstance that made it necessary for the government to fight the battle with the Huguenots absolutely to the death, that is, to the complete abolition of the military and political organisation of the Huguenot party.

The government had hastened to make peace internally because it needed to free its hands for action abroad, in northern Italy. The king went without delay to Lyons, near the frontier, and the greater part of the army was concentrated there. The remaining regiments stayed behind as garrisons in Languedoc, while the recently recruited units were disbanded.[2]

In this situation any further campaign against the Huguenots would be waged not in the South but in the West, against La Rochelle. For that purpose, however, as has already been shown, a fleet of sailing ships would be needed, and this the government did not have. Time and money were needed for the creation of such a fleet, and these the government also lacked. The fierce struggle for power which went on at court in 1623–4[3] temporarily pushed into the background everything that was not connected with this struggle, or with the pressing problems of foreign policy. This gave the Huguenots a breathing-space which enabled them to prepare for further struggles with the aim of recovering all the positions they had lost.

This struggle might take a variety of forms, entirely depending on the composition of the government, its financial resources, the external situation connected with the Thirty Years War, and many other factors.

The Huguenots might gradually, little by little, using various peaceful or semi-peaceful methods, recover their lost cities in the South. If France were to become involved in open war abroad, it was highly probable that the troops stationed in Languedoc would be withdrawn; indeed, this could be considered certain. In that event, the cities (for it must be remembered that they had undergone no radical changes in their internal organisation) would naturally resume their former status as urban republics. It was because they foresaw such a possibility that the city authorities were doing all they could to delay the demolition of their fortifications. If the government, though not

---

[1] Cazenove, loc. cit. no. 56, pp. 516, 517. [2] Fontenay-Mareuil, op. cit. p. 171.
[3] See Chapter 5,

involved in external war, nevertheless found itself obliged for one reason or another to reduce the forces stationed in the southern cities, the Huguenots would be able to make use of any excuse and any favourable concurrence of circumstances that offered to eject the royal garrisons by force from the cities they occupied, and even perhaps from the South as a whole.

The struggle between different groups at court in 1623-4, which the Huguenots followed with close attention, gave the latter encouragement and inspired substantial hopes, for the weakening of the government which resulted from this struggle was something very much to their advantage. However, La Vieuville's moves towards the formation of an Anglo-French alliance gave them cause for serious worry. The point was that, of all the forces of European Protestantism, the only one which the Huguenots could count on for help was England. Developments in Germany ruled out all thought of obtaining any help from the German Calvinists. Holland was already at war with Spain, and at that time the military situation was unfavourable to her. England alone, which had hitherto remained aloof from the war which was raging ever more fiercely in Germany, was in a position to help the Huguenots. James I, and after him Charles I, had promised aid more than once, and had even attempted on several occasions, though not very persistently, to influence the French government at moments of danger for the Huguenots. But it had to be taken into account that so long as military operations were proceeding mainly in the South, England could not render military aid even in a concealed form, and in the diplomatic sphere her hands were tied because she needed French support for her efforts to restore Frederick V to his Palatinate. The prospect of a marriage between Charles I and Louis XIII's sister meant that an alliance between England and France was a possibility, and there could be little doubt that the treaty of alliance would include an article whereby England undertook not to help the Huguenots.

Thus, by the natural course of events, in which religious interests were being finally ousted by political calculations, the Huguenots were compelled to seek support in the last possible quarter, and from the power which was at that period France's principal national enemy, namely, ultra-Catholic Spain. Many contemporaries suspected that the Huguenot approach to Spain had begun much earlier than the siege of La Rochelle. The very strict secrecy which surrounded Rohan's dealings with Spain made it impossible, however, to do more than suspect, drawing conclusions from the general situation.[1] Richelieu possessed other, more precise information on this

---

[1] An account of these dealings was given later by a very well-informed Huguenot officer who was close to Rohan (J. Bouffard-Madiane, 'Le livre de raison', *Bulletin de la Société de l'histoire du*

point,[1] which strengthened his resolve to maintain peaceful relations between France and Spain throughout the period of the final campaigns against the Huguenots, as he brilliantly succeeded in doing.

Returning to the actual situation in 1623–5, we must draw particular attention to one circumstance. The government was not able to wage open war against the Huguenots, because it lacked both a fleet and the money to build one. At the same time, it did not propose to launch any expeditions abroad, it had not withdrawn its troops from Languedoc, and it maintained a strong garrison at Fort-Louis, blockading La Rochelle from the landward side. In other words, it was not giving up the positions it had conquered, but counted on using them, when circumstances were more favourable, as bases for a new advance. At the same time, the government took certain steps which tended to encourage the Huguenot nobles in Languedoc, Guyenne, the Vivarais, the Cévennes and other regions to come over to Catholicism,[2] so as to weaken Rohan and the Huguenot army. Secret agents of the government negotiated with many nobles, offering them, in the king's name, pensions, gifts, military and civil offices, and so on. It was typical that their most effective argument was the assurance that the king would compensate them for having to give up the church property which the nobles had seized during the civil wars of the sixteenth century. 'For it would not be easy', reported one of the agents to his royal master, 'to attract them if they were to be obliged to lose the income from these properties.'[3] Other agents reported in great detail on the situation inside the cities, on the strategically most important roads, river-crossings, mountain passes, and so on. They maintained that many citizens could be seduced by the offer of important municipal offices. This measure made use of the internal antagonism in the Huguenot cities between the merchants and the existing municipal authorities. The smaller cities were easier to win over to the king's side than the larger ones;[4] in the event of success, fortresses should be built in them and they should be placed under the rule of Catholic noblemen. Strategically important castles should be bought back from the Catholic noblemen at

protestantisme en France, LVI (Paris, 1907), pp. 22–5; see also M. G. Schybergson, 'Ein neuer Beitrag zur Geschichte der drei letzten Hugenottenkriege, 1621–1629', Historische Vierteljahrschrift, neue Folge, I. Heft (Berlin, 1901), pp. 355–65.
[1] Rohan's negotiations with Spain had begun already in 1625, in Piedmont, with Savoy as intermediary. A secret agent of Rohan was arrested in April 1626.
[2] Very interesting documents of this kind, for 1624–5, were published by Griselle in Documents d'histoire, I, 74–9, 397–412; II, 194–8, 363–78.
[3] Documents d'histoire, II, 372. Conversion to Catholicism would oblige them to give back the church property they had seized.
[4] As has been shown, the smaller cities had no chance of resisting the king's forces, and Rohan sacrificed them in order to preserve the larger cities.

present holding them. In short, a broad, many-sided and well-thought-out campaign was being waged to weaken the Huguenot party from within. Subsequent events in the South showed that this campaign was undoubtedly successful, resulting in numerous noblemen renouncing Calvinism. The chief reason why they had felt compelled to become Huguenots was their concern to keep the church lands they had laid hands on. Now, if the king promised either to let them keep these lands, or to give them others in exchange, or to pay them adequate compensation, they were quite ready to abandon their Calvinism since, in the highly probable event of a government victory, they feared being deprived of all their possessions.

This was the situation in Languedoc, Guyenne, and the Vivarais. In the Pyrenean provinces (the counties of Foix, Comminges and Bigorre, not to mention Béarn) the government had no success. Not only did the nobles stubbornly hold to their Calvinism, which they firmly associated with the political independence of this region, and saw as a direct continuation of the Albigensian doctrine, but also the entire population, regardless of religious belief, was inclined towards separatism, and hated the North French (*franchimans*).[1] A government victory meant for them the end of their *de facto* independence, free from royal officials and state taxes.

In the large cities of Languedoc and Guyenne the royal agents operated mainly by way of agitation among the rich and well-to-do citizens, whose royalism, though it went back more than two decades, had wavered in the circumstances of 1620–2 and was dependent on many factors. Now, seeing royal garrisons in their cities, they were more worried than ever about what was to become of their fiscal and municipal privileges, and were ready to listen to those who assured them that only submission to the king could save these privileges. Consequently, Rohan's position in the wealthy cities of Lower Languedoc and Lower Guyenne (which was not very strong, in any case, as the events of 1621–2 had shown), was still further weakened.

As early as 1623 the royal governors appointed for Montpellier and Milhau began interfering in the election of municipal authorities, and ensured that Catholics as well as Huguenots were elected as consuls in Montpellier. In 1624, despite the fact that the city's fortifications had been razed, the garrison of Montpellier stayed on, and the governor imposed a tax for its upkeep.[2] Rohan, after remaining more than two years inactive, at last became convinced that time was working for the government, and seized the first opportunity to rise in revolt.

At the end of 1624 Richelieu went over to an active foreign policy. The

---

[1] Cazenove, loc. cit. no. 57, p. 15; Tucoo-Chala, op. cit. pp. 54 ff.
[2] Cazenove, loc. cit. no. 56, pp. 520–1.

Grisons were occupied by French troops, and the Constable Lesdiguières, together with the Duke of Savoy, laid siege to Genoa. Control by the French of the Grisons and the Valtelline, and their capture of Genoa, if they brought it off, would cut communications—after 1621 especially important—between Spain on the one hand and Germany and the Netherlands on the other. France also sent financial help to Holland, and subsidised Mansfeld. But the military operations, after a good start, began to drag out; money proved, as before, to be insufficient, and Richelieu's position was precarious. It was then that Rohan and Soubise decided on an open revolt in La Rochelle. At first, even in this Huguenot citadel, they had no success, and were unable to win over the city council to their view. Though it was torn by a fierce struggle between the old members and the new ones who had entered the council in 1614, the established oligarchy of royalist sympathies nevertheless held firm. But Soubise's victory in 1625, when he seized the islands of Oléron and Ré, covering La Rochelle on the seaward side, produced a sudden change in the balance of forces. The new members of the council, supported by the bulk of the citizens, forced the council to line up with Rohan and his brother. It was not so much religious fanaticism that lay behind this (though that factor must be given its due weight) as the anxiety of the masses to save themselves from the king's taxes and the king's officials.

The Huguenot operations, which began promisingly, were not adequately backed up in the South, where the cities very much wanted to remain at peace.[1] On the whole, Languedoc and Guyenne stood aloof from the revolt.[2] During the summer campaign of 1625 Rohan had great difficulty in recruiting forces and in keeping on his side even a few cities in Upper Guyenne and Upper Languedoc. His biggest success was merely that he was able to prevent the king's army from penetrating into the Cévennes.

For the struggle against La Rochelle Richelieu used ships obtained from Holland and England. Soubise was beaten at sea. The situation became very unfavourable to the Huguenots; nobody was helping them, and Holland and England were even helping the government against them. But there was another factor that did help them, namely, the government's awkward situation internationally. Spain and the pope lost no time in exploiting the Huguenot uprising for their own advantage, and the result compelled Richelieu to make peace immediately with the Huguenots (5 February 1626). The conditions of peace were fully acceptable so far as the South was concerned: the Edict of Nantes was confirmed, and those few fortresses that

[1] They even tried to make separate peace treaties with the government without the consent of the Huguenot party as a whole.
[2] Schybergson, op. cit. pp. 362–4.

were at that moment still in Huguenot hands were to be retained by them for another three years. For La Rochelle, however, the conditions were very much more severe. The pre-1614 structure of the city council was restored, that is, power passed once more to the oligarchy of shipowners. A royal commissioner was appointed to reside in the city and see to the fulfilment of the peace treaty. Catholic worship was restored, and secularised property was given back to the church. Left on its own, La Rochelle was obliged to submit.

Subsequent events, in 1627–9, are well known so far as La Rochelle is concerned, which has always attracted the lion's share of attention from historians, as it did from contemporaries. The situation in the South has been less fully covered in historical writing, and its connexion with the events of the siege of La Rochelle given insufficient consideration.[1] Yet this was of great importance for the outcome of the campaign as a whole.

Let me outline the principal facts of 1627–8. After making peace with the Huguenots and thereby freeing his hands for action in Italy, Richelieu then came to an agreement with Spain about the Valtelline and withdrew from the war, so as to secure a breathing-space to prepare a decisive campaign against the Huguenots. England hoped for France's aid in the war she had begun with Spain, and therefore, in her own interests, promoted conciliation between the French government and the Huguenots, at the expense of the latter. However, Richelieu disappointed England's expectations, relations deteriorated, and Charles I promised military and financial help to La Rochelle.

It was significant that the negotiation of the treaty between Buckingham, who was sent to La Rochelle but was not allowed to enter the city, and the city council (now composed of the old members only), proceeded with great difficulty.[2] Taught by bitter experience, the Rochelais did not trust the English, assuming that the latter were first and foremost following their own political interests. It would have been different if the cities of the South had openly and effectively risen in revolt along with La Rochelle; then, English support would have been merely of secondary importance, while the chief contribution would have been made by Huguenots as such, and they could have been sure of fully retaining their 'liberties'.

Meanwhile, the rich men and royal officials in La Rochelle were as royalist as ever in their sentiments and feared an open break with the government.

---

[1] Valuable material on events in the South is included in Cazenove's work, which is based on contemporary records.

[2] On events in La Rochelle see P. Villemain, *Journal des assiégés de La Rochelle, 1627–1628* (Paris, 1958). The author describes the history of those years in fictional form, but makes extensive use of unpublished documents, diaries kept by Rochelais, and local chronicles. For a detailed diary kept by a contemporary, see P. Mervaux, *Histoire du dernier siège de La Rochelle* (Rouen, 1643).

The agreement with England was not signed until the end of October 1627, under strong pressure by Rohan and his supporters, when Rohan himself also signed a parallel agreement. He looked forward to receiving help from the English in Guyenne, and made preparations in advance to link up with them as soon as they should land somewhere on the coast. But the English did not appear on the coast of Guyenne, and the southern cities were even more determined than in 1625 not to break with the government. Frequently Rohan had to force them to join him; after entering a recalcitrant city, he would remove the ruling authorities, sometimes going so far as to take severe repressive measures, and replace them by his own adherents.[1] His strained and often hostile relations with the cities put Rohan in a very awkward position for money, since the cities were his main source of financial contributions. He was able to raise soldiers now only in the Cévennes, but the manpower resources of this mountainous region were almost exhausted. In these very unfavourable conditions Rohan displayed his outstanding talent as a commander and stubbornly fought against Condé and Montmorency, winning victories over the royal forces. But the latter steadily confined him to a comparatively small territory around the Cévennes, which inexorably shrank smaller and smaller. The depressing news from La Rochelle only strengthened the royalism of the Southern cities; the beleaguered city's appeals for help remained unanswered. Languedoc had been completely devastated by the war, trade had ceased, the population was in the grip of famine. Rohan was surrounded by a sinister void, and his army was breaking up. His only hope was Spain and the financial and military aid she promised.

The events of the siege of La Rochelle are well known. After the siege had begun, the opposition party triumphed in the city, the old royalist-tending council was overthrown, and the defence was headed by a new mayor, Captain Guiton. Their only hope was help from England; by itself the city could not withstand a siege by the large royal army which completely blockaded it on the landward side. Access to the city from the sea was covered by the royal fleet, and work was in progress on the building of a mole. This was located sufficiently far from the city for cannon-fire from La Rochelle not to be able to damage it. The stormy ocean frequently helped the besieged by breaking through completed parts of the mole and hindering the work.[2] Eventually, however, the mole was built, and the English fleet could not get through to the completely blockaded city. The inhabitants of La Rochelle, especially the poor, suffered severely from the shortage of food, and died in great numbers. Already in August murmuring began against

---

[1] Bouffard-Madiane, op. cit. pp. 29–32; Schybergson, op. cit. pp. 362–5.
[2] Soon after the fall of La Rochelle the mole was carried away by a storm.

Mayor Guiton and the members of the city council, and this murmuring spread wider and wider. But the city's leaders would not hear of surrendering while a spark of hope remained that help might come from England. At last, on 28 October, the exhausted city surrendered.[1] The king and Richelieu entered La Rochelle, once so proud, now vanquished, 'a city of ghosts, not people'.

The surrender terms deprived La Rochelle of its special privileges. There passed irrecoverably into history the unique independence of the city-republic on the Atlantic coast, and the former structure of urban self-government was destroyed. But the property interests of the citizens were safeguarded, and freedom of worship for the Calvinists was maintained.

The fall of La Rochelle meant the fall of the South as well. Rohan's submission took another eight months, however, for the king's army was hastily transferred from La Rochelle to Italy. England continued to incite Rohan to further resistance, promising that she would not make any peace with France which did not safeguard the rights of the Huguenots. But Rohan no longer believed these promises (which were, indeed, not kept) and relied only on Spanish gold—which, however, he did not succeed in obtaining. After his rapid and fortunate settlement of affairs in Italy, Richelieu quickly returned the army to Languedoc, and Rohan was now no longer able to offer resistance. The peace of Alais concluded, on 16 June 1629, a war which had gone on for ten years. The Edict of Nantes was confirmed only so far as its basic text was concerned, that is, excluding the additional articles which guaranteed the political rights of the Huguenots. All fortresses and city fortifications were to be demolished, but the fiscal and some other privileges of cities and provinces were to be maintained.

Nearly all Rohan's officers, together with La Rochelle's Mayor Guiton, entered the king's service. So, eventually, did Rohan; after a few years of voluntary exile in Italy, he became the best of France's generals, whose victories over the imperial forces contributed greatly to his country's success in the Thirty Years War.

The Huguenot republic had ceased to exist. La Rochelle was condemned to become an ordinary seaport, and the south-western cities to become ordinary French cities. Their economic development proceeded thereafter as a function of conditions in France as a whole. The Huguenot bourgeoisie was reduced in most, though as yet not all, respects to a level of equality with the Catholic bourgeoisie. Its history after 1629 forms an important and very interesting chapter in the history of seventeenth-century France.

[1] In 1627 the population of La Rochelle was 28,000; at the time of the surrender it was 5,400, many of whom died soon afterwards, of exhaustion.

CHAPTER 5

The financiers and the absolute monarchy

IN this chapter I propose to examine in detail another important task which confronted French absolutism—the need to put the state finances in order.

The two years between the autumn of 1622 and that of 1624 were difficult in every respect. The financial situation was especially difficult. There was no money in the treasury. Once again, and this time in an even more acute form, the question arose of what the government's financial policy was to be, for the possibility of consolidating French absolutism both at home and abroad depended upon the solution of this urgent problem. The need to find financial resources, the urgent measures to be taken in the field of foreign relations, and further policy in relation to the Huguenots—these were the problems, closely interrelated, which became crucial as soon as peace had been signed with Rohan, at the end of October 1622.

The way to solve these problems, the order in which they should be dealt with, the attitude taken towards them by different powerful social groups—all this became matter for disputes and conflicts between various individuals and the groups behind them. The struggle for power within government circles became extremely bitter, and without describing the persons involved in this struggle one cannot explain with sufficient clarity the course and out-come of this struggle, which had a most direct influence on the country's political life.

The two years occupied by this struggle, 1623 and 1624, have long attracted great interest in French historical writing and in foreign historical writing generally. These were the years when Cardinal Richelieu was advancing to the leadership of state affairs. Relying on pamphlet literature and on the numerous memoirs (including the so-called *Mémoires de Richelieu*, which were composed not by the cardinal but by confidential agents of his, on the basis of his papers and under his supervision), all the great French historians of the second half of the nineteenth century and of the twentieth century have set forth an impressive picture of the cunning intrigues and artful diplomacy by which Richelieu attained his ends. He did not find this easy, for nearly everyone in the king's entourage, and the king himself, vigorously opposed them. Consequently, a detailed description of the cardinal's activities (they are described in greatest detail in Hanotaux's book) is also a description of the development of his diplomatic and other talents, which were manifested in their full brilliance immediately after his accession to power *ad majorem Franciae gloriam.*

When today we study the works relating to this period, and also the sources from which they were drawn, it is impossible not to perceive that both contemporaries and the historians mentioned were to a large extent justified in their opinions. All contemporaries, participants in or observers of the struggle recognised in Richelieu not only brilliant and sound qualities but also, and especially, exceptional abilities, intelligence and dexterity.[1] Though historians have hardly ever been able to refrain from taking a retrospective view of events, sometimes making their assessment of the cardinal's conduct in the period when his powers were at their height apply to the whole preceding period of his career, their presentation of the chief stages on his road to power and the destruction of his enemies has been largely correct. But these colourful episodes, following one from another, so logically, it would seem, linked together in a close chain of events which at last brought Richelieu to the place of honour as first minister in the king's Council and *de facto* ruler of France, took place within the walls of the Louvre and the other royal palaces. The conflict between ambitions, grand and triumphant in the case of the central figure, petty and ridiculous in that of his foes, the waverings of the indecisive Louis XIII, the stubbornness of the short-witted Queen Mother—this is the basic canvas on which the design of Richelieu's advance to power is embroidered in red silk. Social forces play no part. Since a few significant events did, after all, occur during these two years (chiefly in the diplomatic sphere), something has to be said about them, but almost always very little, and they are dealt with in the spirit of the *Mémoires de Richelieu,* that is, in a tone of unreserved condemnation of the cardinal's enemies.

In order that the reader may more easily follow both my criticism of historical writings and my exposition of events, I must mention the principal changes of government in 1622–4.

A few days before the signing of peace at Montpellier, Condé left for Italy and thereby quitted the political scene for the time being.

---

[1] Particularly valuable in this instance are the opinions given in the despatches of the Tuscan and Venetian ambassadors, since they were expressed in the very years and months when this struggle was going on, and there is no element of 'wisdom after the event' in them. (See B. Zeller, *Richelieu et les ministres de Louis XIII de 1621 à 1624* (Paris, 1880.)

On 2 August 1622 the Cardinal de Retz, a member of the king's Council, died, an event which opened for Richelieu, should he succeed in being made a cardinal, a possible place in that Council. Richelieu did in fact soon afterwards (5 September) become a cardinal, and this brought him considerably nearer to his goal, though he had to wait another year and a half to achieve it.

From the death of Luynes in December 1621 to February 1624, affairs of state were directed by the Brûlarts—Chancellor Sillery and his son, Secretary of State Puisieux. On 21 January 1623 the Marquis de La Vieuville was appointed *surintendant des finances*, and this resulted in the dismissal of both the Brûlarts on 4 February 1624, with La Vieuville becoming the chief man in the Council—though only for a short time, as on 29 April of the same year Richelieu joined the Council, so taking another step nearer to power. Less than four months later, on 13 August 1624, he got rid of La Vieuville and occupied the highest position. He had attained his end.

The traditional interpretation by French historians of these events is that La Vieuville ousted the Brûlarts with Richelieu's help and then Richelieu ousted La Vieuville and so became master of the situation.

V. V. Biryukovich introduced important changes into this exposition. He criticised this outline and examined the events of 1622–4 on a broader sociopolitical basis. He devoted a long article[1] to studying the struggle for power between the four principals—Sillery, Puisieux, La Vieuville and Richelieu—and the social groups behind them, as a clash between different social interests and programmes. According to him, the Brûlarts were the representatives of the ruling circles of the landowning official caste, merged with the higher nobility,[2] while La Vieuville headed the first government of the financial plutocracy in the history of France,[3] and Richelieu came forward as the representative of the interests of noble and bourgeois circles.[4]

It was important to raise this question for consideration. The author was principally concerned to see how the interests of the estates and groups of which society was composed, and which were struggling against each other,

[1] V. V. Biryukovich, 'The French "financiers" in the political struggle of 1622–1624' [in Russian], *Istoricheskiye Zapiski*, III (Moscow, 1938), 181–240. This article forms part of a considerably more comprehensive work devoted to clarifying the political role played by the French financiers in the first half of the seventeenth century. Unfortunately this work, which was presented in 1939 as a thesis, has remained unpublished. Two other articles based upon it have, however, appeared: 'Popular revolts in Bordeaux and Guyenne in 1635' [in Russian], *Istoricheskiye Zapiski*, II (Moscow, 1938) and 'Popular movements in France in 1624–1634' [in Russian], *Trudy Voyenno-politicheskoi Akademii Krasnoi Armii*, IV (Moscow, 1940).
[2] Biryukovich, 'The French "financiers"', *Istoricheskiye Zapiski*, III, 186.
[3] Ibid. pp. 237–9.
[4] Ibid. pp. 191 ff.

were reflected in politics. This was the standpoint from which he studied the political conflicts of those years.

In publishing Biryukovich's article, the editors of *Istoricheskie Zapiski* noted that the author's conception of a direct struggle for power on the part of usurers' capital in the early part of the seventeenth century implied a certain 'modernisation'.[1] This is true, and in this connexion we must analyse Biryukovich's argument and his conclusion more closely, since they have a very direct bearing on the subject of this book, and on this chapter in particular.

A great deal of material from memoirs and pamphlets is used in Biryukovich's article, but nothing from records. The author had what might seem good reason for this omission. The bulk of the documents of this period which have been published relate to foreign policy, to which Biryukovich gave only casual and passing attention, and that mainly on the basis of the available secondary works and not of independent research. Moreover, because of the principal subject of his work, he focused his study on the financiers and their role in the government's financial policy. There would be nothing to say against this approach if the financiers and their doings had been studied on the basis of an analysis of the entire activity of the government, that is, if the totality of political problems then confronting French absolutism had been analysed (which does not mean, of course, that all the relevant facts should have been set forth in the article, but only that they should have been taken into account in the author's process of investigation). However, he undertook no such analysis.

As in many of the writings of Soviet historians of the 1930s, we find in Biryukovich's article valuable and original ideas about the essential character of the social and economic relations prevailing in French society in the first half of the seventeenth century. Soviet historical writing performed in that period a very great and important task: it demonstrated the enormous role played in history by the class struggle, together with the roots of this struggle in class antagonisms. But political history as such did not then receive the same attention; it was mentioned only incidentally, when events in the class struggle obliged the historian to give some consideration also to the policy of ruling circles. Consequently, the course of political history caught the attention of the historian only at particular, mostly isolated, moments, that is to say, it was deprived of its organic completeness. Thereby the comprehensive view absolutely necessary for an all-round appreciation both of political history as a whole and also of particular events was inevitably obscured, or even disappeared altogether.

---

[1] Ibid. p. 181, note.

Biryukovich's view of the structure of seventeenth-century French society was based on the study of an extensive amount of writing devoted to this matter, which the author had thought over and reduced to an original system of ideas. But although many features of this system have stood up to the test of comparison with the sources, as well as to the test of time, he produced no equally well-thought-out conception of political history. This is particularly true where foreign policy is concerned. Biryukovich implicitly assumes that the government was able to follow whatever foreign policy it liked. This assumption permitted the historian to accord only the very slightest attention to what then seemed the boring hither-and-thitherings of diplomacy and the military operations which had been so frequently described.

The picture drawn by Biryukovich of the political struggle within the government in 1622–4 is open to objection because it takes no account of the entire complex of problems facing French absolutism in both the internal and external fields. Nor does it sufficiently allow for the real possibilities open to the government, or to particular social strata and groups. Only one of these groups receives attention, the 'financiers', and the description of their activity is given disproportionate scope in the article. This lack of proportion is connected with the fact that Biryukovich ascribes an independent political programme to the financiers. Also, the government's policy towards the Huguenots, together with the diplomacy of the predecessors of La Vieuville (according to Biryukovich, a representative of financial capital), is not studied independently by the author, so that La Vieuville's diplomacy is wrongly seen as pursuing an original line.

Later on, in the course of describing the events of 1622–4, we shall consider Biryukovich's detailed argument, which aims to show that financial capital not only gained access to government circles, in the person of La Vieuville, but also determined the course of policy in its own interest. Although I disagree with this view, I think it is important to pay attention to the financiers and study the role they played. The activity of the financiers as state creditors and financial officials (but not as politicians) did assume greater and greater importance in the 1620s, with the growing importance of the state debt and of credit in the financial system of absolutism. The activity of the financiers had already become a necessary condition for the functioning of the state machine and one of the characteristic peculiarities of French absolutism. For this reason, it is impossible to show sufficiently clearly the meaning of numerous measures taken by the government unless one considers and outlines this activity, however briefly.

These are the considerations which have determined the structure of the present chapter. I preface my account of the events of 1622–4, leading up to the entry of Richelieu into the king's Council, with an outline of the structure of the state budget[1] and the government's system of borrowing.

Like all the phenomena of social and economic life in the age of the rise of capitalism, the state finances of France underwent substantial changes in the sixteenth and seventeenth centuries, the fundamental significance of which was the increasing relative importance of indirect taxes, that is, of those taxes which, in a society with a bourgeoisie not completely developed, may be called 'bourgeois' taxes.[2] Internal state loans assumed unprecedented dimensions, through the issue of *rentes*, the extortion of forced loans from officials, and the sale of offices in the bureaucratic state machine. They became one of the chief sources from which government was financed, and led to the creation of a state debt of colossal size for those days,[3] which played a big role in the process of primitive accumulation.

In connexion with this, the social aspect of the state budget also began to change. The increase in indirect taxation, reflecting the intensive development of commodity and money relations, meant not only additional burdens for the masses, hastening their expropriation, but also increased taxation of the new class then being formed, the bourgeoisie, which in France enjoyed no exemption from the payment of taxes. The state appropriated part of capitalist profit, and the question of how large this part was to be was already becoming acute, as the bourgeoisie formed its own idea of the 'just' share of its profits that it was prepared to offer to the royal authority in return for the latter's work of centralisation and protection. Bourgeois accumulation was also drawn upon by the treasury in the form of state loans, which created a financial bourgeoisie and a broad stratum of *rentiers*—elements which were thereafter to be characteristic of French society.

The changes in the composition of the state's revenue, and the increasing importance of the latter in the life of society as a whole were noticed clearly enough by contemporaries, and this was expressed in special treatises as well as in polemical pamphlets. They also noticed another feature—the archaic system of apportionment and collection of taxes. Inherited from the Middle Ages, these features had evolved extremely slowly and did not provide a uniform system for all France. On the territory of the royal demesne (that is, in northern and central France), in what were called the *pays*

---

[1] An analysis of the state budget is necessary also for studying the Assembly of Notables of 1626–7 (see Chapter 6).
[2] Marx and Engels, *Sochineniya* [*Collected Works*], 2nd edition, XXX, 292. [Marx to Engels, 12 June 1863: *Selected Correspondence*, 1934 English edition, p. 151.]
[3] The exact amount of this cannot yet be determined; contemporaries considered that the value of the offices sold came, on its own, to not less than 500 million *livres* (see p. 182).

d'élections,[1] direct taxes and some demesne revenues[2] were levied by royal officials while the collection of indirect taxes, customs dues and also the remaining demesne revenues were farmed out. These provinces bore the main burden of taxation, providing every year not less than 90 per cent of all the receipts from direct taxation alone. The border provinces, however (Languedoc, the Dauphiné, Burgundy, Provence and Brittany), incorporated comparatively recently, retained numerous provincial 'liberties' and even—except the Dauphiné—their own estate representation, in the form of local 'States',[3] which was why these provinces were called *pays d'états*. These assemblies voted *dons* to the government and themselves carried out, with their own machinery, the apportionment and collection of direct taxes, and, in part, of indirect taxes as well. As a result, they paid comparatively little into the treasury.[4]

Unification and a measure of substantial reform of the taxation system[5] was obstructed by the deeply rooted practice of sale and inheritance of offices throughout the financial apparatus. This situation rendered impossible a simple abolition of out-of-date financial institutions, or a reduction of their establishments, for any reform of this sort entailed for the government the need to buy back offices from their possessors, that is, it involved expenditure which was frequently beyond the resources of the treasury.

The obsoleteness of the financial system was also shown in the fact that the items on the income side of the budget were mainly grouped according to the *method of collection* of taxes and levies; thus, the section covering revenue from farmed-out sources included indirect taxes, customs dues, payments from the demesne, and so on. Naturally, each of the farms figures separately in the detailed list of revenues, but, unfortunately, an adequate number of these detailed budgets has not become available to scholars. The historian

---

[1] The *élection* was the primary district for tax-paying purposes. In the period under review there were about 150 of them. The financial officials in the *élections* were called *élus*.
[2] See below, pp. 228, 229.
[3] The local States survived in Normandy, but were, as contemporaries put it, merely 'the shadow of the States', and played no serious role.
[4] The fiscal privileges of these provinces were so extensive that, for example, Languedoc paid in 1620 only 223,900 *livres* in direct (plus some indirect) taxes, and Provence, including wealthy Marseilles, only 170,000 *livres* altogether, while in Normandy direct taxes alone amounted to 2,274,000 *livres* (in round figures). The difference in the tax burden borne by the *pays d'élections* and the *pays d'états* was so great (and in the period under review so lacking in any continued justification) that the government made attempts at the end of the 1620s and the beginning of the 1630s to abolish the fiscal privileges of the *pays d'états*.
[5] It must be mentioned that at this time the question of abolishing the fiscal privileges of the first and second estates of the realm was raised only rarely and hesitantly. Thus, the advocate Du Crot, though regarding it as unjust that the *taille* is exacted only from the unprivileged strata, nevertheless does not call for the abolition of fiscal privilege (L. du Crot, *Traitté des aydes, tailles et gabelles*, 3rd edition (Paris, 1628), pp. 112 ff.)

has to make do with the summary of the state finances for 1598–1708 which was compiled at the beginning of the eighteenth century by Mallet,[1] an official of the financial administration, on the basis of documents most of which have since been lost (or which have not yet been found). The figures quoted by Mallet are sufficiently exact, as has frequently been confirmed by comparison with other sources, but they are not always complete. The problem is that he used documents which reflected the arrival in the central treasury (*Épargne*) of what were called *revenans bons* (net revenue). However, a considerable proportion of the money collected in the provinces was spent immediately on the spot. The royal financial officials or the local States met out of these sums their expenditure for local needs, the cost of the local administrative, judicial and financial apparatus, and also paid the interest on forced loans from the local officials. All this expenditure was called *charges*, and was as a rule not included in Mallet's tables,[2] or at most given in merely summary form. This makes it hard to carry out a detailed analysis of the budget; one cannot, for example, determine the dimensions of such an important item of expenditure as the payment of local officials. We have already mentioned the similar absence of a breakdown of receipts from direct taxes and from indirect taxes in the *dons* offered by the *pays d'états*, as a result of which all receipts from these sources must be listed under direct taxation, because income from the latter made up the bulk of these sums.

The main items on the income side of the budget were, in fact, constituted by the direct taxes (the *taille*, the addition to this called the *grande crue*, and the levy for the upkeep of garrisons, incorporated in the *taille* and called the *taillon*) together with the indirect taxes (the *gabelle*, or salt-tax; the *aide*, which was a tax on wine and other victuals, and so on). All these fell principally upon the people. The *taille* had long since become almost entirely a tax paid by the peasants, while the indirect taxes were mostly paid by the peasants and the townspeople. During the entire period following the death of Henry IV in 1610, the government had taken care not to increase taxation, considering, rightly, that the people were overburdened with taxes beyond all measure. The revolts which broke out in a few places in 1624–5 still further confirmed this policy of forced caution.

The nobility of all ranks, both the old nobility and the new[3] (that is, those

---

[1] *Comptes-rendus de l'administration des finances du royaume de France pendant les onze dernières années du règne de Henri IV, le règne de Louis XIII et les soixante-cinq années de celui de Louis XIV …Ouvrage posthume de Monsieur Mallet* (London and Paris, 1789) (henceforth referred to as 'Mallet').

[2] Mallet, op. cit. p. 211.

[3] We must remember that all the higher officials and a considerable part of the officials of middle-rank belonged at that time to the new nobility.

nobles who were of bourgeois origin), paid direct taxes only in Languedoc and Provence, where the *taille réelle* was payable on non-noble (*roturière*) land regardless of the order to which its actual owner belonged. In the other provinces, that is, over the greater part of the territory of France, the nobles were free from the payment of the *taille* and of some indirect taxes.

The clergy paid the government part of its land rent, that is, it paid a direct tax, in the form of a yearly *don* which was voted by the assemblies of the clergy.[1]

The officials also paid over a considerable part of their income chiefly in the form of the forced loans connected with the payment of the *paulette* (this revenue was called *parties casuelles*).[2] The government showed at that time a certain caution in creating new offices, and mostly restricted itself to the establishment of minor offices in the provinces. The revenue from these, together with loans from the tax-farmers and financiers, was called *deniers extraordinaires*.

An important place in the budget was occupied by internal and external customs dues and levies.

Last in their importance in the budget but first in historical origin were the receipts from the royal demesne. These consisted of many items, the principal ones being (1) revenues from royal fiefs and *censives* paid to the king as feudal lord; (2) levies from the extremely numerous demesne officials (mostly collectors of the *taille* in rural areas of the demesne); (3) a mass of miscellaneous feudal levies (court and office dues, and the like) and local duties; (4) revenue from the exploitation of the state forests.

In the thirteenth century, the revenues from the demesne made up the greater part of the income of the centralised state, then in process of formation. But by the end of that century the relative importance of these revenues had begun to decline, first, because, although these revenues were not increasing, state taxes were, and secondly, because the practice of mortgaging royal property was beginning. In principle, the demesne was inalienable state property, but in practice 'temporary' mortgaging of parts of it, with the right of compulsory redemption, became widespread, constituting in effect a way of borrowing by the state without a definite period for repayment.

Receipts from fiefs and *censives* on the demesne, together with the various dues, were mortgaged and re-mortgaged. Demesne offices were sold and became the property of petty office-holders. Substantial interest-payments were made on these mortgages to the state's creditors, the *de facto* owners of

---

[1] See below, p. 292.
[2] A. D. Lublinskaya, *Frantsiya v nachale XVII veka (1610–1620 gg.)* [*France at the beginning of the seventeenth century, 1610–1620*] (Leningrad, 1959), pp. 63–8; see also p. 231 of this book.

the revenues from the demesne, who came to feel that by prescriptive right they were the owners in the fullest sense, and jealously defended their pretensions.

By the beginning of the seventeenth century only small amounts of revenue were being paid from the demesne into the treasury. This does not mean, however, that these were insignificant in themselves; they had become relatively minor owing to the numerous mortgages. In periods of financial embarrassment, the government resorted to mortgaging various payments from the demesne, all the more readily because in practice this was the simplest and at the same time most profitable way of raising money. In the 1620s it was calculated that during the fourteen years following the death of Henry IV it brought into the treasury not less than 200 million *livres*.[1] This figure may not be an exact one, but the fact that revenue was constantly being extracted from the demesne not by way of direct exploitation of it but by way of mortgages is beyond doubt. On the other hand, when circumstances became more favourable, the question of redeeming mortgaged demesne revenues always came up.[2]

For the purpose of this work I need only give the total figures for revenue under each head (see table 1): direct taxes,[3] indirect taxes,[4] sale of timber,[5] income from *parties casuelles*,[6] extraordinary income.[7] I have set out expenditure under the following heads (see table 2); the court,[8] the army,[9] pensions to noblemen, debts to foreign countries,[10] bridges and roads, extraordinary expenses.[11]

---

[1] Du Crot, op. cit. p. 39.

[2] See below, p. 295.

[3] Let us recall that, in so far as we cannot distinguish, in the totals of *dons* received from the *pays d'états*, between direct and indirect taxes, we must assume that the totals of direct taxation include a certain, even though small, element of indirect taxation.

[4] Also included in these are customs duties (that is, a particular form of indirect tax) and, in addition, some purely feudal receipts from the demesne, such as *péages*.

[5] In all the summary tables this item is included separately. It relates to sales of the timber itself, not of forest land. This was almost the only way in which the royal demesne was exploited directly.

[6] That is, from the *paulette* and forced loans from officials.

[7] Sale of new offices, issue of *rentes*, internal loans.

[8] This item included expenditure incurred not only for the upkeep of the court as such but also on the diplomatic service, the king's council, and so on.

[9] Expenditure on the army was subdivided under the following heads: maintenance of the army, guards, garrisons, expenditure on the navy, on the artillery and on fortresses.

[10] These debts were incurred by the French government during the civil wars of the sixteenth century. Payments of principal and interest on debts to England, Holland, Switzerland, Tuscany, Lorraine, and so on, were especially large in Henry IV's time and immediately after 1610. Later, external debts were mostly payable to Switzerland.

[11] This item of expenditure is not broken down and it is also the largest. At this time it included various cash payments for 'state matters' which were not subject to accounting and checking, payment of interest on internal loans, and so on.

TABLE 1. *Income, in livres*

Items of revenue	1607	1620	1622
Direct taxes	11,306,200	11,446,500	9,872,500
Indirect taxes	5,589,700	7,013,300	8,145,600
Sale of timber	447,900	415,600	447,900
Parties casuelles	1,842,600	13,267,600	20,052,100
Extraordinary income	10,656,400	6,812,500	11,415,500
Total	29,842,800	38,955,500	49,933,600

TABLE 2. *Expenditure, in livres*

Items of expenditure	1607	1620	1622
Court	4,047,700	8,142,200	6,273,100
Army	4,370,700	13,428,400	22,678,400
Pensions	2,010,600	5,422,700	4,214,800
Debts to foreign countries	3,123,700	821,800	409,400
Bridges and roads	842,200	153,900	120,300
Extraordinary expenses	15,551,200	8,758,500	15,601,000
Total	29,946,100	36,727,500	49,297,000

In order to analyse these figures and compare one year with another,[1] I have taken the budgets of 1607, 1620 and 1622. The budget of 1607 was the last 'peacetime' budget in the first half of the seventeenth century.[2] For a long time, nearly down to the period of Colbert, it served as a model worthy of imitation.[3] The budgets of 1620 and 1622 are interesting because they give a picture of state finance at the turning point from the period of civil war in 1614–20 to the period of war against the Huguenots and *guerre couverte* against the Habsburgs. The budget of 1622 is important also because the appointment of La Vieuville as *surintendant* was caused by the critical financial situation in that particular year.

In analysing these budgets I will touch upon the elements which seem to me to be of maximum significance.

[1] All the figures which follow have been taken from Mallet's tables, rounded off to hundreds of *livres*.

[2] In 1608–10 taxes were already increased in connexion with the expected war with the Habsburgs. In 1610–20 the civil war had a marked effect on the budget. The budget of 1607 is fairly well known (see J. H. Mariéjol, 'Henri IV et Louis XIII', in E. Lavisse, ed., *Histoire de France*, VI, part 2 (Paris, 1908) 63, 64). The distribution of the amounts between items is a little different from that shown in Mallet, but the totals are almost exactly the same.

[3] Sometimes (see below, p. 308) the budget of 1608 served as such a model, though it was a little bigger than that of 1607. The financial history of Henry IV's reign will soon be studied, we may hope, since in 1955 Sully's papers were deposited, after many misadventures, in the French national archives (*Les papiers de Sully aux Archives Nationales. Inventaire par R. H. Bautier et A. Vallée-Karcher* (Paris, 1959)).

The stability of the amount received from direct taxation leaps to the eye: between 1607 and 1620[1] it hardly changed. Its decline by one and a half million *livres* in 1622 was due to the enormous amount in arrears (*non-valeurs*) and not to an actual reduction.[2] In contrast, indirect taxes increased in 1622, as compared with 1607, when they amounted to only half as much as direct taxes, by two and a half million, and came near to bringing in the same amount as direct taxes.

Extraordinary income (that is, internal loans in the form of *rentes* and the sale of new offices) fell considerably between 1607 and 1620, but increased markedly between 1620 and 1622. The fundamental cause of this was that in the second decade of the century new *rentes* were not issued, and new offices were created on a moderate scale only, whereas in 1622 the government resorted once more to these devices.

The most remarkable increase occurred in respect of 'casual' revenue, chiefly from the *paulette* and from forced loans at the expense of the officials.[3] In 1620 this item was almost seven times as large as in 1607, and in 1622 more than eleven times as large, amounting in all to 20 million *livres*, that is, to 40 per cent of total revenue. Under this one head alone the government obtained in 1622 a sum equivalent to two-thirds of its entire revenue in 1607.

Revenue as a whole was 9 million *livres* greater in 1620 than in 1607 (an increase of 30 per cent) and in 1622 20 millions greater (66 per cent more), this substantial increase having been achieved primarily through taxation of the officials, and in the second place through increased indirect taxation.

Analysis of the expenditure side of the budget of 1622 shows what happened to the money obtained through this extra taxation. It was spent on war, on the expeditions against the Huguenots. Expenditure on the army absorbed more than 22 million *livres*,[4] making up not much under a half of total expenditure, whereas in 'peacetime' 1607 no more than 14 per cent had been spent for this purpose, an amount which exceeded only slightly the costs of maintaining the court and the central machinery of government. By 1622 the court and the state machine had become half as expensive again as in 1607.[5] Pensions to the princes and nobles had doubled, though they

[1] The same situation prevailed all through the 1620s.
[2] For the same reason, in 1627 the *taille* was again officially reduced (see below, p. 309).
[3] It must be remembered that the advantages of the *paulette* (that is, guaranteed inheritability and saleability of offices) were granted after 1620 only on condition that these forced loans were contributed (see p. 181).
[4] Of these 22 millions, 3·3 millions were spent on the artillery, almost as much as in 1635–6, that is, during the first years of open war with the Habsburgs.
[5] In 1607 the only 'establishments' at court were those of the king and the queen, their children still being small. In 1622 there were also the establishments of the Queen Mother (Marie de Médicis) and of Gaston d'Orléans.

came to somewhat less than in the years of the regency of Marie de Médicis and of the civil wars of 1614-20 (when they amounted, on the average, to between $4\frac{1}{2}$ and $5\frac{1}{2}$ million *livres* a year).[1]

It is significant that extraordinary expenditure amounted in 1622 to the same figure as in 1607, whereas in 1620 it had fallen to half of that figure. The reason was that under Henry IV many *rentes* which were unprofitable from the state's point of view were redeemed, and substantial sums were paid out for this purpose. Interest-payments on loans were in 1620 comparatively small (compared, that is, with the enormous sums paid out on this account later on, in the 1630s, which came to between 50 and 60 million *livres*), but in 1622 they increased sharply, in proportion to the sharp increase in state borrowing.

It must also be noted that the balancing of the budget in 1622 was fictitious, since the item 'extraordinary income' conceals advances obtained from the tax-farmers which were to be made good out of the money collected by the latter in taxes in the following year, 1623.

The general conclusion to be drawn from an analysis of the budget of 1622 is clear: the budget was strained almost to breaking-point. The two years of war against the Huguenots had cost vast sums of money. On two campaigns, in 1621 and 1622, nearly 42 million *livres* had been spent, a sum greater than the entire annual revenue of the state in 1620. The total amount of revenue from taxes received in 1622 was not greater than in 1620, the increase in receipts from indirect taxes merely covering the arrears in payment of direct taxes (the *taille*). In order to conduct the war, the government resorted to loans, which also reached huge dimensions, some short-term ones being obtained, moreover, only on condition that they were repaid out of the first receipts of the following year, 1623. It was the state's creditors who financed the war; ordinary revenue was obviously inadequate for this purpose.

The task of the historian investigating the system of government credit in this period presents considerable difficulty owing to the scarcity of available material. The subject has been given very little attention in historical writing.[2] Pamphlets, treatises and memoirs offer only general information about the tax-farmers and financial officials, while the mass of archives which describe

---

[1] This tendency for pensions to be reduced continued throughout the entire reign of Louis XIII; the amount varied between 2·5 and 3 million *livres* a year.

[2] The only work calling for mention is Heumann's article in which he traces, on the basis of records, the financial activity of Antoine Feydeau, one of the biggest tax-farmers of the period under review and gives some information on tax-farming in general (P. Heumann, 'Un traitant sous Louis XIII: Antoine Feydeau', in *Études sur l'histoire administrative et sociale de l'Ancien Régime*, ed. G. Pagès (Paris, 1938)).

their activities (mainly the decisions of the king's Council) have not been published and have as yet been little used by historians.

Before embarking on an examination of this question, I must draw attention to one important circumstance. My concern is exclusively with the organisation of state credit from national sources, if the expression may be allowed. In the 1620s the French government refrained almost entirely from borrowing from abroad. This was due to two causes: the increased wealth of French tax-farmers and the absence in those days of any possibility for the French government to borrow from foreign banks.

The history of state credit in France can be briefly summarised as follows.

In the fourteenth century the charges of the Crown of France—or, more precisely, the costs of the wars waged by the rulers of France—were met principally by borrowing from the northern Italian banking houses, some of whose representatives came to stay in France and undertook the farming of indirect taxes. In the fifteenth century, French merchants and tax-farmers began to compete successfully in this field, having acquired great wealth through the Levant trade and through tax-farming. The most notable of them, though not by any means the only one, was Jacques Cœur. They were unable, however, to take over the whole of state credit at that time, the Italians, and later (from the end of the fifteenth century) the Germans too, being considerably richer than they were.

All through the long period of the Italian wars (1494–1559) the French kings borrowed money in Lyons, which was then one of the chief centres of banking, because Lyons was on French territory, whereas the greatest money-market of those days, Antwerp, was inaccessible for France owing to political factors: the bankers of the Empire (that is, the Dutch, Spanish and some German bankers) were financing Charles V. Even in the French city of Lyons, however, the French government's chief creditors were Italian and German merchant-bankers who had settled in France (the Strozzi, Gadagne, Sardini, Albizzi, Cléberger, Welser, Tucher, Obrecht, Minckel and other families), while French financiers played a secondary role.[1]

In the second half of the sixteenth century the situation began to change to the advantage of the French. Their Italian and German competitors suffered from all the heavy consequences of the economic and political decline of Italy and Germany. In the same period the fierce conflict in Lyons between Catholics and Protestants, French and foreign, ravaged the town and deprived it of its former position. Many Italian and German financiers went bankrupt,

[1] G. Zeller, 'Deux capitalistes strasbourgeois au XVIe siècle', in *Études d'histoire moderne et contemporaine*, I (Paris, 1947); D. Gioffre, *Gênes et les foires de change: de Lyon à Besançon* (Paris, 1960).

fled the country, or were banished. Those who remained preferred to become naturalised Frenchmen, but their wealth was already no longer what it had been.

These developments, bringing disaster to the rivals of the French merchants and tax-farmers, were most favourable to the latter. Moreover, although as merchants they also suffered from the economic ruin of the civil war period, as tax-farmers they greatly benefited. Lacking its former opportunities of getting credit abroad, the French government began to issue *rentes* on an unprecedented scale, and also to sell newly created offices. The state's internal debt increased with extraordinary speed, so that under Henry III it was much bigger than the state's annual revenue. And all this borrowing by the state was completely met by Frenchmen.

At the beginning of his reign, Henry IV, not yet *de facto* king of France, was unable to make use of these methods, and was obliged to borrow from Venice, Florence, Mantua, and so on. These were difficult and financially disadvantageous transactions, which also involved long-drawn-out negotiations. For this reason, after he had established himself on the throne he abandoned these sources, and the French tax-farmers had a real monopoly of state credit.

In the early years of the seventeenth century another process was completed, namely, the breakaway of the French tax-farmers from commercial and industrial activity and their total fusion with the state's financial machinery. Both aspects of this process were extremely important.

In 1604 Sully reorganised the system of farming the indirect taxes (*aides*). Until then they had been collected on the spot by petty tax-farmers, mostly officials of the government's financial apparatus (*élus*), many of whom were also engaged in trade. As merchants, these men were interested in reducing payments of *aides* to the treasury, because indirect taxation was a burden on trade. The *surintendant*'s struggle against their cheating of the state was unsuccessful, so he brought all these tax-farms together to make one large tax-farm which he entrusted to the Parisian financier Moisset, whose preoccupation would be a different one, namely, to extract the maximum income from his farm. For this reason, both he and his *sous-traitants*, who were not merchants either, ruthlessly put down all abuses in the levying of indirect taxes. The significance of the reform, apart from the possibility which it created of more effective supervision of tax-farming, was that the amount of money obtained from the farm increased sharply and went on increasing. While in 1604 it had amounted to half a million *livres*, twenty years later, in 1624, it came to three times as much, and along with this the state was relieved of all the cost of maintaining the numerous body of tax-collectors.

In short, the system of large-scale tax-farms proved very profitable to the government; following the example of the *aides*, the farming of the salt-tax (*gabelle*) was soon afterwards concentrated in the same way.[1]

The reform introduced by Sully had a great influence on the nature of the activity of all the tax-farmers; being obliged to abandon commerce, they gave all their attention to financial operations. Finance became for 'men of money' at all levels their exclusive sphere of activity. All their capital was invested and put to use outside the sphere of purely bourgeois activity, exclusively in the collection of taxes and furnishing of credit to the state. As a result, this capital increased, in many cases, at fabulous speed; in the course of ten or fifteen years, the luckiest—and, of course, the most thievish —of these operators acquired enormous fortunes, became a byword, and by their luxurious way of life gave rise to widespread indignation.

The absorption of the tax-farmers into the state's financial machinery was something quite unavoidable under these conditions. The tax-farmer could not remain an outsider in relation to this machinery. Having taken over the farming of the indirect taxes, levying these taxes by means of his own employees, and sometimes meeting local expenditure out of the money raised,[2] he eventually became an integral part of the state's fiscal machinery. Furthermore, the selling of offices gave him access to any office he chose in the financial machine—treasurer, collector, controller, or anything else. As these offices were extremely costly (only the highest offices in the administration and the judiciary were comparable in price), they were within the reach only of the wealthiest men, that is, the tax-farmers.

Owing to these circumstances, the French government obtained credit not from bankers who were more or less independent of it, and not from commercial or industrial companies, but from its own financial machine. When they said that 'these leeches swell themselves with the king's money and then lend it to him at exorbitant interest' (this saying was current at the time) contemporaries showed an exact understanding of just what was happening. One must not forget, however, that this situation—paradoxical at first glance—actually freed the government's hands in dealings with its creditors. When circumstances were favourable, that is, when there was no pressing need for extensive and urgent credit, the government could take measures against its creditors—judicial prosecution, confiscation of property, and so on—which in the seventeenth century were impossible so far as foreign or otherwise independent creditors were concerned. True, such

---

[1] In the treatise already mentioned, Du Crot describes in detail the system of farming the *aides* and the *gabelle*, his account agreeing with that given by other sources (Du Crot, op. cit. pp. 64 ff.).
[2] See below, p. 240.

235

action usually stopped short at threats to investigate creditors who were also financial officials, as the latter hastened to pay a few million *livres* as 'smart-money', and that was the end of that. Payments of this sort were more profit-able to the government than a real investigation or confiscation would have been, because the use of coercion risked undermining the basis of credit. For this reason it was much easier for the government to squeeze a substantial sum out of the 'tax-farmer leeches' than to try to force them to lend; in the latter case, each tax-farmer retained some freedom of decision.

All this reflected what was, in my opinion, the still *feudal* nature of state credit in France.

Let us now go on to examine the mechanism of the tax-farms and of loans to the state, and also those aspects of the financial machinery which were connected with tax-farming and the raising of loans.[1]

I have already mentioned that the collection of all indirect taxes, customs dues and demesne revenues had been farmed out. This was done at public auctions. The starting price of the farm was determined by the finance department, usually by the *surintendant* himself, on the basis of whatever information he possessed, which was sometimes the outcome of special inquiries. This price and the date of the auction were made known in accord-ance with long-established practice, announcements being posted in certain places. All who wished to take part in the auctions were obliged to name as sureties of their solvency some sufficiently well-known and credit-worthy persons; other tax-farmers, officials of the finance department, rich mer-chants. The farm was awarded to whoever offered the highest bid 'while the candle was burning', that is, before a definite time was up. Then the contract was drawn up (the *traité de ferme*, or *parti*, from which the terms *fermier*, *traitant*, *partisan* were derived, to describe the tax-farmer); the period for which the farm was let was finally laid down (usually between six and nine years), together with the total sum to be paid and the procedure for paying it. The contract, confirmed by the king's Council, was entered in its register and in the registers of the *Chambre des Comptes* and the *Cour des Aides*. Only then could the tax-farmer, having assumed responsibility for fulfilling the contract, proceed to carry it into effect.

This was the procedure laid down by law. Practical necessity, however, introduced a number of modifications.

First, in order that there should be no interruption in the collection of

---

[1] The material for this has been provided by the works, mentioned above, of Heumann, Mallet and Du Crot, together with the *arrêts* of the king's Council in 1616 and 1622 (microfilms of the MSS in the Bibliothèque Nationale, Paris, in the possession of the Department of MSS of the Saltykov-Shchedrin Library, Leningrad).

taxes, fresh contracts were concluded and registered a long time—one or two years—before the previous ones had expired. Preparation for the conclusion of the new contracts was carried through, as a rule, in an atmosphere of intense competition between tax-farmers.

Secondly, this competition had the result that the government could at any moment cancel an existing contract with a tax-farmer. It was enough for another person to offer a sum larger than that laid down in the contract, to give the necessary guarantee, and so on, for fresh auctions to be arranged, with a new and higher starting price for the farm. Consequently, no tax-farmer had any assurance of uninterrupted fulfilment of his contract during the entire period indicated in it. Nor was there any guarantee that the price of the tax-farm laid down in a contract would remain constant, since, when new offers were made, the tax-farmer often agreed to pay a higher price merely in order to prevent the cancellation of his contract and the announcement of another auction.

On the other hand, the tax-farmers themselves could apply to the king's Council with a *requête* for a *rabais* in the price of a farm, should there be a fall in receipts from indirect taxes, dues, and so on, as a result of natural disasters or of political anarchy (during the civil wars the princes' troops seized, on the roads and in captured towns, the cash-boxes of all the king's tax-collectors and tax-farmers). The granting of such reductions was quite normal, but the reason given for the need for such a reduction did not always correspond to the facts.

For all these reasons, tax-farm contracts were very frequently broken and transferred from one person to another, with changes in both term and price.

Furthermore, having signed the contract, the tax-farmer only nominally received the entire tax-farm. In practice he became a sort of chief administrator, for immediately after the registration of the contract he handed over the tax-farm in sections to several *sous-traitants*, who in their turn divided their shares among their own *sous-traitants*, and so on, so that a three-tier or even four-tier structure was created. In other words, the principal tax-farmer stood at the head of a whole group of several dozen men who were scattered all over the country. It was they who actually collected the taxes, dues and so on, while he himself was mainly occupied with seeing that his own interests and those of the group as a whole were safeguarded, and sticking up for his rights before the king's Council, the central treasury (*Épargne*), and so on. The *sous-traitants* of all ranks paid over to him the money due under their sub-contracts, and he paid it into the treasury himself, for in dealings with the finance department the only official and responsible person recognised was the chief tax-farmer, whose signature was on the contract.

His relations with his *sous-traitants* were his own affair, and any disputes about money or anything else that might arise were matters for the ordinary courts.

This situation had come about gradually. As late as the sixteenth century tax-farms were, as a rule, not large as regards the amount of money involved, and operated over small areas only. Sully, by consolidating the tax-farms through amalgamating many of them, considerably eased his own task as *surintendant*, as he thus had to deal with only a relatively limited number of tax-farmers. Consistent unification of the system, eliminating all or most of the numerous *sous-traitants*, was, however, in the conditions of that time, not a practical possibility: the country was too large in relation to the means of transport and communication then available, complete centralisation of the financial accounting system had not yet been achieved, and so on. The basic reason why it could not be realised was the fact that accumulations of money were so widely dispersed. The large sums paid for tax-farms, amounting to several million *livres*, were made up of many small sums. The large amounts of capital invested by the financial 'big-shots' of those days did not consist entirely of their own money. What made the tax-farming system work was not so much the individual capital of particular rich men as the aggregated capital of many persons, whose fortunes were far from being similar in size.

The largest tax-farms in the period under review—though we must not lose sight of the fact that all of them were based on the same system of *sous-traitants*—were as follows: the salt-tax in the heartland of France, that is, the northern and central regions (*gabelles de France*); the salt-tax in the border provinces,[1] which enjoyed considerable privileges (*gabelles de Langue-doc*, etc).; the taxes on wine and other forms of food and drink (*aides de France*); what were called the *cinq grosses fermes*, embracing customs dues; and the city dues payable in Paris and Rouen.

These major tax-farms were not all managed in identical fashion. In the farm of the *gabelle* the work was done mainly by *commis* appointed by the chief tax-farmer, together with *capitaines des archers* and *gardes* whose responsibility it was to protect the *greniers à sel*. The chief tax-farmer was also responsible for purchasing salt (free trade in which was not allowed in northern France), putting it in all the *greniers à sel*, the keys of which were held by his *commis*, and selling it at the price and in the quantities laid down by the government. If we consider the large extent assumed by trade in such a necessary article as salt, we can appreciate the large scale of the administrative and commercial activity carried on by the chief farmer of the *gabelle*.

Wine and all other items of food and drink were sold freely, and so the

---

[1] These were Languedoc, Provence, Dauphiné and the Lyonnais, and later, Lorraine.

exaction of the dues payable on them could not be centralised. The tax-farm covering these goods, the *ferme des aides*, was in practice dispersed among *sous-traitants* of varying importance, with the chief tax-farmer figuring only as the official representative, who collected these indirect taxes from his *sous-traitants* and paid them into the treasury. Financially, however, the *sous-traitants* were closely tied to their chief. Any change in the price of the farm, whether an increase or a reduction, affected them directly; if the farm-contract were cancelled by the government before it was due to expire, their money would be in as much danger as the chief farmer's. In the provinces this farm was organised in the following manner: in the chief town of each financial district (*généralité*) there were *sous-traitants* who entered into contracts with the chief farmer. They received the money collected in the other towns and the rural areas by second-grade *sous-traitants*, who in their turn dealt with third-grade *sous-traitants*, each responsible for collecting the dues payable on particular goods. In Paris the chief tax-farmer delegated to *sous-traitants* the farm of each separate commodity (e.g. the dues on wine, sea-fish, river-fish, and so on).

Sous-traitants at every level were vitally interested in tracking down and punishing persons who evaded paying indirect taxes and dues, and there were always plenty of these. Some of them claimed immunity from taxation (documents to prove such exemption were often forged), while others bought on the 'black market'. It was no easy task to bring such offenders to justice, not only because of the slowness and clumsiness of the judicial and administrative machinery, but also, and mainly, because of the obstacles put in the way of the *sous-traitants* by the local authorities, first and foremost by the royal treasurers who were also engaged in collecting taxes (direct taxes and demesne dues). The spheres of operation of the *sous-traitants* and these treasurers often coincided, while in other cases the boundary between them was debatable. This was a source of inexhaustible hatred and implacable conflict between them. In most instances the *sous-traitants* at first suffered defeat in these local conflicts, but then the chief tax-farmer took the matter to the king's Council, where, as a rule, he won his point; and this sometimes entailed the imposition of penalties on the local officials who had given trouble.

The chief tax-farmers in the capital, and all the *sous-traitants* in the localities, were at the same time treasurers responsible for paying a considerable share of the government's expenses (*charges*), in Paris and other places: officials' salaries, interest on *rentes*, pensions, and so on. These functions, at first sight unusual for them (which was also the reason for the unceasing conflicts between the royal treasurers and the *sous-traitants*), were derived from the fact that, according to the schedules of the budget, specific expenses were to be paid out of specific revenues. In so far as pensions, salaries, interest on *rentes*, and so on, were assigned as payable out of receipts from indirect taxes which had been farmed, the local *sous-traitants* paid these local *charges*, and the chief tax-farmer did likewise with those payments which were due in the capital (e.g. interest on the *rentes* issued by the municipality of Paris) and which were assigned for payment out of receipts from the chief farm of the *gabelle* or the *aides*.

In other tax-farms (customs dues, internal tolls, levies on trade in manu-factured articles, etc.), much the same system applied as in the farm of the *aides*.

The income received by tax-farmers at all levels was directly dependent on the economic and political condition of the country. It rose in years of good harvest and when trade and industry were booming, and it fell when the harvest failed, there was an economic depression, or civil war was raging. Some figures which are available, though only fragmentary, nevertheless give us some idea of how much the tax-farmers made. Thus, for instance, the *sous-traitant* of the *aides* in one of the financial districts (Poitou and the Limousin) received during our period an average of 30,000 *livres* a year, net income; the chief tax-farmer collected in four out of his twelve districts alone more than half the amount he paid into the treasury according to his con-tract,[1] and his net income was equivalent to about 30 per cent of the price of his farm, which meant approximately 300,000 *livres* and was equivalent to the capital of a very rich merchant, or the income of a very highly placed grandee.

Tax-farming was a profitable business. It was on this fact that the govern-ment founded its system of forced loans from the chief tax-farmers, turning the latter into its creditors.

During the period 1610–29 it even became the normal thing for the tax-farmer who had succeeded in the public auction actually to register his contract only after he had offered the treasury a substantial loan (*prêt*). In theory this loan was made out of the future revenue of the farm, which, therefore, was paid in with a corresponding reduction. However, the loan grew at simple and compound interest; one loan had not been paid off before another one was contracted; despite the existence of an unpaid loan, the treasury sometimes insisted on the payment of the full price for the tax-farm, and so on. Thus, for example, a debt of five and a half million *livres* was owed by the government in 1620–5 to the farmer-general of the *aides*, in the form of forced loans, and so much money was exacted from the farmer-general

---

[1] Heumann, loc. cit. p. 198.

of the *gabelle* in 1622 that the entire receipts from the *gabelle* were *mangés* for the three years following.

The task of raising these forced loans (appearing under the head of 'extraordinary revenue') was also apportioned by the chief tax-farmer throughout his whole network of *sous-traitants*. In this way a considerable group of persons, of varying fortune, were drawn into providing credit to the state, so that the amounts lent to the treasury by the smallest *sous-traitants* were quite small. Just as in the organisation of tax-farms, what functioned here was an aggregate of many units of capital which, though lent to the treasury through the mediation of the chief tax-farmer, was actually drawn from hundreds of *sous-traitants* scattered all over France. The responsible lender, however, was always the chief tax-farmer himself, and he alone.

Besides these forced loans imposed when contracts for tax-farms were signed—loans which were similar to the forced contributions exacted from officials when they paid the *paulette*[1]—the government took money, occasionally in large amounts, from all its tax-farmers and the officials of the finance department. This was sometimes a matter of 'individual loans' in the strict sense of the word, that is, a given person lent what really was his own capital. As a rule, however, the loans came from companies of financiers, many of whom got their contribution together by borrowing from relatives, friends, and so on. Interest on such loans, which were usually short-term, was very high.

This system of state credit, already complex and fantastic enough, was complicated still further by the fact that usually the more or less large-scale tax-farmers and state creditors were at the same time officials of a finance department—treasurers, controllers, or whatever it might be. In order to become a member of purely financial institutions, such as the central treasury, the office for the collection of *parties casuelles*, the army finance department, and so on,[2] the tax-farmer had only to purchase the appropriate office. As a result, these institutions coincided almost completely, as regards their personnel, with the richest group of tax-farmers.

The biography of Antoine Feydeau (1572–1627), one of the richest financiers of the 1600–29 period, illustrates this.

Belonging to a provincial bourgeois family, many of whose members were ennobled in the sixteenth century in connexion with the judicial offices they held, while others specialised in financial operations, Antoine Feydeau began his career at the end of the sixteenth century as a collector of the *taille*, later

[1] See above, pp. 181–2.
[2] These did not include the judicial and administrative organs connected with finance, i.e. the *Chambre des Comptes* and the *Cour des Aides*.

becoming a collector of all forms of royal revenue (*receveur général des finances*) in several provinces. In 1615 he purchased the office of treasurer in charge of the payment of pensions (*trésorier des pensions*). At the same time he was in 1611–15 the chief farmer of the *aides* and in 1622–4 the chief farmer of the *gabelle*. In 1625 he obtained the very expensive office of treasurer of the central treasury, and also acquired the rank of *conseiller du roi*. The *curricula vitae* of other financiers are merely variants of the career of Antoine Feydeau.

The penetration of state creditors into the state's financial administration was due to a number of reasons. The chief of these was the instability and insecurity of the capital invested in tax-farms and loans, as a result of which many financiers ended in bankruptcy and flight (Antoine Feydeau did not escape this fate). This insecurity was caused first and foremost by the complex and insufficiently stable system of credit among the tax-farmers themselves and all their *sous-traitants*. As has been shown above, the capital lent to the treasury was made up of numerous 'shares', and was therefore very vulnerable for a variety of economic and political reasons. The ability of the chief tax-farmers to give credit was to a considerable extent based on the ability to give credit possessed by a whole host of 'partners' (the word *partisan* also had this meaning). The degree of solvency of the debtor, namely the treasury, was very important. It was not to the advantage of the state's creditors, but rather meant a risk to them, if the treasury fell too deeply in debt; such a situation really did 'undermine the state's credit'.

Possession of an office provided the tax-farmer with a reliable security for the capital he had invested in his farm and in loans to the state. Thanks to the system of sale of offices, the latter already constituted, in themselves, a profitable and secure sphere in which money could be invested with the possibility of realisation at any moment, through selling the particular office —perhaps, even, at a profit. This was why the tax-farmers especially sought the highest offices in the financial administration, purchase of noble estates and *châteaux* being of secondary interest to them,[1] since these offices were from their point of view a sort of financial reserve fund. It was also a consideration that these offices brought their possessors considerable social prestige.

Secondly, by getting themselves into the state's financial administration, the state's creditors obtained very useful opportunities for evading any serious supervision of their transactions. Every *surintendant* always complained, and on good grounds, that the accounting system of the central

---

[1] Their children, who married representatives of the highest noble families of France, usually led a purely aristocratic life.

treasury was as confused and complicated as it could possibly be,[1] and this, of course, facilitated abuse by the officials of their positions.

The forms assumed by this abuse are described in detail in an interesting memorandum which was submitted to the king in August–September 1624, that is, after the dismissal of La Vieuville.[2] The author was a certain Marsilly, whose office I have not been able to discover.[3] The facts he cites largely corroborate the information known from other sources,[4] but are distinguished by greater detail. Their gist is that the *surintendant* himself needed to be supervised, because he was allowed excessive independence in the use of funds, while at the same time his real power to supervise the doings of his treasurers and tax-farmers was too slight. Marsilly's reference to *les financiers ...ayant tout l'argent de la France* is also very interesting. If we recall the points made earlier about the aggregated capital applied to the financing of state expenditure this view of his will not seem exaggerated.

The description here given of the system of state credit could be extended by including additional facts of a similar nature. But for the purpose of this book there is no need to go any further. The main thing is to make clear that in France in this period the system of state credit and the state debt was already not merely united with the state's financial administration but formed an integral part of it. It was based on two inherent features of French absolutism: the sale of offices, and a fiscal system founded on preserving the privileged status of the ruling class as regards taxation, while correspondingly overburdening the entire third estate, especially the mass of the people. Only radical reforms could have broken the link between financial capital and the state machine; namely, abolition of the sale of offices and introduction of a completely different system of taxation. It is well known that such reforms were beyond the power of any of the statesmen of the *ancien régime*. These foundations were destroyed only in the course of the bourgeois revolution.

We will now turn to the events of 1623–4, in order to study the political and financial policies of Richelieu's immediate predecessors.

---

[1] It must be taken into account that, as a rule, each office of treasurer, etc. was held in turn by two, three, and sometimes four officials, each for a single year only, and they handed over their affairs to each other at the end of each year.

[2] *Mémoire du sieur de Marsilly touchant les abus commis par les financiers*. Paris, Archives du Ministère des Affaires Etrangères de France, 779, folios 101–2 (microfilm in the Department of MSS, Saltykov-Shchedrin Library, Leningrad).

[3] This may have been Dominique de Marsilly, *grand-maître des eaux et forêts*. In any case he knew about the activities of tax-farmers and treasurers behind the scenes, and named many of them in his memorandum.

[4] For instance, from the facts given in the address of the *surintendant* d'Effiat to the Assembly of Notables (see chapter 6).

The biography of La Vieuville, especially the question of his social origin and position, is of considerable interest in establishing the role of the financiers in the politics of the 1620s.

The Marquis de La Vieuville did not come from the higher nobility. His father, Robert, Marquis de La Vieuville, who died in 1612, was originally *maître d'hôtel* to the Duc de Nevers, and was described by contemporaries as a *simple gentilhomme*.[1] Later he became governor of the town of Mézières, and at the same time was involved in the collection of indirect taxes.[2] In 1608 he was appointed *lieutenant-général* in Champagne and the Rethelois. This signified that from the service of one of the most important of the grandees, the Duc de Nevers, governor of Champagne, he had passed into the service of the king, who showed him much favour, giving him the office of grand falconer in 1606, presents of money and estates, and so on.[3] It is notable that his appointment as *lieutenant-général* in Champagne must have put him on bad terms with the governor of this province, Nevers; Henry IV always tried to make sure that there was no unanimity between the two chief men in any given province, and in his policy towards the grandees who were provincial governors he relied on his own henchmen, the *lieutenants-généraux*, who were not usually recruited from the *noblesse d'épée*.

Thus, in the career of La Vieuville senior, military, administrative and court functions were of major importance; among the court nobility he was regarded as a fairly important person, because the post of *lieutenant-général* in Champagne, a frontier province, was one of some significance.

La Vieuville junior (Charles, marquis de La Vieuville, *c.* 1580–1653) inherited his father's military and court positions.[4] During the years of civil war, 1614–20, he supported the government and came into open conflict with the Duc de Nevers. He did not have to wait long for his reward. In 1620 La Vieuville was given the office of captain of Louis XIII's bodyguard (*capitaine des gardes du corps du roi*), and in that capacity arrested the Cardinal de Guise on 25 March 1621, by order of the king.[5] In January 1623 he stood guard at the door of the Queen Mother's apartment during her interview with the king.[6] It was La Vieuville who brought the news to Lyons that

[1] G. Tallemant des Réaux, *Historiettes* (Paris, 1960), I, 10.
[2] Noël Valois, *Inventaire des arrêts du conseil d'État* (Paris, 1893), nos. 7456, 8443.
[3] Ibid. nos. 10986, 12454, 12793, 13382, 15576, 15581.
[4] These offices did not, however, conceal from contemporaries the not entirely noble origins of the Marquis de La Vieuville. In one pamphlet (*Remerciement de la voix publique au Roy, 1624*) it was stated that he was 'equally hated by the nobility, as being a *métif* [i.e. not a genuine nobleman], and by the third estate, from whose ranks he came' (quoted in M. Deloche, *Autour de la plume du cardinal de Richelieu* (Paris, 1920), p. 238).
[5] L. Vaunois, *Vie de Louis XIII*, 2nd edition (Paris, 1944), p. 250.
[6] Ibid. p. 287.

Mansfeld had removed himself from the borders of Champagne; he brought with him a large body of troops, from the force which had been raised to resist an invasion by Mansfeld and which were now to increase the strength of the army prepared for the Italian campaign.[1] La Vieuville was thus no presumptuous provincial nobleman, well-known only on account of his marriage with the daughter of the important financier, Beaumarchais. He was the captain of the king's bodyguard, a man close to the king and trusted by him, well known at the court and even in wider circles.

Could he have aspired to the office of *surintendant des finances* even if he had not been Beaumarchais's son-in-law? By virtue of all his other advantages, he could have done so, especially with the prospect of war in Italy. Fontenay-Mareuil testifies that the king wanted to have a military man in this post, and he states that all La Vieuville's efforts to get Schomberg's place would have come to nothing but for the death of Monsieur Senecey, whom the king intended to appoint as soon as it was decided to dismiss Schomberg.[2] Henri de Bauffremont, baron and later marquis de Senecey (1578–1622), president of the chamber of the nobility in the States-General of 1614, was a typical military man of his time (governor of the town of Auxonne, *maréchal de camp*), who also sometimes carried out diplomatic functions as well. It is characteristic that the *surintendant* Schomberg, after his brief exile to his estates in 1623, also turned again to military activities and was made marshal and governor of Languedoc. Thus Sully, Schomberg and La Vieuville all combined the administration of finance and important military functions, not because of some fusion or other of the higher nobility with the plutocracy,[3] but because of the conditions of the age, in which this kind of 'pluralism' was advantageous and desirable from the government's point of view.

The circumstances in which La Vieuville was appointed *surintendant* were as follows.

Having arrived in Lyons in December 1622, La Vieuville became convinced that the king and his Council were extremely dissatisfied with Schomberg both as head of the ordnance and as *surintendant*. At the instigation of Sillery and Puisieux he began to lay claim to these offices, describing to Louis XIII the lamentable condition of the state finances. Advances had been made from all the revenues of the following year, 1623, and this money

---

[1] *Relation des choses mémorables arrivées depuis l'année 1616 jusqu'en 1624*, Bibliothèque Nationale MS fr. 15644, fo. 234ᵛ (microfilm in the Department of MSS, Saltykov-Shchedrin Library, Leningrad). The manuscript is a copy with numerous corrections, apparently by the author, whose identity has not been established; the text seems to have been put together in 1624.

[2] Fontenay-Mareuil, *Mémoires*, in *Collection Michaud et Poujoulat*, 2nd series, v (Paris, 1837), 172.

[3] As Biryukovich thought, supposing that La Vieuville was made *surintendant* thanks only to his kinship with the tax-farmer Beaumarchais and as an instrument of the group of financiers as a whole (loc. cit. p. 196).

had already been spent; consequently, the king possessed no means for waging war in Italy. Moreover, the king's credit with the financiers had been undermined, as the money destined to make up for the advances had been otherwise spent.[1] In other words, La Vieuville told the king that Schomberg had so disposed of the income for the following year that the royal creditors could not be reimbursed for their advances and therefore could not give further credit.[2]

The events of December 1622, and the preparations for the Italian campaign, obliged the king to pay attention to La Vieuville. He was alarmed by the gloomy picture which La Vieuville painted, though, according to Fontenay-Mareuil, the colours were laid on rather thick. This alarm related both to the financial situation itself and to the intended campaign, which could not be undertaken without money or credit. If La Vieuville, making use of his connexions with Beaumarchais, could get credit from the financiers, which had been imperilled by Schomberg's actions, then it would be possible to fight in Italy, or at least to threaten Spain with war. This meant that La Vieuville must be appointed, and all the more because Schomberg had compromised himself not only by his poor management of both finance and ordnance but also by his ties with Condé. It was characteristic that, when he dismissed Schomberg in January 1623, Louis XIII announced that Condé's servants could not be his servants. When Condé, in Italy, learnt of Schomberg's dismissal, he decided not to return to France, despite the king's command to do so, because he feared confinement in the Bastille.[3]

It is interesting that Fontenay-Mareuil, who published his memoirs many years after the events with which we are concerned, and after Richelieu's death, recorded a very important reflexion on these events. In his view, the financial situation at the end of 1622 was nothing like so bad, if account be taken of the fact that several hundred million *livres* was spent, out of extraordinary income, in the following years, under Richelieu, and yet there was enough left to get by. His point was that then, before Richelieu's time, it was not the practice to overburden (*surcharger*) the people and fleece private individuals on various pretexts. If, however, this restraint had been continued, the country would have fallen victim to Spain, that is, France would have lost the war.[4] From all this we can draw some conclusions, supported by an analysis of the budget, about the general line of Louis XIII's financial

---

[1] *Relation des choses mémorables*, fo. 235; Fontenay-Mareuil, op. cit. p. 172.
[2] It is obvious from this evidence by Fontenay-Mareuil that one cannot speak of any 'friendship' of the financiers for Schomberg such as Biryukovich supposes to have existed. On the contrary, Schomberg undoubtedly sacrificed their interests in order to cover the costs of war.
[3] B. Zeller, *Richelieu et les ministres de Louis XIII*, pp. 173, 176.
[4] Fontenay-Mareuil, op. cit. p. 172.

policy in those years. Like his predecessors, he feared to increase to any large extent the taxes that were paid by the people. At the same time, a still heavier taxation of the clergy and the officials was regarded as being risky. For these reasons, La Vieuville was appointed *surintendant* on 21 January 1623, having assured the king that he would put the state's finances in such good order as they had never known before.[1]

At that stage the Brûlarts had no reason not to trust La Vieuville or to fear his candidature.[2] They possessed all political power; the seals, the king's chancellery, the *secrétairerie des princes* (that is, foreign affairs); in the king's Council for financial matters (*Conseil de direction*), to which La Vieuville reported, the chancellor was in the chair. The Brûlarts took into account the opinions of the Queen Mother, who had achieved reconciliation with the king.[3] Richelieu was still remote from power, and he was the only person they feared.[4]

Thus, one cannot regard the appointment of La Vieuville to the post of *surintendant* as the first example of penetration by a representative of the plutocracy into the government. The new *surintendant* was certainly a man who had connexions with the financiers, but he was not the first; it is enough to recall the big businessman and financier Barbin, in the government of d'Ancre.[5] The reasons why La Vieuville was made *surintendant* were, in my view, rooted in the actual situation at the end of 1622; the wretched prospect of finding himself without money convinced Louis XIII that he must choose the man who promised to raise what he needed.

These circumstances determined the line of policy followed in 1623. Negotiations for an alliance between France, Venice and Savoy, and preparations for the formal conclusion of such an alliance, brought the necessary pressure to bear on Spain. The two powers agreed to put the Valtelline into the pope's trusteeship, and the French ambassador in Rome, was instructed accordingly. The basis for negotiations continued to be the Treaty of Madrid,

---

[1] Ibid. p. 174.
[2] Biryukovich's view that La Vieuville won the Brûlarts' favour by helping the chancellor to obtain the post of Keeper of the Seals is not confirmed by the sources. Traditionally the chancellor was also Keeper of the Seals, and the chancellor's principal importance lay in the fact that he held the seals of state. A chancellor was irremovable, so that the way to diminish his actual power was to take the seals from him and give them to somebody else. Separation of these two functions was unusual and each time it occurred this was effected for different reasons. In this particular instance what happened was that in 1616 d'Ancre had taken the seals away from Sillery, so depriving him of practically all his functions; then the seals had been held by Luynes, and after his death by other persons; the return of the seals to Sillery in January 1623 was quite a normal proceeding, and there is no reason to suppose that La Vieuville had anything to do with it.
[3] B. Zeller, *Richelieu et les ministres de Louis XIII*, pp. 177, 178.
[4] Ibid. p. 182.
[5] Lublinskaya, *Frantsiya v nachale XVII veka*, ch. 6.

and agreement had to be reached as soon as possible, so as to eliminate the source of conflict between Spain and France, in the Valtelline. In order to strengthen her position, France continued, in January–February 1623, to maintain forces in the Dauphiné, on the border with Savoy, but in Rome the view was taken that neither side wished to fight, and that both of them realised this; warlike attitudes were only intended to frighten the opponent. Besides this, Spain tried to put off surrendering the Valtelline to the pope because she calculated that war with the Huguenots was about to begin again in France.[1]

In fact, however, France brought off a notable diplomatic triumph: on 7 February 1623 a treaty of defensive and offensive alliance was signed between France, Venice and Savoy. When he knew that this was about to happen, Sillery in Rome brought vigorous pressure to bear upon the pope, and the latter in his turn upon the Spanish ambassador. As a result, Spain agreed to evacuate her forces from the Valtelline forts and to hand the valley over to the pope. Thus, the Brûlarts' diplomacy at the beginning of 1623 had a favourable outcome.

There was another knot of contradictions on the Rhine. The Palatinate was completely occupied by Spain. James I, endeavouring to help Frederick V, had tried to make an alliance with Spain. This alliance would threaten France; she feared the presence of powerful foes on the Rhine, close to her eastern frontiers. It must be kept in mind that French diplomacy in Germany was always somewhat complicated and contradictory. While backing the Union of the Protestant princes, France at the same time, if this was to her advantage, refrained from quarrelling with the Catholic League. In the given circumstances the Brûlarts supported Bavaria's claim to electoral status (filling the vacancy caused by the expulsion of Frederick V and the occupation of the Palatinate), but at the same time tried to avoid estranging the Protestant princes. The Duke of Bavaria sent the Capuchin Valeriano Magni to see the Brûlarts (probably without Louis XIII's knowledge) and propose an alliance between France and the Catholic League, under which the latter would undertake to prevent the Huguenots from obtaining aid from Germany, while France would undertake to oppose any strengthening of the Habsburgs' position in Germany. The story of this secret mission is far from clear,[2] but what matters for us is its result: the Duke of Bavaria became an Elector with the aid of France. Thus, on the Rhine as in

[1] B. Zeller, *Richelieu et les ministres de Louis XIII*, pp. 184, 185.
[2] Maximilian of Bavaria sent Count Vaudémont in March on a mission to Louis XIII (letter from Regensburg, 15 March 1623, in Saltykov-Shchedrin Library, Leningrad, Avt. 5, no. 21), but the nature of this mission is not revealed in the letter.

Northern Italy, France's diplomacy had proved successful, and this meant that the need for external war had been eliminated for the time being.

It is in the light of these circumstances, of great importance for the years in question, that we must consider the course of internal affairs, and in particular the nature of La Vieuville's activity as *surintendant*.

He began his work of balancing the budget and finding money for the Crown's purposes by reducing the size of the army—but not touching those regiments which were stationed on the frontier with Savoy and in Languedoc, only the garrisons of fortresses in the interior. He disbanded some of these garrisons entirely, and cut others by half. He took similar steps against persons in receipt of pensions and salaries. All these measures were fully supported by the king.[1] He also proposed to the financiers that they buy themselves immunity from any inspection of their activity.[2] Later came some increase in the *taille*, the tax paid by the peasants, and the introduction of new levies in the towns, including the transformation into 'offices' of the work of supervising the packing of goods and the sale of oysters—in other words, the overseers and pedlars engaged in this work had to make a once-for-all payment in order to continue in their 'offices'. In this way, La Vieuville tried to get by without burdening the coming year, 1624, with any loans.[3]

How did public opinion react to La Vieuville's measures? The answer is to be found in numerous pamphlets published in 1623.[4]

The question of the financiers was not seen in isolation by writers or by public opinion, either in the years we are considering or in the entire period since the start of the century. This resulted from the fact that finance and

---

[1] *Relation des choses mémorables*, fo. 236ᵛ.

[2] Biryukovich regards this measure as 'a pretence of prosecuting the financiers' (loc. cit. p. 203).

[3] Biryukovich sees these measures as merely an endeavour to appease public opinion and divert the imminent threat of a draconic settlement with the financiers, which he sees as constituting the fundamental demand of 'the bloc of the nobility and the third estate'.

[4] Biryukovich describes in detail in his article some of these pamphlets which had already provided material for the extensive researches of French historians such as Zeller, Fagniez, Deloche and others. His attention was naturally attracted to those pamphlets which mainly discussed questions connected with the management of the state's finances, the struggle against the financiers, and so on. He overlooked, however, other and very numerous pamphlets. Biryukovich set up a somewhat artificial construction, making it appear that the pamphleteers concerned themselves only with the financiers and ways of combating them. In fact, the abundant pamphlet literature of the period discussed in detail all the burning questions of state policy, both internal and external, putting forward a variety of programmes and methods for carrying them out. There are no grounds for reducing this wide miscellany of political thought and public opinion either merely to a fight for power carried on long and ably by Cardinal Richelieu, as some French historians do, or merely to a struggle around the financiers, as Biryukovich does. Such restriction of the subject distorts the overall picture.

those who were in charge of it were seen not as a self-contained subject but as the means of realising one or another programme of action. A full treasury, with sound and reliable sources of revenue, made it possible to carry out a certain programme, whereas deficits and debts hindered this or made it quite unrealisable. Moreover, everyone appreciated that any particular financial policy had social implications, being carried out either at the expense of certain classes and orders or else safeguarding their privileges or taking into account their difficult material position. For this reason the pamphleteers of that age nearly always outlined, each in his own way, the *general* situation of the country and its classes, and only then put forward their programme and their views on how to find the means to carry it out. This is what makes them interesting. I have already remarked that in many ways these writers present the problems of the day much more broadly and deeply than in the sixteenth century, when, during the fierce civil and religious wars the interests of the Huguenots and Catholic *parties* often took precedence over considerations of importance to the state as a whole, both in economic and in political matters. In this respect the pamphlet literature of the time very clearly reveals the higher level reached not only by economic but also by political thought in France.

In giving a general description of the pamphlets of 1623–4 we must focus attention on two fundamental questions: (1) the necessity of war against the Huguenots (or, at least, of maintaining the *status quo*), that is, the chief nodal point of internal politics; and (2) relations with Spain and other states which had already been drawn into the Thirty Years War, that is, the main nodal point of France's external politics. The pamphleteers put forward different answers to these questions, according to their respective programmes, but they invariably see these as the urgent topics of the day.

One typical pamphlet, not from the pen of any well-known and brilliant writer and not distinguished by any literary merits, came out in 1623, under the title: *Consultation de trois fameux advocats sur les affaires publiques.* The pamphlet is set out in the form of speeches by the advocates Choppin, Choüart and Robert. These characters do not contradict one another, but each of them stresses what he regards as the most important idea. The combination of these ideas gives us grounds for the following conclusions.

The first advocate considers that for the sake of lasting peace in the country and consolidation of the royal authority (and this is the motto of an enormous number of pamphlets, their initial premise, one might say), it is necessary to destroy the Huguenot republic and abolish the political independence of the Huguenots. Guyenne and Languedoc had already succumbed, and so had the Huguenot nobles, but La Rochelle still stood, the hotbed of unceasing revolt. This must likewise be brought to submission. It is cause for alarm that the government seems to have put this matter out of its mind. Forts must be built around La Rochelle on the landward side, and a mole on the seaward side. Until the Huguenots have been completely put down, France must remain aloof from external conflicts.

The second advocate, while agreeing that the existence of a republic within a monarchy is monstrous, emphasises that a still worse misfortune is the poverty of the people. This poverty is great and incurable, but the king does not even know it exists. The tax-farmers and other 'leeches' hide it from him, while they oppress the people, especially the peasants, who are in dreadful want. The countryside is being turned into a desert.

The third advocate sees the root of the evil in the licentious conduct of the soldiery and the extortions carried out by the financial officials. This was shown especially vividly in the recent civil wars (i.e. the wars against the Huguenots in 1621–2). The soldiers proved to be bad, untrained, and cowardly, and they plundered the population. The army and the régime prevailing in it are bad. The soldiers should be paid regularly, and the whole country should enjoy the benefit of the system existing in Burgundy, the Dauphiné and Provence, where the troops are paid by the local authorities. Chaos reigns in the financial administration, and the chief reason for this is the pensions paid to the nobility.

If we are to try to evaluate this pamphlet in terms of the social and political interests of its author, we have to emphasise the following elements in it: (1) the stress laid on desire for internal peace and strengthening of the central authority, on the need to carry through the struggle against the Huguenots to the end, that is to the capture of La Rochelle; (2) the concern for the needs of the people and their poverty, with the desire to spare them the most frightful of evils, looting and plundering by the soldiery; (3) the proposal for reform of army pay arrangements; and (4) the proposal to reduce the nobles' pensions. All this amounts to a programme of the Third Estate, and actually coincides with its mandate to the States-General in 1614. At the same time, in the conditions of the period, the pamphlet also has a royalist character, because it corresponds exactly to the government's policy towards the Huguenots and in relation to the international situation, and anticipates the demand for reform of the method of maintaining the armed forces which was to be discussed at the Assembly of Notables in 1626.[1] As for the statement that the root of the evil of financial disorder was to be found in the pensions paid to the nobility, this was a view widely held at the time precisely in bourgeois circles.

[1] See Chapter 6.

Does the absence from the pamphlet of any demand for judicial inquiry into the activities of the financiers mean that it comes from circles favourable to La Vieuville and the financiers? Not in the least, for the financiers and their methods are severely condemned. This merely means, as can be confirmed by other examples, that the demand for prosecution of the financiers was not so unanimous and widespread and did not preoccupy the minds of contemporaries so exclusively as Biryukovich supposes.[1]

Let us now look at the actual sources used in Biryukovich's article and which in his view are most significant for their hostility to the financiers; first of all, Bourgoin's pamphlet *Offres ou propositions au Roy*, which appeared in 1623 and was indeed directed against the financiers. It contains no general political considerations, consisting merely of a plan for the reform of the finance department. The writer notes that the treasury is empty and that the financiers are responsible for this, because the revenue goes on payment of interest on the loans they have made, and this means that taxes have to be increased. Bourgoin considers that the blame for these evils lies with the plutocracy,[2] and he proposes that the king undertake 'a hunt for thieves', that is to say, an investigation of abuses in the financial administration; this, in his view, would best be carried out not by way of a judicial prosecution but by purely administrative procedure, without resort to confiscations. The pamphlet's contents as a whole show that it can hardly be called a furious attack on the financiers. Bourgoin certainly lays the dark colours on thick in his denunciations, but essentially he is making only one charge against the financiers—namely, that they take excessively high interest on their loans, and the remedy he proposes consists in reviewing, without any uproar or scandal, the loan agreements which have been concluded with the financiers and reducing these interest-rates. Thus, the pamphlet amounts to nothing more than a call for restoring normal relations between the treasury and the state creditors. If we take into account the fact that Bourgoin's pamphlet appeared precisely at the time when La Vieuville was putting through his measures for cleaning up the state finances, it becomes still harder to regard it as 'thunder and lightning upon the heads of the financiers'.

Thus, we must record that in the pamphlets of 1623, for all their attacks on the financiers, the only concrete measures proposed are a revision of the relations between the treasury and its creditors and a reduction in the interest provided for when loans are contracted from the latter.

Let us now look at the budgets of 1623 and 1624, in order to see if we

---

[1] Biryukovich, loc. cit. p. 204.
[2] But not for all the evils in general, as Biryukovich supposes.

can find confirmation in their figures for the statements made in the pamphlets.[1]

In 1623 total revenue amounted to about 37 million *livres*, and expenditure to about 32 millions. In 1624 both revenue and expenditure came to about 34 millions. Thus, the budgets of these two years were considerably less than those of previous ones; very much reduced in comparison with 1622 (50 millions), rather less in comparison with 1620 (39 millions).[2] On the income side we must note a reduction in receipts from indirect taxes, but even more from 'casual' and extraordinary sources. On the expenditure side the reduction affected two principal costs: the army (little more than half of what had been spent in 1622) and pensions. The latter came to 2·7 million *livres* in 1623 and 3·5 millions in 1624, as compared with 5·5 millions in 1620 and 4·2 millions in 1622.

Thus, La Vieuville did succeed in somewhat improving the condition of the state's finances, by reducing expenditure on the army and suppressing some garrisons. This, it would seem, explains the favour he undoubtedly enjoyed with the king all through 1623.[3] To what extent did the 'régime of economy' which he introduced correspond to the interests of the financiers? Biryukovich considers that 'the appointment of La Vieuville as *surintendant* placed all the financial resources of the state at the disposal of the financiers'.[4] But the documents do not support this view; in some instances, La Vieuville even increased the prices of tax-farms.[5] He genuinely tried to balance the budget, and this primarily served the interests of the government. It has been said above that the state's creditors also needed the king's credit to be strengthened. There is no evidence whatever, though, that La Vieuville used his position as *surintendant* to cover up any irregular dealings by the financiers with the state treasury.

Quite soon La Vieuville began to intervene in 'high politics' too, especially in the French government's diplomacy, which was in the hands of the Chancellor and of Secretary of State Puisieux.[6] He was pushed in this direction by the very régime of economy which he had introduced. The *surintendant* could maintain this line of financial policy with some degree of consistency only if expenditure on the army were to be kept at the new, reduced level. Consequently it was necessary to follow in foreign policy a strictly diplomatic

---

[1] The figures are taken from material in Mallet.
[2] See p. 230.
[3] *Relation des choses mémorables*, fo. 236.
[4] Biryukovich, loc. cit. p. 237.
[5] In 1623 he increased the price of one of the largest tax-farms (that of the *aides de France*) by 400,000 *livres* (Heumann, loc. cit. p. 195).
[6] *Relation des choses mémorables*, fo. 236.

line, avoiding any occasion to get drawn into the Thirty Years War. As regards the Huguenots, the government must bide its time.

These views were in no way opposed to the policy of the Chancellor and Puisieux, and the disagreements that developed between them and La Vieuville were not on matters of principle. Their conflict was purely a personal one. La Vieuville was younger and more active than his rivals; his vigorous activity made an impression on the king, to whom he freely promised successes in diplomacy as great as those he had achieved in the financial sphere.

We have already mentioned that at the beginning of 1623 French diplomacy had prospered to a certain extent in the two directions which were then of greatest importance, namely, in the Valtelline and on the Rhine.[1] Sillery and Puisieux could at that time look upon this as a triumph for themselves.

However, the pope and his Nuncio in France were endeavouring to upset the alliance between France and Savoy and Venice. They were especially afraid of the possibility that Mansfeld might appear in Italy, in the service of the allied states. The Nuncio informed Rome in March of the reassuring news that La Vieuville had reduced expenditure on the army, so that no war-preparation was to be observed in France, which was perfectly true. The pope agreed to take the forts of the Valtelline into his trusteeship, but he wanted to install his own garrisons there and preserve the freedom of the passes for Spain. When he learnt of this condition, which violated the Treaty of Madrid, Ambassador Sillery announced that he must inquire his government's view of the matter, which was expected to be one of complete disapproval. Meanwhile, the pope, without waiting for the French reply, sent his brother to the Valtelline. At the end of April Sillery gave his consent to this expedition, that is, he made a concession without the king's authority to do so. The question of the freedom of the passes was of great importance, both to the Spaniards and to the French. France's allies—Savoy and Venice —did not agree to the handing over of the forts to the pope, although the latter explained that he had received Sillery's consent and that the measure was needed only in order to avoid war. Finally, Feria surrendered the forts— except for the most important of them, at Chiavenna[2] and Riva, without which the surrender of the rest was an empty formality. The pope, calculating that all these difficulties would cause Venice and Savoy to break their alliance with France (another of his demands), did not press Spain to make a full settlement of the conflict. The purpose of Spain and of the pope was clear—

[1] See pp. 247, 248.
[2] The valley of Chiavenna lies to the north of Lake Como, and leads to the Splügen pass, and so to the valleys of the Upper Rhine and the Inn.

to drag the matter out so that Venice and Savoy would quarrel with France, which was holding back from active operations.[1]

Thus, the situation was that Sillery, trusting in the pope, had agreed to the despatch of papal troops to the Valtelline, and this had angered France's allies. The pope and the Spaniards had outwitted the French ambassador, for the most important element in the Treaty of Madrid—French monopoly of the use of the passes—had been violated. The reaction of Savoy, and more especially of Venice, to this violation of the treaty is comprehensible. The Valtelline, occupied by Spanish and papal troops, was now closed to Venice, as it had been in the past.

The affairs of the Valtelline had thus taken a turn to France's disadvantage. However, on 8 June Pope Gregory XV died, and his successor Urban VIII was more favourably disposed towards France.

In Germany, the transfer of the electoral dignity to Maximilian of Bavaria alarmed the Protestant princes, since it still further weakened their position in the electoral college, and in general the balance of political forces in Germany. For this reason, the Electors of Saxony and Brandenburg did not recognise Maximilian as an Elector, and prepared themselves for war. Bethlen Gabor got ready to attack Austria. Denmark took steps to enter the conflict. All this had been set in motion by Spain's success in the Palatinate and in the Lower Rhineland, together with the emperor's successes in Bohemia and Hungary. Consequently, the situation in Germany too called for active intervention by France. But the Brûlarts (principally Puisieux) endeavoured as before to smooth everything over by diplomacy. The reason for their attitude is clear, and it was clear to contemporaries. France had no money with which to fight a war. In such circumstances, however, really effective diplomatic efforts were out of the question, as well: they were not backed by sufficient strength. It made little difference when, on the demand of Urban VIII, Chiavenna and Riva were eventually handed over to the papal forces. The very position of the pope as one of the princes of Italy obliged him to manœuvre all the time between the great adversaries, Spain and France.

These circumstances were all exploited by La Vieuville in getting the king to dismiss the Brûlarts. Louis XIII was particularly sensitive to the poor success of French foreign policy because it tied his hands in relation to all other matters. A diplomatic blunder had been committed by Ambassador Sillery, as a result of which the pope had become *de facto* master of the forts in the Valtelline and Spain's freedom to use the passes had been retained; the Treaty of Madrid was virtually nullified, and along with it—this mattered

[1] B. Zeller, *Richelieu et les ministres de Louis XIII*, pp. 245, 254.

255

especially—France's alliance with Venice and Savoy. Spain also gained the advantage, given the situation in the Valtelline, of greater freedom of action in Brabant and in Germany. Spanish diplomacy, under the direction of Olivares, had shown itself a formidable adversary to French diplomacy, and a statesman of Puisieux's calibre was not equal to it.

At the same time a plan of Chancellor Sillery to take La Rochelle by means of the treachery of one of the Huguenot officers failed to come off. This failure also contributed to damaging the Brûlarts in the king's opinion.[1]

La Vieuville held a trump card in the mistakes made by the Brûlarts at La Rochelle, in Paris and in Rome, especially the error of Ambassador Sillery. Their actions were repudiated at the end of 1623 by a special procedure—the dismissal of the entire French diplomatic service.

Before considering the fall of the Brûlarts and the formation of a new cabinet, we must deal with some other circumstances preceding these events. On 20 November there was a revolt in Rouen provoked by the implementation of decrees concerning new taxes.[2] Members of the Rouen *parlement* who went into the streets to calm the people's discontent were assaulted. Following a judicial investigation of these events, three 'rioters' were hanged.

This was the first anti-tax revolt of the masses for many years, and it made a big impression. Moreover, it raised the question once again as to whether an increase in taxation was in general possible. In principle, this question had been answered, ever since the death of Henry IV, in the negative: in a situation marked by civil strife and weakening of the central authority, popular disturbances were fraught with the gravest of dangers. For this reason, the government drew first upon the gold reserve accumulated by Sully in expectation of war with the Habsburgs, and then raised loans from the financiers. From 1620 onwards the government resorted in particular to loans, obliging the clergy to pay subsidies and the officials to submit to forced loans when they paid the *paulette*. As we have seen, however, all these resources proved inadequate to meet the great tasks of internal and external policy. Yet an increase in taxation would immediately produce an outburst by the people.

No facts about the decisions taken on this matter in the king's Council are available. It is only possible to deduce them by examining their results, namely, that no substantial increase in taxes was made either in 1624 or in the subsequent two to three years.

In circumstances like these, diplomacy continued to be practically the chief instrument of government policy as a whole. However, the course of events in Italy and Germany could only be steered by French diplomacy to

[1] *Relation des choses mémorables*, folios 237–237ᵛ.   [2] See p. 249.

THE FINANCIERS AND THE ABSOLUTE MONARCHY

a limited extent. Opposed to it were forces striving to obtain advantages from the difficult situation in which the French government was placed. This meant, first and foremost, Spain, where the ruling statesman, the Count of Olivares, Richelieu's future rival, was successful in finding a variety of resources to enable him to develop the gains he had already made.

At the end of 1623 the situation was that (1) restriction of state expenditure continued to be achieved by reductions in the size of the army and in the pensions fund, and that (2) French diplomacy had met defeat in Italy. In so far as French diplomacy was guided by the Brûlarts in person, they had to be dismissed. In so far as the reductions in pensions and in the army harmed the nobility (and all the more so because there was no war, since wars, whether internal or external, brought the nobles an auxiliary source of income), it was necessary to do something about this, though neither pensions nor the army could be restored to their previous levels. Furthermore, the princes must be rendered harmless politically, to which end Condé must be brought back to France and admitted to the king's Council—not, of course, in order to give him any share of power, but to keep him under constant supervision and prevent him from linking up with foreign rulers or the nobility in the provinces. This was not accomplished without difficulty, for Condé at first did not want to come back, fearing that he would be put in the Bastille. Even after he had returned to his own province of Berry he feared to go to the capital, and only after a diplomatic approach by his wife did he consent to appear at court. He was merely a decorative figure in the king's Council, but this office prevented him from taking the lead in a revolt by the higher nobility. The Queen Mother had to be brought into the king's Council for the same reason. Under these conditions the princes, deprived of slogans and of the support formerly given by the armed forces of the Huguenot party, already found themselves unable to undertake open revolt against the government. In consequence there was no organising centre around which the *noblesse d'épée* could rally. Moreover, part of the army was maintained in readiness, in garrisons in the South, and especially around Lyons. The government's political policy of isolating the grandees was also followed by denying any appointments or favours to the Guises, Condé, d'Epernon and others, at the end of 1623, although they solicited them.

A very favourable situation now existed from La Vieuville's point of view. Neither the Brûlarts nor the princes constituted any danger to him. As before, the king did not wish to hear anything about Richelieu.[1] The régime of economy impressed Louis XIII. The rudeness shown by the *surintendant*

---

[1] The cardinal's enemies assured the king that Richelieu was *un grand fourbe* (*Relation des choses mémorables*, fo. 237ᵛ).

towards the princes and nobles whom he offended was not new to the French court; Sully had been known for the same style of conduct.

Amid the chaos of antagonistic interests and crafty court intrigues which aimed to push him towards one line of action or another, Louis XIII, trusting no-one, not even his wife, his mother or his brother, felt ill at ease and lost. He tried to spend as much time as possible away from the Louvre, hunting, or in secluded *châteaux* in the country around Paris. In this difficult situation he made no gross political mistakes, declining to accede to the vigorous insistence of the pope and the clergy that he immediately resume the war against the Huguenots, and also resisting the no less insistent demands of Condé and the princes that open war against Spain be begun; and he supported La Vieuville in his financial policy.

All this was passive, however, and though it showed that the king had a certain sense of political reality, and feared taking risks, it showed nothing more.

The dismissal of the Brûlarts was a measure of the same order.[1] Undoubtedly, La Vieuville had a hand in it, counting on being left as the king's only minister; not for nothing did contemporaries call him 'a man of initiative'. On the first day of 1624 Sillery was called upon to surrender the seals (I have already mentioned that the chancellor could not be removed, but the appointment of a new Keeper of the Seals could deprive him of real power). Rumours circulated that the king was going to give the seals to some person of little influence, so that the latter should be dependent entirely on him. These rumours were justified by events, for the seals were conferred upon a worthy official named d'Aligre, to whom the king said: 'J'ai fait élection de votre personne de mon propre mouvement; vous n'en avez d'obligation à qui que ce soit...'[2]

At the end of January the king forbade the foreign ambassadors to deal with Puisieux and asked them henceforth to approach him in person. Finally, on 4 February, the Brûlarts were dismissed, and left next day for their estate. The entire diplomatic representation abroad was changed, together with all the secretaries of state. These facts testify convincingly that it was the unsuccessful diplomacy of the Brûlarts that caused their dismissal. The king told the Nuncio that they had concealed from him the majority of their dealings, for example, the mission of the Capuchin Valeriano Magni, that Puisieux had from time to time given instructions to ambassadors without

[1] The circumstances of the dismissal of the Brûlarts are described in detail in *Relation des choses mémorables*, folios 237ᵛ–8ᵛ.

[2] B. Zeller, *Richelieu et les ministres de Louis XIII*, p. 239. D'Aligre was appointed against La Vieuville's wishes. Louis XIII, in fact, wanted to have as Keeper of the Seals a man who was not dependent on any party at court.

informing the king, sometimes even changing the orders the king had given them, that Sillery had appropriated a substantial amount of the money assigned for payment of pensions to foreigners in Germany, Flanders, Italy and so on.[1]

The new cabinet was composed as follows: there was no chancellor, and the Keeper of the Seals, d'Aligre, was completely dependent on the king; foreign affairs was shared between four secretaries of state, and not concentrated, as earlier, in one man. (Puisieux had been in charge of all diplomatic activity, of war and war finance, while the other three secretaries of state had been confined to internal affairs, each being allotted a group of provinces.) Their duties were now shared out as follows: d'Herbault was responsible for relations with Spain, Italy, Switzerland and the Grisons; Ocquerre for relations with Germany, Poland, Holland and Flanders (that is, with the Spanish Netherlands); La Ville-aux-Clercs for relations with England, Turkey, and the whole Levant; de Beauclerc, the new secretary of state appointed in place of Puisieux (formerly secretary to Anne of Austria and controller of her finances), took charge of war and war finance.

All four were subordinate to the king's Council, the chief member of which at that moment was (in the absence of the chancellor) the *surintendant* La Vieuville.

What was the significance of this reform?[2]

The king's Council lacked its natural chairman, a chancellor,[3] and also a minister for foreign affairs. The secretaries of state found themselves in an unusual situation, and none of them had any experience of diplomacy. The men really at the head of things were the king, the Keeper of the Seals d'Aligre, who owed his appointment to the king, and the *surintendant* La Vieuville. In other words, the king and La Vieuville *had* to direct all branches of state policy, since the secretaries of state had become mere executives.

What did contemporaries make of the reform?

We know the views of the Italian ambassadors (the Nuncio and the representatives of Tuscany and Venice), which in such cases reflected the views of French political circles. The ambassadors considered that the new régime would not last long, both because of La Vieuville's inexperience and incapacity and because of the unusualness of the position and functions of the secretaries of state. Later developments showed that this view was sound.

---

[1] B. Zeller, *Richelieu et les ministres de Louis XIII*, pp. 240–2.
[2] Biryukovich mistakenly places the reform in June 1624, that is, in the period of La Vieuville's rule (loc. cit. p. 220).
[3] Officially, the chairman of the king's Council was the king himself, but he was far from always present at meetings.

The king and La Vieuville were so much afraid of Richelieu's aspirations to become a member of the king's Council (which were obvious, thanks to the continual applications on his behalf by the Queen Mother), that it was proposed to send the cardinal to Rome. However, he managed to get out of this 'honourable' mission. Richelieu was 'feared by every minister, as an excessively astute man, whom it is best not to have too near one', and the king was worried by 'the cardinal's haughty and domineering spirit'.[1]

These were the circumstances of the dismissal of the Brûlarts and the formation of the new cabinet. As we see, there are no grounds for supposing that Richelieu had any hand in the matter.[2]

What was La Vieuville's policy after he had become, in February 1624, *de facto* head of the king's Council? What were the tasks facing the new government?

As regards the Huguenots, the same line was to be followed as in 1623, for there was not the slightest possibility of undertaking the siege of La Rochelle, which would require vast expenditure. It was necessary to keep firm hold of what had been conquered in 1620–2 and to pursue in the South a cautious policy of attracting the Huguenot nobles and cities to the king's side. All this was done, and with some success.

The most urgent measures to be taken were in the field of international relations. Matters in the Valtelline and on the Rhine could not be put off, the less so because in Spain Olivares had now taken the reins of government into his hands, and all the diplomats in Europe at once began to feel his power.

On the question of the Valtelline the French government declared, at the end of February, that it rejected Spain's claim to use the passes. At the

---

[1] B. Zeller, *Richelieu et les ministres de Louis XIII*, pp. 242–4.

[2] Biryukovich offers a different explanation. He considers that the opposition of the aristocrats who had been offended by La Vieuville's régime of economy was dangerous to him and threatened to ruin the entire financial policy of La Vieuville and Beaumarchais. The *surintendant* was too weak to take on the Guises and other grandees as well as the Brûlarts. He was helped by an 'active and impressive ally', namely, Richelieu, whose path to the king's Council was still barred by the Brûlarts. La Vieuville was an incomparably less dangerous adversary for the cardinal than they were; he could first support him and later attack him (Biryukovich, loc. cit. pp. 208, 209). It may be that the cardinal did reason along these lines, as Fontenay-Mareuil testifies (op. cit. p. 175). If the inexperience and incompetence of La Vieuville in 'high politics', that is, mainly, in diplomacy, was clear to the Italian ambassadors, it can hardly have been hidden from the penetrating Richelieu. However, such calculations on Richelieu's part do not provide grounds for assuming that the cardinal also acted in the same spirit. At that stage he quite simply lacked any means of influencing the king, on whose decisions everything depended. Biryukovich gives no details of the aid alleged to have been rendered by the cardinal to La Vieuville in the matter of the dismissal of the Brûlarts. There is therefore no basis for his conclusion that after this event 'the plutocracy became a political power exercising direct influence on the destiny of French absolutism'.

beginning of March, Urban VIII proposed the following compromise: the forts in the Valtelline to be demolished, the valley to be restored to the Grisons (who should be forbidden to maintain armed forces there), and the Spaniards to be accorded the right of passage in one direction only, from Italy into Germany. The Valtelline was to be demilitarised and in that state returned to its former masters—in other words, the *status quo ante* 1600 was to be restored. Venice (to whom it was particularly important that Spain should not bring troops over the Alps into northern Italy) would also be given the right to use the passes. Ambassador Sillery, who at that moment did not yet know that he had been dismissed, agreed to these conditions, since they were considerably more advantageous to France than the situation which existed at the end of 1623, when the Valtelline was occupied by the papal forces, and in practice Spain ruled the roost there. When La Vieuville learnt from the Nuncio on 22 March of Urban VIII's conditions and of Sillery's acceptance of them, he disavowed him once more, declaring that the ambassador's agreement had no force, as he had already been recalled; as for the proposal to allow Spain the right of passage, even if only in one direction, this was contrary to the interests of France. The Nuncio was able to show the French government, however, that when the conditions were discussed, Sillery had not yet received the order for his recall.[1]

For the French government it was nevertheless useful to repudiate their ambassador, in order to get out of agreeing to the pope's proposals. The point was that at that moment France was striking a blow at Spain from another direction, and so it was not considered appropriate to show tractability in the matter of the Valtelline. The blow was struck in the following way.

Anglo-Spanish diplomacy revolved at that time around the awkward question of the Palatinate. James I counted on recovering it for Frederick V, not by force (he did not want to fight in Germany) but by negotiation with Spain. This was why a plan was drawn up for an Anglo-Spanish marriage, and why Buckingham and the future Charles I made their romantic journey

---

[1] Moreover, comparing the dates of these events, the Nuncio reported that in February (this can only have been in the very first days of that month) the king had commanded Puisieux to write to Rome that the ambassador must not enter into negotiations about the Valtelline until further orders; however, owing to his dismissal, Puisieux was unable to send the despatch, and this instruction never reached Rome. It was not until 16 February that the Nuncio himself received the news from the king that he had sent a new ambassador (Béthune) to the pope, before whose arrival there could be no discussion of the Valtelline question. On 24 February he wrote to Rome that the proposal to allow Spain one-way passage across the Alps had been rejected by France. Thus, Ambassador Sillery genuinely did not know about the changes in France when, at the beginning of March (that is, before the Nuncio's letter had arrived in Rome), he discussed the pope's conditions with him and agreed to them.

incognito to Madrid, where they were made fools of for some time, in the Spanish manner, and then sent back home with a formal promise to conclude a marriage-alliance.[1] However, events in England ruined this plan: Parliament declared against the alliance with Spain, and public opinion demanded the restoration of the Palatinate to the Protestant Elector by armed force. French diplomacy was thus presented with a trump card, which it produced from under the table, proposing to England that negotiations be renewed for an Anglo-French marriage, between the future Charles I and Louis XIII's youngest sister Henrietta. This marriage was needed by France for many reasons: first, it would put an end to the possibility of an Anglo-Spanish marriage-alliance, and secondly, it would oblige James I to refrain from helping the Huguenots (more precisely, La Rochelle) in the coming campaign.

Another blow to Spain was Mansfeld's preparations to invade the Palatinate. As mentioned earlier, Mansfeld's army had been hired by the allies (France, Venice, Savoy) and held in readiness. They frightened both the pope and Spain by declaring that they would send Mansfeld into the Valtelline if the pope and Spaniards behaved there as before; this was a real threat, and it actually compelled the pope to make concessions. Mansfeld was already moving against the Palatinate to drive the Spaniards out.

Undoubtedly, the French government concentrated the main effort of its diplomacy in this direction not because it had decided to act on the Rhine rather than elsewhere but because in that quarter it had to secure itself against England no less than against Spain. Let us recall that the Palatine Electorate had been transferred to Bavaria through the good offices of France. The restoration of Frederick V to the Palatinate was very dangerous and undesirable from the French point of view on account of the Huguenots, who had to be isolated both from England and from the German Protestants. This was why French diplomacy turned its attention at the beginning of 1624 mainly to the North, in the hope that the Valtelline would be won indirectly, as a result of French successes in England and on the Rhine.

Following these events of February–April 1624, which developed favourably on the whole for the French government, on 29 April Richelieu was appointed to the king's Council. This came about in the following way.

Not long after Richelieu's appointment, the well-informed ambassador of Tuscany wrote in his despatch that the king had brought a new minister into his *conseil étroit* because important foreign affairs demanded (the secretaries of state being inexperienced in these matters) the presence of a far-seeing and skilful man with great talents and qualities which he had already shown not only as the Queen Mother's adviser but also as first

[1] See above, p. 177, note 1.

secretary of state (*primo segretario*).[1] Having become a cardinal (and in this capacity Richelieu could be automatically brought into the king's Council), Richelieu had striven to be admitted to the Council, but the Brûlarts and La Vieuville had advised the king against this. He had been admitted to the Council on the insistence of the Queen Mother. The restrictions imposed on him amounted to his being forbidden to talk with foreign ambassadors (*négocier*) and also to work with anyone at all on state affairs at his own residence, though he would be summoned to the Council to give his opinion when required. In other words, the king wanted to keep a check on Richelieu where diplomacy was concerned.[2]

In the *Mémoires de Richelieu* the story is told that the cardinal at first refused with displeasure, but later accepted the royal favour. He told the Tuscan ambassador that, owing to bad health, he could not receive anyone at his house. The ambassador also writes that all the members of the Council, and even the king himself, gave Richelieu a poor welcome, and the cardinal tried to conceal his discontent with this by misrepresenting the circumstances of his appointment. However, he was so ambitious that in time he would attain all he desired. Most people were sure that he would soon become head of the Council through his great gifts, for he had 'no equal in intelligence', and as a cardinal he could formally lay claim to the first place.[3]

The king's resistance was overcome by the arguments not only of his mother but also of his confessor, and of the head of the congregation of the Oratory, Bérulle, who convinced Louis XIII of Richelieu's uprightness. Many courtiers, and especially those circles which were particularly close to the king (consisting largely of petty nobles), confirmed that there was no cleverer man in the world than Richelieu, and that he alone was capable of conducting a firm, strong and consistent policy, 'worthy of so great a king'.[4]

Thus, Richelieu entered the king's Council as a result of the efforts made on his behalf by his protectors—Marie de Médicis, prominent ecclesiastics, and courtiers; in short, as a result of a long and complicated 'court intrigue'. His success was determined, however, not merely by the actions of interested individuals, to which a group of pamphleteers added their voices. Louis XIII's stubborn hostility to the cardinal could be overcome only by the king's realisation of all the difficulties of the situation and of the need to

---

[1] Richelieu's work in 1616–17 is meant.
[2] B. Zeller, *Richelieu et les ministres de Louis XIII*, pp. 280, 281. Despatch dated 10 May 1624.
[3] Ibid. pp. 282, 283. Literally at once on his entry into the king's Council Richelieu claimed his right to take precedence of the chancellor and the constable, yielding first place only to the senior cardinal, La Rochefoucauld, and he received the king's sanction for this. After La Rochefoucauld's resignation he became the first in rank.
[4] *Relation des choses mémorables*, fo. 237$^\text{v}$.

have an experienced and skilful diplomat in the Council. That this was at first the role assigned to Richelieu is shown by the conditions already mentioned, on which he was admitted to the Council.[1]

It must be stressed that Richelieu was from the start accepted into the Council as a full member. The conditions imposed on him related only to the procedure which he had to observe in diplomatic dealings with ambassadors.[2]

Let us now pass on to the events of May–August 1624, when state policy was under the direction of two men—La Vieuville and Richelieu. During May and June the negotiations with England proceeded very sluggishly and indecisively. In May a basis for them was still being sought through talks with an unofficial English agent, Lord Kensington. At the beginning of June a plenipotentiary of James I, the Earl of Carlisle, arrived in Paris with a proposal that France should openly break with Spain, something which certainly did not enter into the French government's plans, since, for financial reasons, it was seeking to avoid external war.

At the same time, negotiations were under way with Holland, culminating in the signing at the beginning of June of a treaty of defensive and offensive alliance, under which France was to lend her ally 1,200,000 *livres* in the course of 1624, and another million *livres* in both 1625 and 1626. Catholic worship was to be permitted at the residence of the French ambassador in The Hague. On the French side the treaty was signed by Lesdiguières (the constable), La Vieuville (the *surintendant*), and Bullion (the chief military *intendant*). D'Estrées was sent to Switzerland to try to raise the Protestant cantons against Austria and Spain.

Richelieu could not have played the leading role in all these negotiations and decisions, if only because they had been initiated before his entry into the king's Council. He could not have condemned La Vieuville's diplomacy as a whole, for there were no grounds for this. He could perhaps have adopted

---

[1] Fontenay-Mareuil also explains the appointment of the cardinal by the difficulties in the field of foreign policy. He adds that the king did not regard La Vieuville as capable of dealing successfully with these difficulties (op. cit. p. 175), but this addition arouses doubt; the memoir-writer was writing after Richelieu's death, so that he was evaluating events with the benefit of hindsight.

[2] Basing himself on Avenel's opinion (Avenel, *Lettres, instructions et papiers d'État du cardinal de Richelieu* I (Paris, 1853), 783), Biryukovich supposes that La Vieuville, having found himself unable to prevent Richelieu's appointment, urged the king to allow the cardinal only a consultative voice in the Council, and set up the *Conseil des dépêches* specially for this purpose. Richelieu became 'chairman of this mute council'. This view is mistaken. The *Conseil des dépêches* had long been in existence, and Richelieu was never its chairman. The structure of the king's Council is described in great detail in R. Mousnier, 'Le conseil du roi de la mort de Henri IV au gouvernement personnel de Louis XIV', *Études d'histoire moderne et contemporaine*, I (Paris, 1947), 29–67, and also in his larger publication 'Les règlements du conseil du roi sous Louis XIII', *Annuaire-Bulletin de la Société de l'histoire de France, Années 1946–1947* (Paris, 1948), pp. 93–211.

some other position. But which? An open break with Spain, followed by war? There was no basis for this. Accordingly, he set himself to carry on an intrigue against La Vieuville in which he made use of the considerable diplomatic blunders committed by him in the negotiations with the English envoy. It was not merely a matter of blunders, though there were some very unfortunate ones. Richelieu took into account the king's constant attitude of suspicion, which pardoned no-one for unauthorised actions (the cardinal himself, later on, was never allowed any). He directed Louis's attention to the fact that, acting in this way and without informing the other ministers (that is, Richelieu), La Vieuville had proposed to the English envoy that they agree on the inclusion in the marriage treaty of points about freedom of Catholic worship in England (which the pope insisted on, refusing otherwise to allow the marriage of a Catholic princess to a Protestant), which were to be treated as a mere matter of form, without any obligation to put them into effect. The French ambassador in England also told Louis of this strange proposal by La Vieuville, and by interrogating all the other members of his Council the king convinced himself that La Vieuville really had done this on his own and without their agreement. In addition, the *surintendant* had secretly sent to England an agent of his, the Capuchin Raconis, of whose mission the French ambassador in England only learnt accidentally. The mission of the *conseiller* Marescot to Germany was similar in character. La Vieuville supplied him with instructions which differed from those compiled by the secretaries of state in accordance with the decision of the king's Council.

At the same time as he was exposing him in this way, Richelieu delivered an attack on the *surintendant* by means of the press. Let us consider two pamphlets by the very alert publicist Fancan, who was close to Richelieu in those years and wrote more than one work inspired by the cardinal.

The first, called *Le mot à l'oreille de M. le marquis de La Vieuville* (1624), speaks out for the grandees and nobles[1] 'offended' by the *surintendant*, that is, who had been deprived by him of their pensions and army appointments. The writer emphasises that La Vieuville had ruined and deprived of their livelihood 'a multitude of completely innocent people'. This circumstance is confirmed by Fontenay-Mareuil, who was himself a courtier and a soldier and who in his memoirs devotes much attention to matters relating to the army and the court. In this instance he also notes that, when he reduced the pensions fund, La Vieuville did nothing to find out who were receiving pensions and for what, 'whether the man was serving or not, and

---

[1] Biryukovich interprets the tendency of this pamphlet in too limited a way, considering that Fancan was defending the grandees only and striving to rouse public opinion against the plutocracy as a whole.

this set a lot of people against him, who later took their revenge on him for it'.[1]

Fancan vividly describes the indignation of those who suffered from La Vieuville's 'miserliness' and his mocking attitude to suppliants. The *surintendant* told everyone that there was no money in the treasury because the king's debts had to be paid. But why had the king got into debt to the financiers? They were robbing the treasury and thereby forcing the king to borrow back his own money, which they had stolen from him. Instead of squeezing this band of robbers as he ought to have done, La Vieuville had deprived many deserving people of their pensions.

Further on, Fancan shows in detail the ways in which the treasury is robbed. He accuses Beaumarchais and other financiers of taking excessive interest on their loans (*denier six*, that is, 16·66 per cent). In future they should restrict themselves to the rate prescribed by ordinance,[2] if they do not want to be subjected to a judicial inquiry.

Comparing this proposal with the demands already put forward in Bourgoin's pamphlet, one cannot avoid noticing their common view of the measures to be taken in dealing with the financiers. Both writers want to lay down a definite rate of interest for the state's creditors, and in general to bring the latter under supervision. Fancan's pamphlet contains nothing stronger on this point than had appeared in previous works of the kind. But another note is prominent in his pamphlet: out of the whole range of La Vieuville's doings, only his régime of economy, his reduction of pensions, is subjected to sharp condemnation and derision; this is not done, however, in order to gain the favour of the grandees, but in order to speak openly of the king's need to have the young, active Richelieu as his sole adviser. La Vieuville cannot get along with him, for they both have the same desire—to rule alone.

Thus, bringing order into the relations between the government and the state's creditors, review of the indiscriminate cutting of pensions, and summoning Richelieu to power as sole adviser—these are the fundamental purposes of the pamphlet.

In the other pamphlet, *La voix publique au roy* (1624), Fancan criticises the whole range of La Vieuville's activity, accusing him of treachery and insidious betrayals. The radical way to put things right, he says, is to set up a special judicial commission of inquiry—and to transfer all power to Cardinal Richelieu.[3]

[1] Fontenay-Mareuil, op. cit. p. 173.
[2] This was at that time about 5–6 per cent.
[3] According to Biryukovich the pamphlet envisaged, besides a judgment on the financiers, another line too to be taken by the future government, namely, an anti-Spanish and anti-papal policy corresponding to the interests of the nobles and the third 'estate'. In fact the author had a different

Biryukovich ascribes decisive importance to this pamphlet, directed against La Vieuville and in defence of Richelieu's pretensions, in bringing about the dismissal of the *surintendant*: 'The waves of public indignation [against the financiers] now began to beat more and more strongly against the walls of the Louvre, menacing the monarchy with new upheavals.'[1] Marie de Médicis and others suggested to the king that La Vieuville be replaced by the cardinal. The king began to yield to the pressure of public opinion and incline toward the view that he would not be able to manage without Richelieu. Guessing what Louis's intentions were, La Vieuville asked at the beginning of August about the possibility that he might be dismissed, but was given no answer. Within a few days, however, on 12 August 1624, it was decided not merely to dismiss him but also to put him in prison, and next day he was taken to the *château* of Amboise.[2] Beaumarchais and other financiers hastened to withdraw to their estates. 'Such was the miserable end of the first attempt made by the financiers to become the ruling group in society.'[3]

There are several things that are not clear in this conception. Why was it necessary to *replace* La Vieuville by the cardinal? La Vieuville was *surintendant des finances*. Richelieu never aspired to this position, nor could he have occupied it, being a cardinal. The régime of economy carried out by La Vieuville was undoubtedly supported by the king, and, indeed, had this not been so, he could not have put it into effect. He was not the first to reduce pensions—it is enough to recall the reforms of Luynes. Furthermore, provided he possessed the king's support, he need have no fear of the opposition and intrigues of the nobility. It was very characteristic of Louis XIII that, once he had taken a decision, he showed the greatest persistence in carrying it out. For this reason, the aristocratic opposition to him could not in itself have presented a danger to La Vieuville. It was significant that he did not abandon his régime of economy during the entire period that he was *surintendant*. What were the political difficulties that persuaded Louis that he would not be able to manage without Richelieu? Biryukovich considers that we must see behind these difficulties the public discontent of a 'bloc' of nobles and officials, stirred up by pamphlets which were inspired by Richelieu. But would a few pamphlets, and the discontent of the nobility, have been enough to persuade the king to dismiss La Vieuville? Many pamphlets had once been

aim: it was necessary to 'clear' Richelieu (a cardinal of the Roman church!) of the suspicion that he was inclined to support Catholic rulers at the expense of Protestant ones. This unfounded suspicion is reflected in other pamphlets as well as this one.

[1] Biryukovich, loc. cit. p. 234.
[2] La Vieuville escaped from France in 1625 and was condemned in his absence. He returned after the death of Louis XIII, received the title of duke and peer, and served again as *surintendant des finances* from 1651 until his death in 1653.
[3] Biryukovich, loc. cit. p. 236.

written against Luynes and his policy which was dangerous to the grandees, and much fiercer ones, too (some of the pamphleteers were sent to prison for writing them), but they had no effect either on Luynes's position or on the policy he pursued. In general, the influence of public opinion on the appointment of particular persons to the king's Council could not in those days be decisive, though it doubtless counted for something. My principal objection is that Biryukovich does not deal at all with the events which took place between May and the middle of August, that is, in the period when La Vieuville and Richelieu were both members of the king's Council. Having ascribed to the cardinal during all that time a silent and passive role as chairman of the *Conseil des dépêches*, Biryukovich considers, apparently, that during the summer months of 1624 Richelieu never showed himself in the political field, and that La Vieuville, had no political successes. In fact, he successfully concluded an alliance with Holland, even though he did fail in his negotiations for an Anglo-French alliance.

The causes of La Vieuville's dismissal—his diplomatic mistakes—were listed in a circular from the king to the ambassadors of France, which was drawn up on 13 August, that is, on the day after his dismissal. 'This is what has obliged me to go further than dismissal, and to arrest him, though I do not yet know what may be discovered by inquiry into how he has conducted his office [as *surintendant*], for, whatever may come to light, in itself it could not lead to his arrest.'[1] Further on, the king directed[2] that the question of the English Catholics be smoothed over in a conciliatory spirit (for otherwise the very possibility of an alliance with England would be endangered), and that in future (a very noteworthy point) he must be informed of every happening.

It is hard to suppose that such serious charges would be made both in public declarations and in secret diplomatic circulars if they were merely pretexts behind which other, genuine causes of La Vieuville's dismissal were concealed. But there are other, more solid grounds for believing in the charges brought against La Vieuville. These are provided by an analysis of the diplomatic activity of Richelieu, as his successor.[3]

How, in the light of these facts, are we to evaluate La Vieuville's activities in the year and a half of his administration (1623–July 1624)?

The régime of economy introduced by La Vieuville, carried out by reducing expenditure on the army and on pensions, was no novelty. Luynes had had resort to it in 1617–18, and the consequences, that is, complaints

---

[1] Avenel, *Lettres*, II (Paris, 1856), 22. The same explanation is given in Louis's letter to the *parlement* of Paris, 13 August (ibid. pp. 25, 26).
[2] Avenel prints the copy of this circular which was sent to the French ambassador in London, the Marquis d'Effiat.
[3] See Chapter 6.

from those who suffered by it, could be foreseen. In 1619 these consequences even took the form of open war by the grandees and nobles against the government. In 1623 a repetition of this revolt was not to be feared: the grandees had no leaders and the Huguenots (except for La Rochelle) had been subdued and could not support them. The régime of economy had the king's backing, and it was continued after La Vieuville's fall; the *parlements* made no protest against it.

La Vieuville had pursued two aims. The first was to put the state's finances in better shape; in the circumstances, only this aim could have ensured to the *surintendant* the support of Louis XIII. His second aim was to increase the credit-worthiness of the treasury, and the king was interested in this, too, for without the constant availability of credit the absolutist government could not survive. The very nature of the chief items on the receipts side of the budget, and their size, necessitated the employment of every form of credit, short-term and long-term loans alike. In strengthening the government's credit-worthiness, La Vieuville undoubtedly also served the interests of the financiers—if only by paying them back the money due to them in respect of their loans.

But La Vieuville did not want to be merely *surintendant des finances*, he wanted to direct state policy as a whole. He hardly needed this supreme power in order to keep control of state finance. Circumstances developed in his favour and he hastened to take advantage of them. He did not make a success of diplomacy, a branch of state activity which it was hard to conduct in those days without experience, knowledge and the appropriate qualities. He lacked self-control, patience, the ability to look ahead; in short, all those diplomatic talents with which Richelieu was richly endowed. Contemporaries judged the comparative abilities and characters of the two men very accurately and were not wrong in their estimates of what would become of them.

To what extent did La Vieuville's administration (it must be remembered that he was *completely* on his own for only three months, from February to May 1624) constitute a period of political rule by the financiers? I do not think it was any such thing. I have shown above why I find Biryukovich's arguments unconvincing. His thesis about the existence of a 'bloc' between the nobles and the third estate, directed against the financiers, is also unconvincing. The struggle against the plutocracy, through pamphleteering and by other methods, certainly united all the estates of the realm, but this had also been a feature of the preceding years, 1614–20, when there could be no question of any such 'bloc', since the *noblesse d'épée* were in revolt against absolutism while the third estate were supporting it.

Richelieu did not come to power as the protégé of a party formed to carry out the programme of any such 'bloc'. The principal efforts to make him a member of the king's Council were made by Marie de Médicis and the courtiers. The endeavours made by the pamphleteers to denigrate La Vieuville and popularise the cardinal might have remained fruitless if the balance of forces within the government itself, and its composition, had been different. We cannot close our eyes to the conflict between different cliques at court, which at that time were decisive in the appointment of one individual rather than another. The cardinal did, of course, very skilfully exploit for his own benefit the mistakes and blunders committed by La Vieuville in the sphere of foreign policy, that is, in matters where Richelieu was incomparably stronger than his rival and which at that time were, owing to the war, of extreme importance for France. By giving Richelieu in 1624 a certain share of power (for he still remained at quite a distance from supreme power), the king enabled him to show his abilities and talents in dealing with the very difficult and sometimes even contradictory tasks confronting French absolutism. Success or failure in coping with these tasks would determine the fate of Cardinal Richelieu.

The idea that 1623–4 saw a phase of rule by the financiers should thus be dismissed. They had no aspirations to political power. The policy pursued by La Vieuville was prompted not by their interests but by the general tasks facing French absolutism, which I have described. Among them were such measures as a régime of economy in the field of military expenditure and pensions, the strengthening of the state budget as a whole, alliances with the enemies of the Habsburgs (to be accomplished without breaking, for the time being, with the Habsburgs themselves), and so on. There was nothing in La Vieuville's policy to mark him off from his predecessors. Moreover, Richelieu continued his policy in many respects. But La Vieuville not only acted arrogantly and abruptly, not allowing sufficiently for the king and his specific psychology, he also showed himself a clumsy and careless operator in the field of diplomacy, where the greatest dexterity and foresight were needed.

As regards the attitude of the financiers to the French government, all through the first half of the seventeenth century this was determined by what was the most important consideration for the financiers, namely, the solvency of the treasury. They always desired, of course, to receive the highest possible rates of interest on their loans but, after all, they could obtain these only if the budget were more or less balanced. State bankruptcy, whether complete or partial, was not at all to their advantage. Strange as it may seem at first sight, what their essential interests required was a strong government, able to pay them the agreed rates of interest on their loans. This strong government which they wanted must also, however, be strongly in need of credit from them. From this standpoint, Henry IV's policy was unprofitable for them, but Richelieu's was beneficial. They were sufficiently experienced businessmen and financiers (not so much through their individual experience, though this is not doubted, as the collective experience of the state's creditors, which had been accumulating over more than a hundred years) to appreciate quite well how deeply the government was involved in the system of state indebtedness and how much, therefore, it stood in need of their capital. It would need money even more acutely if it were to pursue a vigorous foreign policy. War was very profitable to the financiers.

The attitude of the government to its creditors was two-sided. On the one hand, it needed to have them always available, so as to be able to obtain money whenever this was needed; on the other hand, it did not want to pay too dearly for this credit which had already become indispensable. In wartime these two considerations usually proved incompatible, and the cost of credit had to be temporarily forgotten. It cannot be said that the government did not seek a way out of this dilemma in another direction, that is, that it did not concern itself with increasing the income side of the budget by methods other than loans or increased taxes. I shall examine these attempts in the next chapter.

CHAPTER 6

The first years of Richelieu's administration (1625-1627)

THE beginning of Richelieu's administration was long treated in historical writing as a period in which his efforts were mainly exerted in three directions: (1) the conduct of a *guerre couverte* against Spain, that is, in the direction of diplomatic activity; (2) the struggle against the Huguenots; and (3) the strengthening of his own position, in conflict with the parties at court.

A very important correction to this conception was contributed by Henri Hauser's interesting book devoted to Richelieu's economic policy,[1] which showed that it was in 1624–30 that his most important economic measures were taken. Considering these with the rest of the cardinal's internal policy brings one to the conclusion that, in general, these first years of his ascendancy were rich in wide-ranging plans for a variety of reforms.[2] It is very likely that further study of the records will add many new features to this picture, but it is already clear how limited was the traditional notion of Richelieu as mainly a diplomat, to some extent an administrator, and also a political thinker (as author of the *Testament politique*).[3] There can now be no doubt that his activity embraced all aspects of policy, both internal and external. This truth, simple as it now seems, was attained by historians only after many years of research, though it is most fully in conformity with absolutism as a form of government, the principle of which is the independence of the ruler, obliging him unfailingly to co-ordinate his actions in

[1] H. Hauser, *La pensée et l'action économiques du Cardinal de Richelieu* (Paris, 1944). Books on the economic policy of Richelieu published before this one present no interest, as regards either the material they contain or the conclusions they present: F. Palm, *The economic policies of Richelieu* (Illinois, 1922); Georg, Herzog zu Mecklenburg, *Richelieu als merkantilistischer Wirtschaftspolitiker und der Begriff des Staatsmerkantilismus*, Jena, 1929. Cf. the justified criticism of them in Hauser's book (pp. 8, 9). A great deal of material from the records, dealing with economic matters, was used in the book by Boiteux from which we have frequently quoted.

[2] See V. L. Tapié, *La France de Louis XIII et de Richelieu* (Paris, 1952) (quoted above) and the material contained in my Chapter 3.

[3] This notion was largely due to the fact that in the collection of Richelieu's letters and papers published by Avenel, the editor's attention was chiefly concentrated on the documents of a diplomatic nature. Cf. also A. D. Lublinskaya, 'Richelieu in the works of historians of the nineteenth and twentieth centuries' [in Russian], *Voprosy Istorii* (1946), no. 10.

every sphere of policy. The cardinal's contemporaries, in estimating his authority as not only all-powerful but also all-embracing, grasped this better than the historians of the nineteenth and the early twentieth centuries, who understood absolutism mainly as mere unlimited power, and for a long time supposed that Richelieu worked with a narrow circle of secretaries and confidential agents, receiving from 'the other departments' merely whatever information he needed. In actual fact the entire machinery of government was in his hands, and all persons in responsible positions were at the same time his *hommes de confiance* and his advisers. These men stand forth in recent historical work in ever greater relief; from mere executives they have grown to the stature of statesmen.[1]

In the light of these facts and ideas it has become clear that what is needed for the period 1624–7 is an investigation of the co-ordinated and purposeful nature of the government's actions. Unfortunately, historians do not yet possess sufficient material to deal fully with the problem; a great many documents, especially important for the history of internal policy, still await publication.[2] Nevertheless, in my presentation of the events of these years I shall try to give some idea of the connexions between them.

As we saw in the preceding chapter, it was questions of international relations that were most acute at the moment when La Vieuville was dismissed, in August 1624: the conflict with Spain and the papacy about the Valtelline, and the conclusion of an alliance with England, which had very nearly foundered owing to La Vieuville's blunders.

In the course of the following years, between the autumn of 1624 and the summer of 1626, both of these great matters were settled. Though it soon became apparent that the improvement in the situation in the Valtelline was only temporary (such temporary improvements in that area continued to occur, however, all through the period of the Thirty Years War), and though subsequent events led to the breakdown of the alliance with England, nevertheless Richelieu's initial successes played a positive role in this situation. They gave the government time to prepare for more decisive acts, and also strengthened Richelieu's own position as minister.

These successes have always aroused enthusiasm in the admirers of the

[1] Cf. O. Ranum, 'Léon de Bouthillier, comte de Chavigny, créature de Richelieu et secrétaire d'État aux affaires étrangères', in *Revue d'histoire diplomatique*, LXXIV (October–December 1960), 323–34, and *Richelieu and the councillors of Louis XIII* (Oxford, 1963).
[2] The existence and importance of these documents is obvious if only from Hauser's book. The unpublished documents in the Saltykov-Shchedrin Library, Leningrad, though very plentiful for 1633–6 and 1643–8, include very few for 1620–5, and those for 1626–30 are mainly concerned with foreign policy.

cardinal's political genius, who see in them a miraculous solution of what had seemed insoluble problems: opposing the Habsburgs with the help of the Protestant princes while at the same time fighting the Huguenots, that is, the Protestants at home, without damaging the alliances with foreign Protestant powers.[1]

Sounder judgments are expressed in the article by Pithon.[2] Unfortunately, the events of 1621–4 do not receive independent study in this article, being described in the traditional manner and without fresh documentation. For this reason the writer does not adequately evaluate the international position in which France found herself at the beginning of Richelieu's administration. He does show convincingly how difficult Richelieu's first steps were and how he had to reckon with a situation which it was beyond his power to change in a radical way. Pithon regards Richelieu's diplomacy in those years as uncertain and vacillating in accordance with the needs of the moment. He sees the reason for this in the fact that Richelieu could not have had any general plan of action at that stage; the programme set out later in the *Testament politique* was drawn up after the event. I consider this opinion groundless. Richelieu's famous programme, for suppressing the political power of the Huguenots and princes and struggling against the Habsburgs, was not invented by him. By 1624 it was already the quite long-established and fully understood line of government policy, directed towards the strengthening of absolutism.[3] Richelieu formulated this programme felicitously, but since the programme existed before he took it up, the question of when this formulation was actually propounded is of no importance.

At first, Richelieu's freedom of action was greatly restricted. His personal position was not firmly established; he still had to win the king's complete confidence, without which he would not allow himself to take any risks. The government's position was itself not an easy one, either. In spite of two years of peace, 1623–4, and La Vieuville's régime of economy, money was lacking. In October 1624 the government announced legal proceedings against the financiers, which was already by then a normal method of bringing pressure to bear on them in order to extract a fine, of larger or smaller dimensions. This time, the financiers bought the government off with 10 million *livres*. The whole of this sum was evidently not exacted,

[1] G. Hanotaux, *Histoire du cardinal de Richelieu* (Paris, 1933) III, 1 ff.; Saint-Aulaire, *Richelieu*, 2nd edition (Paris, 1960), pp. 106 ff.; the same viewpoint is found in many other biographers of Richelieu.

[2] R. Pithon, 'Les débuts difficiles du ministère de Richelieu et la crise de Valteline (1621–1627)', in *Revue d'histoire diplomatique*, LXXIV (October–December 1960), 289–322.

[3] See Chapters 4 and 5, and also A. D. Lublinskaya, *Frantsiya v nachale XVII veka (1610–1620, gg.)* [*France at the beginning of the seventeenth century, 1610–1620*], (Leningrad, 1959), pp. 278, 279.

however, since as early as July 1625 a royal decree exempted all the farmers of indirect taxes from paying the fine.[1] The reason given for this exemption was that the farmers concerned had rendered and were rendering the king important services. This meant something quite normal in the practice of the French monarchy, namely, that the government once more found itself in need of a loan from the financiers. In addition the government, as before, created and sold new offices,[2] asked the provincial States for more money,[3] and so on. In other words, financial policy underwent no changes in those years; the same caution was shown as previously in the matter of increasing taxes. Yet impressive diplomatic moves needed the backing of impressive military moves, or, at the very least, a demonstration of readiness for such moves. His limited resources compelled Richelieu to rely mainly on the flexibility and skill of his diplomacy.

This really was very flexible at that time, so much so that it often confused contemporaries. During 1624–6, that is within about two years, France was at one moment at war with Spain in Italy, and then concluded a treaty of peace with her; at another moment, in 1625, war was being waged against the Huguenots, and then peace was made with them too; an alliance made with England was soon broken off. It must be emphasised that all these sharp changes of course also signified veerings in the orientation of French foreign policy towards one religious camp or the other. Undoubtedly, with all the rulers of that period, political considerations predominated over religious ones, and Richelieu, though a cardinal, was no different in this respect from his colleagues in high positions. It was different, however, where the masses of the people in the various countries of Europe were concerned; furthermore, important groups among the nobility, the officials and the bourgeoisie in France itself, both in the capital and in the provinces ,were also lacking in that opportunism which was characteristic of the government. Gallicanism (which had long since become traditional with these groups, and acquired a political character) was not reconcilable with sharp turns in favour of the papacy and Spain. On the other side, the politically weighty opinion of the leaders of the Counter-Reformation movement made itself loudly heard whenever the government 'indulged' the Huguenots or broke with the Catholic powers and Rome. The hail of pamphlets which fell thick and fast

---

[1] *Declaration du roy en faveur de tous les fermiers et autres personnes qui sont entrez et interessez aux partis*... (Paris, 1625) (Library of the Leningrad Section of the Institute of History of the USSR Academy of Sciences, press-mark II 54/1303).

[2] R. Mousnier, *La vénalité des offices sous Henri IV et Louis XIII* (Rouen, 1945), p. 376; *Cahiers des états de Normandie sous les règnes de Louis XIII et de Louis XIV. Documents relatifs à ces assemblées recueillis et annotés par Ch. de Robillard de Beaurepaire*, II (Rouen, 1877), 295.

[3] *Cahiers des états de Normandie*, p. 89.

18-2

around Richelieu in 1625–8 was far from harmless to him, especially because this 'paper war' was waged on an all-European scale and the cardinal was abused in all countries and all languages. He had to defend himself against these onslaughts not only in France but also abroad.[1]

Richelieu set forth his programme in an extensive memorandum (later included in the text of his *Mémoires*) which he drew up on 6 May 1625 for Louis XIII.[2] The trend of the programme was towards ensuring peaceful relations with Spain by settling the quarrel over the Valtelline, since only by that means could favourable conditions be prepared for a final solution of the question of Huguenot independence. 'So long as the Huguenots retain their power in France the king cannot be master in his kingdom, nor undertake any glorious deeds beyond its borders.'[3]

In accordance with these views, Richelieu at first took no far-reaching decisions. His acts in the sphere of foreign policy were restricted to securing a period of external peace, even if only a temporary one, sufficient to make possible the preparation of the siege of La Rochelle.[4] His acts against the Huguenots were restricted to not allowing them to add to their strength at a time when attention was focused mainly on international affairs.[5]

Richelieu knew that his appointment to the king's Council had been received with satisfaction in Rome because there they counted on him to take care, in negotiating the marriage-alliance with England, of the interests of the English Catholics. At the same time he took into account the apprehensions existing in London (at that point England was extremely interested in an alliance with France) that, being a cardinal, he would oppose the marriage of a Catholic princess of France with a Protestant, or at least would insist on conditions unacceptable to the English. He therefore urged the pope to agree to the marriage, impressing upon him how important it was for the English Catholics and for the church as a whole.[6] In return for this service

---

[1] There are works, by Fagniez, Dedouvres and others, specially devoted to this pamphlet literature. The most detailed treatment will be found in M. Deloche, *Autour de la plume du cardinal de Richelieu* (Paris, 1920). Of great interest is the pamphlet entitled *Le Catholique d'estat*, written in September 1625 under Richelieu's editorship, in which the theory of *raison d'état* is developed and counterposed to international Catholicism. The author declares that 'heretic' rulers are none the less legitimate rulers of their states and, therefore, one can have friendly relations with them. He also says that one cannot apply the theological yardstick to wars between states, and so on. Richelieu took care to ensure that this pamphlet had a very wide circulation (Deloche, op. cit. pp. 281–323).

[2] Avenel, *Lettres, instructions et papiers d'État du cardinal de Richelieu*, II (Paris, 1856), 77–87.

[3] Ibid. p. 83.

[4] For what follows I have used Richelieu's correspondence (Avenel, op. cit. II, 18 ff.).

[5] See Chapter 4.

[6] He arranged through the French ambassador in England for the English Catholics to send petitions to this effect to the pope and the Nuncio in Paris.

he asked for the pope's help in settling the question of the Valtelline. To the English he expounded all the advantages to be gained from an alliance with France,[1] and asked James I not only for promises of a gracious attitude to his Catholic subjects but also for special pledges. In England Richelieu's success was complete, in Rome only partial. The pope's agreement to the marriage was obtained, but the situation continued to be unsatisfactory in the Valtelline.

As early as the end of 1624 the French general d'Estrées (who in 1626 became a marshal) had been sent with a small army into the Grisons, where he incited the Protestant population of those cantons to revolt successfully against the Austrian occupying forces. He was unable to exploit his success, however, because the passes into Lombardy were blocked by the Spaniards. At the same time Lesdiguières, the constable and governor of the Dauphiné, the French province bordering on Savoy, laid siege to Genoa, in alliance with the Duke of Savoy. The aim of this campaign was to cut communications between Genoa and Milan, which would seriously hinder the movement of Spanish troops not only into the Valtelline but also into Germany and the Netherlands.[2] This siege too, however, ended unsuccessfully; the allied forces were inadequate to the task, and Venice failed to join them, since she wanted more decisive actions to be undertaken, directly against Milan. Richelieu would not agree to such actions, because they would have drawn France into open war with Spain, which he was doing everything to avoid. His negative attitude harmed France's relations with her principal allies in northern Italy, Venice and Savoy. It was then that, taking advantage of the government's difficulties, the Huguenots rose in revolt, seizing the islands off La Rochelle. Richelieu considered it impossible to begin a long war against the Huguenots in such a difficult international situation, and at the end of 1625 conditions for a peace pact with the entire Huguenot party were worked out, and ratified by the government on 5 February 1626.[3] Confirmation of the treaty by La Rochelle and the cities of the South took another month, however, so that only at the beginning of March (these dates are very important in connexion with the analysis of negotiations with Spain, below) could the matter be regarded as finished and settled.[4]

[1] Let us recall that this alliance was important not only for England; it was no less important for France since it meant that the English would undertake to withhold the aid they might otherwise have extended to the Huguenots.
[2] Genoa and Milan were vital points on the lines of communication of the Habsburg powers from Madrid through Barcelona, Genoa, Milan and Innsbruck to Vienna, and via Milan and the Franche-Comté and up the Rhine to the Spanish Netherlands.
[3] See above, p. 216.
[4] Letters from Secretary of State d'Herbault to Césy, the French ambassador in Turkey, 9 and 10 March the (Saltykov-Shchedrin Library, Leningrad, Avt. 94, nos. 2-1 and 3).

Parallel negotiations were conducted with Spain regarding the Valtelline, consummated by the signing of the Treaty of Monçon (Monzón). The history of these talks has not been fully brought to light, owing to insufficient documentary evidence,[1] and for this reason historians' views of it diverge. Some (for example, Hanotaux) follow Richelieu's opinion as expressed in his description of the treaty, in his *Mémoires*, as a victory for himself. Tapié considers that the terms of the treaty were a shock to Richelieu and that he wanted to reject it out of hand, but that he was forced, most reluctantly, to ratify it.[2] Pithon seeks many explanations in the circumstances surrounding the cardinal, and hesitates in his ultimate verdict, not knowing whether to see the treaty as a mistake or as a success on the cardinal's part.[3] The fact that I have some unpublished material at my disposal,[4] and the importance of these events for the history of 1626–7, makes it incumbent upon me to discuss the matter more fully.

The point was that without settling the unhappy question of the Valtelline it was impossible even to think of consolidating French absolutism within the country, and thereafter for it to be able to pursue an independent line in international affairs. We have seen that Richelieu, like his predecessors at very dangerous moments, did not stop short of taking military measures in the Valtelline and before Genoa. In reality, these measures meant war with Spain, but officially France was merely helping her allies, the Grisons and Savoy. It did not enter in the least into the calculations of the French government at that time to render more substantial and decisive aid, though all the allies of France, both in Italy and beyond the Alps (Holland, England, the German Protestants) were extremely dissatisfied, and exerted all possible pressure to draw France finally into open war with the Habsburgs, in which they themselves were to one degree or another already involved. In surveying the situation as it existed towards the end of 1625 it is impossible not to take this circumstance into account. The situation was still further complicated by the fact that the operations of the French army, limited as they were, called forth retaliatory operations by the pope, who despatched his forces to the Valtelline as well. Richelieu was confronted (and let us not forget his position as a cardinal) by the highly disagreeable and dangerous prospect of war with the pope.

---

[1] In another article, Pithon examines these events from the standpoint of Franco-Swiss relations (Pithon, 'La Suisse, théâtre de la guerre froide entre la France et l'Espagne pendant la crise de Valteline (1621–1626)', *Schweizerische Zeitschrift für Geschichte* (1963), XIII, no. 1, pp. 33–53.

[2] Tapié, op. cit. p. 188.

[3] Pithon, *Revue d'histoire*, LXXIV, 314–22. Elsewhere Pithon discusses this treaty as a misfortune for Franco-Swiss relations (*Schweizerische Zeitschrift*, XIII, 52).

[4] The reference is to unpublished letters from Louis XIII and d'Herbault to Césy, 1626–8, which are in the Saltykov-Shchedrin Library, Leningrad.

The overall situation was an unfavourable one. Nothing useful had come out of the negotiations with the pope, the Grisons, Savoy and Venice. The military expedition had proved more difficult than could have been expected, and though it had produced partial successes (in the Grisons), on the other hand it threatened to bring about armed intervention by the pope. Only one way out remained—to open direct talks with Spain, the chief cause of these difficulties. (I have shown earlier why open war with Spain was out of the question for France at that time.)

One very important factor played a part in all this, however, a factor to which we have already directed attention, namely the fact that France had allies: Venice, Savoy, Switzerland. For them the situation in northern Italy held the threat of infinitely worse consequences than could befall France, since the integrity of their territories was directly endangered. This situation has been little considered by historians, though the secrecy surrounding the French negotiations with Spain was due precisely to the anxiety felt by France's allies.

The basic facts concerning the Treaty of Monçon are these. The responsibility for entering into absolutely secret negotiations with Olivares, the *de facto* ruler of Spain, was entrusted to the French ambassador in Madrid, Du Fargis, as early as the end of 1625. In January 1626 the main lines of the treaty were decided; in February and March the French government modified and added to it; and in May it was ratified by both parties. The allies learnt of the treaty in March. Their indignation knew no bounds, and it cost Richelieu enormous trouble to smooth this over and to make up even a little for the damage done.

The negotiations proceeded in the following manner. For France the most important question connected with the Valtelline was the monopoly of use of the Alpine passes between the Grisons and the Valtelline. In other words, both of these territories must be accessible to French forces. This was the aim pursued by France, and the means for achieving it was to establish the sovereignty of the Protestant Grisons over the Catholic Valtelline and regulate their mutual relations in such a way as to avoid conflicts between them.

Du Fargis settled the main point, about the passes, quite successfully with Olivares. Spain's tractability sprang from the fact that at that moment peace with France was very necessary for her, in order to free Olivares's hands for action against the Dutch and the English in the north—in the Low Countries and the Palatinate. Given a treaty of peace with France, the Italian theatre of war became of secondary importance to Spain for the time being. That was why the French government was given satisfaction on the most important point. The other points of the treaty, however, on the relations between the Grisons and the Valtelline were formulated, at Olivares's insistence, in such a way that whenever Olivares himself, or the pope, should so desire, the main point, about the passes, could be nullified. It is not surprising that, in the letters sent by Richelieu and by the king[1] (that is, likewise by Richelieu) on 4 February to Du Fargis, he was instructed to obtain changes in these points. In the event of agreement by Olivares to the text proposed by Richelieu (which made more precise and firm the rights of the Grisons), the ambassador was to explain to the Nuncio and to the ambassadors of the *confédérez*[2] that he himself, 'without authority from the king and on his own personal responsibility' (*sans charge et au hazard de vostre teste*),[3] was concluding and signing the said treaty. This was to their advantage as well, in so far as the questions of the passes and of the sovereignty of the Grisons were solved in a positive way. Should Olivares refuse to sign the treaty as revised, Du Fargis was to leave for France immediately, after securing Olivares's agreement to keep the negotiations absolutely secret, and without leaving a single document behind him with any bearing on these negotiations, so that nobody could ever prove that the ambassador had authority from the king to conclude a treaty without the agreement of the allies.[4]

Thus, the essence of the matter was that the negotiations were carried on without the participation of France's allies and behind their backs.[5] Du Fargis was to be the scapegoat; Richelieu had earlier prepared him to play this role, so as to be able to clear himself to some degree in the eyes of the allies. Thereafter, everything proceeded perfectly, as though rehearsed.

On 20 March, Secretary of State d'Herbault wrote to Césy, the French ambassador in Turkey,[6] that two days previously (on 18 March) news had reached Paris from Du Fargis, 'to everyone's surprise', that the treaty had been signed on 5 March, in the revised form,[7] and that Du Fargis had declared that he had done this 'on his own responsibility' (*au prix de sa teste*),[8] considering that the treaty would be for everyone's good, in restoring peace. The king, wrote d'Herbault, was very angry at such irregular conduct by his ambassador (*sa Majesté a montré de grands sentimens de ce procédé extra-*

---

[1] Avenel, op. cit. II, 187–93. It should be mentioned that the practice at that time was for the king's letters to ambassadors to set out the official view, while in letters to them from Richelieu or the secretaries of state, sent at the same time, a commentary was provided and recommendations made.

[2] Here, Venice and Savoy are meant.   [3] Avenel, op. cit. II, 188.

[4] Ibid. p. 189

[5] It must be mentioned that, besides this, the interests of Venice were flouted by the use of the passes being accorded to France alone.

[6] Saltykov-Shchedrin Library, Leningrad, Avt. 94, no. 4.

[7] The new version of the text, containing clarifications and additions by Richelieu, was summarised for Césy in a special document (Saltykov-Shchedrin Library, Leningrad, Avt. 30, no. 5).

[8] As we see, the expressions of 'unauthorised action' coincide.

ordinaire) and had made a declaration to this effect to the Venetian ambassador and to the Prince of Piedmont, with whom he had decided to discuss the treaty in detail.[1]

This discussion took rather a long time, for the French government ratified the treaty only in the second half of May.[2] Richelieu had to put in a great deal of work, as Venice and Savoy submitted substantial claims. In the end, however, faced with the *fait accompli* of the unity of the two great powers, they were obliged 'de se contenter de leurs raisonnables interests'.[3]

The Treaty of Monçon did great harm also to Holland in her struggle with Spain. Richelieu had to reconcile these contradictions too.

The facts cited show convincingly enough that the treaty with Spain must be seen as a 'separate peace', concluded not only without the knowledge and agreement of the allies but also against their interests.[4] That was why they were kept completely in the dark about the negotiations. When the latter became public, the 'blame' for them was placed on an 'irresponsible' ambassador.[5]

Whatever the price paid for this success—and it was undoubtedly a success—Richelieu had grounds to be satisfied with the results of his efforts[6] and to proceed to other urgent affairs. For this reason the Treaty of Monçon was useful and advantageous to France.

The urgent affairs demanding the French government's attention at the beginning of 1626 were the need to balance the state budget and to find the means for war against La Rochelle, that is, for the final abolition of the Huguenot 'state within the state'.

This was also the reason for the constant attention accorded by Richelieu

[1] Saltykov-Shchedrin Library, Leningrad, Avt. 94, no. 4. The Duke of Savoy's son, the Prince of Piedmont, was in Paris for talks on joint military operations against the Spaniards in northern Italy. As clearly emerges from d'Herbault's letter to Césy of 9 March 1626 (Saltykov-Schedrin Library, Leningrad, Avt. 94, no. 2-1), the French government was encouraging him to hope for such a campaign.

[2] The date of ratification of the treaty by France is usually taken to be 2 May, but this date was evidently inserted later, since on 15 May d'Herbault could still write to Césy that, Spain having already ratified the treaty, Louis XIII intended to follow suit within a few days (Saltykov-Shchedrin Library, Leningrad, Avt. 94, no. 7b).

[3] Letter from d'Herbault to Césy, 3 April 1626 (Saltykov-Shchedrin Library, Leningrad, Avt. 94, no. 5).

[4] See above, p. 279.

[5] In the light of these facts Pithon seems mistaken when he opines that Richelieu agreed to the ratification of a dubious treaty under the pressure of the Catholic party (that is, of Marie de Médicis and others), for the sake of his own safety, and so on (Pithon, 'Les débuts difficiles', *Revue d'histoire*, LXXIV, 318).

[6] It can also be regarded as a success that Spain withdrew from Milan Feria, who had been the principal executive of all Spain's military and diplomatic activities in northern Italy and had initiated 'on his own authority' the operations against the Valtelline. As we see, both powers regularly made use of the 'unauthorised acts' of their officials.

at this time to all questions of trade, shipping and the navy. He concerned himself with organising large-scale trading companies, protecting trade, and creating a fleet for both commerce and war, all of which entailed a number of measures and reforms, and also the convening at the end of 1626 of an Assembly of Notables, that is, of representatives of the privileged orders.

In preparing his measures Richelieu went in for wide consultations with merchants, shipowners, sailors, naval officers, financial officials, French ambassadors and so on. He ordered that reports be compiled, he summoned particular individuals before him, he demanded information from local authorities, he despatched special commissioners to check on the spot the state of the shipyards and ports and of the coastal defences. He closely studied all the memoranda and reports he received, made notes, additions and corrections on them, and then used them in his memoranda to the king, in his speeches and at sessions of the Council, in his *Mémoires* and his *Testament politique*. In 1626 he created eight offices of *inspecteurs-généraux des affaires de la marine*, and appointed to fill them men whom he trusted. They operated in the maritime provinces, their functions being similar in character to those of the *intendants*. They concerned themselves a great deal with economic matters and did a considerable amount of good.[1]

The establishment of trading companies and the creation of a navy proceeded simultaneously and side by side. It must be emphasised that at this time the difference between a fleet for commerce and a fleet for war was insignificant. All merchant vessels carried guns and stores of munitions for defence against attack by pirates, and their crews were armed and trained to fight,[2] while warships could easily be transformed into merchant ships. In fact, the difference lay rather between the royal (that is, the state) fleet and private ships, and this also frequently disappeared in practice, since private trading vessels were used for warlike purposes, while the king's ships were sold to shipowners and merchants. Therefore, in creating a royal fleet, the government aimed not to make use of it only for war. Moreover, the task of effectively defending the coast and protecting merchant ships on the high seas could only be carried out by a fighting navy.

In establishing trading companies Richelieu encountered resistance not only from the merchants of certain cities but also from the *parlements*,[3] and in creating a fleet he came up against difficulties of a material order, which I have already mentioned, and against the limited amount of his resources.

---

[1] L. A. Boiteux, *Richelieu 'Grand maître de la navigation et du commerce de France'* (Paris, 1955), pp. 26–30, 121, 122.
[2] Ships for whale-hunting were built at Saint-Malo, with specially reinforced hulls. These ships could be turned into warships in a very short time.
[3] See below, pp. 288, 289.

Yet nevertheless, as a result of his vigorous activity, France acquired a substantial navy within a short time.

In 1625 the government possessed not a single vessel in the ports of the Atlantic and the Channel, and in the Mediterranean only ten galleys. Within ten years there were three squadrons in the northern seas,[1] and in the Mediterranean a squadron and twenty galleys. Richelieu did the main organisational work for this between 1626 and 1630; thereafter matters followed more or less a course already laid down. Together with his advisers, the cardinal worked out a plan for the creation of dockyards and the improvement of ports and harbours; he organised the purchase from abroad of ships and material for ships; in person and through his 'literary staff' he carried on extensive propaganda, striving to attract people and capital to the work in hand.

In 1626, even before the Assembly of Notables (to which the government presented a wide-ranging programme for the formation of trading companies and of a fleet),[2] and, consequently, without waiting for their approval and sanction, Richelieu ordered the building of eighteen large ships in private dockyards in Normandy and Brittany, and at the beginning of 1627 another six.[3] Some of the materials—timber, iron, hemp—had to be obtained from Holland, and Richelieu sent special agents to Amsterdam for this purpose. As buying from the Dutch proved expensive, he tried to restore France's direct commercial links with Danzig and Sweden,[4] which had been disrupted by war and successful Dutch competition, but he did not bring this off completely, and for a long time thereafter the French government was still obliged to deal with the Dutch. Besides the shortage of materials, another kind of difficulty also made itself felt. There were not sufficient experienced shipbuilders in France, so that Englishmen, Dutchmen and Flemings had to be invited in, and their work paid for at high rates. The government actually ordered a number of vessels (in 1626 five, in 1627 twelve, and so on) in Holland.[5] In brief, organising a national shipbuilding industry proved to be a hard task. And yet at the siege of La Rochelle Richelieu already had a squadron of thirty-five ships; though, to be sure, only thirteen of these were really large vessels.[6]

The organisation of trading companies began in 1625, when the plan was

[1] The North Atlantic and the adjoining northern seas were known together as *les mers du Ponant*, or simply as *le Ponant*.
[2] See below, pp. 322, 323.
[3] The orders were put out to public tender, and contracts for them drawn up by notaries.
[4] French merchants carried salt, wine, vinegar and spirits to these places, and brought back timber for masts, hemp, and resin.
[5] Boiteux, op. cit. pp. 57–63.   [6] Ibid. p. 56.

drawn up for the *Compagnie des cent associés de Morbihan*[1] with a nominal capital of 1,600,000 *livres*. At the outset, however, there were only four *associés*, and their number never exceeded twelve. The basis of this company was to be the new free city and port of Morbihan. Within the walls of this town the company wielded full power; in addition, it was authorised to build ships and even to cast guns, which in France was a royal prerogative, that is, a state monopoly. The Morbihan company was given exclusive rights of trade with the East and West Indies, Canada ('New France') and the Levant; it was empowered to establish colonies. The document constituting the company was signed by the four founders and Richelieu on 31 March 1626; Richelieu was its head, in his capacity as *surintendant du commerce du royaume*, but this was only a temporary arrangement—after the cardinal's death the company was to be headed by a syndic (that is, a representative) elected by the *associés*.

Within another six weeks, another company was formed, with the fanciful name of *Nacelle de Saint-Pierre fleurdelysée*.[2] The chief participants were three merchants: a Dutchman, De Witt; a Fleming (perhaps of Italian extraction), Billotti; and a Frenchman, Du Maurier. Richelieu, who headed this company too, was described in the founding charter as *surintendant et réformateur général du commerce de France*. Two free ports were to be established for this company as well—one on the Mediterranean coast and one on the Atlantic.[3] The chief tasks of the company were to be the regulation of the import of cod and herring, the working of ore-mines, the draining of marshes, and the building of new manufactories to produce pottery, cut-glass ware, lace, carpets, and fine linen, as well as sugar, cheese and so on. The area of this company's activity was to be restricted to north-western Europe and Barbary.[4]

[1] Morbihan is the name of a small bay in Basse-Bretagne, between Lorient and Vannes. The coast there is much indented, and nearby are a number of islands which shelter it. Besides its suitable situation for the building of a port, Morbihan was also of special interest because a fleet based there would be able to control the trade routes linking Spain with the Spanish Netherlands and La Rochelle with England and Holland.

[2] *Nacelle de Saint-Pierre* means, literally, St Peter's boat, and, figuratively, the Catholic church. The adjective *fleurdelysée* refers, of course, to the lily emblems of the Crown of France. On the significance of this title for the company, see below, note 4.

[3] Richelieu and the organisers of the company strove to attract to these free ports as many as possible of the people who were ready to leave the Spanish Netherlands out of indignation that at that time Spain monopolised all trade with these possessions of hers. Discontent really was very great there, and many wanted to emigrate to France. Richelieu hoped to bring back in this way some of the Huguenots who had fled, and 'reconcile them to France' (Boiteux, op. cit. pp. 229–32).

[4] One of the organisers had the intention of redeeming Frenchmen who had been taken prisoner by the Algerian pirates, with money raised by selling exemptions from keeping fast-days. The pope issued such indulgences, and it may be that the name given to the company signifies that it was intended to place it under the high patronage of the pope, on the one hand, and the king, on the other.

The news of the formation of these companies caused considerable alarm in Holland, England and Spain. Flemings were forbidden to take part in their work, that is, to emigrate to France. At the same time, France's competitors calculated that nothing might come of the scheme, after all, because the *parlements* would not agree to register the edicts creating the companies. As we shall see, these calculations were justified.

It must be stressed that, in the course of establishing the companies, and thanks to their emergence, Richelieu acquired certain new functions, expressed in his new title of *surintendant du commerce*. These were stages on his way to becoming, in effect, minister of trade and navigation. It was the first time this office had appeared in France, and it accorded badly with Richelieu's red robe and with his position as the king's first minister. Contemporaries were astonished to see a minister and a prelate taking charge of commercial matters and the building of a fleet. Richelieu did not hesitate to justify himself: in one of the pamphlets put out by his 'literary staff' it was stated that he had been asked to undertake this work by the merchants who had founded the companies, and that trade, together with a navy, was of essential importance to the kingdom.[1] Amazement at the cardinal's concern with commercial and nautical activities was soon dissipated, however, and at the sessions of the notables (that is, within eighteen months) everyone appreciated the importance of the chief minister's possessing these functions.

The need for protectionist measures in the sphere of trade was perfectly clear to everyone, together with the fact that only the government could implement them. Then the events of 1625 showed everyone how important it was for France to have her own war fleet: in order to defeat the Rochelais and Soubise at sea, the French government had to buy ships from the Dutch and English, and this was accompanied by embarrassments and complications in the field of international relations.

The appearance of a new office and the appointment to this office of none other than the cardinal had an important political consequence. If the reforms expected as a result were to succeed, then the Duc de Montmorency must cease to be admiral of France. Only Richelieu could deprive him of this title.

The Duc de Montmorency, representative of one of the noblest families of France, and hereditary governor of Languedoc, was also hereditary admiral of France. This office was one of the highest in the realm, its origin going back to the earliest times, and like all other such offices, it belonged to the higher nobility as a piece of hereditary property. The position was complicated by the fact that for Montmorency it was not merely a lucrative sinecure. Between 1612 and 1625 he had gathered into his own hands, by

[1] Boiteux, op. cit. pp. 32, 33.

way of inheritance and purchase—these offices were bought and sold exclusively among the families of the higher nobility—all the admiralty jurisdictions along the Atlantic and Channel coasts,[1] together with the office of Viceroy of Canada. From 1614 onward he was styled *Amiral général de France*. In addition, he was active not only in safeguarding his own prerogatives and interests but also in establishing trading companies.[2] All Richelieu's measures in the field of establishing a fleet and forming companies did great harm to the admiral's position. They reduced his formal standing to secondary importance, and in practice they threatened him with the loss of all his functions. And this affected the interests of the higher nobility as a whole, who even without this had plenty of reason to be afraid of the cardinal. In May 1626 (let us recall that the creation of the companies and the establishment of Richelieu's new office took place between March and May), the 'conspiracy of Chalais' was organised, so named after one of the conspirators —by no means the chief one. The king's closest relatives took part in this conspiracy: his brother Gaston, his half-brothers the Vendômes (natural sons of Henry IV), his cousins Condé and Soissons, and along with them some grandees of the court and certain noble ladies, including the Duchesse de Chevreuse. The queen, Anne of Austria, knew of the conspirators' plans to kill Richelieu and depose the king. They had links with foreign states (the Duke of Savoy and other Italian princes), and they were ready to exploit the hostility of Holland and England towards France, caused by the Treaty of Monçon.

The cardinal managed to escape death, and the conspiracy was exposed. Chalais paid with his life, the Vendômes were arrested, the Duchesse de Chevreuse was banished from France, the queen was disgraced. Gaston, however, was brought into the king's Council and given the title of Duc d'Orléans; as the heir to the throne of the childless Louis XIII he was a person to whom no severe measures could be applied. But he was placed under strict surveillance, which, however, did not achieve the desired results. Gaston d'Orléans continued to figure as the nominal and decorative head of all the conspiracies of the grandees, right down to the birth of the Dauphin (the future Louis XIV), when his role as heir to the throne came to an end.

The conspiracy of Chalais was an attempt by the court nobility, who had been finally ousted by the cardinal from any participation in affairs of state, to settle accounts not only with the man responsible for their 'situation without rights' as they described it, but also with the king who gave his support to Richelieu, and who should be replaced by a more agreeable

---

[1] The Admiralty of the Mediterranean was held by the Duc de Guise.
[2] See above, pp. 137–8.

figure, from their point of view, the young, weak-willed and frivolous Gaston. It is significant that the conspirators were recruited entirely in court circles, and that there was no question of any open armed revolt against the government, such as had taken place as recently as in 1620. It was already impossible to lean for support upon either the provincial *noblesse d'épée* or the Huguenots.

The judicial investigation of the circumstances of the conspiracy, carried out by the first of those special commissions which thereafter Richelieu established on a number of occasions, brought to light facts which finally ruined Louis XIII's relations with his family (except, for the time being, his mother). On the other hand, his confidence in Richelieu was greatly strengthened. He was much stirred by the conspirators' appeal for aid to foreign powers, which threatened France with very grave dangers. From this time on, the king and his minister, right down to their (almost simultaneous) deaths, were firmly and immutably joined in both their political and their personal interests.

It is noteworthy that the execution of Chalais and the stern treatment of the other conspirators aroused no protest, except among the reckless nobles of the court, whom Richelieu and the king proceeded vigorously to subdue, inflicting the death penalty for duelling. Wide circles among the politically influential sections of society accepted the political line of the king and the cardinal, and it was later officially endorsed by the notables. Richelieu, moreover, made the most of the favourable situation and effected changes in the king's Council. The seals were taken away from D'Aligre, who had shown fright at the moment of the conspiracy, and entrusted to one of the cardinal's own men, Marillac, one of the two *surintendants* appointed after the dismissal of La Vieuville,[1] and D'Effiat became *surintendant des finances*.[2] As a result, the 'working part' of the king's Council was thenceforth made up entirely of adherents of Richelieu.

The collapse of the conspiracy of Chalais hastened the dismissal of Montmorency and even gave this a certain political significance, since the Duke, like all the higher nobles, had been mixed up in the conspiracy. In August he was deprived of his office as admiral of France, and his functions were transferred to 'whoever will be in charge of trade'. This proved to mean Richelieu, whose new office was finally established by an edict issued at Saint-Germain in October 1626, in which he was named *grand maître, chef et surintendant général de la navigation et du commerce de France*. In January 1627 the office of admiral of France was completely abolished,[3] together with

[1] See above, p. 267. [2] See below, p. 304.
[3] Richelieu settled the financial side of the matter with Montmorency by redeeming his office of admiral for 1,200,000 *livres* (Boiteux, op. cit. p. 96).

that of constable, the last constable, Lesdiguières, having died in September 1626.[1] Through the abolition of the supreme command of the armed forces on land and sea, which had been in the hands of the grandees, the higher nobility found themselves deprived of great military appointments which had also possessed considerable political significance.

But while Richelieu succeeded fairly quickly in dealing with the higher nobility, his task in relation to the *parlements* and the merchants, though not so dangerous, was complicated. The edict of Saint-Germain involved the appearance in France of a department of state which was new both in form and in content—an administration governing trade, shipping and colonies. In itself this alarmed the *parlements*, especially in the maritime provinces, because it threatened to deprive them of some of their functions, as indeed happened. Still greater misgivings were aroused by the formation of the companies. The granting of the hundred *associés* of the Morbihan company of monopoly rights over trade, and the placing of this company under the supervision of the cardinal himself, which meant that in practice it was immune from interference by local authorities, provoked a vigorous protest from the States of Brittany and the *parlement* of Rennes. They denounced this 'dangerous innovation' which threatened harm to the trade of the other cities of Brittany. The situation was made more complicated by the arrest, in connexion with the conspiracy of Chalais, of Vendôme, the Governor of Brittany, who had many supporters in the province. For these purely political reasons, Richelieu did not consider it possible to press matters to an issue, and the decision to create the companies was not put into force. The *Nacelle de Saint-Pierre* project was abandoned. True, within a year, in June 1627, there was formed instead the *Compagnie du Saint-Esprit*, headed by the same De Witt and two Breton merchants. The purposes and privileges of this company were identical with those of the vanished *Nacelle*. The Paris *parlement* agreed to register the edict, but only on condition that a number of the company's proposed privileges were cancelled. Without these, however, the company lacked its power of attraction, and nothing more was heard of it.[2]

Richelieu encountered a great deal of trouble in obtaining registration of the edict appointing him to his new office. Even the Paris *parlement* took until March 1627 to register it, and the *parlements* of Rennes and Rouen did so

---

[1] Guise kept the office of admiral of the Mediterranean, but not for long. In 1629 Richelieu's functions as *grand maître de la navigation et du commerce* were extended to the Mediterranean as well. Guise resisted and, in his struggle against Richelieu, gave help to the revolt which broke out in Provence (at Aix) in 1630; in the following year he was obliged to leave France. Montmorency headed a revolt in Languedoc in 1632, and after its defeat suffered execution.

[2] A detailed account of the history of these companies is given in Boiteux, op. cit. pp. 85–104, 221–34.

only in April—the former, moreover, not without substantial reservations—and the *parlement* of Bordeaux as late as May. It is significant that among the men appointed in 1626 to the offices of *inspecteurs-généraux des affaires de la marine* which have been mentioned there were a number of members of provincial *parlements*; Richelieu sought by this means to smooth the execution of his task.[1]

Thus, the first attempts to set up large trading companies suffered a reverse. The reason, of course, was not only to be found in the opposition of the *parlements* and of certain groups of merchants. The structure of the companies had not been adequately thought out, capital was not attracted in sufficient quantity, and the aims and spheres of operation assigned to them were too broad. To a large extent these companies were copied from the great Dutch companies, but it proved impossible merely to transplant to the soil of France these institutions which were models for their time. In addition, Richelieu had to draw yet another conclusion from this experience: the need to get the approval of the *parlements* not only for his plans of financial reform (this had been plain to him even before the failure of the companies) but also for the establishment of the companies and of the navy. To this end he decided to convene an Assembly of Notables.

The Assembly of Notables held in 1626-7 has a twofold interest for the student of the history of France in the first third of the seventeenth century. On the one hand it was an important event in the life of the country, and on the other it constituted the last example both of this particular form of representation of the estates of the realm and of such representation in general, on a country-wide scale. These two aspects are related and need to be considered together.

In 1614 the last meeting of the States-General before 1789 was convened, and in 1626 the last assembly of notables before 1788. Historians have long held the view that the cause of the dying-out of representation of the estates was the increasing consolidation of French absolutism. On the whole this explanation is sound, but it is too general and not wholly free from retrospectiveness: if absolutism was consolidated, this 'must' have meant that representation of the estates disappeared. It is sufficient, however, to look at certain peculiarities of France in this connexion, and also to compare them with the peculiarities of England and of other countries where representative institutions were retained, in one form or another, right down to the bourgeois

[1] Ibid. pp. 91–104. The *parlements* of Toulouse and Aix did not register the edict, and Richelieu's authority as *grand maître de la navigation et du commerce* was not recognised there until 1631 (see above, p. 288, note 1).

revolutions in these countries, to realise the significance of certain very important factors. By itself the development of absolutism did not in any way exclude the existence of representation of estates on a national scale; not to speak of provincial assemblies, which, despite absolutism, continued to exist in France almost up to the date of the revolution. Moreover, the abolition of this representative institution by the central power could take place only where there was no resistance on the part of the estates concerned or of other social groups. In other words, the ultimate outcome depended on a relationship of forces, and this in its turn was determined by the social and political weight of the estates and groups in question.

In order to elucidate these ideas, we must detach ourselves somewhat from the history of the 1620s to see the general line of development of estates representation in France both in the form of States-General and in that of assemblies of notables.

Down to the middle of the fifteenth century it was the States-General that, broadly speaking, voted certain taxes; then the royal machinery of government began to collect these taxes without the preliminary consent of the States. Between the end of the fifteenth century and the early seventeenth century (1484–1614), States-General were convened mainly for the purpose of examining particular political questions, which after 1614 were decided by other methods, without any representation of estates.

The history of the assemblies of notables, in many ways parallel to this, has so far been insufficiently studied. It is clear, however, that they cannot be regarded as States-General in miniature. So far as can be judged by the fragmentary information in the documents, the assemblies of individuals invited by the king in the thirteenth century—that is, before the appearance on the scene of States-General in the strict sense of the word—were, in essence, assemblies of notables. The king invited certain persons, sometimes to sessions of his Council (which is why these instances have been regarded by many historians as being merely enlarged meetings of the king's Council), sometimes to special gatherings, and put particular problems to them. The composition of the invited group depended on the nature of the problems to be considered, and the different estates specialised, to to speak, in dealing with those matters which fell within their respective competences. The selection of those invited was made in accordance with the offices they held. From the clergy it was bishops who were invited, as a rule, and from the nobility, men of trust who held offices about the court. From the king's *bonnes villes* came mayors and a few *échevins*.

Notables were convened very rarely between 1302 and 1558. Down to the middle of the fifteenth century they were absorbed, as it were, by the effectively functioning States-General. The assemblies held in the second half of the fifteenth century and the first half of the sixteenth have hardly been studied at all.[1]

In 1558, in connexion with the difficulties of the war situation, an assembly was convened which contemporaries spoke of, by force of habit, as a meeting of the States-General. In reality, this opened a fresh chapter in the history not of the States but of the notables. There appeared at this assembly a fourth estate made up of representatives of the officials, among whom were the most important and influential office-holders: the *premiers présidents* of the supreme courts, who very sharply marked themselves off from the third estate, the government sharing their view on this point. Two years later, in 1560, only three estates were present at the States-General, in the usual way, the higher officials being absent. Together with the fact that in 1558 the representatives of the estates were invited and not elected, these facts show that 1558 saw the revival in new conditions and in a new form of the system of consultation with invited individuals, that is, with 'notables'. The assemblies held at Rouen in 1596 and 1617 were of the same kind.[2]

By 1626 these assemblies were already governed by a definite tradition. They were made up of comparatively few people, and the selection of their members was determined, as in the thirteenth century, by the office an individual held. The king invited ten archbishops and bishops, about the same number of court nobles, and all the *premiers présidents* and *procureurs-généraux* of the supreme courts (about twenty-five to thirty people). This way of selecting those to be present resulted in the assembly consisting exclusively of the most greatly privileged and highly placed persons in the kingdom.

The people as a whole had no say in determining the composition of the assembly of notables. No mandates were drawn up in the localities before the assembly met, and the notables themselves were not required to formulate requests (though they did sometimes voice certain requests), whereas the work of the States-General, in 1614 for example, consisted precisely in the chambers consolidating the mandates drawn up by their respective estates at provincial level into a single statement, and presenting this to the government. The work done by the notables was of a different kind: the government put before them a list of questions on which it wanted to know the assembly's opinion. Discussion took place not estate by estate but by all the

---

[1] The list compiled by Major shows not a single meeting between 1506 and 1558 (J. Russell Major, *Representative institutions in Renaissance France, 1421–1559* (Madison, 1960), p. 152). This gap is perhaps explained by the fact that assemblies of invited persons were regarded as enlarged sessions of the king's Council.

[2] See, on the notables of 1617, Lublinskaya, *Frantsiya v nachale XVII veka*, chapter 7.

notables together, and they voted by counting heads, as a result of which the officials present had a small but constant majority over the bishops and nobles taken together.

The notables had one other important distinctive feature. The clergy and nobles who attended these assemblies did not represent their estates. As early as the middle of the sixteenth century it had become traditional for the clergy to hold regular assemblies at which the representatives of the entire clergy of France voted subsidies (*dons gratuits*) and discussed their relations with the government and the affairs of the church.[1] The ten or twelve nobles who attended the assemblies of notables could not represent the entire nobility, speak in the name of their estate as a whole, or, still less, take any decisions affecting the interests of this estate. The *noblesse d'épée* had at this time no special organisation in France for safeguarding their rights, a fact highly symptomatic of the decline in the social weight of this estate.

The situation differed for the officials. The *premiers présidents* of the supreme courts (that is, of all the *parlements, chambres des comptes* and *cours des aides*) really did represent their corporation, each one representing his own, and the group as a whole representing all the supreme judicial and administrative institutions of France. For this reason the decisions taken by the notables bound the supreme courts to carry out these decisions.

The distinctive features of the notables which I have listed show that this was a unique representative organ, with the estates participating in it on an unequal basis. Essentially, the main role fell to the representatives of the most powerful corporations of the state machine, while the old nobility, and to some extent the clergy as well, remained in the background. As regards the formal aspect of the matter, on this level too the government supported the officials. It was significant that, in the sessions of the notables as elsewhere, the hostility that divided the old nobility and the new (that is, 'official') nobility found expression. The officials would not agree to give their votes after the noblemen, while the latter would not yield on this point and demanded that they rank second only to the clergy, as in the States-General. At the Assembly of Notables in 1617 the government had got out of this difficulty by seating members of every estate on the same level so as thereby to recognise that they were all on an equality, and this had once again aroused the helpless fury of the old nobility.[2]

If we take all these points into account, together with the fact that the notables lacked authority to vote subsidies, it is possible to conclude that the

[1] P. Blet, *Le clergé de France et la monarchie. Étude sur les assemblées générales du clergé de 1615 à 1666* (Paris, 1960).
[2] Lublinskaya, *Frantsiya v nachale XVII veka*, p. 269.

government's aim in convening the notables was not so much to find out the assembly's opinion on particular questions, as to be able to bind the *parlements* to carry out the decisions taken by the notables, that is, to prevent any opposition on their part, whether open or concealed, to the fiscal edicts, taxation measures and other acts of the royal authority.

By assembling the notables in 1617 the government intended to compel the *parlements* to agree to the abolition of the *paulette*, that is, to the abolition of a system of legalised inheritability and saleability of offices which was highly advantageous to the officials. Let us recall that, after the States-General of 1614, at which the question of the abolition of the *paulette* was at the centre of attention, the *paulette* had been abolished, but that after three months the furious protests of the *parlements* compelled the government to restore the *status quo*. At the Assembly of Notables in 1617 the *parlements* did not succeed in defending the *paulette*, and thereby they lost the ability to protest against its abolition.[1]

In 1626 the situation was more complicated. The question of the *paulette* had lost its former sharpness for the *parlements*, since the *paulette* had now been guaranteed to them (and to them only) by the government.[2] Richelieu had a different aim in view.

The reason for the summoning of the notables is expressed differently in different historical writings.[3] Hanotaux considered that Richelieu, having found himself up against court opposition to all his plans, in both internal and external policy, sought to find support in public opinion.[4] In accordance with the economic bias of his book, Hauser considers that Richelieu convened the notables in order to obtain from them approval merely of his plans for economic development (formation of trading companies and a fleet, strengthening of protectionist measures, and so on). He adds this comment: 'One cannot force a nation to work, even for its own enrichment, against its will and without its consent.'[5] It is hard to concur with the view that Richelieu was going to obtain the consent of the whole nation at an assembly where only a few prelates, princes and higher officials were present.

Tapié gives a good deal of attention to the notables of 1626, and in the main agrees with Hauser, though he considerably widens the scope of the projected reform. He examines the proposals drawn up by the cardinal in 1625 and comes to the conclusion that at that time Richelieu had decided on

---

[1] Ibid. chapters 4 and 7.
[2] See above, pp. 181–2.
[3] I have not succeeded in consulting J. Petit, *L'assemblée des notables de 1626–1627* (Paris, 1937). Cf. Pithon's note on the difficulty of finding this book even in France (Pithon, 'Les débuts difficiles', p. 315, note 1).
[4] Hanotaux, op. cit. IV, 102 ff.   [5] Hauser, op. cit. p. 48.

a plan for very extensive reforms, and that the notables were called together to consider these reforms, or at least to approve the principles underlying them. He regards the assembly as having fulfilled a positive function, since it gave support to Richelieu's plan and thereby cleared the road for the renovation of the state. External war, however, prevented the reforms from being realised.[1]

This opinion seems to me correct in so far as the reforms planned by the cardinal are concerned, though these reforms were, I think, more modest in scope. There is, however, one point in Tapié's argument which I find hard to accept.

Tapié supposes that Richelieu intended to carry out his reforms during a period of six years, as he stated in his address to the notables. This undertaking itself, and especially the brevity of the period indicated, puzzles the writer, and he comes to the conclusion that so far as Richelieu was concerned this was either an oratorical trick or else he did seriously count on France being able to enjoy complete peace, externally and internally, for the next six years, an expectation which, as we know, proved false.[2]

If we put Tapié's choice of possibilities in a more clear-cut way, what we get is this: either Richelieu deliberately misled the assembly as regards the time required, or else, if he really expected to enjoy a six-year peaceful breathing-space, he revealed an incomprehensible lack of appreciation of the situation both inside France (the Huguenots) and in Europe (the Thirty Years War) which was quite unlike him, and which itself calls for explanation.

From what he goes on to say it becomes clear that both Tapié's puzzlement and his suppositions are based on a misunderstanding of the significance of the financial reforms put forward by the cardinal, which were the key to the government's future programme. And this misunderstanding is explained by the inadequacy of work on the history of Richelieu's financial policy.

Over a hundred years ago, Michelet wrote: 'L'histoire de Richelieu est obscure quant au point essentiel, les ressources, les voies et moyens. De quoi vivait-il, et comment? On ne le voit ni dans les mémoires ni dans les pièces.'[3] Michelet's shrewd remark is not yet out of date. The history of the state finances under Richelieu has still not been made the subject of special research, though the material in the records on this subject is extremely rich. The documents which have been published contain some (though far from complete) information, but the possibility of using them correctly depends on a proper interpretation of their special terminology and an understanding of the structure of financial administration in France in the first half of the

[1] Tapié, op. cit. pp. 204–14.   [2] Ibid. p. 213.
[3] J. Michelet, *Richelieu et la Fronde* (Paris, 1858), p. 12.

seventeenth century. Lack of attention to these points leads to incorrect treatment of many aspects, including important ones, of Richelieu's policy.[1]

In the previous chapter I gave a brief outline of the state finances in the 1620s and their social implications.[2] In order that the debates in the assembly may be fully understood, we must add to this outline some further information about the royal demesne.

In 1607 Sully had launched upon an operation for redeeming the demesne which was to be carried out in a number of stages.[3] First of all, the mortgaged revenues of the Crown lands were to be redeemed. Sully made a contract with a group of financiers whereby the latter undertook to restore to the owners the value of their mortgages (*rembourser les acquéreurs*), which was estimated at nearly 30 million *livres*. The financiers were then given the right to use the revenues themselves, with the obligation, after sixteen years (that is, in 1623) to restore to the Crown its landed property all free from debt of any kind. A similar contract, for the redemption of demesne offices (worth about 80 millions) was concluded in 1609, also for a period of sixteen years. The treasury paid out not a farthing, but merely waited.

Sully's reforms stirred up a storm of discontent among the occupiers of Crown lands and the owners of demesne offices. But their protests had no effect. The *surintendant* had already taken similar measures on more than one occasion (for instance, in reducing the interest payable on *rentes*), and met this sort of reaction with indifference. If it had proved possible to maintain peace, internally and externally, during the period covered by these contracts (that is, down to 1623–5) the reform would have justified itself. In 1615, however, the civil war led to contracts being torn up and the partly redeemed lands and offices being mortgaged once more.

In 1626 it was very much harder than it had been in 1607–9 to count on a sixteen-year period for contracts; but another line could be followed. The redemption operations could be carried out in a shorter period, say, six years.[4] For this, however, a certain amount of money was needed, which could be used to redeem the demesne gradually, piece by piece, devoting the revenue from those pieces which had already been redeemed to redeeming those that were left. Sully's reform did not involve any expenditure by the

---

[1] Very significant in this connexion are the mistakes made by Hauser in his interpretation of Richelieu's financial plan set forth in the *Testament politique* (Hauser, op. cit. ch. 8).
[2] See chapter 5.
[3] Information about this operation is to be found in many documents of the time, but the information does not completely tally. It is now to be hoped that, with the acquisition of Sully's papers by the Archives Nationales of France, his work in the financial field will be studied on the basis of the most exact documentation (see above, p. 230, note 3).
[4] This period of six years for the redemption scheme has misled Tapié, who takes it as the period assigned for the 'general reform' as a whole. See below, p. 300, note 1.

treasury (the financiers themselves recovered what they spent, at 6 per cent per annum), but on the other hand it required a long period of time (sixteen years), during which the state was not allowed to touch the property being redeemed. The alternative scheme cut down this time to six years, but this substantial reduction, making it possible to receive within six years the entire amount of revenue due from a demesne cleared of debt, also needed a large working fund for its implementation. In 1626 the government did not possess so much money, but it aimed to get this with the help of the notables. It is from this point of view that we must look at the financial and other reforms that the government put forward.

The decision to convene an assembly of notables was not reached at once. At first the idea was to do no more than summon to the meeting of the king's Council on 15 November the *premiers présidents* and *procureurs-généraux* of the *parlements*: an order to this effect was drawn up on 7 October 1626.[1] But by the middle of November representatives of all the supreme courts of France had also gathered in Paris. D'Herbault wrote to Césy on 13 November: 'Le Roy a convocqué à Paris une assemblée des principaux officiers de ses cours de parlements et autres compagnies souveraines de ce roiaume pour prendre leurs advis et bons conseils sur plusieurs propositions qui luy ont esté faictes pour le bien de cest Estat, dont l'ouverture doict estre faicte dans peu de jours.'[2] On 15 November, however, it was decided to summon some prelates and nobles also, and the provost of the Paris merchants,[3] and to open on 23 November a real assembly of notables. Altogether, twelve archbishops and bishops, ten noblemen (mostly important military men) and twenty-eight officials were invited.[4] The reason for the gradual broadening of the composition of the assembly was nowhere stated, but it may be supposed that, in view of the expected intractability of the officials, which had been known about for the past six weeks, the government thought they would do better if representatives of all the privileged orders were present. This supposition is confirmed by the fact that, contrary to the tradition for such gatherings, the king further ordered that the estates sit separately and vote as estates, each having only one vote.[5] In this way the

---

[1] *L'assemblée des notables tenue à Paris ès années 1626 et 1627* (Paris, 1652), p. 2. This detailed report was compiled by the secretary of the Assembly, Paul Ardier, who held the office of treasurer of the Paris financial district (later references to: Ardier).

[2] Letter from d'Herbault to Césy, 13 November 1626 (Saltykov-Shchedrin Library, Leningrad, Avt. 94, no. 22).

[3] Ardier, op. cit. p. 3. In the king's letter to Césy of 27 November 1626 it was stated that the Assembly opening on 1 December would be attended by many prelates and noblemen of the court as well as by officials (Saltykov-Shchedrin Library, Leningrad, Avt. 30, no. 23).

[4] For the list see Ardier, op. cit. pp. 5–10.   [5] Ibid. p. 43.

voting could not reflect the fact that the officials were in the majority among those present.

After stormy disputes about precedence[1] the Assembly opened on 2 December with some inaugural remarks by the king and speeches by the Keeper of the Seals, Marillac, Marshal Schomberg, and Richelieu himself, describing the state of public affairs and the series of reforms that were being put forward.

In considering these speeches, most historians have taken the view that Marillac did not carry out the instructions given him by the cardinal (some even allege that he distorted them) and that this angered Richelieu and caused him to give special emphasis to certain points in his speech.[2] This opinion seems to me groundless. In fact, the three speakers shared out the subjects of their speeches between themselves. The Keeper of the Seals, Marillac, spoke about the general situation, as was proper for the Chancellor, whose functions he fulfilled de facto; Marshal Schomberg spoke about the army; and Richelieu about finance and the plan for redeeming the demesne.

Richelieu prepared his address at the opening of the Assembly with great care. He had got together a large number of despatches from French ambassadors, various memoranda on the state of French trade in general and on France's foreign trade in particular, on the charters of foreign trading companies, documents relating to the navy, and so on.[3]

In a memorandum dated 18 November, Richelieu proposed to Marillac that he should speak about the government's decision to revive maritime trade and safeguard the property and liberty of French merchants by creating a fighting navy of thirty vessels, to protect the coast, keep subjects to their allegiance (an allusion to the Huguenots), and oblige neighbouring countries to reckon with France. Expenditure on the navy would total one and a half million livres a year. On the question of the suppression of the offices of

[1] All the higher nobility stayed away, in protest against the execution of Chalais, and the nobles who did attend took their seats at random in the places that had been reserved for the grandees.
[2] It was Avenel who first drew attention to this, when he published the memorandum on the navy drawn up by the cardinal on 18 November 1626, for Marillac (Avenel, op. cit. II, 290–2). It must be remembered that Richelieu had not long before this been put officially in charge of trade and naval affairs. Hauser thinks that Marillac disregarded some of the aspects of this instruction he received, either because he was then already meditating treachery to Richelieu (which did not reveal itself until four years later), or else because, as a grandee, he despised them (Hauser, op. cit. pp. 50 and 52). It must be said that the conseiller du parlement and maître des requêtes Marillac, whose father was a contrôleur des finances, cannot be classed as a grandee. Tapié mentions these disagreements between historians, but without offering an opinion of his own (Tapié, op. cit. p. 208). Boiteux considers that Richelieu's speech was not delivered extempore, and that it developed in greater detail some points made by Marillac, but he does not explain why it was delivered at all (Boiteux, op. cit. pp. 105, 106).
[3] A list of the records collected together by the cardinal in connexion with the Assembly of Notables is given in Boiteux, op. cit. p. 105.

constable and admiral, and of the transfer to the cardinal of the administration of trade (without additional salary), Richelieu yielded entirely to Marillac's view of what would be best.[1] The latter in fact spoke only briefly about this point, while expatiating in detail on the government's intention to bring about a revival of trade—without mentioning, however, the figure of one and a half million *livres* for the upkeep of the navy. This omission may well have been agreed on between Marillac and Richelieu, all the more probably since the cardinal, when speaking particularly about revenue and expenditure, also failed to say anything about it. Marillac's speech[2] gave a general survey of the difficult situation of French trade and of French government finance. The military campaigns of 1620–2 had dealt heavy blows to the treasury. In 1625 the campaign against the Huguenots and the war in Italy had again called for large extraordinary expenses. As a result, while revenue did not exceed 16 million *livres*,[3] expenditure amounted to 36–40 million.[4] Nevertheless, the government had not increased the *taille* (and was even going to reduce it in 1627 by 600,000 *livres*), nor had it reduced either the interest paid on *rentes* or the salaries of officials.[5]

The need for financial reform was quite obvious. There would be a cut in expenditure on the upkeep of the court, and thanks to the suppression of the offices of constable and admiral (Richelieu taking over their responsibilities without remuneration) the treasury would save about 400,000 *livres*. The king was going to cut down expenditure on the army and revise the schedule of debts, so as to reduce them wherever possible.[6] The main effort, however, must be directed to increasing revenue, but in a way that would not burden the people.

The government saw two chief ways to increase the treasury's receipts. The first was to redeem the demesne, the second to develop trade and shipping.[7] Marillac merely mentioned the first, but he dwelt in great detail on the second, describing it as the best means for enriching the people and

---

[1] 'En vérité, je ne sçay s'il sera à propos de dire cela; je m'en remets à ce que M. le garde des seaux advisera pour le mieux' (Avenel, op. cit. II, 292).

[2] Ardier, op. cit. pp. 23–36.

[3] As mentioned earlier (see p. 227) what was involved here was only the 'net revenue' (*revenans bons*) received by the central treasury after the provincial treasurers had met the expenses arising from local needs.

[4] According to Mallet's figures, in 1626 revenue came to nearly 18 million *livres* and expenditure to 43 million.

[5] The deficit was partly covered by forced loans from officials and loans from financiers (see above, p. 231). At the time when the Assembly began, the state debt amounted to over 52 million *livres* (Ardier, op. cit. p. 81).

[6] The reference is to a review of the rates of interest paid on long-term loans.

[7] What is actually spoken of in all the documents is not a development but a restoration (*rétablissement*) of the former condition of France's trade.

restoring the injured dignity of France. Making extensive use of the material collected by Richelieu, he described the bad state of French trade, caused by its lethargy during many years, which had been exploited by neighbouring countries so as to put French merchants in a subordinate and very disadvantageous position. France possessed very rich resources for the expansion of trade and shipping. Moreover, if the Seine and the Saône, and also the Seine and the Loire, were to be linked by canals, France could be transformed into a great trade route connecting the Levant with the European countries of the Atlantic seaboard, which would mean a severe loss to Spain, since all that country's trade would be controlled by the ports of Provence and Brittany. Cardinal Richelieu had already convinced the king of the importance of taking such measures, and it had been decided to do everything possible to bring about an upsurge of trade. The notables had the task of discussing the draft plan for measures to this end.

After Marillac, Marshal Schomberg spoke of the need to find extraordinary sources of revenue and on the government's intention to reorganise the army's system of pay and supply. The draft regulations for this purpose were also to be considered by the assembly.[1]

In his short speech, Richelieu mainly focused attention on the need to make the most of a situation of internal and external peace in order to carry through reforms, especially in the financial sphere, which would constitute one of the chief ways of strengthening France.[2] The proposed reduction in the amount to be spent on the upkeep of the court, and other economy measures, would reduce state expenditure by three million *livres* a year. This would not be enough, however, to eliminate the budget deficit, not to mention the huge burden of debt. It was not possible to introduce new taxes, for the people would not be able to pay them (*les peuples ne sçauroient plus porter*). There was only one way to solve the problem: by redeeming the demesne.

Richelieu immediately went on to stress that what he had in mind was redeeming mortgaged royal properties, not confiscating them from their present occupiers, for the government was concerned to retain public confidence (*foy publique*), which was of great importance to it as an inexhaustible well of further resources. Redemption of demesne revenue, which amounted to about 20 million *livres*, would make it possible to balance the budget permanently, and that would be a great benefit. It would become possible to

---

[1] Ardier, op. cit. pp. 36, 37.
[2] Ibid. pp. 37–42. Richelieu's address was printed at the time in the *Mercure françois* for 1626 (XII, 756 ff.), and frequently reprinted later. Avenel published it on the basis of six manuscript copies (Avenel, op. cit. II, 297–305). On the omission of this address in the new edition of Richelieu's *Mémoires*, see Hauser, op. cit. pp. 51–3.

relieve the people, 'qui contribuent maintenant, plus par leur sang que par leurs sueurs, aux despenses de l'Estat'. Internal disturbances and conflicts with enemies from outside would not take the country unprepared, for there would always be the means needed for defence. It would not be necessary to pay court to the tax-farmers in order to raise loans from them. The supreme courts would not need to register new fiscal edicts. In brief, the age so much wished for by all would have arrived at last.

It might be objected that these splendid plans would be hard to put into practice. However, declared the cardinal, 'J'ose dire en la présence du Roy qu'il se peut trouver des expediens par lesquels dans six ans on verra la fin et la perfection de cet ouvrage.[1] Le Roy, Messieurs, vous a assemblez expressément pour les chercher, les trouver, les examiner et les résoudre avec vous.'[2]

Analysis of all three speeches brings out an interesting fact which has not been developed in historical writings, and has been left unexplained, namely, the division of the subjects between the speakers, or more precisely, between Marillac and Richelieu (Schomberg, as was appropriate, spoke about army affairs only). The Keeper of the Seals set forth, and in great detail, the measures to be taken for improving trade and shipping, although it was Richelieu who not so long before had headed this 'administration', an innovation in France. The cardinal himself chose[3] for his topic the reform of the state's finances, although the government included a *surintendant des finances*, the Marquis d'Effiat, who might well have been the minister to speak on these matters.[4] The significance of this strange division of labour, in my view, is to be seen not merely in the fact that it was effected on the basis of the importance of the subjects concerned, but also in the fact that it was in itself an innovation. At the opening sessions of meetings of the States-General and of assemblies of notables, the address on the tasks before the assembly had always been made by the chancellor, after which the assembly at once began its work. In 1626 the Keeper of the Seals, taking the place of the chancellor, composed his address on the traditional lines, but at the same time put the main emphasis in it on one of three important subjects, namely, trade. Schomberg undertook the task of speaking about the army. Finally,

[1] The mention of a six-year period shows that Richelieu had in mind redemption of the demesne by means of a working fund. Moreover, the way it is mentioned leaves no doubt that this period was being suggested only as the period for carrying through the redemption scheme, and not for the programme of reforms as a whole.

[2] Avenel, op. cit. II, 302–3.

[3] The allotment of subjects was undoubtedly made by Richelieu himself, as can be seen from the memorandum of 18 November mentioned above.

[4] D'Effiat contributed a special report on 11 January 1627 (see below, pp. 303 ff.).

the most powerful man in the king's Council, Richelieu, directed the Assembly's attention to the most important point, finance, stating that the notables had been assembled specifically for the purpose of financial reform.[1]

After these speeches were over, the king ordered the estates to separate, each going to the room assigned to it (the meetings took place in the Tuileries), and begin discussing the draft regulations for the army and for the state's finances. As already mentioned, the estates were also to vote separately, each having one vote only.

The officials immediately protested.[2] They did not want the Assembly to vote by estates, and demanded the procedure of voting by counting of heads, referring to the established tradition on this point. They expressed misgiving that under the system of voting by estates they might be treated as part of the third estate; as I have mentioned, however, there was hidden here the more substantial fear of being left in a minority of one against the two votes of the clergy and the nobility. In order to back their protest by deeds, they refused to accept the copies of the draft regulations offered to them for the purpose of their discussion, or, in other words, they refused to start work. Marillac assured them that it never entered the king's head to regard them as belonging to the third estate. Although the prelates and nobles supported the procedure proposed by the government, the *premier président* of the Paris *parlement* continued to object, in the name of all his colleagues. The king then made the following proposal: the estates should sit together and discuss all matters together, but if there should be disagreement between the estates, each estate would be allowed to vote individually. This proposal was, like the previous one, to the disadvantage of the officials, but they could not object to it, in so far as it ensured them freedom to express their views. The discussion of the drafts began.

The plan for the army[3] included measures to strengthen military discipline, to regulate recruitment, to organise supply-depots, for the payment of the soldiers, for the holding of inspections, and so on. Discussion on it continued until 23 December, and in the main it was approved. The notables introduced a number of clarifications and corrections, taking care, amongst other things, to make sure of their own exemption from having troops billeted on them.[4]

Matters proceeded much less smoothly where the reduction of expenditure and the redemption of the demesne was concerned. The notables (especially

---

[1] Hauser supposes that Richelieu spoke after Marillac either because he was dissatisfied with the latter's speech or else in order to reinforce it with his own authority (Hauser, op. cit. p. 52). In other words, the decision to speak must in either case have been taken by the cardinal, on the spot, during the Assembly. This view seems to me groundless.

[2] Ardier, op. cit. pp. 71–8.

[3] Ibid. pp. 47–70.   [4] Ibid. p. 90.

the officials) took a very long time to decide on their opinions, all the more so because differences constantly arose between the estates. The nobles wanted all offices about the court to be confined to the *noblesse d'épée* and to be available free of charge. The officials rejected this proposal, which encroached on their interests, because not only had court offices long been bought and sold (the deals being effected privately and this saleability of the offices in question not being recognised by law), but they had in very many cases become the property of members of the new, that is, the official, nobility. The nobles demanded one-third of the places in the king's Council, but the officials would not agree. At the same time, the officials proposed that the pensions fund be reduced—and pensions were paid almost entirely to the princes and *noblesse d'épée*—to the level of 1607, that is, to two million *livres*, with the provision, moreover, that pensions be given the lowest priority for payment, after all other items of government expenditure.[1] As had happened previously, each of the contending estates tried to put the state's burdens on its adversary's back.

In order to see the situation clearly it must be realised that public opinion reacted in a very lively way both to the government's plans for reform, which became widely known, and to the debates which took place in the Assembly. A multitude of pamphlets appeared, with criticisms of the financial system, a variety of plans for reform, advice to the government and to the estates, and so on.[2]

The dragging out of the Assembly's business, the disputes between the estates, and their repeated appeals to the king with claims in defence of their respective interests, compelled Richelieu to intervene in the work of the notables.[3] Accompanied by the *surintendant* d'Effiat, and some financial officials, he appeared on 11 January 1627 in the Tuileries, at a plenary

[1] In circumstances of chronic deficit, these measures might result in more or less complete non-payment of pensions.

[2] I will mention the two pamphlets corresponding to the government's interests which were re-printed in the *Mercure françois* (xii, 762 ff., 774 ff.). The first of these was written by Nicolay, *président* of the *Chambre des Comptes*, and was aimed against payment to the financiers of un-reasonably high rates of interest on loans, against the enormous number of pensions, and against abuse of the fund for unchecked expenditure (*comptans*). The latter went mainly on various kinds of subsidy, presents (for example, to the Huguenots, on the signing of peace treaties with them), and secret service payments. According to Mallet's figures, in 1626 this type of expenditure came to 17 million *livres*, at a time when ordinary expenditure stood at 27 millions. The other pamphlet, entitled *Advis à messieurs de l'Assemblée des notables* supported the government's reform plan in almost all its points.

[3] At the beginning of January it was far from clear to the government what the outcome of the Assembly would be. D'Herbault wrote to Césy that the Assembly was still going on and that it would be necessary to wait until it ended before one could see what sort of service it might render to the king (letter from D'Herbault to Césy, 6 January 1627, in Saltykov-Shchedrin Library, Leningrad, Avt. 94, no. 28).

session of the Assembly, and put forward a list of questions to which the notables were called upon to give clear and precise answers. The questions were read out by the secretary of the assembly, the cardinal following each one by an explanatory statement.[1] Then the *surintendant* spoke, reporting to the Assembly the state of the government's finances.

These speeches have been given very little attention in historical writing, sometimes not even being mentioned. Especially neglected have been the *propositions* put forward by the cardinal, which have not been critically analysed from the sources.[2] It may be that the reason for this neglect is the absence in the cardinal's remarks of any of the general ideas which were abundant in the speeches at the opening of the Assembly. Yet they contain much very interesting information and are important both for the history of the Assembly and for that of the government's policy as a whole.

In my examination of the speeches of 11 January I depart from chronological sequence for the following reason. Richelieu put forward a list of questions to which the answers given would be of maximum importance, and presented with them his *observations* explaining and supplementing each point. D'Effiat supported his remarks, showing the Assembly a picture of the catastrophic condition of the state's finances. By doing this he more or less barred the notables from giving any answers except the ones which the government intended them to give. Both Richelieu and d'Effiat spoke to contemporaries who were quite familiar with the structure of the state machine and especially of the budget. We, however, in order to see clearly the significance of the government's proposals, need to start by considering what the *surintendant* said.[3]

His speech is most valuable as a source for the history of government finance in 1610–26, thanks to the accuracy and wide scope of the reliable and detailed information contained in it, regarding both the cause of the chronic deficit and the main trends in the government's financial policy and its results. Of great interest also are the two memoranda submitted by d'Effiat to the cardinal at the beginning of November 1626, in which he sets out the measures taken by him over a period of five months to put the finances in order.[4] In view of the fact that this information is very important

[1] Ardier, op. cit. pp. 124, 125.
[2] I cannot say whether this is so as regards the special study by J. Petit (see p. 293, note 3). As, however, neither Hauser nor Tapié mentions the matter, it is hardly likely that Petit discussed it.
[3] D'Effiat's report was printed in the *Mercure françois* (XII, 790 ff.).
[4] One of these was printed by Avenel (op. cit. II, 207–11) because he supposed that it had been drawn up by Richelieu himself and annotated by him. Avenel dated it 1 June 1626, relying on the title at the head of it, but this was added later by another hand, and is incorrect. The other memorandum has not been printed (MS in Archives du ministère des affaires étrangères, Paris. *Mémoires et documents, France*, DCCLXXXIII, folios 214–16; microfilm in the Saltykov-Shchedrin

for appreciating the policy of absolutism as a whole, I will consider it in detail, leaving aside only the material on the organisation of the finance department.

The relation between the two memoranda and the *surintendant*'s speech is as follows; the memoranda describe the lamentable state of the finances at the time of d'Effiat's appointment, that is, in June 1626, and enumerate in detail the measures taken by him between June and November, while in the speech these measures are merely summarised, and the main theme is the very grave condition of the state's finances and the need for reforms. The figures given in the memoranda are the same as those given in the speech.

For my purposes the memoranda are of no less interest than the speech, though only the latter was given to the Assembly. The measures taken by the *surintendant* throw light on the relations between the government and the financiers in the period immediately preceding the Assembly of Notables.

It was mentioned above that d'Effiat became *surintendant* as a result of the 'purge' of the king's Council carried out by Richelieu after the exposure of the conspiracy of Chalais. The new *surintendant*, Antoine Coeffier, marquis d'Effiat et de Chilly, baron de Macy, etc. (1581–1632), was one of the men most in the cardinal's confidence, who held his post until his death. His biography is noteworthy in a number of ways. The noble title held by his family was of fairly recent origin. His grandfather and his uncles were mainly occupied with important financial offices, but his grandfather on his mother's side was a secretary of state, and his father had already held office at court as a gentleman of the household of the Duke of Anjou. The career of the future *surintendant des finances* began in 1614, when he became *surintendant* of the mines of France. In 1616 he obtained an important office at court, as *premier écuyer de la grande écurie*; then, at the head of a squadron of light cavalry, he took part in the campaign of 1621 against the Huguenots. In 1619 and 1624 he carried out important diplomatic assignments, notably in connexion with the negotiations for an Anglo-French marriage alliance; in 1626 he was appointed *surintendant des finances* and in 1629 put in charge of

Library, Leningrad, Department of MSS). It is headed *Estat auquel estoient les finances quand Monsieur Deffiat entra en charge, 1626*, this title being written in the same handwriting as that of the first memorandum. Analysis of both shows that they were compiled by the *surintendant* after he had been five months in office; as he was appointed on 9 June 1626, the memoranda must be dated in early November, that is, a month before the opening of the Assembly. The notes on the published memorandum were made not by Richelieu but by d'Effiat. The two documents differ in content; the shorter, which is the unpublished one, is a general account and a request, addressed to Richelieu (the superscription is *Monseigneur*), to give his backing to the inquiry which the *surintendant* had begun into the doings of the tax-farmers and officials of his department. The second and longer one contains detailed information about the checking of tax-farms; it would appear to have followed a few days after the first one, in response to a request from Richelieu for these details.

the ordnance, thus, like Sully and Schomberg before him, combining this office with the management of the state's finances. In 1630 he was *lieutenant-général* with the army operating in Italy. In 1631 he received the title of marshal of France, and in 1632 he commanded the army in Alsace, where he died.

A diplomat, a high-ranking commander, *surintendant des finances*, the Marquis and Baron d'Effiat was one of the most brilliant of those men from the new nobility who, under Richelieu, took over many important offices in the machinery of government and the army. The bourgeois origin of his family (after all, he was only the grandson of a high financial official) was buried beneath the glitter of his acquired seignorial titles and offices of the the highest rank.[1] During his occupation of the post of *surintendant* between 1626 and 1632, d'Effiat carried through a number of reforms: he reduced pensions and court expenses, he increased the prices of tax-farms, and he at least tried to cut down some of the financial privileges of the border provinces (*pays d'états*),[2] and so on.

D'Effiat's initial measures were mainly directed to increasing the amount received from the tax-farmers. His immediate predecessors (after the dismissal of La Vieuville in August 1624) had been Bochart de Champigny and Michel de Marillac, who exercised the office of *surintendant* jointly. Their chief task consisted in getting 'smart-money' out of the financiers, in which they had only partial success.[3] Marillac left the finance department altogether because at the same time as d'Effiat was appointed (as sole *surintendant*), he received the office of Keeper of the Seals.[4] Measures for financial reform began only when d'Effiat took over.

When he began work he discovered that huge extraordinary expenses were being incurred for the army (in the Valtelline, in Languedoc and Guyenne, in the forts before La Rochelle, and so on), which were covered mainly by loans from financiers, in some instances at 30 per cent interest.[5] The accounting system was, moreover, extremely confused, and most of the tax-farmers and treasurers did not submit accounts. D'Effiat began by checking the accounts, and revealed the existence of arrears on a large scale for the previous five years (that is, for 1621–5). In his first memorandum, a brief one, he reported the total amount of the arrears he had brought to light, and in the

---

[1] Contemporaries, however, commented on his *dubia nobilitas* (G. Tallemant des Réaux, *Historiettes* (Paris, 1960), I, 294). His son, the unfortunate Cinq-Mars, was executed in 1642 as a traitor.
[2] See above, p. 226, note 4.   [3] See above, pp. 274–5.
[4] He was removed in 1630 after the events of the *Journée des Dupes*, when Richelieu finally alienated the king from Marie de Médicis. Michel de Marillac was brother to the Maréchal de Marillac who was executed in 1632.
[5] D'Effiat's report mentions the average level of interest as being between 15 and 20 per cent. See below, p. 307.

second he gave a list of the accountable persons, with the sum owed against each name. As a result of his check he was able to recover more than one and a half million *livres* from the treasurers, and the increase he made in the prices of certain tax-farms produced over five million more; the latter method of raising money was not exhausted by his increases, moreover, and he intended to get another two millions in the same way.

However this was still not enough to meet all the state's debts and current expenditure. D'Effiat was able to obtain fresh loans to the total amount of nine million *livres*, at only 10 per cent interest, and paid the most urgent bills, to the amount of about fourteen million *livres*. In this way, part of the state debt was covered by means of new loans, obtained on conditions more favourable to the government. This meant that in the existing circumstances there were no other sources from which expenditure could be met. For this reason, d'Effiat particularly insisted in his memoranda to Richelieu that it was necessary to adjust the system of state credit, to back him up before the king in respect of the measures he had initiated, and to strengthen the state's credit-worthiness, so that creditors would have confidence in the security of the loans they advanced. For this purpose, when setting forth the plan for reform (he evidently had in mind the plan for redeeming the demesne which was presented to the notables) it was necessary to give a firm public assurance regarding these matters; which, as we shall see, was duly done.

Undoubtedly, the memoranda by d'Effiat which I have reviewed provided the basic material for his address to the session of 11 January. But this address, which I shall now analyse, also contained a number of points which were mainly in the nature of historical comparisons. D'Effiat declared that the chief reason for the debt which had accumulated since the death of Henry IV[1] was the regular excess of expenditure over income which had produced a yearly deficit of five or six million *livres*. As a result, the total of payments actually made never coincided with the preliminary estimate drawn up at the beginning of the budgetary years. The money went on various forms of unforeseen expenditure (extraordinary diplomatic missions, pensions, secret service payments, military and financial aid to allies, and so on). All this exceeded the income side of the budget; revenue did not grow but rather declined, because rebates were accorded to tax-farmers on the prices of their farms, in consideration of various calamities (harvest failures, epidemics, and so on).[2]

---

[1] D'Effiat explained the prosperous state of the finances under Henry IV mainly by the conditions of external and internal peace that then prevailed, and, in addition, by the fact that in those days the budget was drawn up so that three or four million *livres* were always 'allowed' for unforeseen expenditure.

[2] See above, p. 237.

In the first years of the Regency (1610–13) the government spent the gold reserve that Sully had accumulated in the vaults of the Bastille.[1] When this was exhausted, resort was had to tearing up the contracts made for redemption of the demesne and mortgaging once more those properties which had been redeemed. In 1616, at the height of the civil war, new offices were created and sold, called *triennaux* (that is, there were to be three possessors of each of these offices in addition to the existing two),[2] and from then on extra-ordinary expenditure grew to such an extent that there was no way of meeting it out of normal state revenues. Every possible extraordinary measure began to be applied: new exactions from officials, sale of new offices, loans secured on the revenue of the next year, and even on that of the next two years. Long-term loans began to be obtained from the treasurers themselves (or, more precisely, from the 'accountable persons', the *comptables*), while money was found only with difficulty to pay the interest on loans already contracted. The same procedure was followed with the tax-farmers, all the more so because the amounts received from them for their farms actually came to no more than two-thirds of the nominal prices of these farms. If money was required by a specific date, and in cash, there was nothing to be done but seek loans from the financiers, who exploited the situation to name 15–20 per cent as their rate of interest.[3] The fact that the same persons were both treasurers and creditors of the state led to extreme (and sometimes intentional) confusion in the accounts. In order to put an end to this, d'Effiat demanded that accounts be rendered to him personally for revenue received during the previous five years, by ten treasurers of the central treasury, more than a hundred collectors-general, 240 tax-farmers,[4] and so on.

It was all the harder to find one's way among all the details of expenditure during the previous five years because the money for the navy, the army and the artillery had been dispensed by the constable, the admirals, the head of the Ordnance and the secretary of state. The king now resolved to abolish the offices of constable and admiral, as otherwise it would not be possible to bring any order into the spending of money on the army and navy. According to the estimates, this expenditure was to total 20–22 million *livres*, but in reality it absorbed more than 40 million; the *comptables* hid behind the instructions they received from their masters, while the latter occupied, by

[1] Nicolay's pamphlet contains the interesting observation that the treasury was full of money, and trade suffered from a lack of it (see above, p. 302, note 2).
[2] See Lublinskaya, *Frantsiya v nachale XVII veka*, p. 67.
[3] This refers to such a decline in the credit-worthiness of the treasury that creditors took care to ensure every possible guarantee for the security of their money.
[4] In the original the tax-farmers are described as *fermiers* and *traitans*; Russian [and the same is true of English] has only the one term covering both groups (they differed in the form of the contracts they signed).

virtue of their birth and rank, such high positions that they were unwilling to account to anyone but the king.

Previous *surintendants* had sought and found with difficulty various sources of revenue to meet the enormous costs of maintaining the army, and then had had to seek additional funds to meet the payments on the loans they had contracted, and so on. The consequence was that the treasury was now so empty that income was insufficient to cover even one-sixth of the most important and necessary expenditure.

The way out of this situation had to be through some strong and immediate measure, for palliatives and delay would not help.

It was necessary to return to the practice of 1608[1] and draw up estimates which took into account possible unforeseen expenditure, otherwise it would not be possible to balance the budget and put an end to the confusion in the accounts. But it was also necessary to take into consideration much that had happened since the death of Henry IV, when, wishing to win the hearts of the people and make them immune to *pernicieuses pratiques*,[2] the Queen Mother had reduced taxes and countermanded edicts which had already been prepared for increases in them.[3] Receipts due from the towns had been cut by over a half, and since then they had paid hardly anything into the treasury. As a result, the income side of the budget had been reduced by nearly 3 million *livres*, while expenditure, owing to increases in pensions to the princes and nobles had increased by 4 millions. There was a gap of 6–7 million *livres*. In the conditions of that time such measures (the reduction of taxes and increase of pensions) were inevitable, but they did not succeed in preventing the outbreak of civil war, as a result of which expenditure increased from 20 to 50 million *livres*; even then, however, money was obtained without burdening the people, by way of the sale of offices and of loans.

The position was that income from the demesne was nil, and that though nearly 19 million *livres* was collected as *taille*, not more than 6 million of this actually reached the treasury,[4] after passing through the hands of, first, 22,000 local collectors, then 160 collectors of the *taille*, and then the 21 collectors-general who dealt directly with the treasury. This sum of 6 million *livres* was spent on military charges and the upkeep of the king's court.

The *gabelle* (the salt-tax) brought in about 7,400,000 *livres*, but of this

---

[1] In all subsequent accounts the year 1608 was taken as the model, because it was the last of the prosperous peacetime years. In 1609, with the prospect of war with the Habsburgs, Sully began to take extraordinary measures (see above, p. 230, notes 2 and 3).

[2] That is, the princes' propaganda.

[3] See also Lublinskaya, *Frantsiya v nachale XVII veka*, pp. 105, 111.

[4] 'Net revenue' is meant (see above, p. 227).

6,300,000 *livres* was alienated (that is, mortgaged), so that only 1,100,000 *livres* actually reached the treasury, to be spent in payment of interest on *rentes*.

Of the total price of the farm of the *aides* (indirect taxes), nearly 2 million *livres* had been alienated, so that two-thirds of the receipts from all the other tax-farms was hardly enough to cover this sum.

This burdensome legacy of the epoch of war and civil strife had to be got rid of. The king desired to have the notables' good advice on how to do it. The public interest demanded that a way be found out of the difficult situation without increasing the load on the backs of the people, and so the king had reduced the *taille* for 1627 by 600,000 *livres*.

Revenue for the first quarter of 1627, and part of that for the second, had already been spent (*mangés*).[1] The army stationed in Italy, in the Valtelline and in France itself was made up of 91,000 foot and 6,000 horse; several regiments were still waiting for their pay for the past eight to twelve months, and about 22 million *livres* were needed for this purpose. Payment of the king's Council and the court would require about 2 million *livres*, and so on. The urgent expenditure referred to in d'Effiat's report amounted in all to around 28 million, and of this about half had been met in the second half of 1626. In concluding his address the *surintendant* said: 'Toute laquelle despense en argent comptant a esté faicte par emprunt dont les interests montent à plus d'un million de livres, qui ont consommé tout ce qui restoit de la recepte de ceste année 1627...Il est nécessaire de trouver de quoy vivre, et couler le reste de l'année.'

The information given in d'Effiat's report enables us to draw some interesting conclusions. First and foremost, there can be no doubt that the financial situation really was critical and called for immediate intervention. In the second place, the *surintendant* showed that the budget could be balanced only provided there was no war, external or internal.[2] Immediately war broke out the equilibrium of the budget was upset. War made taxation policy a very delicate matter because in war conditions it was extremely risky to increase taxes. One resource alone remained: loans, loans and more loans, in almost every possible form (sale of offices, tax-farms, long-term loans, forced loans from officials). The only measure of this kind to which the government did not resort was the issue of new *rentes*, and the probable reason for this omission was that there was no longer any readiness among the public to purchase such *rentes*. External war put an even greater strain

[1] That is, this revenue did not go to swell the treasury's coffers, but straight into the pockets of the government's creditors.
[2] His figures coincide in the main with those given in Mallet's tables.

on the state finances than civil war, because the armies operating abroad were, as we have seen, very large. These figures confirm my view, and that of Trevor-Roper's opponents, that it was not the court or the state machine but war, internal and external, that swallowed up the bulk of the government's resources. One further observation needs to be made.

At the beginning of 1627, after nine years of the European war, there was nobody who entertained any illusions that it would end soon. It was clear to the French government that the war would go on, in one form or another. It was well known that at that stage the government's foreign policy was quite clearly defined: not to enter upon open war with Spain and Austria. This fundamental principle was accompanied by another—to help France's allies, but only to the extent of enabling them to escape from very threatening situations, so that they could return at once to their initial positions, and no more. This second principle was fraught with grave danger, since it involved dragging out the war. The French government's policy of performing only the most unavoidable actions meant that it was weakening its allies, both actual and potential. Moreover, not only did the campaigns of the French armies merely pursue limited aims, which could not bring about any significant weakening of the Habsburgs, they were sometimes incapable of achieving even these limited aims; the aid rendered to France's allies was ineffective. Many contemporaries realised this, and the allies better than anyone else. Historians have interested themselves mainly in the internal situation in France, in the views of its rulers, and so on, that is, in factors which really were important. But in my view the most complete and precise explanation of what happened is this: there was no money for war. Absolutist France could not embark in the 1620s upon a prolonged open war, spending sums which were enormous by the standards of that time, because its budget was already so severely strained that its hands were completely tied. Richelieu saw this, too, after two years at the head of affairs.

Let us now examine the question of what he asked from the notables.

As I have said, he addressed the gathering on 11 January 1627, and proposed, in the king's name, to acquaint them with important matters of state and to express his opinion on these matters. The text of these *propositions* was read out by the secretary of the Assembly and embodied in full in the minutes. On each point of the *propositions* Richelieu contributed an explanatory comment (*observation*). As the text of these comments had not been made available in writing, the secretary merely summarised the cardinal's words in his minutes of the Assembly.[1]

---

[1] Ardier, op. cit. pp. 125, 131–4. In the main this minute coincides with the text prepared earlier by Richelieu (see above, p. 311, note 1), but the numbering of the points is not always identical. In

To facilitate treatment of the subject I will analyse the *propositions* and the *observations* together, taking them point by point.[1]

In the first point,[2] the king proposed[3] to transfer to the provinces the charge of maintaining 20,000 foot and 2,000 horse. The latter were to be paid out of receipts from the *taillon*,[4] while the infantry were to be kept by the provinces, which should set up special funds for this purpose, to be disposed of by themselves. This measure would make it possible to reduce the taxes paid by the people to the treasury, which would be relieved of the burden of maintaining the troops stationed in the provinces. Richelieu explained that in putting forward this proposal the king was endeavouring to ease the burden on the people, who suffered from plundering by the soldiers. When the forces were on the treasury's payroll the funds assigned for this purpose were often spent in other ways, and the soldiers were left to find their own subsistence, which cost the people almost four times as much as they paid in *taille*.

In the second point, the king invited the notables to draw up lists of fortresses which could be demolished, and also to determine the size of the garrisons to be stationed in the remainder, and find means of paying them. The king proposed that the provinces undertake the responsibility of paying the garrisons on their respective territories. The frontier provinces, where there was a particularly large number of fortresses, would receive help in meeting their cost from the interior areas of the country. Richelieu added that at a time when no-one had confidence in the loyalty of the Huguenots and in the obedience of all the king's subjects,[5] it was still not possible to proceed to the demolition of all fortresses, and so this work would for the time being have to be limited to those which were clearly unnecessary.

The third point related to punishments for what was referred to as

my subsequent analysis I shall rely almost everywhere on Richelieu's complete text rather than on the secretary's brief minute, in which are to be found, however, some expressions written down nearly verbatim. I give the numbering of the points as it appears in the minutes of the Assembly.

[1] The texts of both the *propositions* and the *observations* were prepared earlier by the cardinal. The *propositions* have survived in several copies, and are also included in Richelieu's *Mémoires*, but the *observations* are available only in one manuscript dictated by the cardinal Avenel gives the text in two columns, the right-hand one, printed in larger type, containing the *propositions*, and the left-hand one, printed in smaller type, containing the *observations* (Avenel, op. cit. II, 315–34).

[2] In one of the manuscripts used by Avenel this point appears as No. 2, point No. 1 being devoted to finance (ibid. II, 317, 318, note 3). Its text enables us to surmise why it was discarded, namely, that its contents were included in d'Effiat's report. It would seem that Richelieu at first intended not to add anything to this *proposition*, but later entrusted d'Effiat with making a special, extended report on finance.

[3] I keep to this form ('the king proposed') though there can be no doubt that the *propositions* were also drawn up by the cardinal, simply for convenience in exposition, so as to distinguish more easily between the *propositions* and the *observations* made to the Assembly by Richelieu.

[4] See above, p. 227.   [5] The higher nobility were meant.

désobéissance, by which was meant not popular risings but resistance to the king's will by the Huguenots and revolts by the great nobles. Both the contents of this paragraph in Richelieu's address and notes on it to be found in several manuscripts make clear that no other interpretation is possible.[1] The king proposed that such *désobéissance* be punished not by sentences of death (*peine capitale*), which were usually rescinded later, but by forfeiture of all offices and appointments. Richelieu explained this proposal by saying that it was better to apply more lenient measures, but to apply them strictly, than nominally to retain the former severe punishments though these were not actually put into practice.[2]

At first sight this proposal and its justification may seem odd. In reality, it was more profitable to the government to punish rebels (we must not forget that it was not the common people who were involved here) by such measures as removing the Huguenots and princes from the posts they held. Moreover, the government had grounds for considering that such a measure, if really enforced, might well restrain many from taking part in revolts.

The fourth point[3] consisted of thirteen paragraphs enumerating in detail all those actions that constituted *lèse-majesté*: unauthorised recruitment of soldiers; acquisition of guns and munitions of war; pacts with foreign powers; fortifying of cities and *châteaux*; assemblies, whether open or private; publication of political pamphlets, and so on. The most important was the paragraph that forbade any dealings with foreign ambassadors; this soon stirred up fierce disputes among the participants in the Assembly, to which we shall return later.

In the fifth point, the king referred to the severe distress caused to the people by the conduct of those who, without his authority, forced them to pay various levies. Richelieu explained that no measures could contribute to easing the condition of the people and establishing a lasting peace if governors continued to be able to collect money at their own discretion, for 'whoever has money can find as many soldiers in France as he wants'.

In the sixth point,[4] the king proposed to bring into the king's Council

---

[1] Cf. Avenel, op. cit. II, 321, note 3. This note refers to the recruitment of soldiers and assembling of arms, which could occur only when the Huguenots and the great nobles rose in revolt.

[2] Here I give Richelieu's words as they are recorded in the minutes, since the version in Avenel contains only a few phrases of a general character about the need to obey the king and the harm done by rebels to society as a whole. Evidently Richelieu decided to give the notables a more concrete explanation of his ideas.

[3] In Avenel this point is given no number and appears as an addition to point No. 3. As a result, the fifth point in the version given in the minutes corresponds to the fourth point in Avenel's version.

[4] Point No. 5 is lacking in the minutes (so that the later numbers coincide with those in Avenel). In this point the king spoke of the suppression of the offices of constable and admiral and invited the notables to express their views on how far and in what way the functions of the remaining

some *sages gentilshommes*, in order to train them in the management of state affairs. Richelieu added to this that such noblemen were fully worthy of admission to the Council, and the king needed them for the conduct of important negotiations.[1]

The seventh point proposed the setting up of a sort of travelling assize court (*Chambre des Grands Jours*) to visit the provinces and hear complaints against those persons who were too powerful in the localities on account of the offices they held.[2] Richelieu explained that this was especially important for those provinces which were remote from the seats of the *parlements*.

In the eighth point, the king proposed to the notables that they discuss the question of a proper distribution of the burden of the *taille*, so as to reduce the share paid by the poor peasants. Richelieu stressed the great importance of this measure, adding that the notables would do a great work if they would find means of reducing the number of persons exempted from paying the *taille*.[3]

In the ninth point, the king proposed regulation of the trade in grain, so as to keep prices at a level within the people's reach and prevent merchants who bought up grain from selling it too dear. Richelieu added that his purpose was to relieve the people who were being impoverished by the high cost of bread. In so far as the notables (meaning here the *présidents* of the provincial *parlements*) knew best what the actual situation was in the localities, they could give the advice on this matter which the government needed.

In the tenth point, the king proposed to reduce substantially the number of *sergents* (petty local officials), and asked the notables for their opinion whether even more offices should be suppressed. Richelieu described both soldiers and *sergents* as a real scourge to the people, and the *sergents* as leeches sucking their blood.

The eleventh, twelfth and thirteenth points[4] all relate to finance and we

Crown offices, and other major offices, should be reduced. Avenel prints this point, but notes that in the manuscript it is struck through and transferred to the very end. Its absence from the minutes shows that it was not read out at the session of 11 January. It was discussed during the last days of the Assembly (see below, p. 323), that is, after the edict on the suppression of the offices of constable and admiral.

[1] The secretary omitted from the minutes the *observation* uttered by Richelieu on this point, and as a result mis-numbered all the subsequent *observations*.

[2] In the minutes we find the cardinal's explanation that the powerful persons he means are the governors.

[3] Let us recall that the *taille* was not levied in proportion to income but assessed upon parishes and, within parishes, upon their inhabitants. One and the same amount of *taille* might be assessed upon a larger or smaller number of taxpayers; for this reason, abolition of the privileges of persons exempt from paying taxes meant reducing the share which had to be paid by the peasants.

[4] In Avenel, point No. 11, containing the ban on dealings with foreign ambassadors, is cancelled, as this figures in point No. 3 (see above, p. 312, note 3). Consequently, points Nos. 12, 13 and 14 correspond to points Nos. 11, 12 and 13 in the minutes.

will consider them together. Their sequence is: establishment of rational estimates of expenditure for 1627, redemption of the demesne, reduction of interests on debts.

As expenditure involved such huge sums that it could not be met without resort to extraordinary means, the king proposed to the notables that they discuss the estimates for expenditure in 1627 (all this was happening at the beginning of January 1627), and that pensions and salaries be cut sufficiently to bring their charge as near as possible to the corresponding figure in the budget of 1608, 'estant plus à propos de diminuer les gratiffications que de les continuer à l'oppression des peuples'. At the same time it must be taken into account that the other items in the budget of 1608 could not simply be reproduced as well, because in 1627 expenditure was needed, in order to maintain peace within and without, on a different scale from what had been adequate in Henry IV's time. For this reason the king proposed to the Assembly that they review expenditure in every year since 1610 and submit an estimate[1] which could be put to practical use. To this proposal Richelieu added that it would be good to draw upon the experience of zealous stewards of private households (æconomes des maisons particulières), who, when they draw up their estimates, take into consideration unforeseen expenses that may have to be met. For this reason their estimates are not exceeded, whereas estimates drawn up in too mechanical fashion have to be continually corrected, and merely introduce disorder.[2] There is an interesting addition to this in the minutes: Richelieu enumerated in detail the increase since 1610 in the numbers of the standing army, which had entailed considerable extra expenditure of which there had been no need in Henry IV's time.

The king further asked that the Assembly, after determining the amount of expenditure in 1627, should also try to find the funds needed for redemption of the demesne within a few years, taking into account the need to reduce the taille in 1627–31 by 3 million livres.[3] Later the Assembly was asked to find the least offensive ways of reducing the state's debts, to cut down expenditure in future years (what was involved here was reduction of interest payments on rentes and other loans).

These points were set forth very briefly; Richelieu's observations, on the other hand, were very extensive, nearly six times as long as the propositions.

---

[1] An estimate of expenditure only was meant.

[2] One cannot but detect a clearly defined personal note in these observations. The cardinal's management of property was exemplary. Other personal notes are sounded in the frequent comparisons of the state to a sick man. Richelieu was at this time almost continuously ill (see below, p. 315).

[3] The reduction of the taille by 600,000 livres in 1627 (see above, p. 309) was the first stage in the implementation of this reform.

This was a whole speech[1] in defence of the plan to redeem the demesne in a very short time, that is, by means of a working fund. The cardinal's arguments amounted to the following.

Redemption of the demesne was a very difficult but absolutely necessary undertaking. The planned reduction in the *taille* could be effected only provided revenue was increased, and such an increase in revenue could be 'harmless' (*innocent*) only if the demesne were redeemed.

Redemption of the demesne could bring substantial and immediate benefit only if it were carried out in a very short space of time and by means of a working fund. To try to redeem the demesne, without spending any money, over a prolonged period[2] would bring only apparent advantage; it would not produce the desired effect, because it was not in the French character to keep to one resolution for a long time.[3] Just as an exhausted patient who has lost a lot of blood can sometimes be cured by further blood-letting, so it was impossible to enrich the French state 'si par un nouvel effort on ne tire encore une fois un fonds extraordinaire qui en engendre un autre qui soit ordinaire et qui dure toujours'.[4]

Subsequently a very remarkable passage appears, aimed at assuring the assembly that the fund Richelieu was asking for would not be diverted to other purposes. This was the heart of the problem. The notables had to be convinced that their agreement to the creation of an extraordinary fund (that is, to new burdens which, let us recall, were to be borne not by the people but by the privileged orders themselves) would serve exclusively the aim of radically restoring the health of the budget. Richelieu cited as guarantees regarding his proposals both 'la probité de ceux qui les mettent en avant et la seureté que leurs actions passées donnent lieu de prendre en leurs paroles',[5] and the king's own affirmation that he needed the fund only in order to increase revenue by redeeming the demesne, so as to be free thereafter from all need for extraordinary funds. Richelieu assured the notables that all possible steps would be taken to make certain that the fund in question could not be spent for other purposes. The king's Majesty had ordered 'ceux qui ont l'honneur de la servir en ses conseils' (that is, once again, the cardinal himself) 'de tenir religieusement la main à l'exécution de ses volontez sur ce sujet' and so these persons 'ne craignent point de s'y engager de

---

[1] It is merely summarised in the minutes, but with retention of the main ideas and even of some of the actual expressions used.

[2] See above. pp. 295, 296.

[3] '...les françois ne demeurent pas sy longtemps en un mesme dessein' (Avenel, op. cit. II, 330). This widely held opinion had already at that time become proverbial.

[4] Ibid. II, 331, 332. The expressively laconic phrase is highly characteristic of Richelieu.

[5] Richelieu is referring, of course, to himself.

parolle'.[1] 'Il y a beaucoup d'honneur à faire réussir un si glorieux dessein, et on ne peut sans mortification, pour ne pas dire honte, l'entreprendre pour ne le faire pas. Ces considérations sont, à mon advis, de très bonnes cautions du succès de cette entreprise; ce sont des motifs fort puissans, particulière-ment pour ceux qui estiment plus une once de gloire méritée par quelque signalée action que tous les biens du monde.'[2]

Thus Richelieu gave the Assembly his word of honour that he would keep his promises. How the Assembly interpreted this we shall see later; at this point I merely add that Richelieu's concluding words on these points were no less significant. Employing his characteristic method of putting forward a series of alternatives, Richelieu thus defined for the notables the task of their Assembly: (1) they could find some other means of easing the life of the people and increasing the state's revenue, without resort to the creation of extraordinary funds—but this was not possible;[3] (2) they could leave everything as it was—but this would be unworthy of them.

Consequently, the notables were under obligation to find 'des moyens proportionnés aux fins que vous jugerez nécessaires au bien de ce royaume'. This confronted them with the necessity of accepting the decision suggested by the cardinal as the only one possible in the given circumstances.

I have quoted Richelieu's argument almost in full so as to show what a shaky basis it had, despite the strict logic with which it was expounded. To prove this I will summarise the actual situation.

The government had to carry through a financial reform, increasing revenue and reducing expenditure. Not only was it not going to increase taxes, it had already announced that it would reduce them. It intended to reduce expenditure by cutting considerably (by more than half) the pensions paid to the nobles. Thus, the notables had no moral right[4] to propose that the government seek its extraordinary fund by raising taxes, and at the same time they were obliged to accept a reduction in pensions. It was easy for the officials to consent to the latter measure,[5] but the nobles protested against it.

The government was proposing to carry out financial reform by that very means, redemption of the demesne, which everyone had always suggested was the best and most reliable way of strengthening the budget[6] and pre-

---

[1] These last words are written in Richelieu's own hand (ibid. II, 333, note 1).
[2] Ibid. II, 333. This tirade is also highly characteristic of Richelieu.
[3] That is, it was not possible to find any such other means.
[4] The extremely difficult position of the common people was at that time the subject of universal comment, in speech and writing. It provided the reason given by the *parlements* for refusing to register edicts on new taxes.
[5] They themselves had, indeed, already proposed this (see above, p. 302).
[6] The last official expression of this proposal had occurred when it was included in the mandate of the third estate at the States-General of 1614–15.

venting the exaction of new taxes, the practice of forced loans and dependence for money upon the financiers. The notables had no grounds for rejecting this plan, especially as they themselves shared the belief that it would be productive of good results.

Here what was clear and unquestionable in the situation ended, and the difficulties began. How exactly was the redemption of the demesne to be carried out?

The government was unwilling to employ Sully's method because it required the excessively long period of sixteen years.[1] The government proposed a six-year period, but this required a working fund. Where was this to be found? The amount needed was too large[2] to be obtained as a loan from the financiers at normal rates of interest (5 or 6 per cent), and there was absolutely no money available to pay a higher rate. The government could not count on receiving a subsidy, because the notables were not authorised to grant one. In putting forward a plan for redemption within six years and, as we have seen, insisting very strongly upon it, the government had in mind obtaining the agreement of the notables to offering it a long-term loan at a low rate of interest. This loan could be got from the towns and from the church;[3] the *noblesse d'épée* were in no position to lend anything to the treasury.

A loan from the towns would weigh heaviest on the rich and well-to-do sections, that is, on the merchants and the officials. The officials did not want to grant a loan to the government. They had already formed the view long since, and with justification, that the government was encroaching upon their interests, by creating unnecessary offices and offering the *paulette* only with the accompaniment of forced loans.[4] Why should the officials, in addition to the burdens already put upon them, offer the government voluntarily a big loan at low interest? However, they could not say what they thought, for all to hear, or put this forward as their reason for refusing. They justified their

---

[1] I have explained earlier (see p. 296) that the duration of the period was determined by the rate of interest (which in this case was the normal one) to be received by the financiers for redeeming the mortgaged Crown properties. It was for this reason that the actual scheme put forward for redemption of the demesne necessitated this specific period for its accomplishment.

[2] The amount of the working fund is not indicated in the documents at our disposal, but we may make the following surmise. Income from the demesne, at the normal rate of 5 or 6 per cent, came to about 20 million *livres*; therefore the capital invested in the demesne and subject to redemption must have come to between 100 and 120 millions. The working fund could not therefore have amounted to less than 10–15 million *livres*.

[3] Picot mentions a document preserved among Richelieu's papers which contains a *proposition* to the notables to the effect that, in order to constitute a working fund, the clergy and the towns should provide the government with a loan (G. Picot, *Histoire des Etats-Généraux*, 2nd edition, v (Paris, 1888), 41, note 2).

[4] See above, p. 228.

refusal by their lack of confidence that the fund in question, if obtained, would really be used for the purpose mentioned, that is, that it would not be diverted to meeting some other expenditure, so that the demesne would continue unredeemed as before and they would be left as ordinary creditors of the Crown, but on terms unfavourable to themselves. In other words, they were afraid that the proposed fund would change nothing in the financial system and the operation would turn out to be, in essence, just another forced loan.

What could the government do in such a situation? It was in no position to provide any material guarantees. It could only assure the notables of its intentions. This was why Richelieu gave his word of honour and the king's that the working fund would be employed as promised. This assurance was backed up by d'Effiat's report, in which a picture was painted of something like state bankruptcy. But at the same time Richelieu's promise showed that the government possessed no other means whatever of bringing pressure to bear on the Assembly.

The word of honour given by Richelieu conclusively deprived the officials of the possibility of openly refusing their consent to the working fund— they could not publicly express their distrust of him. Subsequent events in the Assembly, which went on for another month, show their attempts to escape from the position which had been definitely established on 11 January.

Before proceeding to these events, however, we must return to the other points in the government's *propositions*. The notables were asked to answer a number of other questions, the two first of which—the quartering of the army upon the provinces, and the payment of garrisons—also required a rearrangement of public finances, since it was proposed that the upkeep of the army became a charge on the provinces. Among the other points there were also some directed against the Huguenots (or, more precisely, against the rebellious Huguenots) and the great nobles: punishment for rebellion, prohibition of unauthorised levies, suppression of the major offices held by the great nobles. The notables could not object to these. The proposal to bring nobles into the king's Council and to establish an extraordinary judicial commission (*Grands Jours*) wounded the interests of the higher officials. The reduction in the exemptions from *taille*, the regulation of bread prices and the reduction in the number of *sergents* were acceptable to all, and these points did not in fact give rise to any dispute.

There remained the point which banned dealings with foreign ambassadors. In principle it was perfectly acceptable to all the estates; argument arose only on the question whether the papal Nuncio was to be regarded as a foreign ambassador. This difference of opinion, however, attained unexpectedly wide dimensions.[1]

How are we to evaluate these reforms as a whole and in connexion with the reform of the state finances?

The proposal to quarter the army on the provinces was not a complete novelty. Sporadically, and also in the case of certain frontier provinces, this had been done earlier. What was new was the proposal to extend it to all the provinces, and that the maintenance of the regiments was to become a provincial responsibility.

There were many difficulties and stumbling-blocks in this scheme from the point of view of the provinces. The frontier provinces maintained the troops stationed within their limits but they also possessed their own provincial assemblies of estates, together with some substantial fiscal privileges. The other provinces had neither *états* nor privileges. The government was proposing that they take on the burden of maintaining the troops, while offering nothing in return except the promised reduction in the *taille*. The situation was similar regarding the payment of the garrisons. Moreover, there was this question to be answered: if the provinces were to recruit and pay the soldiers, under whose orders were the latter to be—those of the governors, of the *parlements*, or of the *intendants*? This was the reason for the prolonged debates in the Assembly and the wrangling that went on with the government.

Why did the government put forward this plan, and how was it linked with the scheme for redeeming the demesne?

What was involved, of course, was only peacetime conditions, when the army could be dispersed and in practice reduced to a network of garrisons. This was a measure which would greatly relieve the burden on the budget. In addition, it would make possible a considerable reduction in the establishment of the finance department, for a very large number of collectors of the *taille* and other small and medium officials would become redundant. That was the financial aspect of the reform, aimed at the same objective as the redemption of the demesne. There was also, however, a political aspect.

At first sight it might seem that the consequence of the reform would be to strengthen the independence of the provinces, and that the presence of regiments quartered there would give more power to the governors and the local authorities, that is, the *parlements*. In fact, Richelieu proposed this reform because he had at his command new rulers for the provinces, the *intendants*, who were subject only to him. Without going into details we can say that by that time they were almost everywhere (and some had been there for several years) and in charge of almost everything. Below, I quote the strong

[1] See below, pp. 320-321.

protests made in the Assembly against the *intendants* by the officials, that is, the *premiers présidents* of all the *parlements*. Here I want to make the point that, because of the *intendants*, the government would gain by the proposed reform in the political sphere as well.

After the announcement of the *propositions*, this list of specific reforms, the Assembly's proceedings took the following course. Richelieu at once proposed that, to save time, two commissions be formed, one for army affairs and the other for financial affairs, and this was done. From then on until the close of the assembly its work consisted of discussion by the estates of the draft resolutions prepared by these commissions.

On some of the points, the simplest ones, decisions were reached almost immediately, without much discussion. Lists were drawn up of the castles in Provence and the Dauphiné which should be demolished, together with lists of the remainder to be retained in the frontier provinces, and those in the interior which were regarded as necessary for coping with rebels.[1] The notables asked that the existing laws for the punishment of rebels should not be mitigated.

Then, on 19 January, the dispute about the Nuncio arose, and the regular course of the Assembly's work was interrupted. True to their Gallican tendency, the officials were for including the Nuncio among the foreign ambassadors, on the grounds that the pope was also a secular prince. The prelates objected, ceased to attend the sessions, complained to the Nuncio, and even held a separate meeting with the Nuncio present. The king was very displeased, because all this complicated relations with Rome most inopportunely, and also might lead to a break-up of the Assembly. When the Nuncio himself lodged a protest, threatening to leave France, the government proposed that he should not be classed as a foreign ambassador.[2] This angered

[1] Only those provinces were reviewed by the Assembly from which the information had by then been received that the government needed in order to carry out the royal declaration of 31 July 1626 on the demolition of castles. These were Poitou, Saintonge, the Angoumois, Provence and the Dauphiné. The position of each fortified place was examined individually, and the reasons given for the decision taken in each case show that the fundamental consideration was the situation prevailing in the given province. Thus, in Poitou it was proposed to retain all the fortresses, because these were occupied by royal garrisons, and the province was inhabited by Huguenots. In the Angoumois, on the other hand, it was proposed that not only all fortifications be razed, but also the walls of the cities, only two of the latter being seen as possible exceptions. In Provence, where the demolition of the fortifications erected in the days of the League around nearly all cities, *châteaux* and even villages, had begun already in Henry IV's time, the notables asked that not a single fortress be left standing (this would include Orgon, which belonged to the Guises), apart from the fortresses on the frontier. The notables specially emphasised the need to demolish all castles (about thirty) belonging to nobles and to the church. A similar proposal was made for the Dauphiné, except for the citadel of the city of Die, situated in the centre of the province, where the population was Huguenot (Ardier, op. cit. pp. 111–21, 135–48).
[2] Ibid. pp. 149–54, 158–60.

the officials and, in defiance of the king's ruling, they continued to uphold their previous point of view on this question and to discuss it.

The notables approved the points on the suppression of unauthorised levies, on the inclusion of members of the lower nobility in the king's Council (on this matter the officials found themselves outvoted), on the regulation of the grain trade and the price of bread, and on the collection of the *taille*. They called for the issuing of a new decree on the *taille*. An interesting incident occurred in connexion with the discussion on the *taille*, when the *premier président* of the Paris *Cour des Aides* proposed that the *taille réelle*, which was levied only in the South,[1] be extended to the whole country. Let us recall that in the South a land-tax was charged upon *censive* land, that is, land which was *roturière*, 'non-noble', regardless of the estate to which its actual owner might belong. If a nobleman bought such land, he paid *taille* for it. In the rest of France, that is, in the greater part of the country, the *taille* was personal, and so was not demanded from nobles for *censive* land in their possession. Consequently, whenever *censive* land passed into noble ownership, this meant an increase in the share of the *taille* that had to be found by the other people living in the tax-district concerned. The proposal made was reasonable and important; it would result in a considerable lightening of the burden borne by the peasantry. But it infringed the fiscal privileges of the noble estate—not so much those of the *noblesse d'épée*, who owned hardly any *censive* land, as the *noblesse de robe*, whose profitable landed possessions were to a very large extent made up precisely of *censives*, that is, of peasant holdings which they had bought. Naturally, this proposal was rejected, 'comme estant de très difficile et dangereuse execution'.[2]

The officials also rejected the point about the *Grands Jours*, declaring that this was aimed directly at their interests. They proposed that these commissions be composed exclusively of members of the *parlements*, which completely emasculated the significance of the measure.[3]

The most prolonged discussion took place on the most important points, those relating to the army and to finance. First, however, I must mention the disputes (*grande agitation*) that arose in connexion with the plan to abolish the offices of the *sergents*. The fact that offices were a form of property turned every reduction in the number of officials into a complex operation of redemption of offices, that is, liquidation of part of the state debt. What the notables discussed was not the reduction of offices itself but the methods for redeeming these offices: should the treasury pay the owners the value of

---

[1] In Provence and Languedoc. In the middle of the seventeenth century it was introduced in the Dauphiné as well.

[2] Ardier, op. cit. p. 162. [3] Ibid. pp. 157, 158.

their offices at once and in full, or should it pay them in *rentes* at $6\frac{1}{4}$ per cent? The latter procedure would mean that though the office was abolished, its owner went on receiving a *rente* for sixteen years, until he had been fully repaid the value of his lost office. The majority of votes were cast in support of the decision which was more favourable to the office-holders, that is, for payment of the full value all at once. It was proposed that all the other offices that had been created since 1617 be abolished in the same way.[1]

These were the notables' decisions on the most important points. They proposed that the demesne be redeemed by the payment of a $6\frac{1}{4}$ per cent *rente* (except in Normandy, where the rate should be $7\frac{1}{10}$ per cent) until all the capital had been repaid, that is, for a period of sixteen years.[2] Thus, the notables declined to provide the working fund they had been asked for. They proposed that the budget be balanced by the complete suppression of unchecked expenditure (*comptans*).[3] They agreed to accommodate the army in the provinces, but in such a way that two-thirds of the cost was borne by the treasury and only one-third by the provinces. In those provinces which had their own *états* and voted the king annual subsidies (*dons gratuits*), the latter would be reduced by the amount which had to be spent on the upkeep of the army.[4]

The government's proposals regarding the navy and trade were announced afresh, with additions, and discussed by the Assembly, on 5–8 February. The notables agreed to the plan to establish a navy, in accordance with the estimate presented to them (45 vessels, costing 1,200,000 *livres*), and also to the plan for the formation of trading companies, provided, however, that the edicts instituting them were registered by the *parlements* (who could, as with all edicts, make *remonstrances* against them). The notables emphasised the need for strengthening the defence of the coast of Provence and asked for an increased number of galleys in the Mediterranean.[5] But they said nothing about either the source from which the building of the fleet was to be financed or about the character of the trading companies. However, it was decided to send a special deputation to the king with the task of setting before him a fully worked-out answer from the assembly on questions of trade. The representatives of the notables were received by Louis XIII on 10 February, when the Bishop of Chartres delivered a long and flowery

---

[1] Ardier, op. cit. pp. 164, 165, 167, 168.   [2] Ibid. pp. 168–72.

[3] Ibid. pp. 173–5. It must be mentioned that the king declared his intention to treat very graciously those financial officials who did their duty honestly (ibid. p. 177).

[4] Ibid. pp. 193–205, 215, 216, 222, 223. It is significant that the government's proposals on this point limited the period for which the army was to be quartered on the provinces to the six years during which the demesne was being redeemed (ibid. pp. 200, 201).

[5] Ibid. pp. 178–83.

speech, the gist of which was that trade and shipping were the best ways of increasing the nation's wealth, that a navy was needed for the defence of the country and the protection of its merchants, and, most important, that Cardinal Richelieu (who was not present) was very well suited indeed for the office of *grand maître et surintendant du commerce et de la navigation.* When it is remembered that the *parlements* were then delaying in every possible way the registration of the edict appointing him to this office, the deputation and the speech can be seen as means of forcing their hand.[1] The king thanked the notables for their support and praised the cardinal's zeal and firmness in putting the plans into practice.[2] For three days the Assembly debated the question of how far to curtail the functions of the major offices and also of those dependent on the constable and the admiral. The notables expressed the view that the king himself should appoint all office-holders in the navy and in the army.[3]

The notables' decisions were presented to the king on 24 February.[4] The nobles and the officials also laid before him their respective petitions (*requêtes et articles*).[5]

The nobles (meaning here only the *noblesse d'épée*) complained to the king about the state of decline and poverty to which they had been reduced as a result of the rise of the third estate (that is, of the new nobility of official origin, whom they stubbornly refused to accept as their equals). They repeated in summary form the demands of their mandate at the States-General of 1614:[6] a monopoly of the ownership of fiefs, that is, of 'noble' land; a third of the places in the king's Council, especially in all its financial sections; reservation to them, free of charge, of one-third of ecclesiastical benefices; establishment of military schools without fees; and so on.

The officials, on their part, particularly insisted on some of the points which were most important for them. They wished, as before, to insert their own amendments into those of the king's edicts which they verified.

---

[1] The means proved effective: see above, pp. 288–9.
[2] Ibid. pp. 206–15.
[3] Ibid. pp. 217, 221. In general, this view remained a pious aspiration, but in the navy Richelieu made many appointments at his own discretion.
[4] During the final formulation of the Assembly's decisions, the question of the Nuncio cropped up again and revived the quarrel between the Assembly and the government. Some of the *présidents* of *parlements* even stayed away from the ceremony at which the Assembly's decisions were presented to the king. By the king's order the Nuncio was given an extract from the decisions containing a formulation favourable to him; not, however, by the secretary of the Assembly (who refused) but by the secretary of state (Ardier, op. cit. pp. 218, 219; *Extraits des États-Généraux du royaume de France*, Saltykov-Shchedrin Library, French MSS, F. II 79/2 folios 409–10. This MS was written about 1650; the section dealing with the 1626 Assembly includes copies of the manuscript protocols of the sessions).
[5] *Mercure françois*, XII, section for 1627, 40 ff.; *Extraits des États-Généraux*, folios 410–16.
[6] Lublinskaya, *Frantsiya v nachale XVII veka*, chapter 4.

21-2

They wished, as before, to deal directly with all matters connected with the administration of the demesne, by-passing the tax-farmers, and asked that tax-farm contracts be submitted to the *parlements* for registration. They wished, as before, to keep under their own control the elections to urban municipalities, and protested against the participation of the lower classes (*menu peuple*) in such elections, which survived here and there. But most of all, and most insistently, they protested against the *grand préjudice* done to them by the *intendants*, and actually called for the abolition of the post of *intendant*.

Summing up these demands of the *parlements*, we can say that they objected to all the innovations introduced by absolutism in the previous twenty or thirty years and called for a return to the régime of the sixteenth century.[1] The only thing they did not object to was the *paulette*, because the form in which this innovation had been confirmed in 1620 suited the *parlements* very well.[2]

So ended the Assembly of Notables of 1626–7. Understandably, the royal declaration issued in connexion with this event contained, apart from the reduction of the *taille* by three millions in 1627–31, nothing but fine words and vague promises.[3]

Thus, the government had not obtained from the notables any solutions to its greatest and most urgent problems. The *parlements* represented in the Assembly had wrecked the plans for financial reform and for putting the budget in order, because these would have required financial sacrifices on their part. They agreed only to whatever required of them nothing more than their passive approval. They left the government to get out of its difficulties on its own.

The notables had rendered no service to the government or to the country. The leaders of the privileged estates present at the Assembly had demonstrated their devotion to the narrow caste privileges which in their minds completely prevailed over the interests of the state as a whole. All the estates, each in its own way, were dragging the country backward. The prelates disapproved of Gallicanism, that is, of a national church, and inclined towards Rome. The *noblesse d'épée* demanded, with stupid stubbornness, first place everywhere and in everything, not appreciating that the course of history had already put an end to this prospect so far as they were concerned. The

---

[1] Lublinskaya, *Frantsiya v nachale XVII veka*, pp. 70–4.   [2] See above, p. 182.

[3] Ardier, op. cit. pp. 225–8. The outcome of the Assembly was reported in the same vague way to the ambassadors of France, the reduction in the *taille* being the only concrete fact mentioned (letter from D'Herbault to Césy, 5 March 1627, in Saltykov-Shchedrin Library, Leningrad, Avt. 94, no. 32). It should further be added that payment of the members of the Assembly cost the treasury 200,000 *livres* (Ardier, op. cit. pp. 228–33).

new, official nobility, the richest and most powerful of all the privileged estates, had also chosen the path of reaction. It could have given a fresh direction to the government's financial policy, but it preferred to turn away from this responsibility. In this sense, the conduct of the *parlements* at the Assembly of Notables was a kind of turning-point in their transition from support of absolutism to opposition to it.

In addition, the Assembly proved to be an embarrassing affair for the estates themselves. The prelates had once again clashed with the militant Gallicanism of the *parlements*, so that the Assembly (in which, having their own organisation of the clergy, they were not greatly interested, anyway) meant only unpleasantness for them, without any positive outcome. The nobles had played no role in the Assembly and could get nothing out of it. It was the king who proposed that they be included in his Council (a promise which, incidentally, was not carried out), while the officials tried to prevent this.

For the representatives of the *parlements* the Assembly proved directly dangerous. It was on them that the acceptance or rejection of the most responsible and most positive (or, as we should now say, constructive) of the resolutions before the Assembly depended. They turned out to be unable to rise to this task, because their first concern was to safeguard their privileges and material interests and this led them to refuse to take the necessary steps. This injured them in the eyes of public opinion and intensified the friction between them and the government, which in its turn threatened them with further encroachments by the king's Council upon their privileges and power.

Consequently nobody was interested in retaining for the future, even for occasional functioning, the institution of the Assembly of Notables. It disappeared because it was of no use to the government and it was not only not needed by the estates but was even harmful to them. The road to the strengthening of absolutism and its release from control by the *parlements* was cleared not so much through Richelieu's efforts in this direction as through the failure of his attempt to obtain help from the notables and to lean upon them in carrying through his reforms. This attempt collapsed, and, as a result, Richelieu was obliged to write off the prospect of help from the estates in general, and from the *parlements* in particular.

How did he proceed after the failure of his plan for financial reform? In order to besiege La Rochelle and wage the campaign in Italy, Richelieu had to have resort to the old method—loans from the financiers. In 1627–9 these loans brought about 18 million *livres* a year into the treasury, or about 40 per cent of total receipts, and this money was spent almost exclusively on the upkeep of the army. Later, taxation began to be increased, and this was followed by its inevitable consequence, a wave of popular uprisings. But though financial reform had been frustrated, nevertheless the notables had agreed, with the backing of public opinion, to the creation of a navy and of trading companies, and this had considerable effect. Moreover, Richelieu had learnt a lesson from the failure of the plans for the original companies, in 1625–6, and was now against large monopoly companies. In 1627 he rejected the plan for two large companies, a *Compagnie d'Occident* for the merchants of Paris and the Atlantic ports and a *Compagnie d'Orient* for the merchants connected with the Levant trade. Richelieu now gave preference to companies with narrower aims and spheres of action. In 1627 a company was founded for trade and colonising activity in Canada (*Compagnie des cent associés de la Nouvelle France*), and later there appeared a company for colonising the West Indian islands (*Compagnie des seigneurs de Saint-Christophe*, also called *Compagnie des Indes Occidentales*), a company for trade with Barbary, and so on.[1] The affairs of all these companies progressed in a not particularly distinguished way, but nevertheless, thanks to them, the colonial and commercial expansion of France across the Atlantic was intensified, and the country's manufactories were developed and extended.

[1] Boiteux, op. cit. pp. 240–60, 286–8, 325–32.

Conclusion

What points need to be stressed in surveying the outcome of this study?

First and foremost, what has it contributed to our understanding of the level of development of capitalist relations between 1610 and 1629, in France and in the other states of Western Europe?

The rise and development of capitalism showed in each of these countries clearly marked peculiarities which had their source in both internal and external circumstances. For this reason the progress of these countries towards bourgeois society proceeded not only in different forms, as is well enough known, but also at different rates, which, though also known, is far from always sufficiently taken into account in relation to particular brief periods.

France in the sixteenth century and in the first third of the seventeenth presents a very interesting phenomenon from this point of view.

The sixteenth century opened for France an epoch of substantial economic advance in all branches of production, which was connected with the appearance of early forms of capitalism. But even by the last third of that century a decline was observed, basically caused by the ferocious forty-year-long civil war, itself a social and political consequence of the earlier economic advance. The ending of civil strife, and the economic progress achieved in the first decade of the seventeenth century, brought about a consolidation and further development of capitalism. At the same time, however, quite clear signs already appeared which pointed to a difference in the level of capitalist development in the different countries of Europe and, as a result, to a change in their economic power to conquer the markets of Europe and overseas. In Holland and in England capitalism developed at a more rapid pace, and penetrated deeply into the very citadel of feudalism, the agrarian structure. In Holland, this economic progress of capitalism considerably strengthened the political position of the bourgeois republic, while England moved in earnest towards the bourgeois revolution. The economic decline of Spain, though it had begun, had as yet not weakened that country politically, and in this period it was still a colonial and European power of the first rank.

The economic interests of these four Western European countries—the principal countries of that age—were closely interwoven with their political pretensions and programmes. To a certain extent, economics had even begun to *determine* their struggles, not so much over colonies (in the period under review this rivalry had not yet assumed an acute form) as for industrial and commercial hegemony in Europe itself. One of the main tasks before each of these countries was the conquest of external markets, which was dictated by the intrinsic needs of early manufacture. The markets of neighbouring countries constituted the nearest prey, and, given certain conditions, offered sizeable profits. Advantages of this sort were mainly won at the expense of the economic development of these neighbouring countries. The Dutch grew rich by exploiting Spain, and above all by exploiting the extensive French market, inflicting heavy losses on French industry and trade and retarding the progress of capitalism in France. The English grew rich at the expense of Spain, and to some extent of France; the French at the expense of Spain, and to some extent of Germany. It was typical that the strengthening of protectionism in Spain in the 1620s immediately had a harmful effect on the interests of French merchants and manufacturers; if the government of Olivares had been able effectively to carry through the line of economic policy it had initiated, and close the Spanish and American markets to all, or nearly all, French goods, the losses suffered by France would have been still more considerable.

The deep interest shown in conquering the markets of neighbouring countries within Western Europe was accompanied by interest in the markets of Central, Northern, Eastern and South-Eastern Europe and the Near East. The struggle for these markets constituted an element in that complex knot of international relations and the series of armed conflicts which are grouped under the title of the Thirty Years War.[1] But even at that time this complex of relationships was not restricted to Europe alone. Although the chief focus of hostilities was in Europe, threads from the conflict extended

---

[1] The fundamental causes of the beginning and the gradual spread of the Thirty Years War as the first all-European war are now being closely and fruitfully studied. So far as this touches on the subject of my own work, I would observe that, in my opinion, insufficient attention is given in the very interesting articles of M. Groch and J. Polišensky to the economic interests of the bourgeoisie in still feudal countries, that is, to the national interests of these countries. Groch regards the Thirty Years War as a conflict on a grand scale within the feudal class in an age when the existence of an all-European market was bound to transform every local struggle into a European one (M. Groch, 'A contribution to the question of the economic relations between the countries of Eastern and Western Europe at the turning-point of the Thirty Years War' [in Russian], in *Srednie Veka*, no. 24 (Moscow, 1963), pp. 236, 237). His conception ignores the tasks and aims of the state policy of the different countries, since this does not fit the idea of a conflict within the feudal class. After the end of the Thirty Years War, moreover, there were numerous conflicts which were far from being all-European in scope. J. Polišensky also stresses mainly the class antagonisms and hidden conflict within the feudal class. (J. Polišensky, 'The Czech question and political relations between Western and Eastern Europe in the first period of the Thirty Years War' [in Russian], in *Srednie Veka*, no. 24 (Moscow, 1963), p. 242).

also into other continents.[1] Besides which it must be emphasised that only a few years after the end of the Thirty Years War real 'trade wars' began (Anglo-Dutch, Franco-Dutch, Franco-English, etc.), through which economic predominance in various markets was secured by one country or another.

It was very characteristic of the France of that time that the general backwardness of its manufactories as compared with Holland and England was intensified, beginning with the decade after 1610, by the subjection of French trade and industry to the interests of English and Dutch merchants and manufacturers. Thus, in the concert of the three countries which had firmly taken the capitalist road of development, France was not only in an unequal position as compared with her northern neighbours, she was the *only* one of these countries which in the given period experienced serious difficulties in this respect.

These conclusions have, in my view, a direct and very important bearing on the critique of the theory of the 'crisis of capitalism' in the seventeenth century. In chapter 1 I repeatedly stressed that the historians who support this theory make, in fact, an exception for Holland and England, in relation to which they rather emphasise their point about the slow pace of development of capitalism generally. France, however, provides them with most satisfactory proofs of the existence of a crisis. Yet analysis not only of the French economy itself but also of its relations with the English and Dutch economies shows us that the difficulties were not caused by obstacles hindering the development of the capitalist mode of production as such (from which, however, one should not conclude that capitalism in general progressed without hindrances). The difficulties encountered were of a special kind, and supply no basis for discussion of a 'crisis of capitalism' in the seventeenth century. On the economic plane, manufactory production had its own intrinsic peculiarities, and in the first place a comparatively slow rate of development and a comparative weakness of capitalist elements, especially at the start. As regards the political sphere, the military power of a particular country, in its activities both in Europe and beyond, played an extremely important role in the conquest of external markets. The specific example of France is, in my view, proof of the absence of a crisis of capitalism in the seventeenth century.

Consequently, French protectionism in the seventeenth century cannot be regarded as a general method of escape from the crisis of capitalism. Its

---

[1] This fact is well known as regards the American colonies. There is interesting evidence relating also to the Far East (P. Chaunu, 'Manille et Macao face à la conjoncture des XVIe et XVIIe siècles', *Annales E.S.C.*, no. 3 (1962)).

purpose was to protect national manufacture from the purely economic competition of the more developed countries, which was at that time too strong for it. It may be assumed that protectionism was essentially similar in other countries too. The complex combination of economic phenomena characteristic of the sixteenth and seventeenth centuries was not rooted, it seems to me, in any crisis that had overtaken the new, capitalist mode of production when it had only just appeared. Whatever meaning one gives to the concept 'crisis'—even the meaning 'crisis of growth'—it corresponds ill with the actual situation in the first half of the seventeenth century, analysis of which in the case of France, alleged to be a 'model' instance in this regard, brings to light quite different causes, which I have already mentioned.

What conclusions can be drawn from a study of the social and political history of France in this period? The social structure of France consisted of a combination of different estates and groups which was, perhaps, unique in that period: (1) a clergy, a body of grandees and a *noblesse d'épée* which were feudal both in essential nature and in origin; (2) a new nobility of highly privileged officials which, though bourgeois in origin, was already almost feudal in its essential nature; (3) a bourgeoisie of trade and industry which, though still without a voice in politics, was well developed economically and complained continually on behalf of its own vital needs, and (4) the masses of the people in town and country, who suffered severely not so much from the development of capitalism as from the inadequacy of this development. French society of that time really was in constant ferment, and the antagonistic relations between classes, as well as between estates, were clearly expressed. This, however, in my opinion, was not at all a preparation for the appearance of the revolutionary situation alleged to have taken shape in the middle of the century. The development of capitalism, that is, of new relations of production, had not yet encountered within the country obstacles which could be overcome only by a bourgeois revolution. The main line of the policy of the absolute monarchy followed a direction favourable to the bourgeoisie, which badly needed a strong central authority, able to defend its economic interests beyond the frontiers of France as well as within them. The very nature of the political conflicts in the period under consideration convinces me that this view is well founded.

The civil wars of the second and third decades of the seventeenth century break down into two main phases. The years 1614–20 were filled with struggle by the grandees and *noblesse d'épée* of both religions, in revolt against the government, and suffering defeat. The second phase, 1620–9, was a period of struggle undertaken by the government against the political party of the

Huguenots, and in this case too victory went to absolutism. In both phases the government's success was made possible not so much by its military might as by the constellation of social forces. As a result, there disappeared from the political scene at the beginning of the 1630s both the most reactionary feudal groups (the *Fronde des princes* was the last splash they made) and the separatist Huguenot 'republic', lacking inner social cohesion, which was incompatible with a centralised national state.

It is very important to stress that in their fundamental features these internal wars were a peculiar expression of the development of capitalist relations inside the country. Without the new phenomena in the economy and in the social structure, the state authority would not have been able to grow so strong that the reactionary groups of grandees and of the old nobility of blood were obliged to fight against it so long and fruitlessly. Otherwise, these groups would simply have seized the leading positions in the state without needing any armed conflict, through a palace revolution; there are examples enough of such occurrences in the Europe of that time. In that event the 'Huguenot state' too might have secured much the same sort of autonomy as (allowing for all the differences between them) marked off Catalonia in the structure of the Spanish kingdom, and this would, obviously, have hindered the process of the welding together of a French national state. Unable to win victory, the reactionary groups and the separatist republic of the Huguenots actively obstructed by their armed revolts the economic development of the country, exhausting its material resources both directly, through the devastation of towns and countryside in the course of the troubles, and also indirectly, by causing increases in taxation made necessary for the struggle against them. A very important feature of the civil wars of the period between 1610 and the end of the 1620s is also the fact that they proceeded almost entirely in the 'pure' form of a fight between the government on the one hand and the feudal strata and the Huguenot republic on the other. The popular revolts of 1624–9, both urban and rural, are not to be compared in number and scale either with those of the second half of the sixteenth century or with those between 1630 and the 1650s. In my view this is explicable by the comparatively slight increase in taxes in this period; in a situation of civil war with the grandees and the Huguenots the government took care not to exacerbate the discontent of the broad masses. Between 1629 and the Fronde there was, of course, a period of two decades which saw an almost unbroken series of popular revolts caused by the unbearable growth of taxation in connexion with the external war. It must be emphasised, however, that the position of the bourgeoisie of trade and industry did not substantially alter in this period. Though taxes pressed quite heavily on them too, they supported on the whole the policy pursued by the government.

I consider that these features of the economy and social structure of France, like its political history in the first third of the seventeenth century, express those very important circumstances which determined the nature and tempo of development of capitalism in France. 'The classical country of feudalism' was not able to settle accounts with the age-old burden weighing upon it as quickly as little Holland, which bore only a light burden of this kind, or England, with its uniquely rapid tempo of penetration by capitalism into agriculture and its 'new nobility' which really became capitalistic. The French bourgeoisie of trade and industry had, then, to pass through a period which was difficult for it both economically and politically, and it could look for help only to the government. But this does not mean that in France there had already objectively been created the conditions for a 'crisis of capitalism', or for a 'crisis of feudalism' and preparation of the bourgeois revolution. Yet the majority of the supporters of the theory of the 'crisis of capitalism' and the theory of 'general revolution' in the seventeenth century regard the three decades of the seventeenth century which we have been considering as the initial phase of these processes.

So far as French absolutism was concerned, the 1620s were decisive for its development in the seventeenth century. This is usually linked with the name of Richelieu, who is alleged to have sharply altered the political course followed by his predecessors. Our study of the political struggle of 1620-4 gives grounds for considering that there was no change of course as such and that Richelieu basically followed a path marked out already before his time. It is, however, beyond question that he achieved unprecedented success. It seems to me, though, that this success was decided by the profound changes in French society itself which took place between 1610 and the 1620s. Without these changes this greatest statesman in the history of absolutist France would probably have had to while away his life in some out-of-the-way bishopric, with no opportunity to display his outstanding talents, or else to end his days in imprisonment or exile.

Richelieu's policy in the first years of his administration (1625-9) is extraordinarily interesting from this standpoint. Although the main lines of this policy had been laid down earlier, its realisation, in very complicated conditions both internally and especially externally, did indeed require great political skill. The ways and means chosen for the attainment of the purposes in view show very clearly that the real possibilities available to French absolutism at that time were still limited. In every field of policy, external and internal, the central authority was restricted by the numerous and baneful privileges, some old and others newly arisen, of the various strata of the ruling class, by its lack of money, by the separatism of the grandees and of the south-western provinces, by its weakness in the international arena, and much else. The events of 1625–9 offer an interesting picture of Cardinal Richelieu's search for means and methods of overcoming the obstacles standing in the way of the economic and political strengthening of France, a search which was not always crowned with success in that period.

In characterising French absolutism in these years we have also to note that the government was very much concerned to increase the wealth of the bourgeoisie of trade and industry, because this was closely linked with the growth of the state's revenues; while the bourgeoisie itself could increase its wealth only with the help and co-operation of the central authority. Consequently the political alliance between these forces was not severed in this period. As regards the nobility, the conflict between its two parts, the old and the new, was also not yet at an end, and this made it possible for the government to strengthen its independence by making use of the rivalry between these two groups, to its own advantage.

The history of Richelieu's administration does not, of course, end with his victory over the Huguenots, crowned by the *Édit de grâce* of 1629. But the history of France between 1630 and the 1650s, including the Fronde, is another stage in the development of capitalism in France and of French absolutism.

333

List of Works and MSS Cited

Angliiskaya burzhuaznaya revolyutsiya XVII veka. [*The English bourgeois revolution of the seventeenth century*], symposium, 2 vols, Moscow, 1954.

Anquez, L., *Histoire des assemblées politiques des réformés de France (1573–1622)*, Paris, 1859.

Ardier, P., *L'assemblée des notables tenue à Paris ès années 1626 et 1627*, Paris, 1652.

Arrêts of the king's Council, 1616 and 1622. (MSS in Bibliothèque Nationale, Paris; microfilms in Saltykov-Shchedrin Library, Leningrad.)

Aston, T., ed., *Crisis in Europe, 1560–1660*, London, 1965.

Avenel, D.-L.-M., ed., *Lettres, instructions et papiers d'état du Cardinal de Richelieu*, vol. I, Paris, 1853; vol. II, Paris, 1856.

Batiffol, L., *Le Roi Louis XIII à vingt ans*, Paris, 1910.

—— *Richelieu et le Roi Louis XIII*, Paris, 1934.

Bessmertny, Yu. L., review [in Russian] of Sweezy *et al.*, *The transition from feudalism to capitalism, Voprosy Istorii*, no. 12, 1955.

Biryukovich, V. V., 'Popular movements in France in 1624–34' [in Russian], *Trudy Voyenno-politicheskoi Akademii Krasnoi Armii*, vol. IV, 1940.

—— 'Popular revolts in Bordeaux and Guyenne in 1635' [in Russian], *Istoricheskiye Zapiski*, vol. II, 1938.

—— 'The French "financiers" in the political struggles of 1622–4' [in Russian], *Istoricheskiye Zapiski*, vol. III, 1938.

Blet, P., *Le clergé de France et la monarchie. Étude sur les assemblées générales du clergé de 1615 à 1666*, Paris, 1960.

Boiteux, L. A., *Richelieu 'Grand maître de la navigation et du commerce de France'*, Paris, 1955.

Bouffard-Madiane, J., 'Le livre de raison', *Bulletin de la Société de l'histoire du protestantisme en France*, vol. LVI, 1907.

Bruhat, Jean, review of Porshnev, *Narodnye vosstaniya vo Frantsii pered Frondoi* (Moscow, 1948), *Pensée*, nos. 29 and 32, 1950.

Cahiers des états de Normandie sous les règnes de Louis XIII et de Louis XIV. See Robillard.

Cazenove, A., 'Campagnes de Rohan en Languedoc', *Annales du Midi*, nos. 55, 56 and 57, 1902–3.

Césy. See Herbault; Louis XIII; Richelieu.

Chaunu, H. and P., *Séville et l'Atlantique (1504–1650)*, vols. I–VIII, Paris, 1955–60.

Chaunu, P., 'Le renversement de la tendance majeure des prix et des activités au XVIIe siècle. Problèmes de fait et de méthode', in *Studi in onore di Amintore Fanfani*, vol. IV, Milan, 1962.

—— 'Manille et Macao face à la conjoncture des XVIe et XVIIe siècles', *Annales E.S.C.*, no. 3, 1962.

Clark, G. N., *The seventeenth century* (1929), 2nd edition, London, 1960.

Coolhaas, V., *Generale missiven van gouverneurs-generaal en raden aan heren XVII de verenigde Oostindische Compagnie: Deel I: 1610–1638*, The Hague, 1960.

Cousin, V., 'Le Duc et Connétable de Luynes', *Journal des Savants*, Paris, 1861–3.

Craeybeckx, J., 'Les industries d'exportation dans les villes flamandes au XVIIᵉ siècle, particulièrement à Gand et à Bruges', in *Studi in onore di Amintore Fanfani*, vol. IV, Milan, 1962.

Czaplinski, W., 'Le problème baltique aux XVIᵉ et XVIIᵉ siècles', *XIᵉ Congrès international des sciences historiques. Rapports*, vol. IV (*Histoire moderne*), Stockholm, 1960.

Déclaration du roy en faveur de tous les fermiers et autres personnes qui sont entrez et interessez aux partis..., Paris, 1625. (Library of Leningrad Section, Institute of History, USSR Academy of Sciences, press-mark II 54/1303.)

Deloche, M., *Autour de la plume du cardinal de Richelieu*, Paris, 1920.

Deschamps, L., 'La question coloniale au temps de Richelieu et de Mazarin', *Revue de Géographie*, vols. XVI and XVII, Paris, 1885.

—— 'Un colonisateur du temps de Richelieu: Isaac de Razilly. Biographie, mémoire inédit.' *Revue de Géographie*, vol. XIX, 1886.

Dessaix, P., *Montchrétien et l'économie politique nationale*, Paris, 1901.

Deyon, P., 'À propos des rapports entre la noblesse française et la monarchie absolue pendant la première moitié du XVIIᵉ siècle', *Revue historique*, vol. CCXXXI, 1964.

Dobb, M., *Studies in the development of capitalism*, London, 1946.

—— *The transition from feudalism to capitalism* ('Our History' pamphlet no. 29), London, 1963.

Documents d'histoire. See *Griselle*.

Doncaster, Viscount, letter from, to Soubise (MS in Saltykov-Shchedrin Library, Leningrad, Avt. 72, no. 19).

Doroshenko, V. V., review [in Russian] of Soom, *Der baltische Getreidehandel im XVII Jahrhundert, Voprosy Istorii*, no. 10, 1963.

Du Crot, L., *Traitté des aydes, tailles et gabelles*, 3rd edition, Paris, 1628.

Duval, J., *Un économiste inconnu du XVIIᵉ siècle: Antoyne de Montchrétien*, Paris, 1868.

Elliott, J. H., *Imperial Spain, 1469–1716*, London, 1964.

—— 'The decline of Spain', *Past and Present*, no. 20, 1961.

Enjalbert, H., 'Le commerce de Bordeaux et la vie économique dans le bassin aquitain au XVIIᵉ siècle', *Annales du Midi*, vol. LXII, 1950.

Erlanger, P., *Louis XIII*, Paris, 1936.

Estat auquel estoient les finances quand Monsieur Deffiat entra en charge, 1626, MS in Archives du ministère des affaires étrangères, Paris. (*Mémoires et documents, France*, vol. DCCLXXXIII, folios 214–16; microfilm in Saltykov-Shchedrin Library, Leningrad.)

Extraits des États-Généraux du royaume de France, c. 1650. (MS in Saltykov-Shchedrin Library, French MSS, F. II 79/2, folios 409–10.)

Fanfani, Amintore, Studi in onore di. See *Chaunu*; *Craeybeckx*; *Houtte*.

Fontenay-Mareuil, Marquis de, *Mémoires. Collection Michaud et Poujoulat*, 2nd series, vol. v, Paris, 1837.

François, M., *Lettres de Henri III, publiées par*, vol. I, Paris, 1959.

Gassot, J., *Sommaire mémorial*, Paris, 1934.

Georg, Herzog zu Mecklenburg, *Richelieu als merkantilistischer Wirtschaftspolitiker und der Begriff des Staatsmerkantilismus*, Jena, 1929.

Gioffre, D., *Gênes et les foires de change: de Lyon à Besançon*, Paris, 1960.

Goubert, P., *Beauvais et le Beauvaisis de 1600 à 1730. Contribution à l'histoire sociale de la France au XVIIᵉ siècle*, Paris, 1960.

Griselle, E., *Documents d'histoire publiés par*, vols I and II, Paris, 1910.

Groch, M., 'A contribution to the question of the economic relations between the countries of Eastern and Western Europe at the turning-point of the Thirty Years War' [in Russian], *Srednie Veka*, no. 24, 1963.

Hamilton, Earl J., 'The history of prices before 1750', *XIᵉ Congrès International des Sciences Historiques. Rapports*, vol. I, Stockholm, 1960.

Hanotaux, G., *Histoire du cardinal de Richelieu*, vol. II, Paris, 1896; vol. III, Paris, 1933; vol. IV, Paris, 1935.

Hauser, H., *La pensée et l'action économiques du Cardinal de Richelieu*, Paris, 1944.

Henri III. See François.

Herbault, D', Letters to Césy (MSS in Saltykov-Shchedrin Library, Leningrad, Avt. 94, nos. 2–1, 2, 3, 4, 5, 7b, 22, 28, 32).

Heumann, P., 'Un traitant sous Louis XIII: Antoine Feydeau' in *Études sur l'histoire administrative et sociale de l'Ancien Régime*, ed. G. Pagès, Paris, 1938.

Hill, C., review of *Angliiskaya burzhuaznaya revolyutsiya...*, *World News*, vol. II, 1955, no. 30.

Hobsbawm, E. J., 'Il secolo XVII nello sviluppo del capitalismo', *Studi storici*, no. 4, 1959–60.

—— 'The general crisis of the European economy in the seventeenth century', *Past and Present*, nos. 5 and 6, 1954.

Houtte, J. van, 'Déclin et survivance d'Anvers (1550–1700)', in *Studi in onore di Amintore Fanfani*, vol. v, Milan, 1962.

Jeannin, P., 'Les comptes du Sund comme source pour la construction d'indices généraux de l'activité économique en Europe (XVIᵉ–XVIIIᵉ siècles)', *Revue historique*, vol. CCXXXI, 1964.

—— review of Mousnier, *Les XVIᵉ et XVIIᵉ siècles* (3rd edition), *Revue historique*, vol. CCXXX, 1964.

justice des armes du roy, La, pamphlet, s. l., 1622.

Kan, A. S., note [in Russian] on Roberts, 'Queen Christina and the general crisis of the seventeenth century', *Voprosy Istorii*, no. 2, 1963.

Kellenbenz, H., 'Autour de 1600: le commerce du poivre des Fugger et le marché international du poivre', *Annales E.S.C.*, no. 1, 1956.

Kossmann, E., *La Fronde*, Leyden, 1954.

Lagarde, H. de, *Le Duc de Rohan et les protestants sous Louis XIII*, Paris, 1884.

Lavalley, P., *L'œuvre économique d'Antoine Montchrétien*, Caen, 1903.

Lefebvre, G., Procacci, G., and Soboul, A. 'Une discussion historique: du féodalisme au capitalisme', *Pensée*, no. 65, 1956.

Lenin, V. I., *Sochineniya* [*Collected Works*], Moscow, 4th edition, vol. III (1941).

Leningrad section, Institute of History, USSR Academy of Sciences, Library of. See Déclaration.

Leningrad State Public Library. See Saltykov-Shchedrin.

Louis XIII, letter to Césy. (MS in Saltykov-Shchedrin Library, Leningrad, Avt. 30, no. 23).

Lublinskaya, A. D. *Frantsiya v nachale XVII veka (1610–1620 gg.)* [*France at the beginning of the seventeenth century, 1610–20*], Leningrad, 1959.

—— 'Richelieu in the works of historians of the nineteenth and twentieth centuries' [in Russian], *Voprosy Istorii*, no. 10, 1946.

—— 'The contemporary bourgeois conception of the absolute monarchy' [in Russian], in *Kritika noveishei burzhuaznoi istoriografii. Sbornik statei* [*A critique of contemporary bourgeois historiography. Symposium*], Moscow-Leningrad, 1961 (*Trudy Leningradskogo Otdeleniya Instituta Istorii*, vol. III).

Major, J. Russell, *Representative institutions in Renaissance France, 1421–1559*, Madison, 1960.

Malingre, C., *Histoire de la rébellion excitée en France par les rebelles de la religion prétendue réformée depuis le restablissement de la foy catholique en Béarn en l'année 1620 jusques à l'an 1622*, Paris, 1623.

Mallet, M[onsieur], *Comptes-rendus de l'administration des finances du royaume de France pendant les onzes dernières années du règne de Henri IV, le règne de Louis XIII et les soixante-cinq années de celui de Louis XIV...Ouvrage posthume de*, London and Paris, 1789.

Malowist, M., 'L'évolution industrielle en Pologne du XIVe au XVIIe siècle', in *Studi in onore di Armando Sapori*, Milan, 1957.

Mandrou, R., introduction to Russian translation of Razilly (see Deschamps), *Srednie Veka*, vol. XX, Moscow, 1961.

Mansfeld, letters to Louis XIII. (MSS in Saltykov-Shchedrin Library, Leningrad, Avt. 5, nos. 59–52, 64.)

Mariéjol, J. H., 'Henri IV et Louis XIII', in E. Lavisse, ed., *Histoire de France*, vol. VI, part 2, Paris, 1908.

[Marsilly], *Mémoire du sieur Marsilly, touchant les abus commis par les financiers* (MS in Archives du Ministère des Affaires Étrangères, Paris; microfilm in Saltykov-Shchedrin Library, Leningrad.)

Marx, K., *Formy, predshestvuyushchie kapitalisticheskomu proizvodstvu* [*Precapitalist economic formations*], Moscow, 1940.

Marx, K., and Engels, F. *Sochineniya* [*Collected Works*], Moscow, 2nd edition; vols. XX (1961), XXI (1961), XXIII (1960), XXV, part I (1961), XXVI, part II (1963), XXX (1963), XXXVIII (1965).

Mauro, F., *Le Portugal et l'Atlantique au XVIIe siècle (1570–1670). Étude économique*, Paris, 1960.

—— 'Sur la "crise" du XVIIe siècle', *Annales E.S.C.*, no. 1, 1959.

Maximilian of Bavaria, letter to Louis XIII (MS in Saltykov-Shchedrin Library, Leningrad, Avt. 5, no. 21).

Mercure françois, vol. XII, 1626.

Merriman, R. B., *Six contemporaneous revolutions*, London, 1938.

Mervaux, P., *Histoire du dernier siège de la Rochelle*, Rouen, 1643.

Méthivier, H., *L'Ancien Régime*, Paris, 1961.

Meuvret, J., 'Circulation monétaire et utilisation économique de la monnaie dans la France du XVIe et du XVIIe siècles', *Études d'histoire moderne et contemporaine*, vol. I, Paris, 1947.

Michelet, J., *Richelieu et la Fronde*, Paris, 1858.

Montauban, Histoire particulière des plus mémorables choses qui se sont passées au siège de, Leyden, 1623.

Montchrétien, A. de, *Traicté de l'œconomie politique dédié en 1615 au roy et à la reyne mère du roy*, ed. Th. Funck-Brentano, Paris, 1889.

Mousnier, R., *La vénalité des offices sous Henri IV et Louis XIII*, Rouen, 1945.

—— 'Le conseil du roi de la mort de Henri IV au gouvernement personnel de Louis XIV', in *Études d'histoire moderne et contemporaine*, vol. I, Paris, 1947.

—— ed., 'Les règlements du conseil du roi sous Louis XIII', *Annuaire-Bulletin de la Société de l'histoire de France, Années 1946–1947*, Paris, 1948.

—— *Les XVIe et XVIIe siècles. Les progrès de la civilisation européenne et le déclin de l'Orient (1492–1715)*, Paris, 1954 (2nd edition, 1956; 3rd edition, 1961).

—— 'Recherches sur les soulèvements populaires en France de 1483 à 1787', *Revue du Nord*, no. 174, 1962.

Munby, L., 'Some problems of progressive historiography in Britain' [in Russian], *Voprosy Istorii*, no. 5, 1963.

Nadal, J., and Giralt, E., *La population catalane de 1553 à 1717. L'immigration française et les autres facteurs de son développement*, Paris, 1960.

Palm, F., *The economic policies of Richelieu*, Illinois, 1922.

Perroniana, Cologne and Geneva, 1669.

Petit, J., *L'assemblée des notables de 1626–1627*, Paris, 1937.

Picot, G., *Histoire des États-Généraux*, 2nd edition, vol. V, Paris, 1888.

Pithon, R., 'La Suisse, théâtre de la guerre froide entre la France et l'Espagne pendant la crise de Valteline (1621–1626)', *Schweizerische Zeitschrift für Geschichte*, vol. XIII, no. 1, 1963.

—— 'Les débuts difficiles du ministère de Richelieu et la crise de Valteline (1621–1627)', *Revue d'histoire diplomatique*, vol LXXIV, October–December 1960.

Polišensky, J., 'The Czech question and political relations between Western and Eastern Europe in the first period of the Thirty Years War' [in Russian], *Srednie Veka*, no. 24, 1963.

Porchnev, B., *Les soulèvements populaires en France de 1623 à 1648*, Paris, 1963, (*École Pratique des Hautes Études, VIe sections, Œuvres étrangères*, IV). (French translation of Porshnev, *Narodnye vosstaniya vo Frantsii pered Frondoi*, Moscow, 1948.)

—— French translation of preface to *Narodnye vosstaniya vo Frantsii pered Frondoi* (Moscow, 1948), *Pensée*, nos. 40 and 41, 1952.

Porschnew, B., *Die Volksaufstände in Frankreich*, Berlin, 1954. (German translation of Porshnev, *Narodnye vosstaniya vo Frantsii pered Frondoi*, Moscow, 1948.)

Porshnev, B. See Porchnev, Porschnew.

Puisieux, letter from, to Léon. (MS in Saltykov-Shchedrin Library, Leningrad, Avt. 106, no. 66.)

Ranum, O., 'Léon de Bouthillier, comte de Chavigny, créature de Richelieu et secrétaire d'État aux affaires étrangères', *Revue d'histoire diplomatique*, vol. LXXIV, October–December 1960.

—— *Richelieu and the councillors of Louis XIII*, Oxford, 1963.

Razilly. See Deschamps.

Relation des choses mémorables arrivées depuis l'année 1616 jusqu'en 1624, Bibliothèque Nationale, Paris; MS fr. 15644 (microfilm in Saltykov-Shchedrin Library, Leningrad).

Richelieu, amendments to memorandum for Césy. (MS in Saltykov-Shchedrin Library, Leningrad, Avt. 30, no. 5.)

Roberts, M., 'Queen Christina and the general crisis of the seventeenth century', *Past and Present*, no. 22, 1962.

Robillard de Beaurepaire, Ch. de, Cahiers des états de Normandie sous les règnes de Louis XIII et de Louis XIV. Documents relatifs à ces assemblées recueillis et annotés par, vol. II, Rouen, 1877.

Rohan, H. de, *Mémoires. Collection Michaud et Poujoulat*, 2nd series, vol. V, Paris, 1837.

Romain, Ch., *Louis XIII, un grand roi méconnu*, Paris, 1934.

Romano, R., 'Tra XVI e XVII secolo. Una crisi economica: 1619–1622', *Rivista storica italiana*, vol. LXXIV, part III, 1962.

—— 'Encore la crise de 1619–1622', *Annales E.S.C.*, no. 1, 1964.

Rudloff, M. P., 'A. de Montchrétien et les problèmes du développement économique', *Revue d'histoire économique et sociale*, vol. XL, 1962.

Saint-Aulaire, Comte de, *Richelieu*, 2nd edition, Paris, 1960.

Saltykov-Shchedrin Library (Leningrad State Public Library), MSS. See: Doncaster; *Extraits*; Herbault; Louis XIII; Mansfeld; Maximilian; Puisieux; Richelieu. Also (microfilms): *Arrêts*; *Estat*; [Marsilly]; *Relation*.

Saulx-Tavannes, G. de, *Mémoires. Collection Michaud et Poujoulat*, 1st series, vol. VIII, Paris, 1837.

Scholliers, E., *Loonarbeid en honger. De levensstandaard in de XVe en XVIe eeuw te Antwerpen*, Antwerp, 1960.

Schybergson, M. G., 'Ein neuer Beitrag zur Geschichte der drei letzten Hugenottenkriege, 1621–1629', *Historische Vierteljahrschrift, neue Folge, I. Heft*, Berlin, 1901.

'Seventeenth-century revolutions', report of discussion, *Past and Present*, no. 13, 1958.

Soom, A., *Der baltische Getreidehandel im XVII Jahrhundert*, Stockholm, 1961.

Stone, L., 'The inflation of honours, 1558–1642', *Past and Present*, no. 14, 1958.

Sully, Les papiers de, aux Archives Nationales. Inventaire par R. H. Bautier et et A. Vallée-Karcher, Paris, 1959.

Sweezy, P., Takahashi, H. K., Dobb, M., and Hill, C., *The transition from feudalism to capitalism* (symposium), London, 1954.

Tallemant des Réaux, G., *Historiettes. Texte intégral, établi et annoté par A. Adam*, vol. I, Paris, 1960.

Tapié, V. L., *La France de Louis XIII et de Richelieu*, Paris, 1952.

Tavannes. See Saulx-Tavannes.

Trevor-Roper, H. R., 'The general crisis of the seventeenth century', *Past and Present*, no. 16, 1959.

'Trevor-Roper's "general crisis"', (symposium), *Past and Present*, no. 18, 1960.

Trocmé, E., and Delafosse, M., *Le commerce rochelais de la fin du XVᵉ siècle au début du XVIIᵉ siècle*, Paris, 1952.

Tucoo-Chala, P., *Histoire de Béarn*, Paris, 1962.

Valois, N., *Inventaire des arrêts du conseil d'état*, Paris, 1893.

Vaudichon, G. de, *Montchrétien (1575–1621)*, Amiens, 1882 (offprint from *Investigateur*, vol. LIII, 1882).

Vaumas, G., *Lettres et documents du Père Joseph de Paris concernant les missions étrangères (1619–1638)*, Lyons, 1942.

Vaunois, L., *Vie de Louis XIII*, 2nd edition, Paris, 1944.

Verlinden, C., *Dokumenten voor de geschiedenis van prijzen en lonen in Vlaanderen en Brabant*, Bruges, 1959.

Vilar, P., 'Problems of capitalism', *Past and Present*, no. 10, 1956.

Villemain, P., *Journal des assiégés de la Rochelle, 1627–1628*, Paris, 1958.

Zeller, B., *Le Connétable de Luynes. Montauban et la Valteline*, Paris, 1879.

—— *Richelieu et les ministres de Louis XIII de 1621 à 1624*, Paris, 1880.

Zeller, G., 'Deux capitalistes strasbourgeois aux XVIᵉ siècle', in *Études d'histoire moderne et contemporaine*, vol. I, Paris, 1947.

Zhordaniya, G., *Ocherki iz istorii franko-russkikh otnoshenii kontsa XVI i pervoi poloviny XVII veka* [*Studies in the history of Franco-Russian relations at the end of the sixteenth century and in the first half of the seventeenth*], part II, Tbilisi, 1959.

Zvavich, I., review [in Russian] of Dobb, *Studies in the development of capitalism*, *Voprosy Istorii*, no. 4, 1947.

INDEX

absolutism
  Assembly of Notables and, 324–5
  estates representation and, 289–90
  French form 'classical', 1
  greater nobles and, 1–2, 92
  Montchrétien's fiscal plan incompatible with,
    131–2, 135
  Mousnier's views on Dutch and English, dis-
    cussed, 31; on French, discussed, 26, 36–7
  official caste and, 324–5
  requirements of capitalist development and,
    139, 146, 167, 225, 330–3
  Richelieu and, 270, 273, 332
  royal victory at Ponts-de-Cé and, 148
  state credit and, 224, 243
  Trevor-Roper's views on criticised, 102
accumulation, primitive
  colonies and, 145
  Hobsbawm's views on, criticised, 60–1, 63–4
  peasantry and, 60–1
  state debt and, 225
admiralty
  offices, 285–6
  abolished, 287–8, 298, 307, 323
Africa, Razilly and, 143
agriculture
  capitalism and, in England and Holland, 327
  capitalism in industry and, 77
  Hobsbawm's views on, criticised, 58–61
  Montchrétien and, 110–11
  Mousnier's views on, criticised, 11–12
  Romano on, 75–7
  Soom on, 49
Agucchi, papal secretary, 209
aides, 227, 234, 238–40, 309
Aides, Cour des, 236, 241 n.2.
Aigues-Mortes, 207
Aix-en-Provence, 288 n.1, 289 n.1
Alais, 184; peace of, 219
Albigensian tradition, 215
Albigeois (district), 191
Albizzi, 233
Albret (dynasty), 170–1
Alès. See Alais
Aligre, d' (Keeper of the Seals), 258–9
Alpine passes, 175–7, 178, 201, 254–5, 261,
    277, 279–80. See also Valtelline
Amazon (river), 141
America
  Hobsbawm's views on, criticised, 50–2

Montchrétien and, 132–3
Razilly and, 143
Richelieu and, 144
Amiens, 36
Amsterdam, 86 n.2; 88; Bank of, 34
anachronism. See 'modernisation'
Ancre, d', 168, 247
Andalusia, 83, 94
Anduze, 184
Anne of Austria (Queen of France), 258, 259,
    286
Antwerp
  Baltic grain imports, 48
  industrial revival, 80
  money-market, 233
  stock exchange, 7
  Trevor-Roper omits, 86 n.2
apprenticeship. See skilled workers
Ardier, P., 296 n.1
Argencourt (military engineer), 208
Arkhangelsky, S. I., 85
army
  critique in Consultation. . . (pamphlet, 1623),
    251
  expenditure on, 91, 229 n.9, 231, 309,
    311
  make-up of royal, 185, 309
  notables and, 301, 309, 311, 319
  reduction by La Vieuville, 249
  Rohan's, 183–5
  See also Constable; fortresses; taillon; war
Arnoux, R. P., 194
Atlantic trade, 52, 53
autonomy, regional, 95. See also separatism
Auxonne, 245

Baltic trade
  Czaplinski, Groch and Malowist on, 49
  Hobsbawm's views on, criticised, 42 n.1,
    48–50, 57–8
  Jeannin on, 50, 79
  Romano on, 75
  Soom on, 49
  Verlinden on, 48
Barbary, 116, 143, 284, 326
Barbin, 247
Barg, M. A., 85
Bassompierre, 177, 178, 179, 180, 191
Bauffremont. See Senecey
Bavaria, 248, 255, 262

INDEX

Savoy, 130, 247–8, 254–6, 277, 279, 280
Savoy, Duke of, 214 n., 216, 277, 286
Saxony, Elector of, 255
Scholliers, E., 48
Schomberg, Marshal, 174, 198, 205, 245–6, 297, 299–300
Seals, Keepership of the, 247 n.2, 258
secularisation in France, 183, 214, 215
Sedan, 174, 207
Senecey, 245
Senegal, 126, 138, 140, 143
separatism, 2, 167, 200, 215, 331
'serfdom, second', Hobsbawm's views discussed, 48, 60–1
Serres, Olivier de, 116
Seville, 52
share-cropping, 55, 60. *See also métayers*
shipbuilding, 138, 145, 283
silk and silk fabrics, 115–16, 125
Sillery, Chancellor. *See* Brûlarts
Sillery, *Commandeur de* (French Ambassador in Rome), 200, 247–8, 254–6, 261
silver. *See* metals, precious
sixteenth-century boom, 8–9, 45, 87, 327
skilled workers, Montchrétien and, 108–9, 113, 119, 135, 144–5. *See also* manufacture
slaves, 52
smart-money, 236, 274–5
Soissons, 286
Solingen, 56
Sommières, 207
Soom, A., 49
Soubise, 141, 159, 174, 187, 188, 203, 204, 216
Sound, the, 40, 48, 50
sous-traitants, 234, 237, 238, 239, 241
Spain
  Power of grandees, 2
  capitalism in, 1, 13–14, 51
  Montchrétien and, 122–3, 124–5
  Franco-Spanish trade, 139–40
  decline of trade with America, 52
  still first-rank power, 327
  protectionism, 328
  Huguenots and, 213–14, 216, 218
  military communications, 277 n.2
  J. H. Elliott on, 93 f.
  See also Andalusia, Catalonia, Olivares
specialisation, regional, 11, 61
spices, 51, 52 n.5
Spinola, 175, 177, 194, 209
Splügen pass, 201, 254 n.
States-General, 107, 111, 120, 129, 135, 141, 171, 251, 289 f.
States, local, 226, 288 290. *See also pays d'états*

Stone, L., 96
Strozzi, 233
subsidies, 63, 64, 71, 72, 145
Sully, 116, 158, 159, 230, 234, 235, 238, 245, 256, 258, 295, 307, 308
Sumatra, 140
surintendant des finances, title of, 197 n.
Sweden, 49, 50, 283
Switzerland, as ally of France, 279

taille, 226 n.5, 227, 249, 298, 308, 313 n.3, 314–15, 321, 324
taille réelle, 228, 321
taillon, 227
Tapié, V. L., 151–3, 278, 293 f.
taxation and taxes, 19, 23, 64, 129, 131, 139, 225 ff., 256, 299, 325–6, 331; direct, 20, 227; indirect, 20, 225
tax-farmers and tax-farming, 17, 130, 145, 226, 232 n.2, 234 f., 306–7
tenanciers, 9
Teutonic Order, 48 n.1
textiles, 36, 39–40, 44, 45–6, 61, 62, 69, 70, 114 f.
Thémines, Marshal, 173
Thirty Years War
  causes of, 328
  international situation in 1620, 175 f.
  international situation in 1623–4, 213–14, 250, 254
  France and, in the 1620s, 310
  French internal policy and, 2, 123, 169–70
  trade depression and, 39 n., 42–3
Thouars, 160
toleration, 164–5
Tonneins, 201
Toulouse, 21, 158, 204, 289 n.
Tours, 181, 200
treaties, commercial, 120–1
Trémouille, 186
Trevor-Roper, H. R., 82 f., 100–2
triennaux, 307
Tucher, 233
Tuscany, ambassador of, 221, 259, 262–3

Ulm, treaty of, 172
United Provinces. *See* Holland
Urban VIII, Pope, 255, 261
Uzès, 203, 208 n., 210, 211

Valais, 130
Valtelline, 176–9, 188–9, 193–4, 201, 205, 206, 209–10, 216, 217, 247–8, 254–5, 260–1, 273, 278
Vannes, 284 n.1
Vaudémont, Count, 248